Love Song for the Life of the Mind

Love Song for the Life of the Mind

AN ESSAY ON THE PURPOSE OF COMEDY

Gene Fendt

THE CATHOLIC UNIVERSITY OF AMERICA PRESS
WASHINGTON, D.C.

The paper used in this publication meets the minimum requirements of
American National Standards for Information Science—Permanence of Paper
for Printed Library Materials, ANSI Z39.48-1984.

∞

LIBRARY OF CONGRESS CATALOGING-IN-PUBLICATION DATA
Fendt, Gene, 1955–
Love song for the life of the mind : an essay on the purpose of comedy / Gene Fendt.
p. cm.
Includes bibliographical references and index.
ISBN-13: 978-0-8132-1485-6 (cloth : alk. paper)
ISBN-10: 0-8132-1485-8 (cloth : alk. paper) 1. Comic, The. 2. Comedy.
3. Aristotle. 4. Iphigenia (Greek mythology) 5. Tragedy. I. Title.
B105.C456F46 2007
809'.917—dc22
2006021105

Metuunt cupiuntque, dolent gaudentque,
et quia rectus est amor eorum,
istas omnes affectiones rectas habent.

—De Civitate Dei 14.9

To all those whom I have not loved properly,
and for Joan Kung, teacher

CONTENTS

PREFACE

"As I remember, Adam, it was upon this fashion bequeathed me by will . . ."

As You Like It I.I.I

This is to be a book about the purposes of comedy, by which I mean in the first instance the dramatic art that the ordinary educated imagination unproblematically traces back from contemporary playwrights and movie makers (like Stoppard) through Shakespeare to Aristophanes. It is written in such a way as to open occasionally on to issues of high or scatological humor, jokes, and recreation, and, still at a distance, to adumbrate a parallel between the dramatic genre of comedy and what might be styled (against an author of my existentialist youth) the comic sense of life. There are voices in Kierkegaard who suggest that the comic or humorous borders the religious, and there is a long tradition that styles human life as a comedy, sometimes with the superscript "divine." Those latter filiations will be more frequent and obvious than the first sort, but all of them—scatological, recreational, cultural, and religious—are shadowy filiations outside the main focus of the present study. It is at least historically fitting that the traces of religious discourse should be more obvious in this discussion, since in both its ancient instantiation and its later medieval rebirth comedy had a place in religious festival and at the very least lived in close proximity to liturgy. It is possible to consider jokes as the last reduction of such liturgy, or perhaps the smallest crumb of its real presence.

To write a book in aesthetics has seldom been a clear-edged project, and it seems altogether more questionable these days, for there are critics who will argue against the very possibility of interpretation, as well as those who will question any particular's validity. The world of aesthetics seems to be one in which any presumed facts are overdetermined by theoretical (or practical, limited frequently to political)—perhaps even unconscious—prejudices,[1] the popularity of which change only slightly less quickly than Paris fashions, and the *terminus ad quem* of which is an ever receding hermeneutic horizon.[2] How, then, does one begin? And why?

I suppose it happens the way it happened to me: art does something. And some people, when that does happen, begin to wonder and to question: How did that happen? Or perhaps, What are the conditions for the possibility of that happening? And perhaps first of all, *What* happened *here*? Is this what the maker meant to happen? And that is how this book came into being. Though seeing and performing in *As You Like It* was not my first experience of art working, it set off and centered a long and very complicated assortment of feelings and reflections and that play is the true, if not the onlie, begetter of these insuing sonnets into philosophy. That beginning is now the middle of this book, the first two sections of "The Exemplary Comic Fiction: Resolution, Catharsis and Culture in *As You Like It*." Some readers may wish to read that part first, for it gives a complete emblematic picture of where this book is going and of the relation of plot, personal psychology, and culture it envisions and will attempt to defend in detail and with such exactness as I can presently muster. Shakespeare frequently has insets of his plays within the play that crystallize the action of the play, or are the play writ small to adapt an image of Plato's; the above mentioned sections on *As You Like It* are that for this book, just as several chapters have their own *mise en abyme*.

That old beginning, I realized even while writing it, presumed much. It presumed a story about the function of art, of comedy and tragedy particularly; it presumed, then, a conception of genre and a means of generic distinction; it presumed also a conception of the human being in society, and of human sociality, of ethos and psychology, the details of which in-

1. "Taste . . . you read as ideology." For a good overview of the difficulties of identifying "art" or "the aesthetic," see Thierry de Duve, *Kant after Duchamps* (Cambridge, Mass.: MIT Press, 1996), chapter 1; the quote is from p. 32.

2. Again, Theirry de Duve:

> [The choices about what counts as art] force you to espouse a philosophy of history for which there is no definition of art except the historical process through which art negates itself and comes to terms with its own negation. This process does not have an essence for its ground; rather it has struggle for its motor. It never constitutes itself as a patrimony but projects the heritage of the past into the future in order to contradict it. When you call this process art, you mean that we, humans, don't need to agree about what art is. On the contrary, we need to struggle for what art should be. Some fight for one conception of art, others for another; yet we all stake a claim to what art ought to be for all of us. (21)

clude presumptions about affectivity, cognition, intention, and agency; it is not unfair to say it presumed a conception of spirituality and of the relation of philosophy and art to religion. All of that should not be in the least surprising, for that it touches, or invades, or is invaded by all these other *problemata* is what makes writing on aesthetics so complicated and fraught with intestine war. If it is the messiest part of philosophy, that is because all of Minerva's owls roost here on occasion.[3] In brief, that beginning in *As You Like It* had all the features of an emblem or coat of arms: it was clear, quickly readable, beautiful, and very presumptuous. This book, which is that earlier article's underwriting, will be less quickly readable, and is my attempt to become less presumptuous and considerably more perspicuous and detailed in its argument. Still, if it is not frequently beautiful, I shall have failed in an important aspect of comic philosophy. At times, at least, beauty itself is the reason, the cause, the purpose.

To write a serious book on comedy is not generally taken as a very serious venture, certainly not as serious a venture as writing a serious book on tragedy. And judging things by that serious democratic standard of counting noses, we will find that the number of serious studies of comedy in the last tragic century is far outweighed by the number of studies of tragedy. It's rather funny, in this circumstance, to remember that Plato (that most serious of ancient men, one shadowed by a figure known to history as Plato *comicus*, of whom, they say, no works survive) ends what is arguably his most comic dialogue (one whose *mise en scène* is the house of tragedy) with an argument that the same poet who composes fine tragedy should also be able to compose comedy.[4] Philosophy (Socrates), drinking from the same large bowl as Tragedy (Agathon) and Comedy (Aristophanes) at the end of

3. That is the philosophers' view of the problem of art. The semiotician suggests that

> signs—and art-signs to a greater extent than those of ordinary exchange—have their own existence; they form a system among themselves, but this system is limitless and overwhelms humans who, thinking to serve themselves by working the system, in fact are worked by it. (de Duve, 25)

But how one picks out which signs are "art-signs" being the first question, the distinction de Duve attempts here between art-signs and signs is merely a white mythology, one that might easily lead to a more medieval understanding of everything in the world being an art-sign, and signed by the artist.

4. If my argument about comedy is correct we might recognize *Symposium* as comic by the lightness of its action, which is perhaps built around this question: Can the young victor at the tragic festival throw a symposium in which there is no heavy drinking? More importantly, we should consider the dialogue's effects, which work through our concupiscent passions (of desire and sympathy)—inspiring some, mocking others—rather than through our irascible passions (fear and pity).

Symposium, sees their fellowship and puts them to sleep with an argument about it. It will take history about two thousand years to actualize the philosophical point—in the person of Shakespeare—which is perhaps an indication that history is slow in more than one sense of the word.[5] It may be true that the owl of Minerva flies only at night, but she seems to reach places that have not yet seen the dawn. At least, it was true in former days.

If Plato's Socrates is right—and that he is right, history, eventually, showed—then there is something seriously wrong with a century more serious about tragedy than comedy. The century would exhibit the same failing as the poet who could only do tragedy—but the century writes its fault more largely. The double capacity Socrates says should be found in the man who writes should be true, *mutatis mutandis*, of the man whether he writes or not, and of the culture within which writing comes to be and those arts have a place. The zeitgeist must be suffering from hamartia, from a serious error of judgment, perhaps a lack of self-knowledge, perhaps hubris when it appears as a one-handed playwright. Even that most well balanced of modern critics, Northrop Frye, seems to feel the pull of zeitgeist gravity when he says,

> It is largely through the tragedies of Greek culture that the sense of the authentic natural basis of human character comes into literature. In romance the characters are still largely dream characters; in satire they tend to be caricatures; in comedy their actions are twisted to fit the demands of a happy ending. (*Anatomy*, 206)

But the symmetrical cosmological program Frye had earlier outlined for literature belies the seeming necessity of this asymmetrical connection between tragedy and authentic human character. According to that cosmological compass (162), where plots remain either within the (figuratively superior) world of romance or within the (figuratively inferior) world of experience, or move up from experience (the comic plot—to the East) or down from romance (the tragic plot—toward the West), there is no *necessary structural* difference between characters who inhabit, or move, in the "between" worlds of comedy and tragedy: the difference is in the world and the way it turns. Further, there is a structural symmetry between the characters of the two kinds of plot that Frye himself exhibits by his patterning of comic

5. There is a report of a poet in Hellenistic times who wrote sixty tragedies and thirty comedies, but none of his work survives. Aristotle (in *Poetics* 4) credits Homer (via the historical inaccuracy of imputing authorship of the *Margites* to him) with being the grandfather to both arts.

character types on tragic types (171–76; cf. 216–19). But if the characters in each genre are structurally similar and the upper and lower worlds between which they move are the same, then the only difference between comedy and tragedy is the movement. So, then, the idea that tragic characters are more "authentic" and "natural" must be a confession of the author's belief that movement into the world of "habit, ritual bondage, arbitrary law"—the tragic world (169)—is more authentic and natural than movement into the world of freedom—comedy's world. The hamartia of the zeitgeist bends him—even him—so. But that world is not more natural; in fact, art is not possible to the soul in complete bondage. That is why art is always seen as a threat by one who would be a real tyrant. There is a deep joke in Socrates' association of tyrants and tragedians (*Rep.* 568), as deep and as wise as the Fool's shadowing of Lear. Art is only possible from freedom, and whatever shadow of that freedom remains is what art speaks to in its audience. Frye's supposal about character, then, is a confession of despair, a failure of faith—or perhaps he is playing the fool.

Already we have overshot our mark, coming to conclusions far beyond what little argument and less explication has so far been presented; but perhaps this illumines some of the more deeply involved problems—social, political, spiritual—that are tied up with any venture into philosophy of art. For clearly the hamartia that so valorizes tragedy over her more happy sister is both a personal and a social—or political—matter, and it is the task of philosophy to attempt to discover and exhibit it. Before daring to attempt such cultural criticism, however, a thinker has to have the concepts at his finger's ends. This book will undertake a smaller task than a critique of religion, art, and society in the twentieth century, but a task that is a necessary preliminary to them: the main aim of this book is to discover and exhibit the purposes of comedy.

Comedy's more well thought of sister must first be allowed her dance; the argument about comedy will then proceed by antistrophe. I suppose that Aristotle's original book on poetics was structured similarly, though *Poetics* now holds only half of the dance. My analysis starts from the aesthetically and critically problematic case of the *Iphigenia in Tauris*. This play is the decisive node and key to the dance of the sisters, for Aristotle said it contained the best kind of tragic pathos—one in which the deed of suffering that threatens *is avoided by recognition*. The modern critic is absolutely stymied by this statement. She thinks *Iphigenia* should be a comedy, or some middle form—tragicomedy.[6] There is no good reason to suspect Aristotle's text of corruption here (though, naturally, that has been done); the problem must be faced and solved. How could Aristotle consider a story with a happy ending tragic at all? I will argue that in order to understand Aristotle's position we must pay attention to the catharsis of the passions of the audience, for this personal and social effect is the final cause of the poem, and it is only by reference to the purposes of made things that we can judge whether or not those things are well made. The first chapter of this book will therefore lay out Aristotle's reasoning about tragedy and its catharsis, and show how *Iphigenia* is the best form of tragedy under this view.

The solution to the problem of the *Iphigenia in Tauris*—why Aristotle calls it a tragedy and why he is right to call it the best exemplar of the type—provides the clue to understanding what the purposes of comedy are. The second chapter of the book will then present and defend an Aristotelian view of comedy, using as its main example Aristophanes' *Acharnians*, and together the first two chapters will limn, I hope, at least the archway—the propylaia—to the argument Plato pretends took place at Agathon's house just before the dawn of a day so many centuries ago. The third and fourth chapters will concentrate on applying the understanding of comic catharsis to two exemplary fictions from other times and cultures: Shakespeare's *As You Like It* and Tom Stoppard's *Arcadia*. We will close by returning to the drinking party where these two sisters were first seen as twins born of the same genius. One might think of the whole book as a long pause in a porch, a thought before a symposium.

The whole book may be seen as defending a double thesis about comedy, namely, a purely philosophical thesis that comedy's purpose was and is catharsis of the passions of desire and sympathy, and a historical-philosophical thesis that this explication is most likely to have been Aristotle's. That comedy transhistorically and cross-culturally does aim at catharsis of desire and sympathy is due to the nature of the finite rational and mimetic creature, which—as finite—is given to suffer pleasure and pain, and—as rational and mimetic—is a maker of poems or, more generally, mimeses, and desires to know. It will be true under this Aristotelian view that insofar as our natural desires and sympathies are culturally shaped (which Aristotle presumes), there will be differences across societies. It is the similarity of human desire

6. See, e.g., Anne Pippin Burnett, *Catastrophe Survived: Euripides' Plays of Mixed Reversal*, and Kitto's "New Tragedy: Euripides' Tragi-comedies," chapter 11 in *Greek Tragedy*.

and sympathy, pity and fear that roots the experience of comedy or tragedy, however. A culture that considers the eating of its children an honorable thing, a great desideratum, will not be able to experience much of Greek tragedy as tragic; the action is, rather, to them, high comedy. Such a culture is not long for this world, though if there are immortal souls, one could imagine such feasting going on forever.

Because this human nature is the source of art, any argument about art proclaims (or hides) a thesis about human nature; this is as true of Nietzsche (a proclaimer) and Derrida (a disclaimer) as it is about Plato and Aristotle, who exhibit the problem perspicuously. So, this book's two arguments (historical about Aristotle and philosophical about comedy) are necessarily interwoven not only because Aristotle sets out the original terms of the discussion, but also because I think Aristotle is right about a large number of things in the areas we will touch upon. In other words, I think this interpretation of Aristotle is a reasonable view of Aristotle, and true about comedy and human beings—or perhaps I should say about the great comedy of being human. It is, of course, possible that readers of Aristotle will disagree with some of my ideas about Aristotle. Despite this, they may find themselves in agreement with the argument about comedy. Being less a historian of philosophy than a philosopher, my main interest is in the latter argument. I do not, however, agree with Harold Bloom that all of our creative thinking is misprision of our intellectual fathers, though that may happen on occasion.

This project's interdisciplinary and transhistorical nature may make the reading difficult in our overspecialized and decidedly historicised age. That the chapters are divided into various sorts of subparts is an attempt to make it less so. But it will perhaps be most helpful to say here why all the various things that are in this book have come to be in it, as a way of explaining how that division is to work. My original purpose was an investigation of comedy, by which I mean, in the first instance, the dramatic genre. But what counts, or ought to count, as a member of this generic category is part of the question at issue, and so one might well be puzzled about how to begin. If one begins with an a priori definition of comedy, nothing in art—like the existence of an *Iphigenia*—will call it into question, and the scholarly dialectic will merely be about diverging uses of terms (like *comedy*) among families of critics. Such a project rightly (*recte et juste*) names sublunary things only by accident or by lawyerly stipulation. Eschewing such nominalism, there is a smaller and more practical (if anything in literary criticism is to be counted "practical") way into the problem, which in fact became a troubling puzzle to me. That practical problem is the status of the *Iphigenia in Tauris*, a play with a discovery and recognition leading from dire threat of horror to a happy ending, which Aristotle calls the best kind of tragedy. The way into the problem of comedy and its purpose for me was to attempt to understand, in properly historical terms, why Aristotle should have considered this to be the case.

That particular investigation threw me (again) into the very deep and much stirred waters of Greek philology and poetry, as well as Aristotle's wider—particularly ethical and political—philosophical concerns, which are tied to his understanding of the nature and purpose of poetry. I cannot expect that every reader will be interested in swimming through all of that water in order to come up in the promised bejewelled and open cove of the comic catharsis to which I first attained by such hard swimming. I have therefore arranged the larger journey (of the book's chapters) after the basic pattern of my own journey of discovery, but broken each into discrete sections of relative independence, not all of which are equally necessary to achieve the final goal. The title and occasional short summary of each section should allow each reader to decide whether or not the section is necessary or interesting for the reader's own purpose. For example, someone interested only in literary criticism of comedy might skip all of Chapter 1; someone interested in both dances, but not in the esoterica of Aristotle's psychology, could easily skip section four of Chapter 1, as I have in giving that chapter as lectures to such audiences, without ill effect. On the other hand, a classicist who wants to know why I think the view I am espousing is Aristotelian will need to read it, but may be less interested in the modern problem about the relative freedom of aesthetic judgments raised at the end of Chapter 3.

Greek theater was part of a civic (political, in the Greek sense) religious festival. In the course of the argument there will be more and less glancing remarks in these regards to contemporary culture, but the serious issue of the relation between religion and drama—especially as it applies to contemporary culture—will be left to the side (or merely figured, as Dante's unnamed *Inferno* a bit above) for future investigation. I want the reader to keep in mind, however, the important question about the relationship of the comic and the tragic to the religious, and read this study under the dawning light of this historical—or better—dramatic question: Whether or not our loss of the civic and religious significance of comedy and tragedy is a comic, tragic, or religious *pathos*? Perhaps, even, a cultural hamartia.

Of course it could be that Plato was not serious about the consanguinity of the tragic and the comic—after all, his *eirōn* is speaking, everyone but he is drunk, the would-be reporter has fallen asleep, and Plato never lets on what the convincing argument is. That dialogue itself is a comedy, and perhaps we should not expect anything too serious to come out of a drinking party. Perhaps that ancient krater does not hold any secret of life, not even the lees of a secret; perhaps Plato did not mean anything by the fact that comedy and tragedy drink from the same large bowl as philosophy throughout the night after the festive communal ritual. In that case this book is only an imaginary gadfly in a real, but decaying, garden.

A NOTE ON KEY WORDS AND REFERENCES

It is difficult to trace what may or may not be intricacies of argument across languages, to say nothing of *tempora* and *mores*. It is particularly difficult if one is not a philologist. Nonetheless, philology is a useful tool for philosophical investigation, and so I have, throughout this text, taken note of where the interested reader may find more philological evidence or argument on disputed points. Most of this book will be in relatively standard English with the addition of several words which, instead of translating, I merely transliterate and leave (after this introduction) unitalicized, hoping that the significance of Aristotle's concepts (or my perversion of them) might become clear in their use. Though many scholars translate these words in various ways, I am of the opinion that the translations beg absolutely essential philosophical or poetic questions and stir up scholarly tempests merely by their presence. The first such word, the centrality of which has already been made obvious, is *mimēsis* (Greek plural, *mimēseis*); it is sometimes translated by representation, sometimes by imitation. It is the central term of art in *Poetics*, philologically absolutely distinct from that famous *eikōn* (515a) of the cave—which is (a representation? an imitation? an imaginary picture?) of our natural state.[1] Mimesis is almost a legitimate English word—it is listed in the *Oxford English Dictionary* (hereafter *OED*) as "not naturalized,"

1. It is not, I think, illicit to contrast the mimetic and iconic functions of language or, more generally, signs. The iconic works as reference or representation *of* something; the mimetic is immediate; we don't just mean things, we fall into patterns of rhythm and tone (as well as word choice) which allow Professor Higgins to tell within a space of six blocks what neighborhood we learned our mother tongue in. That is, he reads our mimetic nature as a sign—that's how science treats everything, but what those things are is the mimetic, not the iconic aspect of our speech. The Athenian Stranger, for example, seems to be trying to get Kleinias to pick up this distinction in what leads up to and away from his remark that "all the arts of the muses are iconic and mimetic" (εἰκαστικήν τε . . . καὶ μιμητικήν, *Laws* 668a). For the application of this distinction, see my "Intentionality and Mimesis."

though it should be in the field of aesthetics, since Aristotle uses the word to identify not only poetry and Socratic dialogue, but also dance, music, and painting. Stephen Halliwell's most recent book is (among other things) an extended argument against translating the word into the more impoverished term "imitation," or the more cognitively penumbraed "representation." In an effort to naturalize its citizenship in English, I will use the word as if it is so already, providing an English plural—mimeses—which follows the usual habitus of English theft and reclamation, simplifying the foreign orthography.

Catharsis (katharsis) was, by all accounts, a term of several arts—religion, music, medicine—even before Plato's time. Its most common translations are purification, purgation, and clarification. To attempt to translate it by reference to one or another of these, however, is to limit the resources of the word—and every translation does so. Such limitation is thoroughly unjustified by the text of *Poetics*—where catharsis appears once—and stands against the multiple meanings available in *Politics* 8.[2] The *OED* treats this word also as not naturalized, and emphasizes its medical meaning—purgation; it traces the word's history in English to the mid-nineteenth century, around the time when Bernays (Freud's wife's uncle) published his influential work on the topic, a work that favored the purgative signification. Let us be suspicious of this Victorian constriction.

The third word I will not touch is *hamartia*—variously translated as sin, flaw, error, miscalculation (a rather large range of moral and nonmoral concepts).[3] It is not so frequently transliterated as mimesis, but as I was not sure when I began this investigation where it would lead in the moral and religious realm, I chose to leave it a Greek blank and see where I ended up. (Perhaps this is a confession of hamartia.) House describes in admirable brevity how this term is linked to discovery and peripety in his discussion (cf. 93–99): "the discovery of the truth . . . [is the] wakening from that state of ig-

2. Halliwell concludes his discussion of the term similarly; see his Loeb translation of *Poetics*, 198–201. See also House, 104–11.

3. Adkins holds that *hamartia* is "not a technical term for any one of the three possible alternatives by which it is rendered in English" ("Aristotle," 82; see also 83, 87–90). Stinton seems to agree; he considers that all of its various meanings are plausible at different points in Aristotle's argument. John Jones gives a brief explanation of the problems engendered by taking the word as necessarily moral (15); Nussbaum argues for a wide range of meanings (*Fragility*, 282f). Golden's thorough review (*Tragic and Comic*, 80–89) argues in favor of a morally nonculpable error of judgment. This seems to be too narrowly specific in the nonmoral direction, after a century (the nineteenth) and more of narrow moralism.

norance [or error in judgment] which is the very essence of 'hamartia'" (98), from (or with) which awakening the peripety follows.

The most famous example of hamartia is another word I wish to leave transliterated—*hubris*, sometimes spelled *hybris*. "Outrage" or "wanton insolence" are not unreasonable translations, but this one I prefer to leave untranslated for poetic reasons: I like its heft, the way it breathes its meaning. Curiously, my *OED* allows *hubristic*, but not the noun. For similar poetic reasons I will use *telos*—end, goal, purpose—as if it were English. It has, to me, always sounded like an arrow hitting its mark.

Philia and its cognates present other problems for translation. "Love" in English is too romantically colored, or too variable; "friendship" too weak—perhaps these problems are not merely linguistic, but cultural. Among other things. Philia is deep and natural to man; our *philoi* are the most important of external goods, and an aid to all the internal ones: the virtues. Gods and beasts may live without *philoi*, men only unhappily, if at all. Philia joins the family together, and friends together too, as well as the philosopher to wisdom. It is perhaps not too much to say that it is what makes a unity of any community, as Aristotle shows in *NE* 8. Several recent and important Aristotelian studies of literature by Belfiore and Nussbaum use the transliteration of these terms as a matter of course; I would be friends with them, though I do not agree with them on all other points.

The last word will cause greater difficulty because it is in all English dictionaries, though there is great debate about whether it means the same thing for Aristotle and in *Poetics* as it does in English. That word in Greek is *philanthrōpia* or τὸ φιλάνθρωπον—philanthropy or the philanthropic. It does not mean, for Aristotle, giving large sums of money to charitable work. Stephen Halliwell's translation of it as fellow-feeling strikes me as pretty good, but, as it may range from broad human sympathy even with sinners and the hamartemic to a more narrow basic sense of justice that discounts that latter group, I thought it best to mark the word here and leave it transliterated.[4]

In all those cases I henceforward leave the word in ordinary type, just as if it were ordinary English. Foreign words and phrases, the significance of which is sometimes technical (e.g., *eikōn*, *technē*, *poiēsis*, *pathos*) and some-

4. See, e.g., Halliwell's translation in the new Loeb edition. Gould discusses the term at xxii, 53f; see also Moles ("Philanthropia"), who tends toward the "moral feeling" or "sense of justice" interpretation of the word. Else opts for "relatively indiscriminate fellow feeling"; cf. *Argument*, 368–71.

times rhetorical (*tempora, mores, fait accompli*), I have anglicized in spelling and italicized. I hope their significance is either known to the reader or figurable from the context. With regard to other Greek words, where I have thought a reader might be helped to keep some things in Aristotle related or distinct, or where I (or another scholar) depend upon a change or continuity in Aristotle's terminology for part of an argument, I have placed the Greek word or phrase as near as practicable to the English word or phrase in question. I have used the universally available Greek version given in Stephen Halliwell's new Loeb edition of *Poetics* as my source in these cases, and the older Loeb editions for other texts in which I have made reference to the Greek.

All works referred to frequently are given abbreviated references after their title. All texts with standard reference (e.g., works of Plato, Aristotle, Augustine, Shakespeare, Kant, Nietzsche) are referred to according to the appropriate scholarly convention rather than page number of any edition. In the case of Aristophanes the line number of the Greek text (Loeb edition) is followed by the page in the translation of his complete plays edited by Hadas.

WORKS AND EDITIONS OF ARISTOTLE

De Anima (*DA*). Translated by J. A. Smith. In *Basic Works of Aristotle*, ed. Richard McKeon. New York: Random House, 1941.

———. Translated by W. S. Hett. Cambridge, Mass.: Harvard University Press (Loeb Classical Library), 1975.

De Motu Animalium (*DMA*). Translated with commentary and interpretive essays by Martha Craven Nussbaum. Princeton, N.J.: Princeton University Press, 1978.

———. Translated by E. S. Forster, M.A. Cambridge, Mass.: Harvard University Press (Loeb Classical Library), 1983.

De Interpretatione (*De Int.*). Translated by E. M. Edghill. In *Basic Works of Aristotle*, ed. Richard McKeon. New York: Random House, 1941.

———. *Commentary by St. Thomas and Cajetan.* Translated by Jean T. Oesterle. Milwaukee, Minn.: Marquette University Press, 1962.

Eudemian Ethics (*EE*). Translated by H. Rackham. Cambridge, Mass.: Harvard University Press (Loeb Classical Library), 1952.

Nicomachean Ethics (*NE*). Translated by W. D. Ross. In *Basic Works of Aristotle*, ed. Richard McKeon. New York: Random House, 1941.

———. Translated by H. Rackham. Cambridge, Mass.: Harvard University Press (Loeb Classical Library), 1962.

———. Translated by Martin Ostwald. Indianapolis, Ind.: Bobbs-Merrill, 1962.

Metaphysics (*Meta.*). Translated by W. D. Ross. In *Basic Works of Aristotle*, ed. Richard McKeon. New York: Random House, 1941.

Parva Naturalia (*PN*). Translated by W. S. Hett. Cambridge, Mass.: Harvard University Press (Loeb Classical Library), 1965.

Physics. Translated by R. P. Hardie and R. K. Gaye. In *Basic Works of Aristotle*, ed. Richard McKeon. New York: Random House, 1941.

———. Translated by Philip H. Wick Steed and Francis M. Cornford. London: William Heinemann Ltd. (Loeb Classical Library), 1970.

Poetics (*Po.*). Translated by Ingram Bywater. New York: Modern Library, 1984.

———. Translated by Leon Golden. Englewood Cliffs, N.J.: Prentice-Hall, 1968.

———. Introduction, Commentary and Appendixes by D. W. Lucas. Oxford, U.K.: Clarendon Press, 1968.

———. Translated by Stephen Halliwell. Cambridge, Mass.: Harvard University Press (Loeb Classical Library), 1995.

Politics (*Pol.*). Translated by Benjamin Jowett. In *Basic Works of Aristotle*, ed. Richard McKeon. New York: Random House, 1941.

———. Translated by H. Rackham. London: William Heinemann Ltd. (Loeb Classical Library), 1932.

Posterior Analytics (*An. Post.*). Translated by Hugh Tredennick. London: William Heinemann Ltd. (Loeb Classical Library), 1960.

Problems. Translated by W. S. Hett. Cambridge, Mass.: Harvard University Press (Loeb Classical Library), 1965.

Rhetoric (*Rh.*). Translated by W. Rhys Roberts. New York: Modern Library Editions, 1984.

———. Translated by John Henry Freese. Cambridge, Mass.: Harvard University Press (Loeb Classical Library), 1967.

ACKNOWLEDGMENTS

Parts of this book have been delivered as lectures at various venues; among them are the Society of Ancient Greek Philosophy meetings at State University of New York at Binghamton and Fordham University as well as their meetings with the American Philosophical Association, the Philosophy of Education Society of Great Britain at Oxford University, and the International Society for Neoplatonic Studies at Orono, Maine. The greatest part of the research was done during a year's sabbatical granted by the University of Nebraska–Kearney Research Services Council for the academic year 1996–1997. Thanks to the audiences for their comments and to the University of Nebraska–Kearney for its funding of the sabbatical and for some of the travel to conferences.

Parts of the book have also been previously published, with some changes in this recension. Thanks to Johns Hopkins University Press, which originally published much of the first two sections of Chapter 3 as "Resolution, Catharsis, Culture: *As You Like It*" in *Philosophy and Literature* 19 (October 1995): 248–60. Thanks also to Blackwell Publishing which originally printed part of Chapter 2, section three, as "*Hippias Major, Version 1.0*: Software for Post-Colonial, Multicultural Technology Systems" in *Journal of the Philosophy of Education* 37, no. 1 (2003): 89–99.

As this book has been under construction for over a decade thanks are due to many readers of various parts and editions. Most helpful of all has been the last reader, Professor Stephen Halliwell of St. Andrew's University, who read a draft I thought finished and offered considerable constructive criticism and suggestions for a bit more research—and then reread the manuscript. I am sure they did not pay you enough! Thanks also to an unnamed reader at the Catholic University of America Press, who (among other things) made me become clear about what I did not want to be taken as doing and also explain why I was not doing it. Thanks to Allen Dunn who read and commented on the whole manuscript during a National Endowment for the Humanities seminar on Literature and Values in the summer immediately preceding my sending it to the Catholic University of America Press for its first reading. Thanks to Owen Goldin of Marquette University for helping me with the Greek, and to Fr. Dan Pekarske, H. L. Hix, and Paul Schollmeier for reading much of the book in early versions. I also owe a debt of gratitude to numerous students through the years who worked through many of the texts utilized in this study in courses on Shakespeare, the philosophy of tragedy, ancient philosophy, and aesthetics as well as the regular introductory courses in philosophy and in ethics; I hope that they found the work sufficiently cathartic and inspiring to our most proper love.

Love Song for the Life of the Mind

PROPYLAIA

In a recent book opening on to many of the issues this one will examine, Stephen Halliwell invokes the shade of Goethe, in particular his essay "Über Wahrheit und Wahrscheinlichkeit der Kunstwerke," as the propylaia for his reexamination of the concept of mimesis.[1] In setting up this propylaia Halliwell follows Goethe, who draws our mind from a simplistic view of mimetic art as "sheer illusionism—like the famous birds reputedly tricked into pecking at Zeuxis' painted grapes" to the mimetic as having "the psychological power to draw its audience into its world, to offer something that is wholly convincing and absorbing in its own terms" (3). Since it is clear that the grapes did achieve this also, at least for the birds, we can see that Halliwell is arguing for an expansion of the concept of "the mimetic" (*to mimētikon*) from the narrow product of representationalism and realism made by the kind of imagination Plato famously represented as a mirror, to something more like the creation of a (hetero-) cosmos by a more powerful demiurge (also called imagination by Plato)—into which cosmos the audience is drawn.[2] For Goethe, the expanded notion of mimesis was one that allowed insight into the "inner truth" of things (2, 4). Halliwell corrects the romantic tendency toward a solipsistic subjectivity this phrase might give rise to by precisely defining a point in the middle distance. He contends that mimesis "depict[s] and illuminate[s] a world that is (partly) accessible and knowable outside art, and by whose norms art can therefore, within limits,

1. Stephen Halliwell, *The Aesthetics of Mimesis: Ancient Texts and Modern Problems* (Princeton, N.J.: Princeton University Press, 2002). References to this book are by page number in the text of this propylaia.

2. In "Two Views of the Imagination" I argue that Plato himself considers the imagination under two distinct metaphors: the mirror and the demiurge of images; for more on this distinction, see that article.

be tested and judged," even while admitting that mimesis is "the creator of an independent heterocosm . . . [which] may still purport to contain some kind of 'truth' about, or grasp of, reality as a whole" (5). This more complex view of mimesis is, he shows, "present in the tradition of thought about mimesis from a very early stage" (5). This ancient sense of mimesis precedes our popular division between realist and representationalist theories of art on the one side and romantic expressionist and emotivist theories on the other. The ancient word *mimesis* plays on both sides of our modern division.

One might, in fact, write a whole history of the philosophy of art within the bounds of "mimesis" so broadly and anciently understood. Little would escape it. As the originally broader term is pruned radically back to "mere" imitation, other terms of art must develop to stake out the phenomena once included in the richer ancient concept. The metaphors of the mirror/depicts and the lamp/illuminates, which have been seen as distinguishing the classical and the romantic, find their air here in this newly pruned area, as does that of the romantic creative genius (a demiurge somewhat forgetful of its "demi" status). This last, we should remember, as the δημιουργὸς εἰδώλων (597d–99a), as well as the first (the mirror), can be traced explicitly to *Republic* 10. Exhibiting the presence and operation of that more complicated view of mimesis in Plato and Aristotle, and tracing it through philosophies of art "from Plato, as one might aptly put it, to Derrida" (6) is what Halliwell's book does.

With Halliwell's project, at once both historical and philosophical, my own efforts in this book have a large measure of agreement and community of purpose. Like his, this project aims to be historical: it aims to build up, from the extant corpus of Aristotle, what his famously missing theory of comedy might have been. It also aims to be philosophical (as Aristotle would have been), for it presents an argument about what the nature and function of that made thing—comedy—is, which, if true, provides grounds for judgment of better and worse forms (as Aristotle does for tragedy in *Poetics* 14 and and Plato famously does in *Republic* for art generally). Clearly, the historical and philosophical aims of my project are intrinsically interrelated for a considerable length. For any attempt to make a historical claim about Aristotle's view of comedy requires more than two steps back into the larger interpretation of Aristotle's philosophy generally. And any attempt to make a philosophical argument about comedy requires a non-question-begging delineation of which of the historically conditioned phenomena are to be accounted for. The interpretation of Aristotle built up in the course of this book (particularly the first half) is not likely to be in complete agreement with anyone else's, but I trust it is also not entirely disagreeable to all other Aristotle scholars; I have a similar expectation regarding literary critics and the view of comedy here espoused. The introduction and particular development of all these (sometimes extremely fraught) matters is always bent toward the explication and resolution of the problem of the nature and purpose of comic drama, which problem I find I cannot rightly set out or answer without taking them up in some detail.

While the manner of this investigation is like Halliwell's in being at once historical and philosophical, and shares some considerable agreement with it about both aesthetics and Aristotle, my scope is considerably more limited. More particularly, it is because of my more limited focus on Aristotle (not all ancient mimetic theorizing) and dramatic comedy (not all ancient arts) that I have been so bold as to appropriate his book as the propylaia for mine.[3] A *propylaia,* as he explains, is an entryway, an architectural portal; in particular, it is the entry into the acropolis at Athens, and also was the title of Goethe's aesthetic journal, in which his above-named essay first appeared. So, let us say I have set my sights on the (missing) temple of the goddess of comedy, and in order to get you to see where it was and how it was built, I set you on a particular step (Aristotle's) and turn your sight through a particular portal (the mimetic theory of art) and, by contrast, to a less catastrophically destroyed sister temple (tragedy) visible through the same portal from that step. That is the purpose of the first chapter. I may then be able to turn you to see how certain broken columns and fragmentary walls might well have fit together to support the missing light and airy temple that we seek (in Chapter 2). This ancient outline will be more particularly filled in by reference to works of Aristophanes (*Acharnians*) and Plato (*Hippias Major* and *Phaedrus*). Having done that, I will then try to show how several other works (Shakespeare's *As You Like It* in Chapter 3 and Stoppard's *Arcadia* in Chapter 4) accomplish, each in their way, the same function as that ancient temple. During the discussions of those particular works I will return to some wider aesthetic and cultural concerns, concerns that affiliate my project again with Halliwell's. I will close with a comic and philosophical read-

3. Halliwell's book was published while I was first looking for a publisher for this book. It is too important not to be taken account of, so I have rewritten all of the Propylaia and some additional matter in order to do so.

ing of *Symposium*, which will show this Aristotelian philosophical project to perhaps have been instigated by (and go a long way to explaining the working of) that Platonic comedy (in the Epilogue). The limitation of scope to an Aristotelian theory of comedy means I will not have much to say about other theories, like Hobbes's or Bergson's. My choice to focus for considerable time on particular works of Aristophanes, Plato, Shakespeare, and Stoppard precludes a wide-ranging menagerie of examples from comic drama, and my focus (as Aristotle's) on drama leaves nondramatic genres of comedy largely on the side. I argue, however, that Aristotle picks drama as his subject in *Poetics* because it is the form of mimesis that includes the means of mimesis all the other arts only use some of, so what applies to tragedy/comedy in drama will apply *mutatis mutandis* (a very generous term, which should always be in Latin in order to mimic the specificity that it precisely avoids representing) to the more limited mimeses (e.g., dance, music, lyric).

It is legitimate to ask, as anyone who has come upon an ancient propylaia in a rain forest or in the welter of a modern city built over the ruins of an older one, Why this particular propylaia? And also, Why is this one where it is? Halliwell shows that "mimesis gave antiquity something much closer to a unified conception of 'art'" than many modern thinkers have been willing to admit (7). He fills out the details of this conception to show that it includes both representational and expressive elements, which modern theories of art separate (7, 13–16, 21–23, 172–73, 188–90, et al.). And he points out how the mimetic conception extends through "a series of grades of imaginative absorption" on the part of the audience, from "quasi-participant . . . to the holding of an attitude of critical detachment" (80; cf., e.g., 88–93, 98–101, 238–39). His explication is more than sufficient to defend the importance and repossess the fullness of significance the mimetic theory of art has.

While that history provides sufficient reason for choosing the mimetic theory of art as one's propylaia for an understanding of comedy, I think Aristotle quite specifically, and the ancient thinkers generally, built this particular entryway because of the things themselves: mimesis is the real entryway into humanness; *homo mimeticus* is the way into *homo sapiens*. Mimesis opens the construction of culture. That the mimetic is not merely the basis for a theory of art, and of artistic importance, but of anthropological import and the root of humanity is stated most clearly by Aristotle: mimesis is natural to us (κατὰ φύσιν 1448b20; cf. 3–8); it is original, the most distinctive instinct of anthropos (σύμφυτον τοῖς ἀνθρώποις; 1448b5), though other animals have it to some degree. And ontogeny recapitulates phylogeny: mimesis is the way in which the individual first learns (1448b7);[4] it is because mimesis works, as Plato puts it, "before reason" that it is both so important and so potentially dangerous (*Rep.* 402a; cf. *Laws* 653b, c; Aristotle approvingly refers to this at *NE* 1104b10–13). It is through mimesis that we are set up for virtue or vice before judgment becomes active, just as one or another "natural virtue" might be found in a soul, but needs rational judgment to become virtue in the full sense (*NE* 1144b3–18).[5] The mimetic animal is shaped in accord with the fears, desires, pleasures, and pains of those around him, just as cognition is given its first objects by repeated perception; all learning seems to be founded on this (*An. Post.* 99b6–100a3).[6] So, this propylaia is far from an accidental cultural construction, or accidentally placed; it marks the birth canal of the human individual and of all culture. The development of individual arts recapitulates that of the individual: certain kinds of character

4. This point is made by Halvard Fossheim in "Mimesis in Aristotle's Ethics," in *Making Sense of Aristotle: Essays in Poetics*: "according to Aristotle, we take our first steps in understanding of the human good by the natural propensity, from childhood onwards, to be thoroughly engaged in and formed by the activity of 'being like'" (84). We take our first steps in evil this way too.

5. Of interest in this regard is the question from the pseudo-Aristotelian *Problems* (30.6, 956a11–14):

> Why should one trust more in a human being than in another animal? Is it . . . because humans alone among animals know (ἐπίσταται) how to count? Or because humans alone believe (νομίζει) in the gods? Or because humans are the most mimetic of all animals? For this enables them to learn (μανθάνειν).

(Cf. S. Halliwell, who invokes this passage at the beginning of his "Aristotelian Mimesis and Human Understanding," in *Making Sense of Aristotle: Essays in Poetics*, 87). The usual structure of these problems is that the last sentence offers the (pseudo-) Aristotelian answer. If our learning and understanding grow out of mimesis (as Aristotle pretty clearly says in *Poetics* 4), and if our linguistic ability is one of those things we begin to learn and understand through mimesis, perhaps even counting finds its source there, as well as opinions about the gods, as this problem suggests. Rene Girard's thesis that the source of religion is mimesis ties belief in the gods directly to "being like the other" in passion and desire, without and before the direction of concept and rationality. Aristotle could go far along this Girardian line, holding that "mimesis has the potential to generate elaborate forms of cultural practice" (ibid., 88). If both religion and learning come through this gate, then the differential attributes of, and the differences between cultures within, the human arise from this fact: "man is the most mimetic of animals." This may not, however, be grounds for trust.

6. Rene Girard claims that the mimetic crisis that is resolved in violence "creates a new degree of attention, the first non-instinctual attention" (*Things Hidden since the Foundation of the World*, 99). Aristotle need not agree about the foundational violence at the origin of signification, but that the mimetic nature of human beings is what first focuses our attention "beyond the purely instinctual . . . , the alimentary or sexual object" (ibid.) he does share with Girard. This kind of attention and "learning"is necessary before anything like the learning *An. Post.* explicates is possible. It is, then, "before reason."

improvised noble mimeses, certain others improvised in a more vulgar fashion (1448b23–27). Perhaps each artist chose which way he would improvise; it is far more likely he *found himself improvising* on what was going around the neighborhood or in the culture at large—and then became conscious of it—and when the neighborhood or culture liked the effects, or the effect was a solution or re-creation of the solution to what Girard calls the mimetic crisis, he continued in them. Having been formed by repetition he became like the things he repeated, and he improvised accordingly. The passivity of original mimesis, this "being taken up by" mimesis, rather than a more cognitivist "proposing to" imitate is important according to Aristotle, even for the seemingly active poet, for the art "demands a man with a special gift for it, or else one with a touch of madness in him; the former can easily assume the required mood, and the latter may be ecstatic" (*Po.* 1455a33–35).

Even these brief lines from *Poetics* 4 suggest a wide range of complex problems in developmental psychology, anthropology, individual and social psychology, and perhaps even comparative biology, tied up with the expected difficulties in philosophy of art, art's relationship to ethics and politics, and philosophy of education for which Plato and Aristotle are still providing the root questions. These lines from *Poetics* suggest that Aristotle (as Plato) is aware of these deeper and seemingly more obscure relations and complexities. Mimesis is, I want to say, of deeper significance and greater import for the ancients than as even the central concept in the philosophy of art. It is the proylaia of all humanity; through it we enter into our city. (Each culture or epoch or city into its own.) In this matter I think that Halliwell does not go far enough, though I do not suppose that extending the import of the concept of mimesis beyond aesthetics is something with which he must necessarily disagree.

Raising the issue of the place and function of mimesis in anthropology and developmental psychology, however, also brings forward a critique of several philosophical distinctions that are presently taken for granted, as is the distinction in aesthetics between representative and emotivist theories of art. Two such distinctions that will be of importance in what follows are the distinction between cognitivist and conativist theories of human action, and the distinction between cognitivist and noncognitivist theories of emotion. Halliwell touches on the second of these areas in his discussion of musical mimesis (in chapters 5 and 8). There he argues that "the patterns of music have properties 'like' the emotional states" and so the experience of music "appears, for

Aristotle, to be a matter of experiencing emotions that are not just indicated or evoked . . . but are in some sense enacted by the qualities of the artwork" (159). This is exactly correct in my view, and correct about Aristotle. However, he interprets Aristotle's story as an iconic—in Pierce's sense of "denot[ing] merely by virtue of characters of its own" (160)—treatment of musical mimesis. Tellingly, this iconic explication of Aristotle is one that "we need to supplement" because of Aristotle's emphasis on the directness of the effect music has on us (160). The problem Halliwell's felt need for a supplement here touches upon is that for music to be seen as an iconic *sign*, and for it to function as such a sign *denoting*, say, some *kinēsis* of "emotional-cum-ethical feelings" (159) implies an altogether too well-developed cognitive and possessively individualist psychology for the immediacy, directness, and simplicity Aristotle presumes for musical mimeses's effects (which even are visible in animals). The mimetic *arts* do, I agree, "*embod*[*y*] or *enact* [their] 'likeness(es)' in [their] own organized form" (190), but their kinesis transfers in a way that is more mechanical (or biologically infectious) than cognitive: perception, pleasure, and pain are all that is necessary. Several of Aristotle's word choices and images will make this point. Socrates' demand in *Republic* for certain kinds of rhythm and tone patterns, and for the dismissal of others, is a recognition of this same mechanism.

So when Aristotle says we learn (μανθάνειν) *first* through mimesis, he must mean that kind of learning that underlies all of what we usually call learning. In *Posterior Analytics* 1.1, he explains that someone who is learning something (μανθάνειν) in a sense already knows (ἐπίστασθαι). But this means, he says, that some kind of learning (μανθάνειν) must already have taken place and preceded the kind of learning *Posterior Analytics* is discussing. Halliwell notes that "the spectrum of *manthanein* continues below the human (*Meta.* 980b21–5)"[7]—just as the mimetic does. These connections of mimesis and the earliest form of learning with the nonrational souls of animals is a good indication that Aristotle has in mind something more mechanical or infectious than rationally cognitivist. Feeling pleasure and pain, desire and fear, as those around us do, is something we "learn" before we know we are learning—indeed, before we are able to know at all, reason not yet functioning in the infant and young child.[8]

7. See "Aristotelian Mimesis and Human Understanding," p. 107, n. 44.

8. This natural mimetic noncognitivism may be hinted at also by Aristotle's remark that "it was not art but chance that made the poets discover how to produce such effects" (*Po.* 1454a10–12).

Thus much on how the mimetic works on the human being—the subjective effects of mimesis. On the other side of the work—as made things, or objects—musical and other mimetic works are admittedly an advance upon the original mimeses in which and through which human beings first learn. Clearly, the artist, as someone with a *technē*, puts the music together with knowledge of how the music works and (in many cases, like drama) the signs denote, but the music works of itself, not as "a sign" "denoting" (even "by virtue of characters of its own") some emotional-cum-ethical feeling. Mimesis understood from this more advanced side has "something like the factor of iconicity" (169) Pierce finds in certain signs, but my point is that the work of mimesis is essentially distinct from and precedes cognition of signs—of which the mimetic artist is well cognizant. The mimetic is that in which we have already participated, and by which we *have already been taken up* (the passive voice is essential here) before any recognitions of likeness—such as that between the movement of a certain piece of music and a certain feeling—take place. This is so much the case that it may even be true of the musician—the one making the mimetic thing, particularly in cultures that have no written music or for instruments (such as the gamelan orchestra) for which writing seems impossible. Aristotle considers that a better poet has this mimetic gift—even being ecstatic. Signs need cognition (and explicating Aristotle via Pierce takes Halliwell in a cognitivist direction), but the musical mimesis only requires that we be taken up into the musical thing itself, not that *we make* cognitive connections to the truth the likeness is like (a feeling, say), though we will point these likenesses out in any philosophical discussion. In fact, mimesis is that through which we first learn, and first become able to recognize, likenesses. If the mimetic learning Aristotle puts first implied the mimetic thing is "a 'likeness' in the sense of something we require an existing grasp of reality to comprehend" (192), it could not, ipso facto, be that through which we *first* learn.

Similarly, the pleasure in mimesis to which Aristotle refers in *Poetics* 4 is not first a pleasure in learning through mimesis, but a pleasure in mimesis itself, the pleasure in becoming like. Mimesis isn't a means, but a natural, and according to Aristotle, pleasant activity: it is a "for its own sake" of our nature, which can take us anywhere from hell to heaven. A similar point about the pleasure in mimetic activity and its nonrationality is made by Fossheim. He concludes in a way that is in line with the Girardian influenced manner of understanding mimesis I intend when he says that "practical reason is in ineradicable debt to something that isn't in itself entirely reasonable."[9] The rational *dunamis* of the human soul is led out by mimesis, a natural activity we share with animals.

It seems, then, that Aristotle focuses on music in taking up the effects of mimesis because music is, even among highly developed *Homo sapiens*, the art form in which the more anthropologically basic mimetic action of art is most clear. In it perception of rhythms and tones mechanically transfers to (or, more biologically—as Aristotle tended to think—infects) even the animals. One might, in an art form that uses language, get hung up on the representative and the intentional.[10] Aristotle's choice of music as the art form around which he discusses the catharses available in mimeses—purposefully, I say—keeps as far from that cognitivism and rationalism as possible. Mimesis is, anthropologically speaking, the *élan vital* that gives rise to such cognitions as representational likeness, and later, ideas. As Rene Girard says, it "precedes consciousness and language."[11] In this anthropological (rather than specifically aesthetic) sense, mimesis is

> prior to gestures, attitudes, manners, and everything to which mimesis is usually reduced when it is understood only as representation. This mode of imitation operates with a quasi-osmotic immediacy necessarily betrayed and lost in all the dualities of the modern problematics of desire, including the conscious and unconscious.[12]

The quasi-osmotic immediacy of primary mimesis is precisely what Aristotle is touching upon when he says that "our souls are changed" (*Pol.* 1340a22–23) as we listen to music, without needing to posit that the hearer "recognizes the emotion 'in' the music" as Halliwell's (161) more cognitivist explication requires. It by-passes (re)cognition; it effects us immediately. Plato's Ion says the same thing: "somehow you touch (ἅπτει) my soul with your words" (535a).[13] Aristotle particularly names rhythm and melody (*Pol.* 1340a19), not

9. Fossheim; see esp. p. 82 and following; the quote is from p. 84.

10. A more extensive discussion of the supplemental use of the mimetic vis-à-vis the intentional/representative in the history of philosophy is in my "Intentionality and Mimesis: Canonic Variations on an Ancient Grudge, Scored for New Mutinies," *Sub/Stance* 75 (1994): 46–74. See also note 13 below.

11. "A conversation with Rene Girard," in *The Girard Reader*, ed. James G. Williams (New York: Crossroads, 1996), 277. Girard reads Aristotle's term *mimesis* (when he mentions Aristotle at all) in accord with the intellectualist translation of it as imitation or representation; this misreading is unfortunate.

12. Rene Girard, *"To double business bound": Essays on Literature, Mimesis and Anthropology* (Baltimore: Johns Hopkins University Press, 1978), 89.

13. John Bremer notes that "the word touch (ἅπτει) strongly inclines the meaning toward a

the words, as the mimeses that produce qualities of character "which hardly fall short of the actual affections" (1340a21–22); an almost mechanical mimesis and psychagogy seems to be the import of both views. The infection that creates a mob, culture's irrational other, presents itself here as well: the human individual is made—and lost—through mimesis.

On the other hand, when we *tell a story about* mimesis, as I am here, we make propositions about how it works and affirm or deny them, but mimesis itself does not require the propositionality or "quasi-propositions" of contemporary cognitivist theories of emotion (or action). In fact, Aristotle (and the truth about human beings) requires that mimesis be precognitive, prepropositional, and the attempt to explain mimesis as dispositional ascription of propositions (which does not presuppose awareness of the particular propositions or beliefs, but merely a tendency to act in accord with what those propositions would entail) is as heuristically valuable—and as true—as to say that two hydrogen atoms want to share their electrons with one of oxygen. It is the way we *think through* what is going on, but that is precisely what is not going on in original mimesis: thinking. Such dispositions or patterns (whether of oxygen or of infant mouthings) are clearly not necessarily cognitive, and to import cognitivity into them is to import a manner of understanding the mimetic that is not available to critical discernment for the matter at stake. We are, as it were, anthropomorphizing our infancy.

Generally, when we anthropomorphize, we are evading the specifically mimetic, substituting for it the cognitive: the mimetic soul is read as *ego cogito*. An explanation of mimeses even as iconic sign seems to presume too much upon the construction and definition of an (modern philosophical) individual and relatively cognitively developed psyche—a miniature Cartesian ego, as it were. That individuality is belied by the lack of individuation produced in, for example, those highly mimetic social occurrences we call panics, and clearly represented in such works as Euripides' *Bacchae*, which exhibits the mimetically induced loss of individuation. Such events must indeed be figured as loss if we *are already* such individualized and cognitively developed psyches as modern philosophy presumes, but the anthropological (and original developmental) import of mimesis goes the other way; it is a claim about how this individual spontaneity develops in a being that is originally neither individual nor spontaneous, but whose nature is mimetic at the

physical act, even though Ion refers, for the one and only time, to the soul" (*Plato's "Ion,"* 284). Socrates' analogy for the poet and rhapsode is the mechanically infective magnetic stone.

core. The creation of such literature as *Bacchae*, and the fact of such panics (or "group swoons") as occurred when the Beatles played in Yankee Stadium, indicates the continuing operation of the mimetic even in the more sapient, developed being. This almost mechanical, quasi-osmotic view of mimesis is brought out, I think, in the ancient references to mimesis as infectious; Halliwell notes some of these.[14] This is clearly a noncognitivist ancient metaphor; and infection can pass by touching, as something in the music touches our souls and affects everyone (*Pol.* 1340a5–25, 1342a9–16). By contrast, the propositional (or quasi-propositional, dispositional) belief ascription of contemporary cognitivist theories of emotion and action seems to require an always already thereness to a kind of cognition which in fact Aristotle and Plato clearly think *develops*—so isn't already there, and can be made to develop in particularly superior (or barbaric) ways by a culture's or neighborhood's particularly superior (or barbaric) actions, emotions, rhythms, manners of speech and dress—all of which are the stuff of infantile (and even animal; cf. *Rep.* 563c) mimesis. The cognition that "this is a that" (1448b17; cf. Halliwell, 187–93) is first possible *after* mimesis embodies or enacts its effect (the likeness) in us. In short, the modern distinctions and debate between cognitivism and noncognitivism of the emotions and in action theory are drawn within a philosophy of mind that is already too possessively individualistic;[15] that modern presumption is precisely what the anthropological import of mimesis in Plato and Aristotle denies.

So, my disagreement with Halliwell's interpretations of both mimesis and Aristotle will center around these points. I am arguing for what I would call a noncognitivist position in understanding mimesis and the emotions engendered by mimeses, but my point is not to plump for a modern understanding of noncognitivism, but to try to get at (and keep in mind) this more basic anthropological conception of mimesis as that *through which* cognition (and self-recognition) comes to be, and also is sometimes lost once it has begun to be. Mimesis exceeds cognition by working beneath it and before it. This excess is why Halliwell felt the immediate need for a supplement when discussing musical mimesis (160). Certainly, once cognition is active, it clearly can have a place in both the effecting of emotions and in the

14. *The Aesthetics of Mimesis*, 60n, 77.

15. See C. B. MacPherson, *The Political Theory of Possessive Individualism: Hobbes to Locke* (London: Oxford University Press, 1964), for a discussion of how modern political theory implies and reinforces a much more individualistic idea of the person than ancient philosophers would have accepted as true.

art of producing mimetic things, but because we are "the most mimetic of animals" (1448b6), we are still (even in our intellectual habits, tics, and desires) affected by this "quasi-osmotic," almost mechanical, possession by the power of something other:[16] an infection that is perhaps purifying, perhaps polluting.

16. In the first chapter of his thorough, but finally overly cognitivist, recasting of Girard's work in *Models of Desire: Rene Girard and the Psychology of Mimesis* (Baltimore: Johns Hopkins University Press, 1992), Paisley Livingston rightly begins with Girard's consideration of "le désir selon l'Autre, 'desire according to the Other'" (1) which is contrasted to the more usual "romantic 'myths' of the individual's spontaneity" (2).

1

THE PROBLEM OF THE *IPHIGENIA* AND THE PURPOSES OF TRAGEDY

The perfect plot, accordingly, must have a single issue; . . . the change in fortune must not be from misery to happiness, but on the contrary from happiness to misery; and the cause of it must not lie in any depravity, but in some great hamartia (1453 a12–15).

But best of all is the last; what we have . . . in Iphigenia, where . . . [*one*] *meditating something irremediable in ignorance* [*of the relationship*] *makes the discovery* [*in time to draw back*] *(1454a5, 7; 1453b35–37).*

I. BACKSTAGE AND THE WINGS: OF *POETICS* AND POETICS

This section will lay out the place of the *Poetics* in criticism and show the filiation of poetry to natural living things on one side and tools on the other. That double analogy shows that constructing poetry is like constructing constitutions, and so criticism of poetry, like criticism of constitutions, will depend upon a correct understanding of final causality in a thing that is not simply a made thing of human choice, but one that also arises out of nature and so is inescapable: *that* mimeses and constitutions exist is natural, given man's existence; *how* they exist is made—but to the purpose.

Near the beginning of the last century, when Lane Cooper attempted a task similar to this book's, he claimed, referring to Aristotle's *Poetics*, that "we possess, all things considered, but a single adequate investigation of a literary type with regard to form and function."[1] Since then, there has been much in the way of war—not all of it bloodless. At the end of that century, having attempted to overcome the hegemony of the dead via the destruction of genre and the dissolution of final cause into grapheme, phoneme, and the shifting phantasms of *différance*, it may be more clear that the hegemony of the *Poetics* is neither accidental nor the political *fait accompli* of the white and the male and the dead. Both the art (e.g., Beckett, Ionesco, Pinter) and the criticism (Barthes, Derrida, deMan, Girard, et al.) of the last half century have aimed their creative powers and engines—directly and indirectly—at Aristotle's unfinished and elliptical, though discipline-founding, ramparts. Through it all some scholars have refused to give comfort to the popular front of the modern and postmodern, in favor of exploring and defending the less politically correct though half-destroyed ancient temple. From the broader community of literary critics, we might see Northrop Frye, Elder Olson, Martha Nussbaum, along with many continually rearguard professors of classics (the inimitable Nussbaum among these also) enlisted on this side. Stephen Halliwell's previously discussed book is the latest exemplar partaking of both natures. The bands of marauders have gone by many names. In all this, as full of sound and fury as this paragraph is of purposed bombast, our latest century has proven not much different from any of twenty others taken at random. It may be that any of these critics, or even Aristotle himself, got one or another support not quite plumb, and so there is a slight rake to the rampart or stage that any of them walk upon. It may even happen in this book, though I have the advantage of having all these fine predecessors, and so have less excuse, and am more to blame—as Aristotle himself says (*NE* 1113b30–1114a3)—for getting it wrong. Be that as it may, I hereby begin my inexcusable, impolitic, and possibly blameworthy project in understanding the poetics of comedy.

Given the constant discussion of Aristotle's *Poetics* in scholarly and literary circles, it would be surprising and indeed suspicious if any author at this late date were to disagree with everything everyone who has written on the topic before has said. Yet I do disagree with nearly everyone about something. Even this much disagreement may strike some people as an expression of bilious humours. For unlike Plato, who never appears in his own name and who is considered by many to have said (under his own name) that appearing in print under one's own name is the surest sign of a lack of serious-

1. Cooper, *Comedy*, 3.

ness a man can give, Aristotle's extant works are neither poetic, nor fictional. They do not fall under the broad category he calls mimeses (as Socratic dialogues most assuredly do), but into the category of enunciative speech (cf. *De Int.* 17a2–5): speech that makes truth claims. His are not doubly reflected, or indirect communications, but direct, and quite frequently openly demonstrative and systematic.[2] Aristotle's works make truth claims about our theoretical, practical, and productive knowledge, and it should have been possible to get these claims clear and see how they work in practice before the dawning of the present age. The only irony in or about Aristotle's texts is that his teacher for so long should have been such a Cheshire cat as Plato. But almost all of Aristotle's extant work looks to be unpolished lecture notes, frequently in need of emendation if not addition on merely grammatical grounds, and *Poetics* itself is particularly fragmented and all but indubitably missing its second half.[3] In the course of time Aristotle's corpus has suffered much more considerable corruption than that of his teacher. This is all well known. I mention it in order to avoid a preemptive dismissal for my coming disagreeableness. There is room for disagreement here.

I have already set out my major disagreement about mimesis generally; I do not present a new idea about mimesis, but argue that Plato and Aristotle understood the concept as more basic and anthropologically central as well as less cognitive than most aestheticians have taken it to be. Their philosophies of art, and their criticism of the arts, follows from their deeper, anthropological sense of the source of art. Plato and Aristotle understand mimesis to be natural to human beings; aestheticians are interested in the rules for making the poetic things and generally overlook the natural aspects of poetry. The major disagreement I have with my predecessors in the more narrowly focused study of comedy is with their views of its particular function, telos, or final cause. While this is the most important aspect of anything, for a thing's nature is most clearly revealed by its telos, it is possible to get a large number of other things right about something (as many critics do about comic and tragic poetry) while not being clear on its fundamental purpose. That an error in such an important point can occur without concomitant and large er-

2. Insofar as he considers Aristotle to be indirect and poetic in *Poetics*, I think that Michael Davis (*Aristotle's "Poetics": The Poetry of Philosophy*) is merely incorrect. Many of his remarks on the relation between poetry and action, however, strike me as insightful, to the point, and even Aristotelian—just not what *Poetics* is directly about.

3. *Rhetoric* 1372a1, e.g., refers to a discussion of the ludicrous in *Poetics*. It is not in the text of *Poetics* we have.

rors in other matters might seem surprising, or argue against the importance of final causality *in toto* as modern sciences pretend. But Aristotle himself, early in *Metaphysics* (I.3 and I.4), tells a history of science that only by fits and starts gets to seeing the necessity of teleology as part of its explanation of a thing—"being forced," as he says, "by the truth itself to inquire into the next sort of cause" (984a18, b10). To give a specific instance, one might be able to say quite a lot about tragedy, and be largely correct, only by considering manner (dramatic, not narrative), means (language with pleasant accessories), and object (serious action). Such an explanation would not, however, be sufficient to allow for proper judgment—either aesthetic or moral and political—about the work. If we do not know what a piece of machinery is to do, we can have no correct judgment about whether or not it does it well: any Rube Goldberg device is as good as anything else; in fact, perhaps a Rube Goldberg device would be considered better than anything else just because it contains a wide variety of objects, manners, and means—that is, it is interesting. Many paths in contemporary criticism go down this general route.[4] Such a position merely hides a belief about the telos of art, but does not dispense with it. It says variety or complexity is not the spice, but the meat. But a very complicated crossword puzzle, which would take significant *technē* (art) to build and solve, would not count as a work of mimesis for Aristotle. Complexity and uselessness are insufficient characteristics for a definition of art.

However one may feel about the use of final causality as an explanatory theme in the science of nature, the science of poetics is not the same kind of thing because poetics is not about the same *kind* of thing. For one thing, mimeses are developed, they are not self-subsistent, self-developing entities like the natural things science studies: it is a construction "like a single and whole animal" aimed to "produce the pleasure proper to it" (1459a17–20). As Aristotle makes clear early on, while it is natural for man to engage in mimesis and to enjoy mimetic things—so the existence of mimeses is natural to our kind of being (*Po.* 1448b5–8)—the specific forms (like comedy and tragedy) are gradual developments. Elder Olson tells a very reasonable story about these developments:

4. That the search for, and love of, the interesting is a moral flaw should be considered demonstrated after *Either/Or*. That Aristotle did not suffer from the modern desire to erect an aesthetic theory independent of ethos and pathos is defended by House (100–111), among others. That he is right to view art this way will be taken up later. The interesting is not the category that delimits aesthetics. Some greater exposition of problems in modern aesthetics will appear in Chapter 3.

> [I]n the first phase, human instinct for imitation for the sake of the pleasure and knowledge . . . is the originating cause. . . . But instinct is perfectly uniform and consequently cannot account for variation in poetry; and in the second phase, in which poetry diversifies . . . , the cause of the diversification lies in the moral nature of the imitator himself. In the third phase, forms desirable in themselves are developed; here we have art proper.[5]

This story, based on *Poetics* 1448b24–1449a8, helps us see how Aristotle can place mimeses between natural living beings—to which both he (*NE* 1050a37, 1050b34–37) and Plato (*Phaedrus* 264c) compare poetry—and the tools human beings make, invent, design, and cause to exist for specific purposes. As *Physics* 2.1 explains, natural living things have an *internal* entelechy—for example, growth and reproduction; these are causes in accord with what the thing is (καθ' αὑτό), internal principles of motion and rest; mimesis is such a principle for anthropos. On the other hand, tools are made with a particular final cause—or set thereof—*in mind*, in some external agent. They are causes κατὰ συμβεβηκός, in accord with what the thing happens to be—as the light above my desk allows me to read because of the way its stuff happens to be put together. The final cause of the tool, as well as its original formal and originating efficient causes, are external to the thing itself and even external to the *kind* of thing it is, for they are in a mind. The final cause preexists the tool in a different kind of being than the tool. On the other hand, the purpose of the acorn, whatever the squirrel or wild pig may do with it, is to become an oak, and by nature (necessarily or for the most part) it will. In nature the formal and the final causes are in the being (and in the kind of being) and while they can exist by abstraction in a mind,

5. Elder Olson, "The Poetic Method of Aristotle: Its Powers and Limitations," 184. It will be noted in what follows that I disagree with Olsen's implication that the causes of mimesis are pleasure and knowledge, considering rather that the causes are the pleasures of doing and of seeing mimeses. The Greek here is ambiguous, so we must consider further matters of Aristotelian developmental psychology to secure any interpretation. First of all, we should remember that pleasure and pain are the proximate causes of animal motion. No doubt the latter pleasure (seeing mimeses) is closely associated with knowledge, but I am not certain that it is the *knowledge* that causes the infant's pleasure rather than *seeing (or hearing) the mimesis*—which pleasure develops into a love of knowledge (seeing that one thing is like another): the movement of the body/soul caused by the mimesis is pleasant. Hardison (*Aristotle's Poetics*) and Heath ("Aristotelian Comedy") give a story similar to Olson's for the development of comedy. Not only is it not necessary to be cognitivist about how mimesis works on us in order to explain its pleasure, it is not, I think, possible to fit all of the ancient examples of mimeses' working into a cognitivist frame: the mad, disordered motions and cries of the infant are the root of music and gymnastic working in the infant and child "lacking intelligence" (*Laws* 672c). Musical mimeses affect even some other animals (by definition irrational for Aristotle) as well as children and slaves (*Pol.* 1341a15–16) who have not developed it.

they don't exist there first. (At least they don't for Aristotle, who thinks the world is eternal, not created from the divine idea.) Poetry, by contrast, is born of both nature and artifice. Aristotle's point seems to be that by nature mimesis is engaged in for pleasure and through it we learn; that is, mimesis is for its own sake as well as for some effects. When we start purposefully making them, for our first mimeses are not purposed, we give these effects finer points, or come to them more finely. The first mimeses (those we are taken up into, those the infant finds himself doing) are for their own sake—in an infantile, animal, natural way.[6] Art will keep this element alive: the sheer pleasure in aesthesis; we may come to call it the freedom of aesthetic judgment when we become philosophers.[7]

The efficient cause of the natural thing's coming to be is in the *same kind* of being. By contrast, artifacts come to be from a *different kind* of being than the made thing. The invention (or coming to be) of a lightbulb took a long time after the final cause was decided upon. Further improvements became possible not by changing the final cause, but by varying and testing the other causes to more effectively achieve the telos the *inventor* keeps in mind. Such a thing does not happen in nature. So, because mimesis is a natural instinct, mimeses are natural to our kind of being; to say human beings are the most naturally mimetic of animals is to say that we mime originally and without a preexisting purpose.[8] We then become innovators—to impose

6. Aristotle's association of mimesis with play or amusement in *Politics* (1336a22–b23, 1337b30–1338a30, 1339a11–1340a5), and Plato's association of mimeses with joy or delight in *Laws* (655c), play, and a charm that is distinct from both benefit and correctness without being harmful (*Laws* 667b–668) bring out this "for its own sakeness"; there is a pleasure in the activity itself, then there may *also* be judgments of correctness and benefit.

7. This hints at a connection to Kant I will try to make more explicit in Chapter 3. We should note here, however, that Kant also has a distinction like Aristotle's between natural and made things. It comes into play in the *Critique of Judgement* (*KU* 372–74) where he distinguishes a "self-organizing being" (like the oak), in which the parts cause the whole and the whole the parts, from an artificial thing, for which a concept that is produced by a will (clearly external to the thing) is the cause. He makes the further well-known distinction that the former final causes are regulative, but not constitutive, while the latter are constitutive final causes. He does not deny that the regulative final causes we use to guide our inquiry into nature exist (Aristotle does make existential, or constitutive in Kant's terms, claims about these), only that we cannot know them to be so in themselves, since our thought and experience are constituted (naturally, it seems) in accord with those regulative ideas.

8. It would be interesting to trace the Derridean theme of the (ab)original back to Aristotle's recognition of the human mimetic nature: How can a being be—originally—mimetic? What is the (de)structure of a being which is so? Perhaps I should write "nature," regarding such a being, under erasure. (This is, effectively, what Girard attempts to explain in his mimetic theory.) But would this not be, almost, a confession, as if the son of man could only do what he sees the father doing, or the sublunary beings only and always attempt to imitate the prime mover?

a certain result, or carry it more timely off, in ourselves and others like ourselves.

The efficient and formal causes of the existence of mimesis are in nature—in human nature most particularly; the human being is going to do that mimetic thing like an oak is going to leave and make acorns. But for human beings final causes can also be purposed. Indeed, it is probably through mimesis that thought about purposes and thought of purposes develops. The laughing child's cry "Do it again!" proposes just such a purpose. Mimesis is pleasant by nature, but its pleasure need not be purposed, and first, in fact, it isn't. We are carried by our mimetic nature; we don't, at first, set about to enact a mimesis. In *developing* mimeses, however, the poet does so purpose, and it is because *we develop* mimeses in accord with a final cause—such as catharsis, or "to achieve the pleasure particular to tragedy" (*Po.* 1453a36)—that mimeses are like tools. They can be made better or worse, more or less effective. Comic and tragic mimeses differ naturally because they affect us differently; without this natural difference[9] in the effect on the audience we could never have picked them out *for development* in their particular ways, or for analysis. Aristotle might well, then, ask "whether or not tragedy is even now sufficiently developed in its types" (1449a7), while maintaining that it had become something definite before Aeschylus (1449a14–17) and that its development so far is in accord with "tragedy's own nature" (1449a23). Based in and coming to be from our mimetic nature, mimeses affect that nature in certain ways. The early tragedians picked out certain of those effects as choice-worthy and developed means to effect them more perfectly. Thus the "what is" of tragedy became stable, and it stabilized around a certain natural result. Aeschylus and Sophocles innovate on the patent, and further innovations are quite plausible (1449b14–18).

Aristotle makes a similar argument about development in politics, against the claim that political change is undesirable—"if politics be an art, change must be necessary in this as in any other" (*Pol.* 1268b38). Change is necessary in an art when there is a better way to achieve the end. Because of other changes in the sublunary realm, like changes in population, means

9. Perhaps I should say "quasi-natural difference," since the differing cathartic effects are deeply tied to morals, which Aristotle thinks are shaped, though not entirely determined, by the polis and its culture. We should remember that polis and culture have natural ends too; some cities and cultures fail to achieve them, and some achieve them effectively for the most part. Comic and tragic mimeses differ because "necessarily or for the most part" they effect us differently. Halliwell calls mimeses "quasi-naturalistic" in the introduction to his new Loeb translation, 9.

of, as well as quality and quantity of production, environment and resources, increase of appetite, or changes in general health and relative strength of emotions, even changes in language, changes in art—medicine, poetry, politics—will always be necessary. It is as if Aristotle, in this remark, is aware that dealing with nature—particularly human nature—requires the use of multivariable iterated equations, though he may not yet have the mathematics to lay them out perspicuously, or the computer to solve them.[10] We may fairly bet that knowing the kind of thing we need, the man will develop them, unless the culture has lamed him for virtue.

The doubleness of the analogy here laid out has caused several problems (as might be suspected). Some scholars have taken the likeness of a poem to a natural thing too far, as we shall see in more detail shortly; on the other side, there have been critics who take poetry as a *technē* (like bridle making) and its products as mere tools—Ion, in Plato's dialogue of that name, being the extant Adam of this particular sin.[11] There is an undoubted likeness between poetry and *technē* as well; it is strengthened by Aristotle's use of medically inflected terms like catharsis, for medicine is a *technē*. Like poetry, medicine no doubt began by trying to strengthen and control the timing of certain natural effects noticed accidentally. If we consider drinking when thirsty, eating when hungry, and seeking warmth when cold as medicinal, then we might consider medicine a natural activity we practice and enjoy from infancy, as mimesis is for all human beings. Even so, for Aristotle, there is an important difference between poetry and medicine. Medicine is concerned with the body, and it is through the instrumentality of the soul that we learn and judge concerning the working of that art (medicine) upon its object. But poetry's aim is for the soul itself.[12] Aristotle's treatment of the arts of the muses in *Politics* indicates that poetics does fall under political science—as it must, since political science is the master science of the good, and mimesis (like every other action, science, and *technē*) aims at happiness. Poetry's particular aims (as those of the music arts generally) are catharsis of the passions, moral education, and intellectual recreation (*Pol.* 1341b37–40). Thus, when it comes to poetry, the well functioning of all our knowledge and feeling is itself at stake, and we cannot reduce this end to a

10. In this he foreshadows the work of Thomasina in Stoppard's *Arcadia*.

11. For a reading of this dialogue, see my "*Ion*: Plato's Defense of Poetry"; the notes therein give wide reference to other interpretations. Now also available in *Platonic Errors*.

12. This is a Platonic point as well, not only in the (in)famous arguments of *Republic*, but also in the argument of *Philebus* (47d–48a), and *Laws* (1 and 2).

series of rules in a *technē* because the rule-making *technē* is precisely part of the "well functioning of all our knowledge and feeling" that is at stake in the purported rule making. So, what has come to be called the objectivity of *technē*—whether exemplified in the teachable rules of medicine or of carpentry—is either unavailable to poetry (as has become popular opinion since the romantics) or must be based on different grounds than objectivity in science and technology (as both Kant and Aristotle argue). Poetry is what Marcel would call a mystery—it involves the thing it is to explain, rather than a problem—which does not involve the thing it is to explain. A nonmusic, nonmimetic *technē* (bridle making, lightbulb invention, surgery) answers problems; a music, mimetic *poiēsis* (tragedy, comedy) involves mystery. Mimeses propagate mimesis in the mimetic being; neither bedsteads nor bridles propagate anything. The poem is not merely made thing; its *technē* is not wholly rule reducible.

In contrast both to the nakedly natural (acorn) and to the artificial or technical (lightbulb), poetry has elements of both. In this poetry is like constitutions of states. While both mimesis and sociality are in the strongest sense natural to man, poetry and constitutions are purposeful shapings of that natural being, self-conscious refinements of natural acts and affects. *Technē* sometimes works a similar line regarding its products; for example, breeding corn to achieve a certain size kernel is a refinement of the plant's natural entelechy. More frequently *technē* involves inventing or imposing new final causes on nature (which is the material cause); for example, the use of diamonds in a machine for the reproduction of sound in an ancient technology. Even where *technē* and *poiēsis* both seem to follow this latter similar line, however, there is the difference that the human being's *technē* directs or shapes the substantial being of some other natural being, but in poetry and politics it shapes and directs his own.[13] Perfect objectivity about these matters, then, is a fiction available only to God.

13. I am not sure I agree, then, with R. S. Crane's interpretation of Aristotle's remark that "art partly completes what nature cannot bring to completion and partly imitates her" (*Physics* 199a15–17). It seems that Crane, rather undialectically, separates what Aristotle had put together: "Sometimes, as in medicine, the first function is more completely explanatory of what the artist does than the second" (48). Poetry, Aristotle said, does both, and all the time. Politics and poetry are each both mimeses of our nature and completions of it. The Aristotelian questions are "on what does the art work?" and "to what purpose?" Perhaps I should say that human nature is essentially unfinished and so mimeses and constitutions—which aim at the human being as a whole—are necessarily always both part bringing to perfection and part imitation of nature (and they accomplish the former through the latter). But this last statement again approaches a religious, rather than being a strictly scientific, thesis, for it requires us to believe that a certain end is man's. Aristotle's own ideas about

There is the further difference between mimesis and *technē* that mimeses—epic, lyric, dance, mime—require not even so much science as writing, and were well developed in the Bronze Age, and probably considerably earlier. Like societies, which while natural and necessary to *anthrōpos* have developed according to various constitutions and with differing degrees of success, so, too, mimeses develop into poetry of various sorts, about which—like constitutions—we should be able to make judgments. These developments (whether in epic, lyric, dance, or constitutions), not their (ab)original being, do seem to require the minimal rational faculty of counting, so only humans—among creatures that might have mimetic tendencies or the incipient politics of a hive—have *developed* them. As Aristotle thought that the purpose of a constitution—a reasoned construction of our natural social instinct—is happiness, and as politics is the art that understands and aims at that good for a society, so poetry must also shape our natural mimetic instinct for a purpose. We see poetics and politics as analogous sciences when we consider their double source in naturally telic human instinct and our more open-ended purposiveness; insofar as politics is the master science of the good, poetry is subordinate. Catharsis and intellectual pleasure are necessary for happiness; happiness is the aim of politics. As disbelief in, or failure to acknowledge, correctly discern, or aim at happiness makes a constitution a failure (*NE* 1103b5), similarly, failure to acknowledge or correctly discern what the aim of different forms of poetry is will lead to concomitant errors in both poetic criticism and construction. That such errors will have a political effect is a necessary conclusion. And the sea flows the other way also: political errors will no doubt lead to errors in art and aesthetic judgment. Illustrations from the last century are manifold. The political errors are not, however, absolutely determinative of artistic ones; for while poetics is subservient to the complete human good aimed at by politics, according to Aristotle poetry does have a nature of its own, which can be discerned and acted upon even under the conditions of political oppression, imprisonment, and the death camp. This, too, has been proven, as they say, by history. That is to say, human beings have proven it by trying the experiment on other human beings.

---

imitation of the divine and our happiness requiring participation in that divine life so far as that is possible to man knock at this door (*NE* 1177b30–35), as we did in note 8 above. Aristotle considers this religious question to be answered by, and so discoverable in, nature. It is not, then, a matter of faith in the ordinary modern sense.

It should be briefly noted that these political and artistic issues are not merely accidentally or analogously related even in modern philosophy. We might date the beginning of modern political theory to Hobbes, whose *Leviathan*, in contrast to Aristotle, distinguishes sharply between "Nature (the Art whereby God hath made and governs the World)" and "the Art of man" which imitates Nature. Art's highest work, "imitating that Rationall and most excellent worke of Nature, Man . . . goes yet further" than the ordinary engine (or lightbulb). "For by Art is created that great Leviathan called a Commonwealth, or State, (in latine Civitas) which is but an Artificiall Man."[14] Hobbes, unlike Aristotle, does not think there is anything natural in constitutions; indeed, the state of *nature is without one*. Politics and art are both wholly made things for Hobbes—imitations that require cognitive activity in order originally to be made. Mimeses do not arise as part of our nature through which we first learn. They are imitations of a nature already known, not natural themselves. It is quite natural for Hobbes's children to consider the same of all art as it considers all constitutions: both are entirely made things, artificial. Mimesis, translated as imitation, falls, in the modern period, to just this artificiality. Constitutions fall with it. Then, almost as a further natural development, one should eventually say of art that it is all the production of the greater automaton, Leviathan, just as "dreames are caused by the distemper . . . of the inward parts of the Body" (17). Freud, blown up large, becomes Marx. And Marxist art critics are shown here to be the direct descendants of Hobbes: art is merely the expression of Leviathan's distempered dreams. According to Aristotle, the first step on this road contradicts nature, for politics is not mere imitative artifice, but an aspect of nature in us; as is mimesis. Continued travel on this wholly artificial road takes one further and further away from the being of the human. Politics, reading Hobbes's title, becomes wholly beastly, but the Leviathan he imagines being wholly artificial, perhaps he should have named his book *Frankenstein*, or *I, Robot*. In any case, art is but the dream of the distempered giant. There is empirical evidence for the truth of this Aristotelian critique. The reduction of aesthetics to politics is a "natural" conclusion from the originating premise about the artificiality of politics.[15]

14. Thomas Hobbes, *Leviathan*, ed. Richard Tuck (Cambridge, U.K.: Cambridge University Press, 1991), 9.

15. There will be further discussion of these matters in Chapter 3.4: The Freedom of Aesthetic Judgment; see esp. 223–27.

The idea that politics is the master science of the good leads Aristotle to consider that aesthetic questions should find a place within that larger frame (viz., *Politics* 8)—one to which they are necessarily related since happiness is the proper and most excellent functioning of our nature. That is, to judge about tragedy "*in itself* and *in relation to the audience*" are different discourses (*Po.* 1449a8–9), but not unrelated.[16] The first cannot be entirely concluded without reference to the second,[17] nor can the second be adequately understood apart from the first. Therefore the New Critics are just as wrong as the Marxists or reader response theorists—and just as right. What we call "aesthetic" and "political or ethical" questions are distinguishable discourses, but the poem cannot be entirely removed from the matrix of their double discourse. What we find Aristotle doing makes sense, then; for he talks about the relation of the poem to the audience most largely in *Politics* and not in *Poetics*, which he attempts to keep as much as possible on the topic of poetry καθ' αὐτό. Poetics attempts to keep that political discussion at bay, without denigrating its importance or necessity. It is because he keeps that discussion at bay that *Poetics* has been read by many as a perfect formalist treatise eschewing all extrapoemic effect and influence. Whether and how the arts, among them the various forms of *poiēsis*, can contribute to our natural end—happiness—is the center of a long and ancient quarrel.[18] It is a quarrel that is both taken up in, and determines the interpretation of, such Platonic dialogues as *Ion*, *Republic*, and *Laws*, among other things less scholarly if not more important. That the question of how the arts fit into the happy life of states and individuals was a question of the first political importance is indicated by the fact that such matters were the first order of business in *Republic* and *Laws*, and last, but decisive, in *Politics*. *Poetics*, while it reverses the polarity of the discussion by taking up poetry in itself (καθ' αὐτό, cf. 1447a

16. It appears to me that the text of Aristotle here allows several kinds of reasoning (or *logos*): a *logos* about whether or not tragedy is sufficiently developed in its types, a *logos* about judging it (tragedy or tragedy's development into types?) intrinsically, and a *logos* about judging it (tragedy?/types?) in relation to the audience. Aristotle seems not to be putting off as another *logos* the argument about whether or not tragedy has sufficiently developed intrinsically, as the remainder of the chapter concludes that it has achieved its nature. He does seem to talk about types (*eidea*) in chapters 13 and 14, where he also mentions some different effects on the audience. He does not otherwise say anything about tragedy's (or its types') relation to the audience. So I propose to take his distinction between a discussion καθ' αὐτό and one πρὸς τὰ θέατρα in the most general way.

17. For a more detailed examination of when and why in his argument about poetry intrinsically Aristotle brings this "extrinsic" factor of the audience into play, see my "The Others of Aristotle's *Poetics*." Parts of that argument will be rehearsed in the discussion of *Poetics* 13 and 14.

18. In order to participate fully in the quarrel, then, one has to know what happiness is, for one is implying a definition of it whether one will or knows. See Chapter 4.

περὶ ποιητικῆς αὐτῆς), never escapes the gravity of politics altogether, for it cannot. That in our current politics matters of poetry suffer wide neglect, while a wider range of critics and artists reduce poetry to a form and venue of political expression are signs that either we are a different species than Plato and Aristotle—one for whom either mimesis or sociality is no longer natural—or that politics and criticism have completely failed to understand their relation or to acknowledge their only true ends.[19]

2. THE PROBLEM OF ARISTOTLE'S EVALUATION OF THE *IPHIGENIA*

One of the greater difficulties facing anyone who would build a theory of comedy out of Aristotle's book on tragedy is that not only does he use several unclear though obviously important terms of art, like catharsis, but there are also places where Aristotle seems exceptionally clear about tragedy, but obviously wrong or self-contradictory. Such a crux comes face to face with any reader in the short space of chapters 13 and 14 quoted as the epigram of this chapter, which seems to be both. Not only does there seem to be a contradiction in what the two chapters say constitutes the best tragedy, but chapter 14 seems to mistakenly identify *Iphigenia in Tauris* as a tragedy despite the fact that brother and sister escape and live happily ever after.

To recall the plot briefly: Iphigenia, rather than being sacrificed by her father at Aulis is secretly spirited away by the goddess to the land of the Taureans. Their custom is to sacrifice all strangers to the goddess and Iphigenia is made priestess of the ritual. The plot of the play begins with the arrival of her only brother, Orestes, who is immediately captured. The ritual sacrifice is ordered, but just before she marks him with the goddess's irrevocable sign, brother and sister are revealed to each other. They plan and successfully carry out an escape—or, as Aristotle says, they recognize each other, "thence comes salvation" (1455b12).

Many scholars have attempted to clear up the tragic difficulties Aristo-

19. That Plato considers poetry and politics both to be ways of loving souls can be seen in *Symposium* 209d–e where Diotima places them together, as well as in *Phaedrus*; in other dialogues (*Republic*, *Laws*) their relation is also clearly dialectical, though the limitation of one by the other is brought to the fore. Plato's *poetic construction of the political* discussions might be the best indicator of his thought about the true relationship of poetry and politics: correlative, not contradictory.

tle seems to fall into in the course of these chapters without any reference to a missing theory of comedy. To try to clear up the problem by reference to such a theory would be to explain the paradoxical by the absent. While this may be an honored method in theology, philosophers and literary critics (excepting Freudians) are not apt to look kindly upon such an effort. Though we cannot approach Aristotle's view of tragedy this way, it should be clear that however one resolves this well-known problem in Aristotle's poetics of tragedy, the solution will directly involve one's understanding of the poetics of comedy. The way out of this problem will have reverberations through the whole of the science. For one thing, if one agrees with chapter 14's estimation that *Iphigenia in Tauris* is the best tragedy, it will be clear that a happy ending cannot be the sufficient condition of the comic genre. Aristotle's understanding of comedy—at least what is *not* comedy—is partially revealed by how one resolves the crux of these two chapters. The case of the *Iphigenia in Tauris* is, then, like one of Kant's antinomies, a model problem, a *quaestio* on both sides of which there are reasonable arguments, and the mind is in chains until a solution is found.

The best way to lay out the difficulty is to summarize the problem-causing chapters. Chapter 13 requires the plot to be aimed at by the poet to be complex (having peripety and recognition) and of single issue. The finest (κάλλισται) tragedies will be mimeses of fearful and pitiable events, which implies we should not see decent people (ἐπιεικεῖς) changing from prosperity to adversity since this is repugnant (μιαρόν). Nor should we see depraved people (μοχθηροὺς) rising from adversity to prosperity; this is the least tragic change of all, being neither pitiable nor fearful nor arousing philanthropy. Nor should we see the utterly wicked (σφόδρα πονηρὸν) fall from prosperity to adversity, which may arouse philanthropy, but not fear (which is felt for one like ourselves) or pity (which is for undeserved suffering). This leaves someone in between—a person not preeminent in virtue—who falls from prosperity into adversity not through depravity (μοχθηρίαν) and badness (κακίαν), but through some hamartia. The finest (καλλίστη) tragedy has such a structure (συστάσεως). Aristotle adds that the structure (σύστασις) with the double outcome—opposite for the good (βελτίοσι) and bad (χείροσιν)—is thought to be best because of the weakness of the audience, but its pleasure is more appropriate to comedy.[20]

Chapter 14 begins by remarking that the better poet aims to educe the

20. This last is, perhaps, a hint that comedy's pleasure is related to an enjoyment of justice.

pitiable and the fearful from the structure of the things done (συστάσεως τῶν πραγμάτων) rather than from the spectacle. As the action must logically take place between friends, enemies, or neutrals, and, if the action is between enemies or neutrals, nothing is pitiable save the suffering (πάθος), it follows that tragedy rightly seeks suffering engendered between philoi, as, for example, when one is about to murder a father, mother, sister, or brother. Aristotle then explains how to make fine use (χρῆσθαι καλῶς) of such traditional stories by presenting four possibilities: (1) The worst is if the action is about to be done knowingly and is left undone. This is repugnant (μιαρόν) and untragic, since it lacks suffering (ἀπαθές). It is the case of Haemon in *Antigone.* (2) The action can occur with knowledge, as when Medea kills her children. This is the second worst action. (3) The action can be done in ignorance, followed by recognition of the relationship, as in *Oedipus.* This is better (Βέλτιον) since there is nothing repugnant and the recognition is thrilling (ἐκπληκτικόν). (4) The best (κράτιστον) is that someone about to do something irremediable recognizes it and so does not do it: the case of *Iphigenia in Tauris.* So while in chapter 13 it seems the best plot is that a protagonist not preeminent in virtue falls from prosperity to adversity, in chapter 14 the best plot is one in which the completely innocent, put-upon, and seemingly goddess-abandoned protagonist, about to kill her only and beloved brother, recognizes him, and salvation follows: from adversity, prosperity.

3. SOME ATTEMPTED SOLUTIONS: THE FALLACY OF ARISTOTELIAN FORMALISM

Getting Aristotle around what looks to be both self-contradiction and error has led to the development of a host of scholarly devices. There is, naturally, the perennial thesis of historical change in the meaning of terms through time.[21] This leads to remarks like "we are reminded that Aristotle's

21. I will skip over entirely the strongest form of this historicist view. A. W. H. Adkins concluded his analysis of the problem, which attempted to show Aristotle's fourth-century use of key moral and evaluative words was significantly different from those of the fifth-century tragedians, by saying that Aristotle's main ideas not only have "no relevance at all to later tragedy, [like Shakespeare, but they also are without] any relevance to extant Greek tragedy," and only have the historical interest of being the remarks of an intelligent and sensitive reader ("Aristotle," 101). If this were true, then neither the art nor the criticism of Greece could have any significance for our life other than being a sort of esoteric entertainment: a Rube Goldberg device for classicists. If such historicism were true, only the fully adequate historian could understand the text, or get anything

definition of tragedy is quite different from the modern one, which places major emphasis on the "unhappy ending."[22] But, at best, the thesis of historical change in the meaning of terms would explain the mistake of choosing *Iphigenia* as the *best* tragedy, not the affirmation of the earlier "correct" definition of a tragic plot, which is entirely in line with our modern terms. Nor does this proposal resolve the contradiction between that "correct" definition and the definition and choice of the following chapter, which places *Iphigenia* over *Oedipus*. We must, then, think that Aristotle lived through a revolution in his own thought between writing chapters 13 and 14—and didn't realize it.

The thesis of historical change in the meaning of terms does not become any easier to believe when we consider Aristotle's further remarks. For example, chapter 13 had rejected the plot with a double issue—"an opposite issue for the good and the bad personages"—by saying "the pleasure here is not that of tragedy. It belongs rather to comedy, where the bitterest enemies in the piece (e.g., Orestes and Aegisthus) walk off good friends in the end, with no slaying of anyone by anyone" (1453a33–39). Here, indeed, "Aristotle appears to be using the word 'comedy' almost in its modern sense of 'having a happy ending'" says the lexical historian, but this "cannot be entirely right because Aristotle considers *Iphigenia in Tauris* a tragedy and calls its kind of recognition, in which the tragic deed is contemplated and then avoided at the last minute, the best kind of all" (Hardison, 188). Such a complex of statements on the part of critics like Hardison confesses that this is not a

---

out of it—and he wouldn't. Adkins, in this article and in his book, treats the Homeric poems as teaching what real men were and ought to be like in the heroic age of shame culture—i.e., he does not treat them as poems.

Vernant and Vidal-Naquet have a similar tendency; see esp. the first chapter of *Myth and Ritual*. The root of the problem here is a deeply philosophical issue; Adkins, and historicists generally, share with the Socrates of *Republic* the view that poetry is primarily a representation (or imitation) of reality, which I would like to distinguish (and I think Socrates would like his interlocutors to distinguish) from poetry as mimesis: something that takes us into a certain set of feelings or even actions: e.g., weeping; Socrates' discussion, and that of the Athenian in *Laws*, allows that there is a difference between the iconic and the mimetic; this distinction seems to be one between what our mind actively builds up and judges, and what imagination is shaped by, so forming our judgment. But then Socrates treats them in an undifferentiated fashion: as if myth were just dogma dressed up: an icon of the invisible, or more simply and more often, the historical truth about the heroes and the gods. That is, Socrates performs as a person who cannot make the distinction, just as his interlocutors (old men who think that in setting the laws they are in control of everything, rather than moved by . . .). Such treatments are thereby marked as palpably incomplete. For further discussion of this problem, see my "Intentionality and Mimesis" and "The Empiricist Looks at a Poem."

22. O. B. Hardison, with Leon Golden, *Aristotle's "Poetics": A Translation and Commentary for Students of Literature* (Englewood Cliffs, N.J.: Prentice-Hall, 1968), 197, cf. 113.

problem for lexical historiography, nor one that can be resolved by philology καθ' αὑτό. The problem with what Aristotle considers "the best" tragedy, and why he thinks it so, is a decisive problem for any philosophical poetics, and central to any discussion of the nature and purposes of comedy: to pull on this string wrongly pulls the whole of *Poetics* out of shape.[23]

Underneath Hardison's remarks there is at work a view I would like to call "Aristotelian formalism." I call it "Aristotelian" not because I believe Aristotle held it, but because it is developed from some of his statements in *Poetics.* I call it "formalism" because it is developed by blowing formal causality into the most significant—if not the only—defining feature of the verbal made thing: the poem. I intend to show that such a view is not only false to Aristotle, it is also false to the things—including the things made by Shakespeare and other artists of a later day as well as those Aristotle knew and was speaking of. What Hardison says about the "modern sense" of comedy implies the modern senses of comedy and tragedy are constrained within this fallacy of Aristotelian formalism.[24] That they do so suffer I agree with; that Aristotle teaches the fallacy is false.

We can see in the remarks already quoted that Hardison is considering Aristotle's outline of possible plots from chapter 13, where, after ruling out several forms as not raising the right emotions, Aristotle says that what remains is the complex plot with a single fatal resolution for the protagonist—who must be a relatively good man suffering due to hamartia. A complex plot is one with peripety and recognition, and he outlines the peripety as being a change in direction of the plot movement; for example, one that seems rising changes to fall. The tack of the unhappy ending that Euripides most frequently takes "is the right line to take" (1453a26). What Aristotle is describing here as the best is the shape of an action that moves the protagonist in a curve approximating the parabola of the mouth on a tragic mask: the

23. One can also pull *Poetics* out of shape by silence. For example, Golden accepts chapter 13's version of the best tragedy (without argument) when he attempts a theory of comedy; see "On Comedy," 286. He avoids discussion of chapter 14 entirely in "Epic, Tragedy and Catharsis"; see especially 83f. where he makes pity and fear a direct function of the character of the tragic hero. He presumes in his silent act what Bywater proclaims openly by bracketing most of the later chapter as an addition.

24. Halliwell similarly complains of this formalist tendency in the introduction to his new Loeb translation, 10. John Jones ties the formalism I am against to the invention of the "tragic hero," whose fate substitutes for Aristotle's emphasis on action; see his section 1, esp. 12–16. Formalism is common to both post-Aristotelian classical and medieval theories of comedy and tragedy through Dante and Chaucer; see, e.g., Coghill, "Basis," and notable examples in Preminger et al., eds.

protagonist climbs from a bad beginning (runs away from impending tragedy at home) up to a relatively superior position (answers the Sphinx and is named king) where the peripety turns the action to his undoing (discovers the queen is his mother). Aristotle also suggests a contrasting complex plot, which Hardison identifies with our modern idea of comedy. The parabola of this action moves down (the protagonist begins to doubt all his ideas) to a peripety (he considers there might be an evil demon deceiving him, but discovers the good God must exist) whose resolution rises to happiness, not misery (he realizes every clear and distinct idea must be true). The plot of *Iphigenia* clearly fulfills this latter formalist criterion for comedy, as Hardison recognizes. As such formalist critics note, Aristotle cannot be talking about a plot that *simply* moves from happiness to misery or the reverse in a straight line, for he has already specified that the complex plot (involving a peripety or change in plot direction) is better than a simple one (Hardison, 165ff, includes diagrams). The structure of the incidents—the formal cause—has become, in the eyes of these critics, all but definitive of the genre, and in summarizing his discussion of structure versus spectacle Hardison seems to go a little further than is necessary ("structure is always more important than content"; 189) for the definition of the genre.[25]

It would follow that all literature, or at least all dramatic and narrative literature, should fall under one of four plot forms: the simple rise from worse to better fortune (a rising line), the complex change from worse to better fortune (a smile), the simple decline from better to worse fortune (a declining line), and the complex change from better to worse (a frown). A formalist might be tempted to go so far as to call the first set of plots comic and the second tragic, but (even without speaking of final causes) Aristotle would not do so, for, as chapter 13 argued, the character of the protagonist has a great influence on how we respond to the play—a supremely good man passing

25. Frye confesses a similar formalism when he says that the "general distinction between fictions in which the hero becomes isolated from his society and fictions in which he is incorporated into it" is that aspect of plot which is referred to by the terms tragic and comic in their larger than dramatic sense (*Anatomy*, 35). He reiterates that formalism in a later sentence, tracing it to Aristotle: "the source of the tragic effect must be sought, as Aristotle pointed out, in the tragic mythos or plot structure" (207). But this sentence is hard to join together with its paragraph-opening counterpart: "Like comedy, tragedy is best and most easily studied in drama, but it is not confined to drama, nor to actions that end in disaster" (207). Clearly *Cymbeline*, one of Frye's examples in this paragraph, is not a fiction that isolates the hero from his society, and it is hard to see why, given what Frye has said about the movement of tragedy, the play should be considered a tragedy at all. A more complex explication of the basic distinction between comedy and tragedy is required than one based solely on *muthos*.

from happiness to misery "is not fear-inspiring or piteous, but simply odious" (1452b34f). Such a movement of such a character therefore cannot function the way Aristotle defines tragedy as functioning: "Through pity and fear accomplishing a catharsis of such emotions" (1449b27–28). Similarly the fall of a braggart, miser, pantalone, or sophist into misfortune is frequently—but not always—comic.[26] Notice that in these last sentences we are implying that we know what comedy and tragedy are apart from the structure of the incidents, and that we will regard some falls of braggarts comic and some not.[27] The formalist mistake is to consider the shape of the plot (or—at best—plot plus character) fully definitive of, and sufficient for, the distinction between the types of drama, whereas Aristotle clearly makes the emotions affected in the audience the decisive criterion for the determination of type.

It is of course neither my argument nor Aristotle's that plot and character are disconnected from catharsis, nor that any reader's response is as good as any one else's. As the fall of the good man is odious, so the rise of a bad man to happiness "is the most untragic that can be; it has no one of the requisites of tragedy; it does not appeal either to the philanthropy in us or to our pity, or to our fears" (1452b35–37). Here we see again that Aristotle must, and does, turn outside of the play—to its effect in the theater, on our pity, fear, philanthropy—in his argument about whether or not a play is tragic, so we should turn (and expect he is turning) to the same criterion to answer the question about which tragic plot is best.

Before we come to that solution, however, there are several other instructively mistaken attempts at resolving the crux formed between chapters 13 and 14. Like Hardison's attempt, we will see that these notions have in common a separation of form from function, or (in the case of Else) a limitation of explanatory scope to that suitable for a perfectly natural thing partaking in no way of the way of being of a tool.

26. As an example of it not being comic consider the scene in *Love's Labour's Lost* (5.2) in which the pedants Nathaniel and Holofernes are mercilessly mocked by the young scholars. After Nathaniel retreats, Costard (the clown), himself having taken part in the driving off, says

> there, an't shall please you, a foolish mild man; an honest man, look you, and soon dashed. He is a marvelous good neighbor, faith, and a very good bowler; but for Alisander—alas, you see how 'tis—a little o'erparted. (576–80)

The clown's speech makes us in the audience feelingly realize we have gone too far ourselves in enjoying the mockery of our neighbor, for we have been laughing at him too—and now the clown chastises us. "This is not generous, not gentle, not humble" (621).

27. Frye himself argues that comedy turns into tragedy depending on the nature of the scapegoated figure and the depth of the scapegoating in *Anatomy*, 42–43, 45–46.

The second attempt to resolve our puzzle focuses on the distinction between single incident and plot of the whole. These scholars appeal to a seeming division of topics in the two chapters at issue. They note that as chapter 12 (an early, but probably spurious, addition) was about the quantitative parts of tragedy, chapters 13 and 14 are about the qualitative aspects, and in chapter 13 he is "thinking of the course and effect of the tragedy as a whole, [while in chapter 14] he is thinking of the emotional effect of a specific incident within the tragedy."[28] It is, however, fatal for this proposed argument that Aristotle has emphasized so much that plots are mimeses of a unified action (1450b23–25), like the *Iliad* (1451a29), in which the episodes follow by probability or necessity (1452a3–20). Further, the kind of action that arouses pity and fear in the *plot* is the same as the kind of *incident* that will do so: the kind that causes "suffering within relationships such as brother to brother" being the best kind (1453b19–21). So in order to carry through this distinction between "play as a whole" and "incident" the poet would need to make the most effective kind of incident—the one which is meditated, or perhaps already in motion, but thanks to the recognition not committed—merely incidental to the main action of the play. The play's total action must be, finally, disastrous. We are driven to the obvious difficulty that "to have an imminent horror with a happy issue as the crucial incident in a tragedy would seem to be incompatible with an unhappy ending of the play as a whole."[29]

Despite its obvious problem, this answer has been exceedingly popular. The reason for its popularity is that it lets us keep our easy unexamined opinion. For one would only wish to make the happy incident of discovery fit into an unhappy whole by virtue of an unspoken appeal to the fallacy of Aristotelian formalism; this appeal begs the question at issue, which is whether a tragedy needs to have an unhappy ending in order to be (1) a tragedy, or (2) the best exemplar of the tragic.

A third group of scholars answers the problematic crux by saying that Aristotle changed his mind about what the best tragedy was. They take the conclusion in favor of *Iphigenia* over *Oedipus* to be his final considered opinion.[30] No one of whom I am aware has considered the *Iphigenia* preference

28. Cooper, "Amplified Version," 46; Moles calls this the "usual attempt" ("Notes," 82).

29. Thus Cooper, about his own attempted solution; "Amplified Version," 47.

30. Bywater, e.g., suggests that 1453b22–1454a9 is a later accretion, thereby cutting out everything specific from chapter 14 as not fitting with the original flow of the argument except the remark about plot being more important than spectacle. Glanville suggested that the changes between the two chapters of *Poetics* devolved from Aristotle's sharpening of his views on voluntary

to be early, and then replaced upon consideration by a preference for *Oedipus*. To my view this sort of explanation at least has the advantage of requiring that the scholar allows Aristotle himself an escape from the formalist fallacy, and while it implicitly accuses Aristotle of sloppiness and forgetfulness of major proportions in not changing, deleting, or clarifying the previous chapter, the admission that Aristotle changed his mind in the direction favoring *Iphigenia* might save us from a hypnotic attraction to the mask of plot form. If a thinker of Aristotle's caliber eventually concludes that *Iphigenia* is both tragic and the best exemplar of the form, we ought to consider why. It is clearly not sufficient to say that the answer to this question "must remain a matter for speculation" (Moles, "Notes," 91), still less to speculate that his final preference "is the manifestation of a jaded critical palate" (Moles, "Notes," 92). Aristotle began the troublesome chapter by saying that tragic fear and pity can be aroused by the spectacle, but the better way is by the structure of the actions (1453b1–3); his rating of plots and actions not only follows this remark but also follows from it, and is neither a disconnected accretion, nor a matter for uninhibited speculation, nor the merely subjective tendence of an old horse.

There is, finally, the case of the critics who give Aristotle the lie direct.[31] Aristotle's critical judgments, says Else,

> were based too narrowly to begin with, on his exaggerated and one-sided thesis of the overwhelming importance of plot as against all other elements; and their interlocking [principles] had the result of narrowing his scope still more, to two species of one variety (the complex plot). It so happened that the knife-edge of his judgment hit square on one masterpiece, the *Oedipus*; but the other play it hit upon, the *Iphigenia*, cannot honestly be called much more than a good melodrama, and meanwhile masterpieces like the *Trojan Women* or the *Bacchae*, to say nothing of the *Oedipus at Colonus* or the *Agamemnon*, remain outside the range of Aristotle's formula. . . . Tragedy in its greatest days comported things that were not dreamt of in Aristotle's philosophy.[32]

---

action between (earlier) *Eudemian Ethics* and (later) *Nicomachean Ethics*. I am not convinced that the alleged change between these books is sufficient to ground such a major change in poetics, and it seems exceedingly strange that Aristotle does not notice the contradiction he creates.

31. Besides Else, we might put Kitto in this group, though he is not quite so direct. When faced with the *Iphigenia*, he says "we have to change entirely our critical premisses" (314), leaving us to remember for ourselves that Aristotle seemed to think his judgment flowed from the premises he had outlined. Even more surprising, Anne Burnett calls the *Iphigenia* "non-Aristotelian, as that term is usually understood" (1) and notes that although he admires the plot, Aristotle "makes no attempt to find a place for it in his system" (2n). It is not clear from her explication of the play (47–72) exactly what is non-Aristotelian about it. It is certain that *Poetics* gives it pride of place.

32. *Aristotle's "Poetics": The Argument*, 446. Else's thesis has been resurrected lately by Martha Husain, *Ontology and the Art of Tragedy: An Approach to Aristotle's "Poetics."*

But Else, besides here marrying Aristotle to the fallacy of formalism, has also interpreted catharsis in such a way that the narrow jacket he has made of *Poetics* has become a straitjacket. First of all, he has interpreted catharsis in the most intellectualist manner, as his use of the word 'demonstration' in what follows emphasizes. He reads Aristotle's phrase μανθάνειν καὶ συλλογίζεσθαί τι ἕκαστον (1448b16) as "learning, inferring what class each object belongs to" (125)—a kind of "learning" that necessarily belies Aristotle's claims about the firstness of learning through mimesis, and overlooks man's sharing of both mimesis and μάθησις with nonrational animals (which also seem to share in some of our pleasure in music). Secondly, other critics generally recognize catharsis as something that occurs, or at least has a reference, outside of the play in the audience, and that idea allows some possibility of correction or escape from erroneous judgments dependent upon the formalist fallacy. For Else, however,

> the catharsis is not a change or end-product in the spectator's soul, or in the fear and pity (i.e., the dispositions to them) in his soul, but . . . the purification of the tragic act by the demonstration that its motive was not μιαρόν [polluting]. . . . This interpretation makes catharsis a transitive or operational factor within the tragic structure itself, precedent to the release of pity, . . . rather than the be-all and end-all of tragedy itself. (*Argument*, 439)

It must be admitted that Else's remark that catharsis should not be considered the be-all and end-all of tragedy has some Aristotelian evidence for it, for Aristotle himself says that plot is the *psuchē* and *archē* of tragedy (1450a38). Further, the plot, which is the end (telos) of tragedy, effects the function (*ergon*) of tragedy (1450a30, 1452b29). Else does not deny that poetry has effects on the audience, he just denies that those effects are part of the complete explanation of the poem's being. Partly his remark seems to be based on something trivial: If we say that the final cause is in the audience, we are placing one of the causes for a thing outside the thing. This seems counter to the phrasing that plot is telos, *psuchē*, and *archē*, since plot is definitely in the play. Aristotle's phrasing, however, does not stand against the fact that catharsis is the final cause of tragedy while plot is its formal cause. That "the soul is the form of the body" and gives it life implies that "all natural bodies are organs of the soul" (*DA* 415b15, 18; cf. 415b10–12), so a similar remark about plot means that all the other parts of the play (thought, character, rhythm) are the plot's organs, plot being the soul. In this way the plot as *psuchē* is the telos that the elements of the play subserve.

But all of that can be true (and is true) of the poem in itself without denying that catharsis in the audience is the final cause of the whole play itself. For the play is not a merely natural thing that springs fully formed from the mimetic instincts of man (like a child from a different instinct); it is *made to a purpose* and that purpose unaccomplished or come tardy off we must say that the play (like a certain axe; *DA* 412b13–18) is a play in name only. The play is not *just* a tool either, but it is a tool as well. Even the fact that *natural* bodies find their telos in the soul does not gainsay that the final cause of the *complete being* is happiness (or, for animals, satisfaction). That is, the final cause neither is nor is in either the soul or the body, rather the final cause is the excellent functioning of the composite. Even in the case of such completely natural things as souls there is a way of understanding the soul's final cause as being outside the being, for it aims at immortality, which the mortal soul cannot get for itself, but only for its species (*DA* 415b5–8), continuing its kind in beings other than itself. Similarly with the play, which is the composite of plot plus other elements, the final cause of which is catharsis: The plot makes the play be the kind of thing it is and the thing aims at accomplishing something beyond itself. The soul makes the body be the kind of body it is, gives it the capacity—really, *is* the capacity—to function as that kind of being should, and in fully natural beings is the guarantor that a certain final cause—maple, oak, happiness—is the final end at which the being—seed, acorn, man—aims. But a poem is not a fully natural thing as Else's rendering of the analogy makes it; the poem has a certain *psuchē* because the artist *is aiming at* a certain effect.[33] That *psuchē* gives the play its particular life and motion, and plot is also the *archē* dictating the choice of other elements: characters, music, thought, language. All of these are chosen for plot's sake and act on its behalf. It is as a pseudonatural thing that we must understand Aristotle's remarks that "the events and the plot are the telos of tragedy" and "the most important thing" (1450a22–23). It is the most important thing considering the play itself καθ' αὑτό (1449a8; cf. 1447a7 Περὶ ποιητικῆς αὐτῆς). If a play were a natural thing, this would be the *only* way to properly understand it, and Aristotle would not have to begin his treatise by par-

33. Halliwell calls Aristotle's framework "quasi-naturalistic" (see his introduction to the Loeb edition, 9); I take it this explanation lays out his reasoning for that choice of terms. It is precisely because the artist is *aiming* at an effect that Kant is somewhat suspicious of the beauties of art; it purposely draws a relation between morality (the good) and aesthetics (the beautiful); see *KU* 301f., and the discussion below in Chapter 3.3 and 3.4. Art is beauty created with an unavoidable reference to the moral good, because created by a being with practical reason.

ticularly picking it out, nor would he have to note that there is another set of problems—those that arise πρὸς τὰ θέατρα. But there is that other side because plays are not merely natural, with an entirely self-subsistent and self-actualizing entelechy. We aim to do something with them; that act is accomplished in the audience. As the final cause of the hammer is driving the nail and that of the axe is cutting, so the final cause of the play is a catharsis of the passions. It is as something like a tool that we must understand this: the final cause of a tool is always outside the tool. Here might be a good place to point out that the extant *Poetics* closes with Aristotle arguing that tragedy is superior to epic because not only is its plot more unified, but also it requires less space for the attainment of its end and these two causes make it better in its poetic effect (1462b15). If, as I am arguing, this poetic effect—outside the tool, in the theatre—is catharsis, we might expect that book 2 would begin by continuing with a more detailed discussion of that poetic effect—that is, the kinds of catharsis. That discussion would allow Aristotle to clarify the distinction between tragedy and comedy—a perfect beginning to that latter topic, which is what the missing book is supposed to be about. So plot is *archē*, *psuchē* and telos for the poem considered in itself. But considering the poem's relation to the audience (which relation is part of its nature as a poem) the telos is catharsis.

Else's idea of catharsis, which makes it a transitive factor in the tragic structure itself—if it can be understood at all—considers tragedy after the model of a *fully* natural thing, with an entelechy that is self-referential and self-developing. This is never the case in art. While mimesis arises naturally and accomplishes its effects naturally, it is shaped by the poet for specific purposes the poet aims to achieve through those natural workings (cf. 1454a10–12). These purposes are outside the poem in the naturally mimetic being from whence the art arises and by whom and for the sake of whom it is made. The telos of everything *in* the poem is the plot, but the telos *of* the poem is not. The medical basis of the word for this telos—catharsis—is no mere happy accident, for ancient medicine developed the same way as drama: noticing a natural effect, the physician sought ways to increase the strength and control the timeliness of the effect, *for the sake of* the being affected.[34] The effect is the end-all of medicine, just as it is of politics, and a

34. Richard Kraut has shown that "for the sake of which" relations are both causal and normative in his *Aristotle on the Human Good* (200f); we should expect, then, that Aristotle's poetics will be, like medicine and politics, doing both descriptive and prescriptive work. We might even

legislator or doctor who fails to achieve the end is a failure. So it is also in drama, as Aristotle says in chapter 25: even "impossibilities . . . are justifiable, if they serve the end of poetry itself (which has been stated), that is, if it makes . . . [the poem] more thrilling (ἐκπληκτικώτερον)" (1460b24–25). Similarly, depravity and improbability are inexcusable "when they are not necessary and no purpose is served" by them (1461b18–20). But the ekplektic has clear connections to passional catharsis, not an intellectual clarification (as the next section will exhibit). The aim of poetry is not "the interesting," but the affectively effective.

In his famous definition of tragedy as "a mimesis of a serious action, complete and having magnitude; in language with pleasurable accessories; dramatized, not narrated; through pity and fear accomplishing a catharsis of such passions" (1449b24–28), Aristotle clearly picks out the formal, material, efficient, and final causes he demands of a complete explanation. As has been almost universally noted, he talks about all the other causes at length in the extant *Poetics*, but the final cause—catharsis—is not clearly discussed anywhere in *Poetics*.[35] I have argued at length elsewhere[36] that Aristotle's reason for largely skipping a discussion of catharsis is that he is considering poetics alone—as his opening line suggests: περὶ ποιητικῆς αὐτῆς (1447a7)—and is leaving to the side as much discussion relating to the audience (πρὸς τὰ θέατρα) as possible in order to keep his little study centered as much as possible καθ' αὑτό (1449a7–9), on poetry intrinsically. He must, and does, make reference to the effect of poetry when he discusses kinds of plot in our problematic chapters because, since everything else in the poem is there for the sake of the plot, what is required or best for the plot must be judged by something outside of the poem itself: unless, that is, one thinks it possible to judge of form without reference to function—the fallacy of (Aristotelian) formalism.

Largely because Aristotle does not speak of it elsewhere in *Poetics* Else brackets the whole phrase introducing the *Katharsisfrage* (1449b28) as a late addition by Aristotle, and raises a host of problems to the usual interpretation of it as referring to the passions of the audience. Most apropos to

---

go so far as to say it is impossible for any poetics, medicine, or politics not to be doing both. Being prescriptive implies that it is possible for the art *Poetics* describes to be turned to ill, as well as good; thus always with pharmacy.

35. Belfiore, like many others, concludes similarly; cf. *Pleasures*, 257–60, 337–39, and her references.

36. See "The Others In/Of Aristotle's *Poetics*," esp. 250–51.

continuing the analysis of the present problem is his discussion of the last phrase, τὴν τῶν τοιούτων παθημάτων κάθαρσιν, of which he says "either (1) τῶν τοιούτων must equal τούτων (these), or (2) there must be tragic emotions besides pity and fear," and then emends the text in the most limiting direction (*Argument*, 228; cf.226–27). Professor Else considers changing the Greek text because as it stands it clearly implies other passions than pity and fear are involved in tragedy, and he considers it unlikely that Aristotle thought so. I am willing to leave the text unemended and accept the consequence that there are tragic passions besides pity and fear, though Aristotle explicitly names no others when he refers to the feelings tragedy should generate—except philanthropy (1452b28–1453a5). He does mention disgust (το μιαρόν; 1453b39) as something tragedy should not evoke.

I am willing, that is, to stay with the ordinary translation that tragedy, "through pity and fear accomplishes the catharsis of such (or suchlike) passions."[37] Note that whatever other suchlike passions there may be, these too undergo a catharsis *through pity and fear*, or perhaps I should say "through the pitiable and fearful things"—which is Aristotle's preferred locution throughout the questionable chapters. In either case fear and pity are still the most significant of the passions (or events)—the ones (or the kind of things) that do the work—in hearing, reading, viewing a tragedy. Tragedy may arouse other passions, but it is through pity and fear being aroused that catharsis occurs. This interpretation might go so far as to allow that tragedy may work either homeopathically (pity and fear providing a catharsis of pity and fear) or allopathically (pity and fear providing a catharsis of some other—suchlike?—passion), depending on how much like each other passions have to be to be considered homeopathically catharsized.[38] The fallacy of Aristotelian formalism reaches its esoteric dead end when catharsis is made a transitive factor within the structure of the play itself. The play no longer does any work: a Rube Goldberg device with no output.

There is a deep problem in philosophical aesthetics beneath this discussion. Else wishes to explain catharsis apart from the feelings of pleasure and

37. Janko likewise leaves the text unemended ("From Catharsis," 350), as does Belfiore (*Pleasures*, 226); Bywater and Halliwell both translate "such emotions." Prior to Else, F. L. Lucas had found no difficulty in holding that tragedy dealt with "feelings of that sort," i.e., grief, weakness, contempt, blame; cf. his *Tragedy*, 43–44. Else continues to think the matter problematic; see his last book, *Plato and Aristotle*, 159–62.

38. Resolving the debate between these two versions of catharsis was the final cause behind Belfiore's finely detailed book.

pain engendered in the audience. I suppose the philosophical aim of such an explication is to attempt somehow to make aesthetic judgments of works of art fully autonomous. Any solution of this problem will require us to take note of Kant (in Chapter 3 of this book) but for the time being let us note that Else's desire to make artistic judgments autonomous is itself no doubt an expression of the desire to free them from the vagaries of mere subjectivity or emotionalism, or—this last century's great problem—political dogma and propagandizing. He apparently thinks that a complete disjunction with feeling is necessary in order to defend that wished-for autonomy. As Halliwell shows in the book that was set up as our propylaia, however, the creation of an autonomous sphere for art is not something at which the mimetic theory of art as understood by the ancients aimed. It is doubtful that Plato or Aristotle could even think such a thing as a real possibility for the being called *anthrōpos*. Further, as Kant's work points out (whether or not it itself escapes from this trilemma), judgments about works of art are either (1) wholly subsumable under a determinate theoretical concept (e.g., pseudobiological: "they grow like this") or (2) subsumable under a practical concept (a version of which the political theories of art accept), or (3) result from a merely pathological feeling (about which no agreement can be forthcoming). True autonomy for art will require something other than one of these three choices. Else's formalism escapes the second and third of these difficulties; but his formalism is still not autonomy even if it escapes the charges of being insidiously and surreptitiously political or melancholically phallogocentric.

Else's attempt to understand tragedy in this intellectualist way is reminiscent of Karl Philip Moritz's argument that a work of art is internally purposive; that is, that it can only be understood as having a purpose and perfection in itself, without relation to feelings of pleasure and pain.[39] In this case God could tell us what the true aesthetic rank of things is, but human beings are most likely to find themselves mistaken. Moritz might have been the first of the New Critics. The effect of a work of art on a being with feelings of pleasure and pain would be superadded or accidental: a political, rhetorical, or social effect on top of the "properly" artistic one. But where Aristotle says these two discussions—politics and poetics—are distinct, he means it in the way he would say that an analysis of political structure can be kept dis-

39. For further discussion of Moritz's view, see Paul Guyer, *Kant and the Experience of Freedom: Essays on Aesthetics and Morality* (Cambridge, U.K.: Cambridge University Press, 1993), 141–47.

tinct from a discussion of happiness. That is, we can see how the elements of a poem (or a polis) are related, how plot, character, and language (or legislative, executive, and judiciary) work and interlock, while leaving the purpose of the whole blank. Modern politics—and the modern state—seems to attempt just that. So modern politics, like the New Criticism (and its dark shadow, deconstruction), attempts to understand its object without the reference outside the object's structure:[40] happiness in the political case, catharsis in the case of poetry. But such rigorous objectivity goes too far—by not going far enough: into the audience. In any case it clearly is not Aristotle's position: to keep two discussions distinct (as he does) is not to say either can be completed without the other (which he neither says nor does).

On the way to resolving the problem of the *Iphigenia*, then, our next questions must not be about plot, but about passion: What other passions could be considered tragic? and How do pity and fear accomplish their catharsis?

4. OF STRONG AND PAINFUL PASSIONS

In this section I will show good reason to think that Aristotle considers tragedy's purpose to be a catharsis of the painful emotions, fear and pity being primary among them. By briefly explicating Aristotle's view of the passions I will try to show that what he says about tragedy requires this more inclusive understanding of the passions involved in the art. Part of the argument in this section is aimed against the idea that the passions themselves are, or need necessarily involve, judgments—which view a consistent intellectualist (about *Poetics*) must hold—and partly the argument is aimed at upholding a bifurcation in the passions between those based on pleasure and those based on pain. Such a bifurcation allows for two broad objects of artis-

40. The problem for an Aristotelian analysis of aesthetics, if I am right about Aristotle's understanding of the final cause of poetry, is how a pleasurable feeling of catharsis can be universally valid. This is required if (as Aristotle claims) some tragedies just are better than others, and audiences can be mistaken. This problem, then, is thoroughly dialectical, raising two opposing orders at once, for it requires us to join an effect on *feeling* with a *universally valid judgment*. Against this double-edged sword many a theory of aesthetics—and nearly as many interpretations of *Poetics*—has raised its head, and fallen. This deeper problem of aesthetics will be taken up more directly in Chapter 3.3 and 3.4. It will be necessary, in those sections, to speak of Kant, who clearly sees that this is the problem.

tic making and catharsis, just as Aristotle suggests by the original two-book structure of *Poetics*.[41]

The first indication that a whole spectrum of the passions—not just fear and pity and perhaps two more for comedy—is involved in Aristotle's understanding of catharsis is his use of the term ἔκπληξις. Aristotle says of the *Oedipus*-type plot that the recognition is ἐκπληκτικον—wonderful, surprising, thrilling (1454a4). The word's literal roots could be translated "to strike forth from" and is related to the term κατάπληξις—shame, self-disgust—or, more literally, "to strike down against."[42] We should note the mechanical or animal impetus invoked by the words here, which connect to the broader anthropological sense of mimesis discussed in the "Propylaia." Besides the kind of thing Aristophanes has Euripides say of Aeschylus's poetry (*Frogs* 962), ἔκπληξις makes Ion's hair stand on end when he recites (*Ion* 535b2), and causes soldiers to flee in panic (Belfiore, *Pleasures*, 219). Socrates uses the root verb to describe his reaction to Agathon's lovely, if inconsequent, speech in *Symposium* (198b5), which he describes as infectious, another hint at a more deeply rooted mimetic effect than cognition. Indeed, Socrates' exactingly cognitive response of questioning Agathon, rather than fleeing or discovering his wits are charmed to stone, makes Agathon reverse his field. Philosophy's difference from tragedy is not merely the content of its speech, but what it makes happen, and on what it works primarily. Perhaps Socrates' praise was itself the disarming countercharm needed to free the obviously excited symposiasts (as well as himself) from the passions excited by Agathon. Κατάπληξις was Pericles' cure for Athenian hubris according to Thucydides (2.65.9). Belfiore argues that ἔκπληξις "is not an emotional effect separate from pity and fear," but is "another term for the same effects" (ibid., 222). Moles considers its primary case to be "the surprise of the audience when things turn out contrary to their expectations" and so is "particularly condu-

41. The division in *Poetics* 2 is ἢ σπουδαίους ἢ φαύλους, on which I have more to say later (Chapter 2.1). *Tractatus Coislinianus* says tragedy has pain, comedy pleasure, for its mother (cf. Janko, *On Comedy*, 23, 25, and the discussion of that text in Chapter 2 below). Aristotle's original book had two parts according to all reports: one part on tragedy, the μίμησις πράξεως σπουδαίας, the other on comedy, the μίμησις φαυλοτέρων.

42. More scholarly discussion of these terms can be found in Belfiore, *Pleasures*, 216–22; see also Moles, "Notes," 89–91, and Heath, *Poetics*, 15–16, 42, 112. Stanford emphasizes the visceral effects of tragedy "being felt in the entrails, womb, liver, heart, midriff, lungs, or head, like a stab" (*Emotions*, 21); see also 15, for its effect in crowds; 28f for ἔκπρληξις particularly.

cive to the arousal of pity and fear" ("Notes," 89). Heath says "it and its cognates are used of any emotional reaction, and particularly of those which are particularly intense" (*Poetics*, 15).

The middle ground seems very solid. It is clear that elsewhere in Greek literature (besides discussions of fearful and pitiable things) ἔκπληξις can refer to a wide range of sudden, very strong, encompassing emotional reactions, not necessarily or exclusively pity and fear. Aristotle's three bare uses of the term in *Poetics* (1454a4, 1455a17, 1460b25) argue against it developing any more specific or technical sense in that treatise. In fact, the middle reference is to the recognition of Orestēs by Iphigenia, which is hardly frightening, but that from which comes salvation. This *recognition* clearly involves judgment, but the sudden influx of joy in the characters, expressed in both movement and voice, is itself ekplektic and mimetically effective on the audience. So, ἔκπληξις may seem more particularly associated with pity and fear in other places precisely because the topic is frightening things; for example, the reference in *Ion* refers to a recitation of particularly fearful scenes in Homer. But Alcibiades' use of the term with regard to Socrates in *Symposium* 215 might refer as much to a sudden influx of an ungovernable love as to fear. Its use in that context might make us suspect that the ekplectic—the wonderful, surprising, or thrilling—will be an effect to aim at in comedy as well. As Heath notes (*Poetics*, 15), the term is sometimes used to refer to both love and joy by the tragedians themselves. Aristotle's own remark that plausible impossibilities are allowable when they can accomplish a greater ἔκπληξις (1460b22–25), taken together with the already mentioned remark about the recognition scene in *Oedipus* being ἐκπληκτικόν (1454a4), should convince us that it is not the harmful or the shameful deed per se that causes the emotion of ἔκπληξις,[43] but sudden or surprising recognition and peripety, which in the case of Oedipus is pitiable, but which may well be a sudden cause of joy or release from fear—as Iphigenia's saving discovery of Orestes.

We should not be convinced that the ἔκπληξις caused by peripety is mostly or largely due to the event that takes the audience by surprise by making things turn out contrary to their expectations. Ignorance on the part of the audience will clearly be able to heighten this effect in some circumstances, but most tragedy in Aristotle's day was based on traditional stories, which even if (a debatable Aristotelian claim) they were "only known to a few, are

43. Belfiore (*Pleasures*, 221), plumps for this view—that the revelation of the harmful or shameful causes ἔκπληξις.

a delight *nonetheless* to all" (1451b25–26). Further, Agathon's *Antheus*—"in which both incidents and names are the poet's invention—is no *less* delightful on that account" (1451b21–23), but clearly these plays should be quite a bit *more* delightful if audience surprise is a primary source of ἔπληξις. Finally, many of the plays of the great tragedians were performed on a regular basis (even as they and Shakespeare are now)—the element of surprise cannot be long lasting, and the play could never be as emotionally effective on a second or third reading (or presentation) if surprise were necessary for ἔπληξις. Nor could Ion's recitations of Homer work so.[44] Not only are these things not the case, but frequently a poem becomes more effective the more we read it. In this regard we should also remember that in many plays—like *Bacchae* or *Hecuba*—the prologue lets us know in more or less detail what will be coming. If this were a flaw, Euripides would hardly win Aristotle's palm as the most tragic of poets. It is the rapid and extreme changes of emotion (as well as the fact of being enacted rather than narrated) that makes drama more effective than epic at producing catharsis. As in epic (and probably all music), it is the production of strong feeling that gives delight (τὸ δὲ θαυμαστὸν ἡδύ; *Po.* 1460a17). Partly this is mechanical: the beating down of the feet of the dancing chorus, the rhythms and tones of the voices, the pull of the descant against the melody and rhythm.

In this regard it seems that intellectualist interpretations of catharsis, like Golden's, are particularly ineffective. If catharsis were an intellectual matter, swiftness and sureness of getting an insight should not matter, and certainly not matter more than the fuller and more nuanced insight available to the longer and more ruminative forms (epic or novel). But if catharsis is a matter of feeling, and of *going through* the feelings, then swiftness, sureness, suddenness, and strength are precisely the important matters.[45] Similarly the suddenness of an action or sureness of a recognition are not matters wholly reducible to propositions, even when the recognition involves a statement of fact. We may think of poetry as more philosophical than history not only because the reflection it engenders regards universals (though why this should not be the case for history as well—which is where most tragedy

44. Nor could a piece of music (something we are more likely to hear several times than a recitation of Homer) work so well depending on this. Yet it does work: you know the descant is coming; you wait for it; it comes; and there you are on the verge of tears again. And if I forget you, O Jerusalem, let my right hand lose its cunning on these strings, and my tongue cleave to the roof of my mouth. And perhaps the descant is not even words, but a saxaphone.

45. On this matter, cf. *Poetics* 1462a13–b15 with Golden, "Epic, Tragedy, and Catharsis," 77f.

gets its stories—is unclear), but because of its engendering of the passions, which are the active universals in the theater.[46] Despite Freud, Oedipus is no more universal than Darius or Nixon, but the passions a well-constructed plot about any of them might be set to work on *are* universal—it is in the passions that we mimic each other, and these too require their exercise and purification. That the mimetism of the passions does not require "a more fundamental" cognitive explanation, but that the natural mimeticism of the human being—which is, according to Aristotle, fundamental to our coming to know—is itself the explanation of the infectious nature of the passions in the audience lends further support to the thesis that the mimetic arts are more philosophical than history and that poetry "more concerns the universal" (1451b7). For history aims precisely at cognition; and abstraction from the (infectious and beclouding, to add the usual adjectives) active universality of the passions.

Halliwell notes that Aristotle's point here is that

> [P]oetic universals operate at a level much less overt, and less susceptible to propositional formulation, than the examples or moral maxims of the orator, still more those of the sytematic philosopher; . . . [they have] a metaphorical presence; . . . understanding poetic universals is a matter of implicit grasp, not—or not necessarily—of explicit articulation.[47]

Such descriptions of the "vituality" of poetic universals in contrast to all usual cognitive universals seem even more applicable to music and dance (which have no *logos*). This explanation of poetic universals also goes along with that anthropologically basic sense of mimesis as working in an infectious, mechanical, or quasi-osmotic fashion, as something *which forms* the human being in accord with it rather than something *upon which* he makes a judgment. The Girardian sense of mimesis goes along with Halliwell's insistence that we consider poetic universals "much less substantial," their work "subtextual, virtual" (102), or my emphasis that the work of mimesis is more infectious than intellectual, more mechanical than cognitive.

I conclude, then, that ἔκπληξις is a sudden, strong, encompassing, visceral, and probably emunctory—Ion's eyes fill with tears, Alcibiades' tears flow—affect; one that can be brought on by, among other things, the recognitions and peripeties of tragedy, recitations of Homer, the speeches of Socrates, the beating of the feet of the chorus or drums, sudden shouts and

46. Again, contrast with Golden, "Epic, Tragedy, and Catharsis," 81, 85.
47. "Aristotelian Mimesis and Human Understanding," 101.

changes in pitch—a range that includes, but does not necessitate cognitive judgment. History does not aim at ἔκπληξις in its recitations, nor does philosophy by turning our agreement to its universals (Socrates' method being considerably different from the usual treatise), but this affect is central to the purpose of poetry, and, since this is so, production of greater ἔκπληξις may excuse the poet from making a plot that contains an impossibility (1460b22–25).[48] Ἔκπληξις, then, seems to refer to a sudden and overpowering intensification—the superfetation—of a passion or pathos, but the range of passions that may undergo this intensification covers both sides of a Pythagorean list, from fear and pity to joy and love.

With a view to clarifying further Aristotle's view of the passions and their importance for drama, we must synthesize a wide range of texts from *De Anima*, *Ethics*, *De Motu Animalium*, and *Rhetoric*. There are even greater dangers of misinterpretation here, since these texts have distinctly divergent aims from our own. For example, vis-à-vis the *Rhetoric*, clearly when one is speaking to convince, one is attempting to move the passions in different ways and for different reasons than when one is reciting a poem. Further, the audience of a rhetorician is in a different emotional set than the audience of a poet. The audience of the poet expects and probably wishes to be moved; here, the deceived is wiser than the undeceived. The audience of the rhetorician may be suspicious and particularly on the look-out for emotional appeals: something of their own is at stake. Aristotle implicates this difference between the rhetorical and the poetic situations when he says that imagination and judgment are different forms of thinking;

> [T]he former [imagination] is an affection (πάθος) which lies in our power . . . but it is not in our power to form opinions (δοξάζειν) as we will. . . . Again, when we form an opinion that something is threatening or frightening, we are immediately affected by it . . . ; but in imagination (φαντασίαν) we are like spectators looking at something dreadful or encouraging in a picture. (*DA* 427b21–25)

In this latter case we need not come to judgment or take action. The rhetorician, on the other hand, is attempting to make us judge in a certain way in a situation where we must judge one way or another. We should remember that "judge" (or "decide") is the last word in *Rhetoric*. In a rhetorical situation it seems like fear would drive out pity, for these passions move us to opposite decisions—for example, "If we defend the French any longer, we

48. Heath makes a similar point in *The Poetics of Greek Tragedy*, 115.

will no longer have the resources to defend our island against the coming invasion"; the opinion that the threat is imminent and great but escapable now does not allow the opinion that the French are to be defended to stand. In the theater, however, we can both fear for Hecuba and pity her. In the theater, then, one passion need not drive out another related passion, but may in fact magnify or enhance it. Close attention to Aristotle's remarks in the two books bears out this point. At *Poetics* 1453a4–6, speaking of the passions the tragic hero's fall engenders, he says, "the one passion concerns the undeserved falling into bad fortune, and the other concerns the likeness. Pity concerns the undeservedness, and fear the *likeness* [to ourselves]." But *Rhetoric* 1385b33 presents a different situation; he notes that people suffering from great fear do not feel pity, being taken up by what *is* happening to themselves.[49] The rhetorical situation is one involving present decision. It has, we might say, existential import, it is not merely "in a picture."

Turning back again to the poetic side, the poet works on imagination. Imagination being in our power, we can decide, when looking at a play or a picture, to let the sight affect us or not. Perhaps we even choose to invent a certain imaginative picture. In a way we let it affect us (imaginatively and passionally); but in a way we do not, not letting ourselves be led to decision and action. When we ourselves are in the dreadful or encouraging picture, however (as in the rhetorical situation), judgment—the power to form opinions—is entailed, and we are immediately affected—in different ways depending on our character and judgment, but it is not in our power *not* to be affected. Our judgment here will not be aesthetic, for it is about the real harms, threats, and goods *we* aim at and *are* involved in, not their *likeness*. This distinction might partially explain why the city of Athens would fine a playwright for presenting a *Sack of Miletus* (see Herodotus 6.21); the event calls up pity and fear, but not the pity and fear appropriate to tragedy; it called up judgment, not imagination, for the sorrow was not *like* their own, but—in fact—their own. One might say such a poet's crime is to take advantage of a poetic venue for rhetorical and political purposes, causing painful emotions—but achieving no catharsis, merely putting us back in our own loss.[50]

49. Golden's view of comedy accepts what *Rhetoric* says about the opposition of certain emotions without considering this problem of the difference between rhetorical and poetic situations of the audience; cf. "On Comedy," 286–87. Stanford, too, presumes too easily on the usefulness of *Rhetoric*'s discussion; cf. *Emotions*, 23.

50. See Heath, *Poetics*, 66f. on this event. Spike Lee's *Malcolm X* suffers from a similar flaw. He accomplishes the rhetorician's purpose, but not the poet's.

Several studies of ancient tragedy emphasize the importance of the effect we might call the tragic shudder (φρίττειν)[51] on the audience. Even in modern times it is considered high praise if a critic can say "there wasn't a dry eye in the house." Of course this should only happen to an audience when it is clear that the acts occurring on stage (or in the film) are not disgusting, but it is not the purpose of the play to demonstrate that fact (as Else affirmed), but rather to have the shuddering or emunctory effect.[52] How does the play accomplish this shudder, and why is it worthwhile? What are these affections or passions the play aims to cause?

The conclusion reached regarding ἔκπληξις above is completely in line with Aristotle's definition of the affections of the soul—πάθη—"formulae expressed in matter" (*DA* 403a25–26). Ἔκπληξις is not the hair standing on end or the weeping or fleeing, but it is the pathos that finds expression in any of these bodily motions (or others) depending on the nature and habits of the individual in whom it comes to be. At this point we must take a few steps back to clarify what goes on in the human passions and how they move us.

In beginning his investigation of the soul, Aristotle broadly distinguishes the soul's affections (πάθη) from its functions (ἔργα; *DA* 402b14–403a4, 403a11); that distinction parallels the distinction of what the soul suffers (πάσχειη) and what it makes or does (ποιείη, 403a8). He makes a similar distinction between activity and passivity when he investigates bodies alone (403b13, cf. 465b15–17). In *De Motu* he makes this distinction take on physical measure and psychological weight by arguing that if one part (of a joint) moves, the other must be at rest (698a15–25). That is, the actor (or mover) and the acted upon (or passive moved) must both be present and yet distinct in being if there is to be any motion. What is unmoved active mover and what is passive moved may change as we go through any motion or change, as the lower arm is unmoved mover to the moving hand, but moved mover to the unmoving upper arm, which in turn is moved mover to the static torso. In *De Anima* Aristotle asks whether any of these things—functions or affections—can go on apart from the body, and so belong to the soul essentially. He answers that "anger, courage, desire and sensation" are clearly

51. See, e.g., Heath, *Poetics*, 11f, Belfiore, 226–28, and Gould, chapters 9 and 17; Aristotle uses the strong word referred to here at *Poetics* 1453b5. All the authors mentioned recognize that the play is aiming to cause this kind of strong, even physically manifested, emotional reaction.

52. The demands of an inferior audience may lead poets to raise this emotional effect in improper ways, but that is the fault of the poet and the audience, not of the art.

enmattered, as is φαντασία (imagination). Thinking is the only possible exception, he says, though if it depends upon imagination "even this cannot exist apart from the body" (403a10).

In this list of passions and functions (403a7–10) we should first point out that it is highly likely that Aristotle is using particular examples to stand for types of physiopsychic occurrence: there is the primary irascible passion (anger), followed by a wider capacity (θαρρεῖν, better translated as being confident than as courage), then the primary concupiscible passion (desire), followed by sensation, and finally thinking. The last two are characteristic functions (ἔργα) of the soul; the first three are either all what we would recognize as passions (πάθη) in the strict sense—in line with the meaning the word has in English—or two passions (anger and desire) and a capacity (θαρρεῖν) to be affected by certain passions in that strict sense. A longer such list immediately follows, in which he calls anger, gentleness, fear, pity, courage, joy, loving, and hating passions of the soul (ψυχῆς πάθη), remarking that when they appear the body is also affected (πάσχει; 403a16–19). We should note that it is never the case in all this that thought or its cognates and nearest relatives—belief, understanding—are called passions by Aristotle. *Phantasia* seems to go both ways; as Schofield says, Aristotle seems to be making room for it "between thinking on the one side and sense-perception on the other."[53] The receptivity of sensation produces something in imagination and this passive imagination gives rise to the soul's anger, spirit, desire; or, thinking imagines some good or evil and this more self-activated imagination gives rise to the soul's passions. Finally, Aristotle corrects this picture slightly when he says,

> probably it is better not to say that the soul pities, or learns, or thinks, but to say rather that the soul is the instrument whereby man does these things; that is to say, the movement does not take place in the soul, but sometimes penetrates to it [as perception] and sometimes starts from it [as recollection]. (*DA* 408b13–17)

Aristotle's construction in these lines exhibits another quite interesting parallelism. Pitying, learning, and thinking are described as types of movement, and these movements sometimes penetrate to the soul and sometimes start from it. Knowing that the last (thinking) is the only one he considers it even plausible to exist without the body, the last description—movement that starts from the soul—applies most clearly to it, as it does to recollection.

53. Malcolm Schofield, "Aristotle on the Imagination," in Nussbaum and Rorty, *Essays on Aristotle's "De Anima,"* 254.

From the other direction, some events penetrate to the soul—as through sense perception—and so move us (for example) to pity. The middle term—learning—seems to go both ways. We think of a hypothesis, we test it, we suffer the consequences: the soul starts one kind of movement and receives another from the world in response. Or the reverse: the mother speaks; the baby, perceiving, imitates the rhythms and syllables. After much babbling he finally names the animals rightly. Embodying and repeating the world is our earliest learning, thinking about those things that have been embodied and repeated by forming general ideas is second.[54] That earliest learning is more a suffering than an activity. Mimesis takes us up before we intend it.

So the things that happen penetrate to the soul and *cause* a passion or a series of passions; *thinking* about those things is a different kind of motion—one in the opposed direction. Thinking starts from the soul and moves out to the world. From the other direction, the harsh or fearful thing happens in the world and it is through the soul's perception of the fearful thing that fear comes to be in the human being. This distinction also goes along with the view of *EE*, where appetition is considered on analogy with force *working on* inanimate objects, but real action requires the capacity for *working from* calculation, which we do not attribute to children (1224a 21–30). Children, who are run by their passions (*NE* 1119b5), learn first through mimesis (*Po.* 1448b8). They may be acting *in accord with* reason and judgment, but not from it. So we first learned language too. Cognition follows after what we suffer (πάσχειν), and we may at some point be able to give propositional descriptions of those sufferings, but affirmation or denial of propositions need not be invoked as the *explanation of* the suffering or passion (πάθος). Such affects, then, do not require judgment, merely perception. So music (rhythm and harmony alone) can cause certain affects even in children and animals, without thought or judgment coming into play. The movement of the sound itself is effective; so too with dance or vigorous gymnastics: the actions themselves are mimeses of character or *ethos*. They work mechanically on the soul, quasi-osmotically; they build up what is necessary for cognition and judgment which are part of true virtue—or they are a mechanism for cowardice and self-indulgence.

In his most detailed explanation of the interlocking activity and passivity of the soul, *De Motu Animalium*, Aristotle reduces all the movers of the ani-

54. Cf. *An. Post.* (99b34–100a8): Perception that persists gives rise to memory and memory of many similar things constitutes experience, which is the universal, when established in the soul.

mal to thought and desire (νοῦν καὶ ὄρεξιν; 700b19). Desire comes to be either through thought, or φαντασία or sense perception (701a36), which latter two hold the same place in the causal sequence as thought (700b20), and desire is the proximate cause of the movement (701a35). This same story would apply to avoidance, so that it is the pleasant or the fearful thing (ἡδέος ἢ φοβεροῦ; 701b21) which through φαντασία or sense perceptions or ideas (701b16) cause the passions, and these cause movement. It seems that Aristotle thinks that *either* our thought of something fearful *or* φαντασία *or* sense perception of it can cause the passion of fear (or alternatively, desire).[55]

> For sense perceptions are *at once* a kind of alteration, and φαντασία and thinking have the power of the actual things. For it turns out that the form conceived of the pleasant or fearful is like the actual thing itself. That is why we shudder (φρίττουσι) and are frightened just thinking of something. (701b17–23)[56]

It would make sense, then, that music could cause pleasure in some animals (*Pol.* 1341a16)—or perhaps fear, going so far as to cause a stampede—without necessarily attributing thought to them: sense perception is sufficient. Similarly, sudden sounds in the theater, or screams, can contribute to the arousal of fear operating merely through sense perception, though most of the play—operating through language—works through the higher power. The work of art can (and does) work through any of the three functions of the soul (thought, phantasy, sense) to arouse the passions it aims at. Perhaps art must begin by appealing merely through sense perception; mimesis clearly works originally through this, no more advanced or rational cognition is necessary. Philosophy and stories—as narratives—don't appeal merely through sense perception, though mother's sweet syllables and warm whispering may be what we first, without learning, love, and so listen to, and desiring, attempt to imitate, and through mimesis learn, at last, to speak. But the first time we say "mama" it is meaningless . . . to us.

55. It may be that φαντασία is the required power that in turn is moved by thought or sense perception—φαντασία presenting the forms of the pleasant or of the painful, which forms produce the passions; in this case there would be three steps (sense perception or thought, φαντασία, passion) instead of two (sense perception or thought or φαντασία, passion) (*DMA* 701b21, 703b19–20). This latter would seem to be Aquinas's understanding of it; it is certainly Schofield's. Which of these two is the case is not a matter we have to resolve for our discussion. On the difficulties of these details, see Nussbaum's essay, bound with her translation of *De Motu*, 227–69; also see Dorothea Frede, "The Cognitive Role of *Phantasia*," in Nussbaum and Rorty.

56. Aristotle uses the same word—to shudder with fear (φρίττειν; *Po.* 1453b5)—as an effect that can be brought about either by spectacle or "merely hearing the events that occur."

One of the things I am hoping becomes clear in this all too brief section is my disagreement with Martha Nussbaum's recent arguments that the passions just are identical with judgments or beliefs.[57] The passions are the embodied moved, which can be moved by thought, φαντασία, or sense perception, and perhaps thought and φαντασία can, by long practice and development of habit, shape passion (originating in the animal from sense perception of pleasure and pain), thereby affecting φαντασία, but there is no necessity to think that the passions themselves are beliefs, judgments, or opinions. Our first, most rudimentary and perhaps most powerful passions cannot be, rising as they do out of primary mimesis. Sense perception (or sense perception and φαντασία) is all that is necessary for the arousal of passion in the animal, and perception is not a function of belief.[58] Of course, whenever we "tell a story" about a passion, as Nussbaum does in *Upheavals of Thought*, it will look like the passion is a judgment or opinion because in telling a story about it we are bringing it into *logos*, taking passion from dumb show and noise into reasoned speech; still dumb show and noise affect us mimetically, as does inarticulate music. Movies still use rapid drumbeats and swift movement—perhaps only of the camera, not the people—as *mechanisms* for the arousal of fear. When reason understands a passion, it understands it in the mode of understanding, but the passions themselves may have a very different way of being, and so a "much less substantial, virtual, metaphorical" way of "knowing."[59] It goes without saying that reasoning (whether true or false) can cause or modify the passions. The passions are not dissociated from reason in the normal human adult. Clearly reasoned investigation is one of the tasks of philosophy, but it may well be that reason, belief, and judgment are insufficient for guiding passion by themselves and therefore mimetic arts (and perhaps even punishment) are necessary.

57. See esp. *Therapy of Desire*, 369–86, and *Upheavals of Thought*, lecture 1. Though she makes this claim about the Stoics, it seems she is in agreement with them. It is important to consider whether it is true that the passions are judgments, because if it is not true it *necessarily leads to the wrong explication of the work of art upon the soul.* One might expect, then, that a Stoic *Medea*, like Seneca's, should be less effective than an Aristotelian one—say Euripides', just because the Stoic has the wrong idea about the passions. (This implies one can be more faithful to philosophy than to nature in one's poetic constructions.)

58. For an argument against Nussbaum's view that emotions necesssarily involve or simply are beliefs, see Sorabji, *Man and Beast*, esp. chapters 2–4, or, more briefly "Intentionality and Physiological Processes," in Nussbaum and Rorty, esp. 195–209. That the appetite *can* be modified by the power of reason is obvious. See, e.g., Aquinas's *Commentary on "Nicomachean Ethics,"* book 2, lecture 1, paragraph 249.

59. Cf. Halliwell's language quoted above, "Mimesis and Human Understanding," 31.

It may even be that reasoned investigation shows why reasoned argument is insufficient and what other, more basic manner of purification is necessary. My argument is that poetry is a requirement for human life, for mimeses *elicit the passions themselves* and by bringing them up rightly or wrongly shape them, purify them, or muddy them. It is through philosophy and the arts together, then, that we humanize the passions, bringing them so far as *their* own nature allows into the life that we share with the god (cf. *NE* 10.7–8). In this matter Plato agrees; we were given the Muses so that, refreshing ourselves in the company of the gods, we might return to an upright posture (*Laws* 653d). And the old need it as much as the young.

It should be clearer now how Aristotle understands the passions to be "inseparable from the matter of living things in which their nature is manifested" (*DA* 403b18–19). The motion of the passions is begun in the body, through the activity of the soul's sense perception or thought, and so—moved by the things that are perceived or thought—the passion (desire or fear) moves the body. It is not proper to say that the passion moves the soul, but rather that the movement engendered in the soul by what is experienced (or thought) is the passion. This does not indicate that passions are "in" the soul literally or that they are the activities of an entirely different kind of thing than thinking is, for

> thinking, loving, and hating are not passions of the mind, but of the individual which possesses mind, insofar as it does. Memory and love fail when this perishes, for they were never part of the mind, but of the whole entity which has perished. (*DA* 408b27–30)

The functions and passions are functions and passions of the same unified being; some functions, like thinking, proceed in the opposite direction from the passions; there are acts, and there are passions: Either the action of the world upon the soul (of man or of animal), or even (for man) the soul's own word-wrought vision—no sensation added—(cf. *Po.* 1453b1–5) acting upon us (or, through φαντασία acting upon us), give rise to passion; the passions—by heating and cooling the blood, and so on—then move the body in the world.[60]

It should also be clear how Aristotle specifies and distinguishes the pas-

60. This explication (and what will immediately follow) is in line with that of Aquinas in his *Commentary on Aristotle's "Nicomachean Ethics"* (book 2, lecture 5, paragraph 291): "Although feeling and understanding are in a way passions (i.e., they suffer change), passions are properly denominated . . . only because of appetite." So (paragraph 292), "the operation of the intellective appetite [which is will] is not properly called passion. It does not take place with a change of bodily organ. . . . The operations of the sensitive appetite, which are accompanied by a change of bodily

sions. They are all enmattered formulae that are caused causes of movement and movement is either toward or away from particular things. "The origin of motion, as we have said, is the object of pursuit or avoidance in the sphere of action" (*DMA* 701b 33–34); "the passions are distinguished by pain and pleasure" (*EE* 1221b37–38). Unlike the motions of the planets, animal motion is based in the fact that any living being that has sensation experiences pleasure and pain, "and that which knows these also has desire; for desire (ἐπιθυμία) is an appetite for what is pleasant (ἡδέος ὄρεξις)" (*DA* 414b5–7). Since "appetite (ὄρεξις) consists of desire (ἐπιθυμία), inclination (θυμός), and wish (βούλησις)" (414b3–4), and appetite and avoidance are identical in act with the feeling of pleasure and of pain, respectively (431a10–13), the passions, then, can be broadly distinguished as those associated with sorrow or pain and those associated with joy or pleasure, those which, in act, entail avoidance and those which, in act, elicit appetite and approach. The well-known medieval distinction between the irascible and the concupiscible passions builds on this distinction as well. The movement that we call the passions is from outside in to the soul, not from the soul out. The passions then move the body. The visceral ekplectic effects noted in the previous section—tears, shuddering, hair standing on end—are among the most obvious movements of the body caused by the tragic events. The passional motions, according to Aristotle, are like a child's cart with unequal wheels, which, by heating and cooling, change (as it were) the relative size of the wheels of the body, and so the machine (body, cart) turns one way—attraction to—or the other—avoidance of—the thing causing the passion (*DMA* 701b1–17). Aristotle's mechanical metaphor here again belies the presumed necessity for a cognitivist explanation of the passions and goes along with the basic anthropological conception of mimesis as mechanical or infectious that we introduced early on.

Both aversive and desiring passions are referred to at the opening of *Rhetoric* 2 as the kind of things "which cause men to change their opinion in regard to their judgments, and are accompanied by pleasure and pain; such are anger, pity, fear, and all similar (τοιαῦτα) things and their con-

organ and which in a way draw man, should be called passions in the strict sense." Willing does require a cognitivist, proposition-based explanation. Sensitive appetite and its passions do not require it. If mimesis works as a mechanism first of all, then its arousal of passions would not require the proposition-based explanation either. Later (paragraph 296), he adds, "All other passions are terminated at pleasure and sorrow." This breaks the passions into two categories, each category involving changes in bodily organs, which differing bodily reactions we might emblematize by the comic and the tragic masks.

traries" (1378a20–22; cf. *DA* 429a8–9). Given this, it begins to look like it is highly unlikely that Aristotle would agree with the "orthodox" Stoic notion that passions are themselves judgments.[61] The two kinds of passion (those accompanied by pleasure and those accompanied by pain) cause changes in judgments, as the throwing of a stone may cause a change in the reflectivity of a still pond. As the stone's motion (down and in) vis-à-vis the pond's wavy reflectivity (out and across), the motion of the passions is in the opposed direction to that of thought and judgment. Thought and judgment, like the pond, reflect out toward the world; passion, like the stone, enters in through sense perception, φαντασία, or thought. The stone (as a perception, caused by a different sort of thing than the soul and coming from outside of it) moves down through the water; the water reflects up and outward (as what is known or experienced by the soul is known in accordance with the nature of the soul). The distinguishing thing for Aristotle is the direction of their motion, since both are motions of the same soul. All that is necessary for passion is sense perception; Aristotle's metaphor for the motions of *pathos*, like mine here, are mechanical, not cognitive.

The rhetorician, like the moralist (*NE* 1104b4–34; *EE* 1220a38–b10), knows that the passions—for good or for ill—help shape, and constitute the tenor of, our judgments, but this no more makes the passion a judgment than the stone needs to be water in order to move the water and so affect the pond's reflectivity. (Of course, a stream of water—as a stream of thought on the soul—could also change the tenor of the pond/soul). Perhaps the rhetorician will wish to raise and use some passion for his benefit—to move us to a certain judgment—but clearly it cannot be the function of the poet merely to raise painful passions like pity and fear, or merely to raise them for the

61. For more on the Stoic notion of the passions as judgments, see Martha Nussbaum, *Therapy of Desire*, chapters 9–11, and *Upheavals of Thought*, first lecture. Sorabji distinguishes the "orthodox" interpretation of the Stoics from his own in "Intentionality" (203–7). Of them he says, "in humans perceptual appearance is . . . tantamount to rational thought" (203). Against this Stoic position, consider further that if the passions were judgments, *it would be possible* for the Stoic project of *apatheia* to be accomplished by a human being; all one would have to do is avoid making judgments of importance, which all of the passions must, on their account, include. But I think Aristotle is more realistic and would consider the Stoic project impossible *ab initio* for a being with a body, not just difficult for a mindful soul to accomplish. If imagination is in our power but judgment is not, *apatheia* is certainly impossible. A body that feels pleasure and pain also has desire and fear of necessity; it need not, having reason as another motive, act on such desires or fears. The connection in the first place is from sense perception (pain) to motion, firstly the passions of the soul—the heating or cooling. Some wheels change size no matter what you believe or affirm (cf. *DMA* 701b). Thus, on the other side, music can make even animals have certain reactions without attributing mind to their operations. See also several notes (55–60) above.

sake of pulling off an impossibility in his plot over the audience's beclouded (or scintillated) consciousness.

Like the rhetorician, however, the poet must know—in the case of anger and all the other passions—"the disposition of mind which makes men angry, the persons with whom they are angry, and what makes them so. For if we knew one or even two of these heads but not all three, it would be impossible to arouse that emotion" (*Rh.* 1378a23–27). While one with the art of making a poem may need to know the same things as the rhetorician, his purpose cannot be the same as the rhetorician's—to lead to decision (the telos of the whole rhetorical treatise is this word: decide)—and according to *Poetics* it is not, for the poet's purpose is, in tragedy, "through pity and fear to accomplish the catharsis of such emotions" (1449b27, 28). The difference between poetry and rhetoric in this regard is that one seeks to engage the emotions and so judgment,[62] while the other seeks to engage imagination (φαντασία) and so the emotions. That the border here is easily and frequently crossed does not mean that there is no distinction in the aims of each art. Aristotle considers that it is practice in virtuous action that brings *phronēsis* into actuality in the youth, and the laws educate us into such acts; just so, through the mimetic suffering of appropriate emotion the passions (at which the law cannot directly aim) are educated—literally, led out—and purified. We learn to feel pleasure and pain appropriately or not by mimesis, which makes us into what perception causes in us. Each kind of thing—the rhetorician's speech, the poet's play, the law's command—seeks to engage a different capacity (δύναμις)—judgment, emotion, action—of the soul. If everything is merely a matter of force, as Thrasymachus thought, then we might say that rhetoric is intellectual blackmail, art is emotional blackmail, and the law is actual blackmail. Still, they work differently.

Evils that are painful or destructive are what we pity and fear, so tragedy's purpose is to accomplish a catharsis of the painful emotions,[63] among

62. The rhetorician must "put his hearers, who are to decide, into the right frame of mind" (*Rh.* 1377b23).

63. Heath considers it "plausible to treat the distressing or 'painful' emotions in general as the specifically tragic emotions" (*Poetics*, 16). Janko ("From Catharsis," 350) and House (103) also argue to this conclusion. Belfiore says that "while the tragic *pathos* is a 'destructive or painful event,' comedy deals with just the opposite" (*Pleasures*, 134) and such events cause the proper kind of emotional reaction for the art form (138); this description certainly does not limit the emotional reaction in tragedy to pity and fear. Else and some others consider the synecdochic use of fear and pity to stand for all sorts of painful emotions as eisegesis rather than exegesis of Aristotle. One purpose of this section has been to argue that the more general allowance is the true exegesis of Aristotle.

which *Rhetoric* lists anger, hatred (for it is produced by painful things, like anger, spite, calumny, even though it is not itself painful, 1382a2,3,12), fear, shame (αἰσχύνη), pity, indignation (νέμεσις), envy (φθόνος), and emulation (ζῆλος). Among these we should point out that pity, indignation, and emulation—though painful—are considered to be emotions a good man will be disposed to according to Aristotle. It cannot, then, be the purpose of art to *rid* us of them, as the translation of catharsis by "purgation" implies. On the other hand, there is no mean for shame according to *NE* 4.9—it can be associated with virtue only in the young; and envy does not even have that much to be said for it—it is opposed to pity (*Rh.* 1388a29) and a characteristic disposition of the base (1388a34); fear, of course, has a proper mean (*NE* 3.6), as does anger (*NE* 4.5); it would seem pity, like indignation (*NE* 1108a35–b2), and emulation (*NE* 4.3,4,7) must have proper means as well. Art helps us get there and stay there: it moves us through an experience of feeling to appropriate feeling.

Since tragic poetry acts on these passions, and "if whenever the active (τὸ ποιητικόν) and the passive (τὸ παθητικόν) are found together . . . it is impossible there should be no change" (*PN* 465b15–17), the particular kind of change in the painful passions which the art seeks to accomplish must be what we investigate next.

5. CATHARSIS

The concept of catharsis, more than that of tragic hero, deserves to be considered the most likely single source—if we wished to so simplify our tracing—for John Jones's remark that "*Poetics* has exerted more influence through the ideas people have read into it than through those which it contains" (11). For, besides the debate about whether what it means is best translated as purification, clarification, or purgation, there is also extensive debate about what it acts on and how Aristotle thought it occurred. We might begin to come to terms with the universe of scholarship on this topic by dividing those who have an emotivist interpretation of catharsis, like Bernays and Janko, from those who consider catharsis to be an intellectual process, like Else and Golden.[64] We may make the division *in tres partes* by adding

64. Golden, *Tragic and Comic*, gives a more developed division than I do here; see 2–39.

that there are even some who consider that catharsis is not important at all.[65] Usually members of this third confess allegiance to one of the other parties before abandoning the question. Among the emotivists there is the further debate about whether catharsis is homeopathically or allopathically engendered. Among emotivists particularly the problem is made more complex since Aristotle recognizes that all the passions vary according to the character of the individual, who may be excessive, deficient, or at the mean. This applies, too, in the audience of the play and so an art dealing with the catharsis of passion will have to consider all those possibilities in the audience and deal appropriately with all members. About these matters there is too much discussion to fairly summarize it in but a piece of a book, so I will simply state my view and refer in the notes to agreeable and disagreeable critics.

I will begin with the view that seems closest to my own. Although she overemphasizes the intellectualist side of both mimesis and catharsis,[66] going so far as to translate *katharsis*, with Golden, as clarification (and *mimesis*, with him, as representation), Martha Nussbaum concludes her discussion of catharsis in a fashion that might come closer to splitting the difference between intellectualist and emotivist versions than to embracing the former.

65. Moles, e.g., considers that catharsis is not something the poet aims, or should aim, to produce ("Notes," 86): The theater is not a hospital. Nehamas maintains that it is "impossible . . . that the catharsis to which the definition [in *Poetics* 6] refers is a process which involves the emotions in any way" ("Pity and Fear in the *Rhetoric* and *Poetics*," in *Essays on Aristotle's "Poetics,"* [Princeton, N.J.: Princeton University Press, 1992], 293). Halliwell wishes we could drop the question, so much has been erected on this single word (*The Aesthetics of Mimesis*, 206 and note). Else, we have noted earlier in the text, considered the katharsis phrase a late addition of Aristotle's, and held catharsis to be the result of an intellectual analysis coupled with moral judgment that the tragic deed is not polluting (*The Argument*, 224–32, 423–47). Golden takes this intellectualist idea of catharsis further, claiming catharsis is an act of intellectual perception, a clarification of the events of the plot through recognition (*Tragic and Comic*, 5–39); see also Paul Schollmeier, "The Purgation of Pitiableness and Fearfulness," *Hermes* 122 (1994): 289–99. On the more emotivist side, there are disagreements about the manner (purification or purgation), the matter (what exactly is purified or purged), the means (homeopathic or allopathic), and a number of other details; e.g., see Belfiore, Heath, and Stanford. The emotivist side has the longer history including such names as Robortello, Milton, Lessing, Nietszche, Bernays, Rostagni, Flashar, and Butcher, and more contemporarily Janko, Halliwell, and Lear. Golden and Lear, as well as Halliwell (*Aristotle's "Poetics,"* 184–201, 350–56) give excellent summaries of the various positions on this too much embattled ground.

66. Cf. the following from *Fragility*: "The value of tragic action is a practical value: it shows us certain things about human life" (380); "through attending to our response of pity we can hope to learn more about our own implicit view of what matters in human life, about the vulnerability of our own deepest commitments" (385); "we might try to summarize our results by saying on Aristotle's behalf that the function of tragedy is to accomplish, through pity and fear, a clarification (or illumination) concerning experiences of the pitiable and fearful kind" (391). It will become clear that I do not doubt that all this can happen, and clearly does with all highly reflective readers, but what may or does happen and what the art does or ought to aim at for all are two different arguments.

> [F]or Aristotle appropriate responses are intrinsically valuable parts of good character and can, *like* good intellectual responses, help to constitute the refined "perception" which is the best sort of human judgment. We could say, then, that the pity and fear are not just tools of a clarification that is in and of the intellect alone; *to respond in these ways is itself valuable, and* a piece of clarification concerning who we are. . . . Pity and fear are themselves elements in an appropriate practical perception of our situation. (*Fragility*, 390f; my emphases)

Let us take it as a matter of course that pity and fear are here being used synecdochically, so it is all of the "suchlike" passions that are elements in "an appropriate practical perception of our situation." There are, then, in Nussbaum's phrasing, two distinguishable effects of reading tragic literature, though I am not quite sure that she would like to distinguish them the way I shall. First of all the (correct) responses of pity and fear *are themselves* valuable and essential elements in a fully human life, and so, to respond in these passional ways to literature is itself a valuable thing. This is, it seems to me, the immediate mimetic effect of a work of art and these passional responses change along with the plot or music changes embodied in the artwork. Such mimetic effects are natural and essential to human beings, and we enjoy them for their own sake. Further, my position, and clearly Plato's too, is that these movements of themselves may be cathartic or polluting. Returning to Nussbaum, these passional responses are also parts of and lead to clarification, "a refined perception which is the best sort of human judgment." They are *like* intellectual responses, but not (I say) themselves intellectual responses. One way they are like intellectual responses is that they can be correct or incorrect. Such responses are the *direct* emotional effect of literature.[67] There is in addition, she says, a second, *reflective*, effect: our responses are a piece of clarification in and of the intellect about who we are.

It is difficult to distinguish these two effects exactly *in vivo*, but let us go a bit further. I would not go so far as to say that this reflective effect is *necessarily* separate in time from the first, for in fact, particularly in an ancient theater,[68] one would very quickly notice that no one else is laughing at what you smile at, or that the people next to you are shuddering with tearful emo-

67. Nussbaum is fond of opposing her Plato and her Aristotle, and so I should point out that even supposed critics of literature—like Plato—agree to this direct emotional effect; the question that should be raised is about the rectitude of the emotional response each work effects. Like Nussbaum (and, I might add, Plato), I think that the difference between great literature and pandering (not to load the dice too much) is an ethical, not merely an aesthetic, distinction.

68. See Stanford, *Emotions*, chapter 2, "The Conditions of Performance," esp. 14 and 15; also see 44f.

tion—the effects are visceral and immediate, and without overtly thinking about it our emotions in such a theater are socially shaped: one can suffer a passion, for example, a desire for a certain pleasure, wrongly—deficiently, excessively, or directed to the wrong object at the wrong time, and so on. But just as such a passion can be aroused mimetically, it can be shaped by mimesis. That is, part of the mimetic effect of drama in such circumstances is also the mimesis of our neighbors—frequently more mechanical or infectious than cognitively based. It may even be that the audience's surrounding reaction will help bring about an emotion in someone though that person does not know exactly what is going on, as happens in some circumstances with children. These examples, however, should probably be construed as part of the direct emotional effect of the art. Tears, like love, violence, and laughter, can be mimetically induced, and this induction is not dependent on reflection; in fact, it may well be that reflection inhibits it (as Euripides *Bacchae* has been considered to exhibit).[69] Of course it may also happen that we do think about the matter overtly, and are made excruciatingly aware of, for example, the singularity of one or another of our responses or how much our own reaction to some event is like that of a person on stage (who is not, perhaps, of the best). This is particularly the case among highly reflective, philosophical audience members. These things can even happen in the anonymous darkness of a modern movie theater. Naturally, the usual audience member is thinking about what goes on in the play throughout the play, for the play is not dumb show and noise but words, so thinking is inextricably interwoven with feeling in drama. But this kind of thinking and judging is necessary for detective stories and romance novels and it may be gone through without much clarification of who we are. How each art or artist makes the reflective effect occur (or at least make it more plausible that it will occur) will differ with the art and artist; some artists may wish to inhibit it from occurring at all—that may in fact be its purpose, as Orwell suggested of popular art in *1984*. While "language is the authentic medium of the idea" and reflection,[70] some arts—like music—may be less capable of moving us to the reflective effect. They are more mimetic than iconic

69. See Rene Girard, *Violence and the Sacred*, 126–44, and *Things Hidden from the Foundation of the World*, 117. Perhaps the reason philosophers want to understand the emotions as cognitive, and so works of art as entirely cognitive, is to escape the possibility that there could be mimetic desire and mimetic violence, a kind of thing cognitive judgment could not affect. Such would be a real terra incognita.

70. *Either/Or*, I, 67.

and referential; they work through *moving us*, not by our *psuchē moving itself* through a series of judgments. Even if the pleasure of learning and the pleasure in mimesis are the two founding pleasures of poetry for Aristotle (*Po.* 1448b4–9), they are, yet, distinguishable. And while both pleasures can be, and generally are, brought together in drama, it does not follow that "the essential goal of both epic and tragedy, then, is an intellectually pleasant learning experience."[71] Aristotle, in fact, says the opposite: skill in construction of plot is shown by the poet "aiming at the kind of effect he desires—a tragic situation that arouses the human feeling in one" (1456a21f). If it is true that the theater is not a hospital, it is equally true that it is not a classroom. Particularly, Plato argues, it is not a philosophical classroom. Poetry's antistrophe in Plato and Aristotle is gymnastic, not rhetoric or dialectic; this argues, again, for its mechanical rather than its cognitive modus operandi.

Let us attempt some further illumination of this distinction by considering music. I do not mean to say that we cannot reflect upon music, just that it is the least likely medium to engender reflection. Not only are certain modes contrary to reasonable and voluntary behavior (*Rep.* 398e–400), we need to adjust music to ordered *logos* most exactly because "rhythm and harmony permeate the innermost part of the soul more than anything" (401d). Music's effects seem to work by osmosis, not reflection. Spariosu makes the Nietzsche-inspired claim that Aristotle would like to subordinate music to logos as indicated by his cursory treatment of it in *Poetics*.[72] Given his use of music as the central and exemplary art in his discussion of catharsis in *Politics*, this view seems highly unlikely. It is more plausible that Aristotle chooses drama as central in *Poetics* not because it is logocentric but because it uses all the means of mimesis the other arts use individually. The *logos/mousikē* subordination relation Spariosu sees here is an accidental reification (on his part) of what is originally a heuristic device (on Aristotle's part). Kierkegaard's analysis of *Don Giovanni* as the most abstract idea expressed in the most abstract medium seems more accurate. Music, like sensuousness, "continually moves within immediacy,"[73] and so is just less likely than the other arts to engender reflection, which is precisely why it is the aesthete's favorite art. It moves one through its mimetic fundamentalism, which we share

71. Golden, "Epic, Tragedy, and Catharsis," 79.

72. Mihai I. Spariosu, *God of Many Names: Play, Poetry and Power in Hellenic Thought from Homer to Aristotle*, 222–23.

73. *Either/Or*, I, 57.

with animals; it acts on us before will and judgment. In the course of his experiences of the opera the aesthete ("A") has to move outside the theater because, unfortunately, the music comes with words—and they may bring one to thought. It seems that the movement to reflection *is dangerous to the enjoyment of the music*—for such a creature as he. He wishes to inhibit that reflective movement. He says that Don Giovanni *is* the music and he clearly wishes to be that himself; that is, he wishes to be the mimetic thing. He wishes *to be taken* by the music, to be one with it, as he was at first. In the wish—more precisely the will act preceding the loss of self to the mimetic fundamentalism of music—is his moral difference from the mimetic, for the wish is an act of a reflective (and so morally responsible) being—which (on his argument) the Don *as music* is not. "A" wishes to return down the birth canal to the prereflective, purely mimetic state: "Don Giovanni is the music"—not a full person.[74] This is the consummation "A" devoutly wishes. Music, because of its immediacy, because we do not need reflection to suffer—osmotically—its effects, is the best choice for an example of how mimeses can purify—or pollute.

Returning again to Nussbaum, while the reflective response—the "clarification concerning who we are"—is not necessarily separate from the direct emotional response, it clearly can be, and in many cases must be. It is, in any case, a different effect. For example, in the case of children, who are clearly not given to, or much capable of, moral reflection on their feelings (though they are eminently shapeable by mimeses), the direct emotional response to a story, as to music, will be the most significant effect; the effect of such motions is not so much clarification for them as education: the music or poem *leads out* a certain emotion. Through mimetic engendering it gives them a kind of practice at feeling the emotions, "for certain rhythms and tones hardly differ at all from the state of character" (*Pol.* 1340a) and feeling the right emotion at the right time and to the right degree is a part of virtue. A good work of art will move us toward the *phronimōteros* in and by engendering and moving us through appropriate feeling, and a bad work leads us the wrong way in feeling. Indeed, for many adults, sympathetic by constitution, and indulgent or sentimental by habit,[75] but unreflective about the

74. See *Either/Or*, vol. 1, "The Stages of the Musical-Erotic."

75. Perhaps this is a more particular problem with adults raised in democracies; in any case, such a character type seems to have been a problem in democratic Athens as well. See Stanford, *Emotions*, 3, 4, 24, 48.

depth or significance of such passions, the direct emotional effect of the play, book, or movie will be the extent of their memory of it: a passional shape, not an intellectual structure is the first, most important, and likely most lasting of the effects of mimeses, from music (using harmony and rhythm) or dance (which uses only the latter means of mimesis) to drama (which uses all). It is because a large segment of the adult population has an (unreflective, as I prefer to think) preference for certain emotional effects that certain kinds of publications and shows consistently sell. It is the motions of certain *pathē* we come back to—whether like men or like dogs. Let us not speak of them, but, as Aristotle, keep in mind the weaknesses of the audience as exhibited in popular choice (cf. *Po.* 1453a33–34).

The idea of catharsis I would like to defend, and which I think is Aristotelian, will agree with Golden that "art is neither psychological therapy for the mentally ill nor a sermon directed at imposing an appropriate ethical and moral discipline on an audience" (*Tragic and Comic*, 106). The famous simplistic criticism of emotivism that he invokes—that a theater is not a hospital—is anachronistic; the Greeks had no hospitals. They did, however, have gymnasia and theaters; and a theater can be as exercising and purifying for the passions as a gymnasium is for the body. More particularly, it seems to me that as in the gymnasium the activity of wrestling works first and directly on the body, so in the theater the art of the muses works first and mainly on the passions. In both cases, as Socrates says (*Rep.* 410–412), the object is the soul, but in the gymnasium it is the wrestler himself who puts his body in motion—so an activity involving spirit and will (*thumos*); in the theater it is what *happens* that moves us—so the passions (*pathē*). In both cases judgment and practical reason may be or come to be involved, but not as directly—and certainly not as purposedly as in a philosophy class, so an increase in practical wisdom per se as a result of either activity is plausible and wonderful, but not the direct aim of the art of wrestling or of theater. The free flowing of the emotions that art both grounds and directs will, as the excercise in the palestra does for the body, *keep* one's emotions supple and balanced *or aid* the emotionally imbalanced in various ways. Art will, by its leading out in a certain order also educate (in the root sense of the Latin) the passions—though not as a sermon teaches; further, by leading them out in a dance that allows feeling's free response art provides a re-creation of feeling for the good person in the audience. If art did not accomplish this latter task, it could not do the others either.

Art does not do its e-ducating work *in the way* a sermon does; art is poetic and in that it is a disinterested speech act; art is not rhetorical and so an interested one. Art is mimetic and builds up a "world" (think of how a piece of music builds up a whole ordered set of feelings) rather than referring to the world (which the piece of music does not do) or even representing a world (which music cannot do).[76] It not only builds that world up, it leads our passions through it in its building; it calls up ethos (as does rhetoric) but in order to work on ethos, not make ethos go out and do some particular work or make some particular judgment in the world (as rhetoric does). A sermon is rhetorical, representative, and referential; so is a scholarly book; art does not need to work in any of these ways; music most clearly does not need to represent or refer, though arts using language are representative without necessarily referring to our usual world. Mimesis aims to make us happier not by educating us *about* passion so much as by *e-ducating passion*: by pathos and through pathos. I do not doubt—nor does Plato (*Rep.* 3, 4, and *Laws* 2) that it can even give shape and nuance to our originally rather thick-fingered attractions and aversions. On the other hand, art cannot and does not impose a moral discipline—it is too brief for that, though it might take our feelings through a set of changes that leaves us with the desire to take one up (for better or worse). Against Golden, however, art does not do its work by leading us "to achieve intellectual insight . . . which represents the essential pleasure and purpose of all artistic mimesis" (ibid.). It may, of course, *also* do this, but that is not its primary or essential final cause. The direct effect of mimetic art is upon the passions, and this is what is essential. It is this emotional effect, more concentrated in tragedy than in epic and therefore more pleasant, which is the poet's most particular aim (1462b1–3, 13–15).

76. Here might be as good a place as any to point out something I would like to read Aristotle as implying. There are three places in *Poetics* where Aristotle mentions that aspect of drama called "the spectacle." In chapter 14 he says the fearful and pitiable can come to be ἐκ τῆς ὄψεως (1453b1), and in chapter 6 he had said that since the actors perform the mimesis, part of tragedy is necessarily ὁ τῆς ὄψεως κόσμος (1449b32), and then later named ὄψις as a distinctive part (1450a9). The middle phrase could probably be translated most literally as the order (or arrangement) of the visible (things); but κόσμος does echo other related meanings, and the idea of the artistic heterocosm, whether visible (in drama) or hearable (in music) is waiting here. It does not seem outrageous to consider that Plato and Aristotle recognize that "in fictional narratives . . . a narrative time, expressed by specific tenses of verbs, is displayed by and within the narrative without any connection to the unique space-time network common to ostensive and nonostensive description" (Ricoeur, 36); this would of course be the verbal order or verbal cosmos. The artist sets up—visibly, verbally, hearably, depending on the media of his art—a space-time network distinct from our ordinary one: we are not seeing Roscius (who shares our space-time situation), we are seeing Bacchus, or his clever servant.

What little Aristotle says more positively about catharsis is in line with these largely negative or very general remarks. His *Politics* concludes with a discussion of musical catharsis (1341b32–1342b33), which takes place in a discussion of education within an outline of an ideal state.[77] In that discussion he considers that there are three benefits of the study of music: education, catharsis, and intellectual enjoyment (1341b36–40).[78] The discussion is elliptical and complex, particularly regarding the second benefit of music, but it allows us to consider how the arts are not only invaluable instruments, but perhaps even ends in themselves. Regarding music's (first) educative function he says that "the ethical modes are to be preferred" (1342a3–4), such as the Dorian mode (1342a29–30), which is of the best and courageous temperament (μάλιστ' ἦθος ἐχούσης ἀνδρεῖον, 1342b13, 14), but he also seems to allow (against *Republic*'s Socrates, but in agreement with the Athenian Stranger of *Laws*) for the relaxed modes, which will be more appropriate for "the period of life which is to follow" (1342b27–29) when the men will not be able to sing such stringent harmonies. The music seems to be a way of developing or strengthening, or, later, saving certain feelings that are requisite for the virtues and have various differing inhibitions at different stages of life. We note that, as in Plato's arguments, this kind of reasoning thins out the available kinds of music. So, too, does reasoning about politics thin out constitutions leading to virtue.

As an aside, let us point out that to consider this thinning out of musics and constitutions a merely ideological quirk of the ancients is a red her-

77. A merely formal reminder: *Republic*'s last book reprises a discussion of the arts, having earlier discussed the matter with regard to education; in that final discussion Socrates invites his interlocutors to change his mind about poetry, with a defense, either in prose or meter, proving that it is worthwhile as well as pleasant (607d–8b). He had concluded the previous book, and—it seemed—the discussion of education and state (for book 10 is a kind of coda), with an argument in favor of a kind of natural slavery (590d–91a)—an argument that Aristotle effectively reiterates at the opening of *Politics* (1252b1–5, 1254a20–a37). One might consider, on these merely formal grounds, that Aristotle is placing his entire discussion of politics, including the conclusion on musical catharsis, between natural slavery and final perfection (the telos of education), and that he is offering a convincing interpretation of *Republic* itself in doing so, for the boys—if they are boys and not the always less than perfectly satisfied passions of Socrates' own soul—the boys Socrates converses with on that holy evening are in exactly that in-between position. Perhaps one of the reasons we need art is because the passions can never be perfectly satisfied; here a Freudian discovers that Socrates preceded him, but Socrates also expects more of human desire—and of art. The enjoyment of art is the *analogia entis* of passional perfection. To call such pleasures "substitutive" is an indication of a poverty-stricken materialist metaphysics.

78. Cf. Janko, "From Catharsis to the Aristotelian Mean," who, rightly, I think, reads Aristotle's discussion of music here as metonymic for poetry and drama as well (343–45).

ring. For if art or politics have *any* purpose, judgments are always required about which of several works or forms achieve them better. Aristotle raises just such a question toward the end of *Poetics* (chapter 26) where he admits it is reasonable to ask "whether tragic or epic mimesis is superior" just as he had asked the same question about kinds of tragic plot in the chapters that provided the problematic clue for this investigation. There he argues that the merely sociopolitical question of what kinds of people prefer it, or who it is said to address among the various classes, does not decide the issue about the art. What does matter is "accomplishing the work" with greater concentration and less dilution. "If, then, tragedy excels in all these respects, as well as in the function of art—for these genres should produce no ordinary pleasure, but the one stated—it will evidently be superior to epic through greater success in achieving its goal" (1462a16–b16). So, the real argument between the ancients and the moderns has to be on the grounds of whether or not there is any natural purpose to art or politics. If both art and politics are entirely artificial (as Hobbes says), then there is no natural purpose to either. Judgment must rest on whatever the invented purpose is. And judgment about which of those purposes is better to achieve is also an invention. So, if there is not a natural purpose, then there can be *no* judgment of better or worse, for one can make one's artifices fit any purpose (or none); there is no shared principle under which they can be compared. (I put to the side for this brief argument a suggestion we might take from Kant, that the beautiful achieves something in every human being because of a *sensus communis* which we share—by nature.) That this is the real issue might be seen by examining the apparent disagreements between the Platonic texts *(Republic* and *Laws)* on this music matter. For the supposed changes in Plato's opinions about the value of certain musics requires absolutely no change or development in Plato's own philosophical position. The differences in the arguments are fully explicable by the audience and interlocutors of the respective lawmaker (Socrates among the fiery young men of *Republic*; the Athenian Stranger among the dry, hard old men of *Laws*). Plato always thinks that music is to re-create and set in motion in us those passions that need the re-creation and educating. To judge we need this is one thing; to mimetically engender the cure is another. For the old, the softer and more plaintive melodies of their forgotten and too much constrained eros—or perhaps even drinking parties—are required for their catharsis. For the erotic young men of *Republic* such music is contraindicated, and a drinking party is a test.

They need a kind of comedy that mocks their eros—one that suggests coed naked wrestling, for example (*Rep*. 452b, 457a).

Regarding the third function Aristotle finds in music—intellectual enjoyment, or διαγωγή—which may also serve to relax our tension and provide rest from exertion (1341b41–42a1), he says even less.[79] It is not suitable to attempt to teach this use of music to the young, for this is an end, and what is incomplete, like youth, cannot attain to or enjoy the perfect (1339a30–32). This end, then, cannot be the main end to be attained by mimesis, which is that through which we first learn, and considering that the end of a natural process is what it accomplishes necessarily and for the most part. The primary natural end of mimesis must be something that works even on children. Perhaps we should use a remark that seems to be about the cathartic effects to enlarge upon this point: "Since the spectators are of two kinds—the one free and educated, and the other vulgar . . . —there ought to be contests and shows for the relaxation of the second class also. And the music will correspond to their soul" (1342a18–23). The children are not yet free and educated, so what will be proper for them later is not yet suitable. They must learn how to make music, however, so that when the intellectual element comes into its own the basic elements of this recreation will be available. Aristotle's discussion of διαγωγή tells us nothing about *how* a particular music will perform the function of providing intellectual enjoyment, except by suggesting that such pleasure differs from that merely common pleasure "which every slave or child, and even some animals" can find in music (1341a15–17). It seems, in fact, that διαγωγή is exactly the kind of recreation that the free soul requires and the natural slave does not, having not that power "which can foresee by the exercise of the mind" which is the definition of the master (1252a32). Though he does not mention the fact, it seems plausible that the end of intellectual enjoyment may include many more modes than the ethical ones used for education. The intellectual aesthete thereby opens the door to the universe of possible musics much wider than the narrow strictures allowed by the ethical educator.

79. Though Aristotle does not say quite as little as the Socrates of *Republic* who asks whether "music, so far as we described it before" might have a power to raise intelligence out of the cave of opinion. Getting the response from Glaucon that it was the antistrophe of gymnastic that educated primarily the spirit (*thumos*) "through habit" and "not knowledge" (522a), he drops the topic. He brings it back, darkly, a bit later (530e–31c), but there he says real music does not have this intellectual power, only unheard ideal music can satisfy. Though Keats might not agree, this seems to me to be equally as serious as jesting.

These two functions and pleasures (moral education, παιδεία, and intellectual enjoyment, διαγωγή) frame the thicket of Aristotle's second-listed and most problematical function: musical catharsis. Before we enter into that we should note that throughout the discussion of the other two purposes of music Aristotle takes note of the various ethical states of soul in order to distinguish the valuable from the less valuable musics. Besides the remarks quoted above, he also claims that some music aims at the improvement of the player (which may involve different things for the young than for the old), and some at the pleasure of a more vulgar audience (1341b13–15), which in turn vulgarizes the performer. These effects are pervasive: "Even in melodies themselves there is a mimesis of character and this is manifest, for those who hear them are differently affected by each kind" (1340a39–43). It is because music reaches to the character and the soul (1340a5–6) that it, like other mimeses, can perform its functions and "moreover, everyone when hearing mimeses, even apart from the rhythms and melodies themselves, is moved to sympathy and pleasure" (1340a13–15). This remark, by the way, seems to give rhythm and melody pride of place as mimetic movers of the passions. Logos is thought's way of moving them. Even apart from the rhythms and melody that directly, and almost mechanically, move the soul in accord with themselves, words also can move to sympathy and pleasure.

Aristotle's discussion of musical catharsis explains that, as the sacred melodies engender enthusiasm and then set it to rest, we can expect various melodies (and even mimeses without melody and rhythms) to do likewise for those natures subject to pity, fear, and other emotions—"which are found to some degree in all." These melodies "provide a harmless pleasure to all" (1342a5–17). This "all" of the audience can be divided along the usual lines of character—that is, virtuous or variously off the mark by excess, deficiency, or drawn to wrong objects, at the wrong time, and the like—as were the various musics and the characters in drama.

All of these various natures, then, are moved by musical mimeses to feel pity, fear, enthusiasm, and so on in accordance with their particular disposition, and to receive pleasure, again according to their disposition, from hearing such mimeses, and "all undergo a kind of pleasing catharsis" (*Pol.* 1342a14–16).[80] The question then arises as to how such a catharsis works for

80. I am assuming in all this that the artist's work is a fine one. Aristotle's work, being both descriptive and normative, invites mathematical difficulties with every sentence. There are, at least, nine possible responses to a work of mimesis, for the response depends on whether the work

all kinds of character. While that question will be our main point in the next section, resolving it might also help us gain further insight into the educative and intellectually recreative effects Aristotle also claims for music, and, by synecdoche, all the mimetic arts. Our question now is about thaumaturgy, what drama effects in the various characters of the audience.

6. THAUMATURGY: *HECUBA*

In this section I will show how the tragic catharsis works on the three types of audience member in the case of *Hecuba*, exhibiting thereby that an emotivist view of catharsis works for every category of audience member.

6.1. The Problem and the Play

The two major criticisms of the idea I wish to defend—that catharsis is an emotional thaumaturgy—are, first, that the morally good man should not need a purification or purgation,[81] and second, that no one who heretofore has defended the theory has been able to show how catharsis can cure *deficiency* of emotion, though many have made "use of the process of purgation to explain the act of removal of excess emotion so we attain the proper mean."[82] Moreover, as Malcolm Heath has recently reiterated, the first criticism is sufficient argument to eliminate catharsis as the particular pleasure at

---

is a mimesis of the good, the middling, or the bad and whether the audience member is virtuous, excessive, or deficient; further divisions within the good and bad, such as Aristotle himself makes in *NE* 7, enlarge the matrix. In order to please all in some way the mimesis must be the kind made by the better sort of artist. Even this may not appeal to the bestial, or to the gods, or those incurably vicious, like Claudius in *Hamlet*. If such a king likes not the play—that only means he likes it not.

81. This problem is one of the major criticisms of Bernays; cf. Janko, "From Catharsis," 346. Janko himself holds that "we are all imperfect" (349) and "'by a conflict of opposites [catharsis] leads to due proportion'" of the emotions (348, quoting Olympiodorus's *Commentary on Plato's "First Alcibiades"*). It is not clear whether Janko hereby reduces the kinds of character to two classes (the imperfect and the bad) or leaves three—though what the imperfectly virtuous would be if not morally weak or incontinent and so excessive or deficient in some way at some time is not clear from *NE* 7, or Janko's remark. Perhaps thinking that we are all only slightly imperfect leads Gould to his conclusion that "the benefit to be expected by the pleasurable 'cleansing' of tragedy is really quite minor, according to Aristotle: potentially troublesome emotions are flushed out" (*The Ancient Quarrel*, xxiii).

82. See Golden, *Tragic and Comic*, 16 (also 101), who considers incapacity of raising deficiency of emotion "a fatal flaw in any purification theory based on a purgation model" (16). F. L. Lucas (for example) thought tragedy could only reduce excess; cf. *Tragedy*, 50.

which tragedy aims. Heath admits that there is a "*prima facie* case in favor of identifying the pleasure of *katharsis* with the characteristic pleasure of tragedy: clearly, the pleasure of a *katharsis* of pity and fear satisfies the condition of coming 'from pity and fear,' and it could be argued that it is (unlike the cognitive pleasure) distinctive to tragedy."[83]

His argument against this "*prima facie* case," which I think is Aristotle's case, is that

> the characteristic pleasure of tragedy must be available to all . . . , and especially to the better members. . . . If *katharsis* is in any sense therapeutic, it will not apply to all members of an audience. For the best members of the audience will (by definition) be least in need of therapy. . . . *Katharsis* must be therapeutic in some sense, so *katharsis* puts right something that is wrong with us; . . . but the characteristic pleasure . . . must be available to the best, [who need no such therapy]. . . . So, the pleasure of katharsis is not tragedy's characteristic pleasure, even though it is a pleasure of tragedy. (ibid.)

The real issue here is whether the virtuous need any kind of catharsis. If we read catharsis as purgation, the answer, as he says, must be no; Heath's conception of it as therapeutic moves in this orbit, coming from its medical use. But if we understand catharsis more along the line of purification, a sense which it has from Greek religion and is used, for example, by Socrates in *Phaedrus* before he gives his story about the chariot of the soul, the answer is not so certainly negative. Even the virtuous must wash their hands in order to stay healthy, or might participate in the religious rituals as a part of virtuous living. In order to exhibit a detailed solution to these problems without begging the question of the *Iphigenia*, let us consider another Euripidean tragedy—a more clearly tragic one than *Iphigenia*, according to most critics—*Hecuba.*[84]

Before the play begins a dead child rises up as Prologue—Hecuba's last son, Polydorus, sent years earlier to Priam's friend, Polymestor, king of Thrace. He is already dead, but Hecuba and the chorus of Trojan women are unaware of it, though they lie with the Greek ships on Polymestor's beaches waiting for wind. Hecuba then speaks of a disastrous dream; the chorus enters with news of the demand for her daughter, Polyxena's, life; Polyxena

83. Malcolm Heath, "Aristotle and the Pleasures of Tragedy," in *Making Sense of Aristotle*, 12.

84. Nussbaum deals with this play in detail to close *Fragility*'s discussion and exemplification of the purposes of tragedy (397–421). It has been badly reviewed by Kitto (216–23), Matthaei (118–57), and others; all begin with a complaint about its lack of unity. Nussbaum moves the discussion in the right direction, for it is a great play. Reckford's article and introduction to the new Oxford translation make points similar to Nussbaum's. The most complete contemporary discussion of the play (though I do not agree with her view entirely) is now Judith Mossman's *Wild Justice*.

is called to hear the news and responds with pity for her mother, and then we see Odysseus gerrymander his way out of a promise made when Hecuba saved his life. Polyxena stands up to Odysseus, who also refuses to allow that Hecuba die with her daughter. After a despairing valedictory by her mother and a choral ode compounded of regret, delusion, and sorrow,[85] the messenger returns and we hear the report of Polyxena's gloriously courageous death. When the serving woman goes down to the sea for water with which Hecuba hopes to wash her daughter's corpse, she finds the body of Polydorus. Hecuba turns from sorrow to vengeance.[86] With the promise of noninterference from Agamemnon, she tempts Polymestor to come to her with his two sons. She and the women kill the sons and blind Polymestor, who returns to the stage like an animal, howling for revenge himself. Agamemnon professes to be "shocked" at what has happened, restrains Polymestor, and judges that he is justly served. Polymestor prophesies Hecuba's fall as well as Agamemnon's. He is gagged and the stage is cleared save for the bodies of his two dead sons.

6.2. Catharsis and the Movement of Emotion

Before deciding whether the chief use of tragedy is to satisfy some habit of the reader—as an idea of art as a consumer-oriented enterprise might hold, or to break down strong habitual barriers—as a theory of the avant-garde might demand, let us consider a way under which all might agree. I suppose that this least common denominator, put in the Aristotelian terms we have been employing, would read thus: poetry engages the imagination, thereby the feelings and mind of the reader without needing to engage his more particular judgment (as rhetoric must). Poetry's work on us allows a fullness of feeling without engaging the hearer *in action* (as rhetoric does—at least the action of judging which speech best praises), and it does so in such a way that through our imagination our mind and feeling come to a satisfaction appropriate to the ethos of . . . the virtuous. (Or, the avant-garde, the consumer, the awakened proleteriat: here is where the division among audience types occurs in modern aesthetics.) According to Aristotle's consideration, while tragedy can provide the pleasures of learning and

85. For a very sensitive discussion of the ode's structure and function, see Mossman, 77–83.

86. At present I wish this statement merely to be taken as a statement about Hecuba's actions, not as a *petitio principii* about the vexed question of the consistency of her character.

catharsis, catharsis of the fearful and painful passions are not only what his definition presents as the telos (1449b27), but is also supported by further comments about the "kind of effect" at which the skilled poet aims, namely, one that "arouses human feeling" (not cognition). Catharsis as telos is supported further in the argument for tragedy's superiority to epic by virtue of providing in a more concentrated manner "that very special kind [of pleasure] we have mentioned" (1462b14). These are just some of the texts in support of the prima facie case, but as Heath notes, in order to please everyone (*Pol.* 1342a14–16), the cathartic pleasure *must* be appropriate to the ethos of the virtuous; for what is not fine would not please the virtuous, and what would not please the good member of the audience could not offer a fine pleasure to any other type of audience member either—though it might satisfy a particular passion. We might be tempted to say that the play must offer the "pure pleasures" of perception, reasoning, and the healthy exercise of emotion in order to accomplish the "incidental" pleasure of catharsis. Just this distinction led Humphrey House to the conclusion that the good man suffers no catharsis.[87] But Aristotle clearly says that some kind of pleasant catharsis is felt by all and cathartic melodies give an innocent joy; if House's *division* of pleasures is correct, the story I am telling must be the truth about their *connection*. I do not, however, think that catharsis is incidental, except in the sense that the "pure pleasures" of exercising seeing, hearing, imagining, feeling, and understanding are the efficient causes that bring it about: thus we are drawn through pleasure to pleasure. The pleasures are distinguishable, but I am not convinced that "pure" and "incidental" quite gets it. The "pure pleasure" or innocent joy such as a child has in mimesis leads in to the pleasure of catharsis, which is a pleasure of ethos. And only the ethos of the virtuous is naturally pleasant. So, in fact, by drawing us—emotionally and intellectually (and perhaps physically)—into this pleasant mimetic exercise, the play (or the music) accomplishes its cathartic task. That task is, however, far from incidental.

a) Catharsis of the Excessive and the Deficient

For the ordinary person the opening scenes of *Hecuba* (through the carrying away of Polyxena) arouse pity for both the ghostly Polydorus and his mother, fear for Hecuba and Polyxena, and indignation regarding both

87. Humphrey House, *Aristotle's "Poetics"* (Westport, Conn.: Greenwood Press, 1978), 114.

Hecuba and her daughter.[88] When we hear Talthybius's report of Polyxena's death, however, our indignation (having been particularly aroused by and against Odysseus) is set to rest—*not* by an act of retributive justice, but by the sheer courage of Polyxena's words and deed. Such excellence redeems the world. This is a thaumaturgic shift in the passions: we are moved out of fear, pity, and indignation to courage, and then from courage to homage. Notice the pattern of this passional shift: it is exactly that which the virtuous undergo in situations inspiring fear, pity, or indignation. For the courageous do suffer fear, but they suffer it properly: this movement is what proper fear and its resolution feel like.

Anyone excessively fearful must feel some shame at report of her, for her (while impending) fear-inspiring and pitiable death is revealed as the kind of suffering on which the gods themselves throw incense. For even the enemies of Troy, even those who cried out for her death, reproach any of their number in the strongest terms (ὦ κάκιστε; *Hec.* 577) who fail to bring tribute to her great-hearted excellence. Over the grave of Achilles they proclaim Polyxena to be of surpassing courage. What was to honor their greatest warrior is become the pyre of an even more glorious girl. Along with our indignation, so effectively built up by the request for human sacrifice followed by Odysseus's legalistic obfuscation, our fear for Hecuba finds some release, for we have seen the highest prize attainable by man attained by a girl not yet eighteen, in circumstances most unlikely and inauspicious. Such an audience member's fear, and perhaps until that point unbounded pity for Hecuba and the Trojan women (especially if given to excess of those passions—the likely extreme in our day), finds a more proper measure, too. For what, then, is there to fear except that we might not be able to light a candle even among friends, where this girl ignited a signal fire in the midst of her enemies? Hav-

88. A rhetorical purist (cf. *Rh.* 1386b9) might wish to hold that indignation drives out pity and fear, or detracts from it, but this is not necessarily so in a poetic situation, whereas it probably is so in a rhetorical one. We have already discussed the problem regarding pity and fear in poetic versus rhetorical situations above (45–46, 54–55). In a *rhetorical* situation like this case, faced with the unjust power of others directed against us, it seems we would react *either* with indignation *or* with fear (depending on the power against us and our character), but the two passions seem antipathic to each other: the more the one increases, the more the other decreases. However, the unjust power of people in a play can never be directed against us actually, it cannot call up the crisis of decisive judgment or action, or threaten our own well-being, which rhetorical situations demand; however, when we see it, it will rouse the painful passion of indignation (which we might also feel on our own account). But in the *poetic* situation that passion can be aroused *at the same time* that we realize such things could happen to us—a thought inspiring fear—and the two can increase together.

ing been brought to the point of homage to the girl, the complaints of the women and the queen no longer strike one as quite on target, their passions no longer feel like they have the proper tone; they exceed in pity, particularly in self-pity; they seem to have missed the point so gloriously made by Polyxena, and when the women plot together to work vengeance on Polymestor the formerly excessive audience member may begin to fear that the women may act excessively also.

Though justice is the desire of the virtuous, and injustice usually the claim but always the effect of the act of the one given to excess, the pity, fear, and moral outrage given voice by Hecuba now seems somewhat off-key. Having just heard one daughter resolve to die as princess of Troy, the queen stoops to pandering her remaining living daughter, agreeing ex post facto to that daughter's slavery so long as she be paid in opportunity for vengeance. Justina Gregory insists that there is no fall from nobility or royalty in Hecuba's suggestion that the nightly embraces of her daughter, Cassandra, ought to be worth some consideration (i.e., she is not really pandering)—after all, she says, Creon talks of the other fields available for his son's plowing (in *Antigone*), and Creon is an honorable man.[89] But until this point Hecuba's arguments have always had reason and public acknowledgment on her side. As she claimed, her speech was grounded in justice (*Hec.* 271): return of a debt of mercy, religious limitations on human sacrifice or killing of those who have won sanctuary at the altars of the gods, the illegality of murder—even of slaves, and the like principles are what she used in the appeal to Odysseus. Now, however, her point turns on the purely private satisfactions of sex and vengeance, granting permission to her daughter's concubinage for their sake.

Reckford comes somewhat closer to the point:

> Hecuba is pursuing her private and primative vengeance not just because she has suffered so much and lost so much, but because she is now living in a demoralized world: a world without justice, without grace, without pity, even without meaning.[90]

In such a world Hecuba feels everything is mere means to private desire—so she appeals to Agamemnon's most private desire in order to open the door to her own. If the premise about the world were true, the conclusion might

89. *Euripides and the Instruction of the Athenians* (Ann Arbor: University of Michigan Press, 1991), 106, 118n.49.

90. "Concepts of Demoralization in the *Hecuba*," in *Directions in Euripidean Criticism*, ed. Peter Burian (Durham, N.C.: Duke University Press, 1985), 114.

follow. But this is not the full story either. On my reading, the mistake (of Reckford's reading and of Hecuba) is that the world is *not* really without meaning; the *universal recognition* and acclamation of Polyxena's courage has just proven it.[91] The meaninglessness of the world and the vacancy of value is the first lie Persuasion tells: chaos follows. Though Hecuba affirms that Persuasion rules the world, the claim is false. In other words, I do not agree with Reckford's claim that "the discovery of Polydorus's mutilated little body *simply annihilates* [the golden values of nobility] for both Hecuba and the world."[92] Hecuba *says* she *believes* it does, but I am not convinced that Euripides believes Hecuba; I certainly do not. The world is not made senseless by Auschwitz; Auschwitz is senseless.[93] Even battle-hardened veterans can see it. It is possible to avoid the mark of slavery even there in Auschwitz or among the Trojan women, and the proof is, it has been done. This proof is given in the play. We hear of it being done in the story Talthybius tells. Polyxena is as a statue of a goddess, which even in a fallen world arouses the desire to do homage. And homage is done by all. She proves Aristotle right:[94]

> No function of the human being possesses as much stability as do activities in accord with virtue. . . . For she will always or to the highest degree both do and contemplate what is in conformity with virtue; she will bear the vicissitudes of fortune most nobly (κάλλιστα) and with perfect decorum under all circumstances. (*NE* 1100b13–21)

Then Hecuba is seen to sell the family so recently redeemed from slavery back into it and miss the mark that we have but recently seen achieved. The deed she plans proves to be so; even the excessively pitying member of the audience will be disgusted and horrified by it, and Polymestor's reduction to howling animality helps bring this emotional change off most effectively. His prophecy, linked to another known to be true, that Hecuba will be transformed into a permanent mark of danger to sailors—the Bitch's Grave—certifies for reflection the point made upon sensation by the howling and beating on the tent. The less-than-virtuous have seen and been tak-

91. In "The Construction of *Nomoi*" I showed how Plato uses a cross-cultural recognition of the necessity of courage as a springboard for a universalizable hierarchy of order among the virtues in *Laws*. Perhaps he first saw that argument under the dress of Polyxena. See the last chapter of *Platonic Errors*.

92. See Reckford's "Introduction" to his translation of *Hecuba*, 16; my emphasis.

93. Contrast Reckford's opposed remark in his "Introduction," 17; this is an example of being carried too far into pity. The weaknesses of our character are revealed in our reactions.

94. Contrast Nussbaum (*Fragility*, "Epilogue") who claims that Aristotle thinks virtue and its happiness is destructible, contra Plato, and that Euripides' *Hecuba* proves the point. No to the interpretation of Aristotle; no to the disagreement with Plato; no to the significance of the *Hecuba*.

en along on the enacting of excessive self-pity and indignation and those less-than-virtuous passions are already steering clear of these. Their excessive fear and pity are being purified by fear of what they led into and pity for the result; they have followed their own excess into horror and are horrified. Not so Hecuba. Hecuba is already an animal; it was not a fall, but a leap; all that remains is to mark the grave of her body, the grave of her soul is marked by the space between the bodies of the two children.

An audience member who is among those with tendencies to be excessive in pity or indignation will have both felt and seen that excess satisfied and become disgusted by it.[95] Such emotions have been purified, and we are less likely to be drawn to act on such excesses ourselves because we have *felt* and been *drawn through* the necessary or probable connection between our excess and our disgust; we have experienced how the one leads into the other; we have been bound and carried through the necessary connections of the passions—whether we reflect further on the play or not. Musical compositions seem to carry us through similar passional permutations. This is the process that is catharsizing, and the better plot (or musical composition) more skillfully arouses and purifies our feeling (cf. *Po.* 1456a18–20). In the play we have also seen and felt the impress of something far superior to and more attractive than the satisfaction of indignation or the excess of pity and have been drawn toward it. The strong moral contrast between the actions of Hecuba and those of her daughter has helped make our desire for the mean and our disgust at the extreme satisfaction of indignation both quantitatively stronger, and qualitatively better directed. Our fear and pity (and, for the excessive, perhaps self-pity), drawn in by the opening of the play and allowed to feed freely, are played out through necessary and probable events into the horrible, and so we have been led by these same feelings into disgust at their excess. That is to say, we have *felt* what the speaker *says* in his lines "Th' expense of spirit in a waste of shame / Is lust in action." The mind learns by going through the speech (logos); the irrational part by *going through the passions*; the body by going through the movements: philosophy,

95. Compare this to a famous scene in *Republic* (439e–440c), where Leontius, wanting to see the corpses, but knowing he should not, goes to look at them and forces his appetite to take its excess in order to disgust it and turn it away. Shakespeare's "Sonnet 129" gives voice to the same transformation of excess desire into disgust. It should be clear from my examples that the catharsis of the passions Aristotle is concerned with could not be replaced by a dietary supplement of rhubarb, or prozac, as Bernays or Lucas might allow. Drugs do not allow for the proper association of action and feeling or feeling with feeling (much less any connection with thought or judgment), which is what is at stake in the mimetic arts, and what is at stake in virtue.

art, gymnastic. In a lyric poem we take on the voice of the speaker and so his feelings. The image of Odysseus being bound, ears open to the Sirens' song, is an image of the work of art: we suffer the natural movement of the passions in a situation where we are not allowed to move. Passion thereby purifies and trains passion. And the music works even if the singing is in no language whatsoever.

We should note here that while Aristotle does say certain plots—a bad man rising to happiness—or situations—like Haemon's attempted killing of his father—are disgusting and therefore worse, he does not imply that being led to disgust at excess or deficiency of certain passions may not be part of how our passions are purified. What seems to be the problem with a plot that moves a bad man from misery to happiness is that the movement of the whole play would leave us in a state with our disgust aroused. This is unequivocally to be avoided (1452b33–38). Certainly, the incident in *Antigone* evokes disgust, but we are not left in that state by the play, for other passions are quickly aroused, including yet more pity and fear. Clearly if the poem is "through arousing pity and fear to accomplish a catharsis of suchlike passions," the play that leaves us in the pitying, fearful, disgusted, or other suchlike state it arouses by its incidents has not accomplished its end. Such works of art leave us in a way polluted, less capable of the emotional responses that are appropriate. That certain musics leave us this way is much clearer—and not only to Plato and Aristotle.

On the other hand, if an audience member were deficient in pity and indignation, Talthybius's story, centered between Odysseus's fudging and Agamemnon's politic effeminacy, is made to raise even such apathetic viewers into more appropriate and stronger feelings. Such disgust in this case is likely also to raise the apathetic person to a more appropriate pity for the Trojans. Odysseus's claim to be giving friendly advice (*Hec.* 299–302), by its disingenuous understatement in response to Hecuba's powerfully principled claims, is only the first shock in a series of utterly empty words. Again, both the object and the strength of the feeling of moral outrage is magnified by the contrasting scenes placed one after the other. The swift changes might lead to an ekplektic inrushing of passion like that suffered by the Greek soldiers who witnessed Polyxena's death. Indeed, it is because it provides such *passional* opportunities (not for mere intellectual interest) that Aristotle values the complex plot over the simple one (1456a20–23). It is the concentration of these changes of emotion even in simple plots that leads him to place tragedy above epic (1426b1–3, 13–15). We should note as well that as pity is raised for the Trojan women, the outrage that is raised is against fellow Greeks, and so the audience's feelings are freed from being merely the passions of self-interest or the extended self-interest of love for one's own. Pity and indignation are thereby given the wider bounds virtue requires: not just for or about our own, but even for the enemy who suffers unjustly. Fear, pity, and indignation are thereby being brought into line with justice rather than the natural animal's self-interest or the supposed necessities of our uncommunal passions. This is no small thing, for there is a natural pleasure in the free run of the proper passions, a run unencumbered by politic concerns (exhibited by Odysseus) or self-protection (which real fearful situations and their rhetoric engender), a run of the passions that is fully human and that by evoking outrage and disgust or fear and pity on either side of homage for an an enemy's courage practices the enlargement of our feelings to include the entire community of man, with whom our nature as passional, rational, and mimetic beings is shared.

The natural pleasure of such right-running passions is both purifying and almost kinesthetically educative. It is the kind of right running Nathan allows David's passions before informing him that he is the man (2 Samuel 12); and that right running is what allows David to *feel* the evil of his waywardness. He feels the evil and is roused (from his clearly unvirtuous ordinary state) by the extremity of the story: even he can see and desire justice and experience outrage under that condition. True judgment of his own case in life is now easier, for his passions have already run through to their proper conclusion in hearing Nathan's story. He is already more human because his passions have run freely to the truth. Just so, the play takes the deficient out of their gray and perhaps self-centered world into one of stark contrasts—a world in which the generals are absolutely craven characters, while the youngest girl exhibits an unequivocal heroism that shakes even feeling-hardened veterans and the bloodthirsty son of Achilles into pity and wonder (*Hec.* 545–580). Further, it makes sense to consider that someone deficient in regard to pity and indignation might also be deficient in the passion Aristotle calls emulation, in which case, as for the excessively fearful, Polyxena's words and acts raise him up: A girl did it. In such a way the pity, fear, indignation, and emulation of the deficient audience member are raised to a more proper level, for such an act as Polyxena's requires tears and emulation, and such respect is a tribute we cannot refuse to pay to merit, whether we will or no.[96] Even a child could be roused mimetically by such a story to fear and pity as Polyxena does, and be driven away from her mother's manner.

We can, of course, analyze the play—is it a tragedy of suffering or of character, is its plot simple or complex, is its main character unified or not?—or use it as a model to show excess and deficiency of certain passions, or present its characters and acts as appropriate objects upon which to practice our moral judgment or through which to elicit the likely moral or political beliefs of the poet or the age—and it may sound as if I have been doing something like that—but none of that is the purpose of the poet, or the primary effect of seeing or reading the poem. The point is that in the playing our own passions are brought into play; as Aristotle says, by the synthesis of the actions, by the way things happen one after another the tragedy achieves its *ergon* (1450a30–32)—and if the passions do not play correctly of their own accord—because of excess or deficiency on the part of the audience member—they are corrected *in the playing*, through the way the poet connects the actions to raise opposing or enhancing passions. The great poet is like the most excellent of coaches, who must correct the athlete's motion in its very practice, and the poet's coaching is both more important and more difficult, for he is shaping the movement of the passions, flexing them in, or into, health. As a coach or physical therapist might have to hold one muscle group firmly while making another move, so, too, the poet, the passions. Various combinations of rhythms and tones are able to do this by themselves, "hardly differing from states of character" (*Pol.* 1340a); the addition of language and plot undoubtedly make these effects—this coaching, as it were—more exacting. Sudden changes in the emotional tenor of the events make the passions of the reader take terrific turns, even without a peripety

96. This view of catharsis as a purifying of the passions—purgation approaching adequacy as a translation only for the excessive—is in line with that of Humphrey House, who says "tragedy rouses the emotions from potentiality to activity by worthy and adequate stimuli; it controls them by directing them to the right objects in the right way; and exercises them, within the limits of the play, as emotions of the good man would be exercised. When they subside to potentiality again after the play is over, it is a more 'trained' potentiality than before" (109). See also Fossheim, "Mimesis and *Nicomachean Ethics*," in *Making Sense of Aristotle: Essays in Poetics*. We can see here that Golden's suggestion that the training of the emotions joins learning to catharsis is true, but the further suggestion that such a learning process "can form a bridge to the view that considers katharsis to be 'intellectual clarification'" (*Tragic and Comic*, 16) turns the process out of its appropriate field: the emotions and emotional habituation. *Even if* such a bridge is formed, the first effect—emotional catharsis—is universal and required and first in time as well; the bridge to intellectual catharsis is secondary in all those ways. Cf. House's remarks on mimeses leading out of the soul (ψυχαγωγία), 118–20. The soul is led out mimetically, not by cognition, which is, if anything, its own work rather than something it suffers to have done to it.

or recognition changing the direction of the action. Placing the glorious yet pitiful report of Talthybius between the scene with the disgusting Odysseus and the scene of discovery of the body of Polydorus—a terrible thing whose horror has been held impending from the opening lines—is a masterful synthesis of probable events. It is masterful because of the way it turns our painful passions. Ἔκπληξις and complexity of plot are important elements of this cathartic process, for sudden events and reversals that cause great emotion are necessary to bring the passions out of their sometimes inadequate, sometimes displaced, sometimes externally hindered ebb and flow.[97]

Showing how a play achieves its aim of catharsis will, of course, have implications for the more intellectual analyses of literary criticism—as Aristotle, I think, is implying throughout *Poetics*. For example, the reading I have given so far implies that it is reasonable to consider *Hecuba* a play with a complex plot. For though the death of the daughter might be thought to be merely one step on a straight downward slope in a tragedy of suffering, but one in the series of Fortune's pummelings that come upon Hecuba from above and both entrances, Talthybius makes us question that simplicity. He concludes his recitation of Polyxena's courageous death by saying, "For my part, / having seen your daughter die, I count you / of all women the one most blessed in her children / and also the unhappiest" (580–83). Polyxena's death has shown her name—"many gestures of hospitality," perhaps even "many blessings"—was the truth; it is because of her most noble action that her mother has the right to title of unhappiest: she has lost the best. But even as in the dark eclipse of the sun there is a nimbus of glory, so we feel at the story of Polyxena's death released from our pity and fear. We know there is no such thing as slavery for the brave; Polyxena has said so (*Hec.* 367–69) and she has done so (547–52). Even her enemies affirm it. She is not on the way down, but is the way up. It is the East, and Polyxena is the sun. Polyxena has won through from cultural slavery to the freedom of virtue. Even Hecuba seems to see her own daughter's heroism in the face of the inevitable when she says

> And yet a kind of comfort comes
> in knowing how well you died. How strange it seems
> . . .
> But human nature never seems to change;
> evil stays itself, evil to the end,

97. Cf. Plato's *Laws* 700c–701b; perhaps then breaking down strong habitual barriers will be what a poem does—for the audience member whose habits are less than virtuous.

and goodness good, its nature uncorrupted
by any shock or blow, always the same,
enduring excellence.

(591–99)

The supreme courage of Polyxena is the high point of the defeated women of Troy. It leads to a recognition of their worth and nobility by the whole host of their bloodthirsty enemy. To speak more formally: at their first entrance the choral community of Trojan women entered in shattered singles and small groups—a stunning and brilliant theatrical turn, probably invented here by Euripides, where the stage tradition is for them to enter dancing as a group. They are first united in voice and dance as a chorus *over Polyxena's removal*; they will be shattered again. Thus the poet lets us see and thereby experience that such human excellence as Polyxena's in the face of being sacrificed like a beast could be contagious among them; it unites the community around it (as Frye said comedy would); it could be imitated even by those who are still slaves, for their one moment of unity is around this light. It is possible to rise above the purposes of slavery even in slavery. Then comes the discovery of Polydorus and recognition of Polymestor's betrayal of philia and the fall to animality and reshattering of the chorus. There will, no doubt, be demurrers among the formalists for labeling the play complex, but the complex way in which it works on the passions of the audience should be clear: it takes us to the mountain with Polyxena, then it falls below sea level, and foretells the drowning of Hecuba as a dog. And having filled our lungs with the pure air of Polyxena's beautiful courage our very bodies are unwilling not to rise from the waters that engulf her mother. And that is a sign of the purification of our passions, which has been brought about in and through the working of the play.

b) Catharsis and the Virtuous

Since both the excessive and the deficient have now been dealt with, there now remains, as a criticism both of the view that catharsis is the particular pleasure at which tragedy aims, as well as of the emotivist view of catharsis, the problem of the virtuous audience member. This more difficult argument against the explication of catharsis I wish to defend is that since the virtuous are (by definition) already at the mean with regard to their passions—neither excessive nor deficient, nor wrongly aimed, nor untimely brought to suffer them—they will have no need for catharsis of the passions, and catharsis is in fact impossible for them.

Then is doomsday near. But this news is not true, for the world has not grown honest. It is true that the habitual feelings of the good man, whose ordinary ebb and flow of passion is the mark at which the poet must aim the whole theater, are not rearranged by the play. However, the good are given a satisfaction such as they probably have not received in the last several wintry months of life—a kind of substitutive satisfaction, though not for the id. For there are many external hindrances to virtue in the world; one may lack the wherewithal for generosity, the opportunity for courage, friends, objects of appropriate honor or reverence, to name but a few. But as a purpose of gymnastic is to keep the healthy flexible, strong, and sufficiently spirited for whatever may occur, so the purpose of poetry is to exercise the passions appropriately for the same reason: to keep them flexible and strong. In children such exercise builds up an ethos; in adults it allows for the free running of a series of strong emotions, one in which all may participate to the fullest emotional extent of virtuousity, despite what may be their own all too real external limitations to those practices. Those limitations must be felt as such in the life of the virtuous, but in the experience of the mimetic art the feelings engendered, not any action to be taken, is precisely the point. The external impediments that all but the most blessed (*makarios*; *NE* 1101a8, 21) human beings suffer are not suffered in the world of the theater. Such unimpeded movement of the virtuous person's emotions must be counted a great pleasure (cf. *NE* 1153a), a recreation with the gods.

The movement of the play, then, purges or purifies the virtuous person's feelings, too, of those irritating, small discontents life requires him to bear, for he has seen—and rightly felt—that Polyxena has borne more than the minor external (and ever-present) impediments to excellent functioning that effect him, and has borne them with a grace and freedom that sets our smaller and more private shocks to rest. The ordinary world does not offer much opportunity for the high degrees of courage and emulation this play evokes, but the good must have these—they must have them to an extreme degree, for excellence is, in this way, an extreme. The play allows this unimpeded activity of their natural state (*NE* 1153a15) its exercise. External impediments are the only kind of impediments the virtuous man may have (and until the world grows honest he will have them); internal impediments are signs of moral strength, moral weakness, or worse. External impediments do, however, have their emotional effects: first among them is the limitation of the passions to the quotidian smallness of life; the play releases us from this for it provides a cosmos in which the only limit to virtue is virtue's own limit of appropriate emotion. We need not all be imperfect, as Janko holds, for the world is, and virtue requires that we overcome it. Tragedy is an aid to happiness because it helps us bear those ills, for in the experience of tragedy we first of all are removed to a world where there are no external hindrances, and then we are moved passionally to overcome far greater ills in feeling than those we are ever likely to have to bear. And thus the virtuous are allowed an exercise of their virtue that ordinarily is neither allowed nor called for. The situation of the good man does not change, nor are his emotions arranged more properly—they are already so; rather, his well-ordered emotions are given a free and unimpeded run such as the world does not much offer as it is. And this is his pleasant catharsis. It is a recreation devoutly to be wished. It is this good that the community established between artist and audience aims to achieve universally.[98]

Mise en abyme: The Hecuba of *Hamlet*—We can see this cathartic effect of playing in *Hamlet.* Immediately after the performance of the first player's Hecuba speech, which he requests upon their arrival (2.2.455–506), the prince is entirely himself and even his huge all-encompassing problem seems to be more lightly borne. He exhibits an almost superhuman excellence, requiring mercy over justice for the players—"God's bodkin, man, much better! Use every man after his desert, and who shall scape whipping?"—and begging the players not to mock the man he himself most mocks (2.2.507–30). He is himself again. How else could Shakespeare have exhibited the effect of artistic catharsis upon the good except by making them superhuman thereafter?[99] It is

98. The incipit of *Politics* (1252a) is that "every community is established with a view to some good." In what immediately follows Aristotle considers the state, the family, the master-slave relationship, and the paternal relationships; he considers the goods achieved by the arts of the muses at the end of the book. Surely there is some kind of community between artist and audience as well—perhaps one kind for slaves, another for the free (1342a13–25). It seems that this relationship between the artist and his audience is more than mere goodwill, for the artist does (or should be) "giving them active assistance in attaining the good and letting himself be troubled in their behalf" (*NE* 1167a9–11). (Aristotle's descriptions—particularly of the human—are tied up with prescriptions because the nature of a thing is defined by its final cause.)

99. It will be recognized that I do not share the famous (German) romantic caricature of Hamlet's character. In Aristotelian terms he is at least virtuous, more plausibly god-like (cf. *NE* 7). Cf. my *Is Hamlet a Religious Drama? An Essay on a Question in Kierkegaard.*

after this that Hamlet becomes reflective, and comes to a piece of clarification about who he is, and what he ought to do. But first we see the sheer joy of upright and freely flowing feeling. Such freedom of passional movement has been denied him for weeks. Having achieved a happy, if momentary, release from the emotional repression the matrimonial court enforces upon his just mourning, and momentarily removed from the world of villainy netting him round and thereby requiring (against *NE* 1124b27–29) hiddenness and deception as to his true feelings and thoughts, he sees the solution to his problem. It is because he is now freer and more adequate, passionally, to the requirements of virtue, that his thinking *is able* to be so suddenly clear and clarifying, and his suggestion to himself about what he ought to do is a true one, and in fact the suggestion of genius: the play's the thing. *It is not the case* that Hamlet cognitively works through what has just happened to his own emotions reflectively, and then sees that it is the play that made this possible, and thereafter concludes that perhaps a good play could even bring a bad king to his knees—and reflection. It is the dramatic speech itself, whose words call up a wholly different world in his imagination, which frees his passions from the thousand and deep shocks over which he rightly sorrows as well as from the angles and poisons set about his real-world situation, and lets his mind and more perfectly exercised passions return to see all the way through the impossible problem of finding evidence for a perfect crime. He comes to a solution. That is the power of catharsis upon the good; and indicates its hoped-for power upon the bad. Mimesis, which calls us out of ourselves and takes us through a passional dance not bound to our real limitations, keeps us capable, passionally, through its cathartic action, of that extremity of passion known as virtue to which the world frequently disbars our feelings and limits our action by its circumstancing and our wherewithal.

6.3. Catharsis and Intellectual Clarification

The case of Hamlet shows as well as anything can that tragedy does not work first so much as a "clarification concerning who we are" and as a felt recognition of "the sometimes enabling and sometimes impeding forces of luck and natural happening" (*Fragility*, 391) as it works as a purifying and purging ritual in which we *feelingly overcome* those impeding forces (when we are good) or are roused or dampened in our imperfect emotions (if we are less than that)—and this emotional perfecting, this truing and freeing of emotional response, allows us to clarify and to recognize. Like water from a rock suddenly struck in the right place, Hamlet's virtuous passions are given a free run, his emotional freedom is given voice, and *then* his idea comes; the other way around would not be believable because it is not true.[100] At times, the world, like a rhetorician (Odysseus) or an unjust man with power (Polymestor, Claudius), raises our irascible and painful passions in ways with which even the best—perhaps especially the best, as Hamlet—can do nothing, and these passions, the inflictions of unfreedom from the world, still affect our judgments, and they certainly limit, if they do not infect, our joy. Catharsis is the process of bringing our character into the mean, or if we are there, of freeing us from the incidental pain of great and lesser ills—at least for as long as the play is on. This freedom may allow us to see what we had not seen beset—at least it is so for Hamlet.[101] But whether it allows such an intellectual recognition into our world and situation or not, the work of tragedy is already purifying, and we have been returned to an unhindered upright posture, and accomplish through mimesis a more full and perfect moving.

Nussbaum's emphasis still falls a bit too much on the intellect, perhaps because she takes the intellectualist criticisms of mimesis made by a certain Platonic character too seriously, and, like that *eirōn*, considers our interest in mimesis to be primarily cognitive.[102] For example, she says that "through attending to our responses of pity, we can hope to learn more about our own implicit view of what matters, . . . about the vulnerability of our own deepest commitments" (385). Bringing an unclear idea into clarity is not what happens to Hamlet in hearing the Hecuba speech. Rather, his passions are purged and *then* and *thereby* he is enabled to think and invent with his na-

100. That other way around—clarification of idea leading to emotional freedom that allows virtuous passion its free running—may well be the way philosophy seeks to work on us; poetry and philosophy are, then, not opposed, but antistrophic, the dances that together make the choral play of being human, dances that keep the golden cord of the gods the one that moves the puppet by keeping the other cords supple (*Laws* 645a).

101. Reckford (*Aristophanes*) gives a similar description of the work comedy accomplishes, which he outlines as relaxation, recovery, then recognition. "Right action depends on right intuition, which springs in turn from the recovery of good feeling and good will. And it is just this recovery which must not be postponed [and which comedy preemptively] manages to accomplish" (4; cf. 19, 57). Festive comedy supplies a "'clarification through release,' akin to the lucidity born of relaxation" (24, quoting Barber, *Shakespeare's Festive Comedy*). I read Reckford's word "preemptive" as an echo of the infectious or mechanical sense of mimesis I have been arguing for, a noncognitive happening that frees us *into* recognition.

102. *Fragility of Goodness*, 388.

tive genius. According to Nussbaum, our "emotional responses are themselves pieces of recognition or acknowledgment of the worldly conditions upon our aspirations to goodness" (390). This, I think, is true; and it is because the most important of our aspirations are those natural to the entelchy of our being and these aspirations are social and rational and only superficially relative to time and place that tragedy can remind us of such things—but we do already know them (the virtuous especially do), and the virtuous certainly feel them (and feel them more finely than those rather overfull of pity or inadequately outraged). But there is something more important than this "reminding," tragedy *frees us in feeling from what binds our feeling*. It is not so much an intellectual recognition (though that too can occur) as it is an *emotional achievement*, a rousing and a letting go. It is this feeling of liberation that allowed drama a place in religious ritual, and makes presenting it a *leitourgia*—a high service to one's fellow citizens. This same process of catharsis through mimesis is at work in music as well: catharsis is the particular pleasure at which mimetic art aims, tragedy using all of the means of mimesis in a very concentrated way to achieve its end. If this be magic, let it be an art lawful as eating.

This ritual, clearly, is not to be understood as getting rid of emotion, nor should we consider it tragedy's purpose "to clean out our emotional lives periodically so that we can get on with more important things" (Gould, 266), for the emotions are important things, they are essential parts of our human lives, and the happy life includes those states and runs of feeling that are proper to humanity. Hamlet's grief, for example, is proper. It is also inhibiting—particularly as its free run has been long inhibited by the jolly marital court. Freed of this and other (unutterably worse) emotional upsets for a moment by and during the Hecuba speech, he sees clearly and plans the solution of his problem. Is he still in mourning for his father? Yes. Is he still shocked at Gertrude's easy neglect? Yes. Does he still grieve over his mother's lust? Yes. Does he still desire justice regarding Claudius? Yes. Does the act that he considers suddenly unite all these passions, binding up the impossibly self-contradictory orders of his father's ghost?

In one sense there is nothing more important for us than our passions, since in our kind of being *pathos* is tied into everything, for pleasure and pain are with us everywhere. Gould goes so far as to say that "what is being flushed out is an admirable emotion experienced by good people, yet a painful emotion nonetheless, one any good person would prefer to avoid if he could" (285). Something about this is false. It is, in fact, a prayer to escape the human condition. Pleasure and pain are indexes to our character (*NE* 2.3), and the man who uses or endures the painful well will be good. He will neither seek to flush out what is admirable nor retain or embrace unnecessary pain. Of course we might hope not to have pain as we hope that there will be no cause in our neighbor's life for our pity—but to hope there shall be no pain nor need for our pity and to desire to escape from feeling pain or pity when they are appropriate are distinct; the hope is unlikely to be fulfilled in our present state, and the desire to escape is softness (*NE* 7.7)—or worse—so long as we are still in this state. External impediment, too, is likely to remain in our lives.

Through the sudden excesses of pity, fear, and horror, every kind of person at the play—except the one who does not allow his imagination to be moved at all (and such a one could hardly be human not being mimetically moved)—can experience some catharsis, some purifying or purgation or clear run of his passions. As these translations of catharsis (and my parenthetical expression) imply, there is a state of health and well-being natural to the passions of the human soul, as there is for the form and moving of the body; similarly one does not have to be sick in order to benefit from a regular regimen of exercise or diet, though one must be healthy in order to judge rightly (cf. *Pol.* 1341a35–41).[103] Indeed, good tragedy is healthful food for the soul, a requirement of the human spiritual diet—so long as man has passions, so long (that is) as man is man, not God. Such works allow us not only to move passionally much better than we deserve (if we are excessive or deficient), but they also allow us to move more fully than we are able (even if we are virtuous), given the real limitations that keep even the virtuous from being fully blessed. It is in and to this state of healthy functioning that tragedy aims to move our painful passions, and the poet who does not achieve this is a failure.

6.4. Other Concomitants of Catharsis

We have now answered all the criticisms that stand in the way of the most clear and obvious interpretation of Aristotle. That catharsis as emo-

103. Aristotle does not succumb to the affective fallacy, for not everyone's affective response or considered judgment weighs equally. Again, consider *Hamlet*: "Now this overdone, or come tardy off, though it make the unskillful laugh, cannot but make the judicious grieve, the censure of the which one must in your allowance o'erweigh a whole theatre of others" (3.2.23–26).

tional purification is, on the face of things, the central pleasure of tragedy is not only the prima facie look of things, but in fact Aristotle's real face. Catharsis of the painful emotions is the central effect of tragedy, and brings along the other effects in its train. The same play that can provide a catharsis for every type of soul at the play is at the same time educative for those not yet among the virtuous. It leads the soul out (is psychagogic)[104] not mainly by discussing moral problems (as Plato pretends to take it), nor so much by revealing the ignorance and trouble-shrouded island our moral choice acts upon,[105] but rather *through* exhibiting action and moral choice about serious and important matters, *it rouses* and catharsizes our passions, *bringing them into line* with those that are good, redrawing their boundaries more strongly against the excesses and deficiencies of pity, fear, indignation, and other such pains our state is heir to. It does so by pulling our feelings mimetically through the actions of the play, making us practice (by suffering) the right feelings as the laws make us practice the right acts. According to *Republic*'s Socrates, musical education was for the spirited and emotional part of the soul, as was gymnastic (410c), and that such exercise is necessary for the continued health of spirit and desire Aristotle agrees: indeed, it is an expression of that health (*Pol.* 1337b27–33, 1338a22–29, 1339b20–30, 1339b41–40a6).

That the spectacle and performance will, as well, be a relaxing entertainment to the multitude (*Pol.* 1339b15–17, 26–40) the popular history of drama and the movies can attest; that the play can also be an intellectual recreation for those who apply their reflection to it no one who is reading this book will deny. Golden's point, that διαγωγή (intellectual enjoyment) is "the highest goal, the end in itself of music, and of art in general"[106] is partly true—it is the highest aim; but it is not the only aim, it is not the *main* aim, and it is not (it seems) an aim that art may achieve with the common run of people; a theory of catharsis that takes it as this kind of intellectual pleasure would be true only for philosophers—for the rest of the world art will be powerless or a confused and confusing shadow-play, as Socrates pretends it is in *Republic* 10.

104. Cf. 1450a33, literally psychoactive; curiously, (pseudo) Plato's *Minos* 321a claims tragedy is the most psychagogic part of poetry after recalling that Minos is called back from the dead with Zeus's sceptre by Odysseus. "Psychagogia" originally refers literally to conjuring souls up from Hades (e.g., in Homer), but is this not the artist's own picture of what his art does—conjuring forth the souls of his listeners? Certainly teachers have to do it, as Plato shows. Cf. House's remarks on ψυχαγωγία, 118–20.

105. Cf. Nussbaum, *Fragility*, 383–91.

106. *Aristotle on Tragic and Comic Mimesis*, 37.

Returning to the emotivist tradition of catharsis need not take away any intellectual beauties or uses our more recent critics have defended in art. As their position insists, it is simply true that a play has the advantage, unlike our more usual intellectual objects—God, the universe, society—of being a completed whole that we can grasp both in its completeness and with particular detail (cf. *Po.* 1450b30–51a6). It offers a highly defined, complex, and completed spectacle, an arrangement not only of the visible, but of the verbal and the hearable. And even here art's emotional catharsis shows itself, for such a world as the work of art creates allows that desire and task that is by nature infinite and human—the desire to know—a finite and completable place to play: a home of its own making. As Aristotle says, "[L]earning something is the greatest of pleasures not only to the philosopher, but also to the rest of mankind, however small their capacity for it" (*Po.* 1448b13–15; cf. *Meta.* 1.1, *NE* 10.7). For this joy we cannot give too much thanks. But this joy too is *through* mimesis, and *of* a passion never fully satisfied in our lives and world: "for men but seldom attain the end" (*Pol.* 1339b27). With regard to this most particularly human natural end we are all constrained by the world and limited by our time and circumstance. Intellectual enjoyment of the arts is the playful enjoyment of what Aristotle considers our highest and most divine part; it allows our love for this activity an uninhibited run, for the length and breadth of this whole world can be covered in but two hours traffic. If our mind can reach so far as Aristotle says, so too must our passions. Even tragedy, then, so far as it provokes διαγωγή, will provide a purification of our eros, a sign perhaps that comedy is the higher art, since, as I shall argue, it aims directly at the catharsis of our desires. As the play offers such a complex of perfecting moral, intellectual, emotional, and imaginative satisfactions, it is not at all surprising that a man might consider some mimetic thing, some poem or song, the best thing he made in his life, a suitable memorial and everlasting gift to his city (cf. *Rep.* 599a–600e)—which is also ours. We might do well to consider him right about that.

It will be noted, then, that though I think the intellectualist view of catharsis is incorrect, there is an obvious intellectual pleasure and clarification that is bound up with the hearing and viewing of tragedy. My disagreement with Nussbaum (in, e.g., *Fragility*) about catharsis strikes me as mainly one of emphasis, for in that book she does agree that the effects on the passions are important. The source of my dissatisfaction is, undoubtedly, her idea that the particular pleasure of mimesis is "cognitive" (388), a view she shares with, among others, Golden and Hardison. The scholarly debate about that particular line of Aristotle's (1448b13) is not as conclusive as she presumes.[107] Nussbaum's reflective emphasis may be a product of her most favored examples: novels, which have a mode of mimesis that seems essentially more ruminative than drama, especially drama with music. For music, as a voice in Kierkegaard says, "always expresses the immediate in its immediacy," and the immediate is that which language cannot grasp for "reflection is implicit in language."[108] Though not his language, it seems something like this is true for Aristotle, too, whose only extant discussion of catharsis of the emotions takes place in the musical discussion of *Politics*, who commends tragedy over epic precisely for having "a substantial role for music and spectacle, which engender the most palpable (ἐναργέστατα) pleasures" (*Po.*1462a15–16), and who gives the palm to drama over epic because its brevity increases the art's emotional power (*Po.* 1462a15–b2, b13–15). While he says tragedy can also work just by reading, it seems the immediacy of music and spectacle are of considerable emotional and cathartic effect (1450b15–16), and perhaps the less reflective audience is more enthralled by such things than the critic (even more reflective than the poet) wishes they were. By contrast, Nussbaum's recent work on the emotions makes clear that her cognitive interpretation of mimesis is of a piece with a cognitivist view of emotions. About that our disagreement is not merely a matter of emphasis.

Let us recall, in closing on this matter, a brief summary of our argument against it. Mimesis is natural to us; and we naturally delight in mimeses. As art, mimeses are directed to increase and more exactly orient the pleasure they by nature produce, which pleasure I take to supervene upon the unhindered or unencumbered run of the passions in accord with virtue. In arts using language such passional mimetism and the cathartic process it moves us through is clearly linked to intellectual enjoyments. Music (used by Aristotle as the example around which his extant story about catharsis turns) and dance clearly have a cathartic effect however, even though in at least one regard Aristotle considers music to be contrary to or at least to lessen the opportunity for intellectual activity, for playing the aulos prevents logos (*Pol.* 1341a); he also considers the impact of such music to be catharsis rather more than *mathēsis*. A like lack is praised in the poet, who may actually be ecstatic (*Po.* 1455a30–35). The naturalness of mimesis and its "firstness" in

107. For more argument on this point, see my "Others," 251–52.
108. *Either/Or*, I, 70.

terms of learning seems to indicate that it is, if cognitive, of a most simple cognitive order, one shared with animals, and so embodying universals that are not only "much less overt, and less susceptible to propositional formulation"[109] than our usual judgments, but about which, in describing their work as "sub-textual, virtual" (102) or "metaphorical" (101), we join an ancient (e.g., *Bacchae*) and contemporary Girardian understanding of mimesis as infectious or mechanical. Such an interpretation of mimesis removes it from an activity of cognition and creative or active imagination and places mimesis in the camp of things imagination suffers, at first not *knowing*. The world (or our neighbor, or the work of art) affects our senses and imagination, shaping us into what already is, but is not ourself. If we live among human beings we are shaped, and begin to be, human; if among wolves, wolf. Perhaps tragedy hangs out with tyrants (*Rep.* 568a, b)—and comedy is the first casualty of war—because the former is the only human thing that can come close to him (comedy's outright mockery gets the death sentence), and perhaps through imitation and overtopping of his *thumos* tragedy can lead him into disgust for the excess itself.

6.5. Conclusions on Some Recent Criticism of *Hecuba*

The contemporary inflection of the mimetic as a highly cognitive, if not intellectual, endeavor, and the deflection of the understanding of catharsis from an emotivist one to intellectualist versions, is concomitant with an equally modern deflection to both the formalist and the thematic, historicist, and political or cultural criticism of art that has won a deep popularity in contemporary aesthetics. But enlightening as such elucidations may at times be—even *about* the emotions—such criticism looks at the work the play accomplishes through the wrong end of the telescope: it keeps at the distance of the intellect what the artist wants to charm forth and shape in its own nature. An emotivist explication of catharsis will allow us to distinguish among the literary critics those that are more and less adequate. For if catharsis of the passions is the purpose of the play, then the best thematic, historicist, and cultural interpretations are the ones that fit in best with the catharsis of the passions of the types of character present in the audience. Such a prin-

109. Stephen Halliwell, "Aristotelian Mimesis and Human Understanding," 101; further notes in this paragraph are to the same essay.

ciple of judgment, at any rate, would seem to be Aristotle's version of the rule of charity in the realm of criticism. Indeed, his *Poetics* offers no hints on criticism of theme or political or cultural construction within the poem, but concentrates on plot, character, and language as the means through which the poet moves the passions. As plot, character, and language are subservient to the final cause of catharsis, I suppose that the other, presently valorized, elements must be similarly oriented and judged useful (or not).

Given this rule, it seems to me that *Hecuba* lines up with what I would consider the Aristotelian ethical theme that fortune is only an accessory to happiness, and is not capable of destroying it entirely.[110] This is not presently a popular view of the play. Reckford, for instance, says

> "Is it not strange" that human nobility can thrive independently of outside factors? Yes, it *is* strange. In fact, it is quite impossible; and that is the lesson (if you can call it a lesson) that the *Hecuba* teaches. Put simply, as Euripides never would: the soul, like the body, is corruptible. ("Concepts," 117).

> Virtue can be un-taught, good character corrupted, nobility destroyed. So Euripides's play demonstrates. (Ibid., 118; cf. also 124)

I demur; this is a counsel of despair. Euripides' play "demonstrates," through the passions the play rouses and strengthens, the precise opposite of what Reckford has said. Nussbaum seconds Reckford, and while she pays some attention to the feelings aroused in the play, her view—that the tragedians would not accept what she calls the Platonic thesis that the virtuous man cannot be harmed, and that *Hecuba* is itself the proof that the destruction of *nomos* and community is the absolute destruction of the good and all possibility to conserve it—would not allow the emotional purification of pity, fear, emulation, and indignation we have traced above. Therefore this view cannot be Aristotle's. In fact, the cathartic experience of attending to *Hecuba* outlined here exhibits precisely that *nomos* and communal recognition of the good *cannot* be utterly destroyed, and that is one reason why the happiness of the good cannot be entirely destroyed either; there is something yet worth loving even in the world Euripides has set before our eyes—and *every soul* that is not destroyed for virtue has recognized that jewel and

110. Nussbaum insists, in *Love's Knowledge* and *Fragility of Goodness*, that this is not Aristotle's view, despite his definition of happiness as activity in accord with virtue and the remark that "no function of man has so much permanence as virtuous activity" (*NE* 1100b11), so much so that even in great misfortune nobility can still shine through (1100b30). She calls the view that the happiness of the good is indestructible Platonic.

found itself desiring her.[111] All this in something Euripides does not set before our eyes: the story is told by Talthybius. Even *within* Euripides' brutal, broken, and unstable Thrace the world takes note of both Polyxena's divine response—she is like the statue of a goddess (l.560)—and Hecuba's more animal transformation. But perhaps the tears of Talthybius are not to move us? nor the barking of Polymestor? nor Hecuba's baiting of the dog? For Aristotle, virtue, like constitutions and mimeses, are not merely cultural or personal constructions; they are all tied into nature, therefore some arrangements are better than others, and we can tell, if we have not been destroyed for virtue. "The starting point is the fact of what is, and . . . one with [the proper upbringing] can easily acquire the foundation" (*NE* 1095b5–8).

And so Aristotle would expect that we, like the Greek soldiers, would be moved by Polyxena's courage, and this is an indication that *nomos* and the communally recognized good are *not* entirely destroyed, though even the king (Agamemnon) and one-time queen (Hecuba) do not follow them, but in fact voluntarily participate in their destruction, and the attempted reduction of *nomos* to mere persuasion. Hecuba's *nomos*-denying excessiveness becomes a landmark from which we should (and are, by the play) steer(ed) clear. More mimetically, the play moves us away from the scene of revenge by the barking of Polymestor, as we may be led to weep by Talthybius's weeping. Our feelings rejoice in the courage of Polyxena, and are repulsed by Hecuba's child killing—if we recognize within ourselves the *nomos*, the rule of human virtue—which also, according to Plato and Aristotle, is natural. Perhaps, these days, some do not recognize such a *nomos*. We might call that a confession, but we need not call it truth. At the end of the play we may not pity Hecuba so much as sorrow that she went so far; but *the process of feeling* an excess of pity and indignation end in such sorrow and unnerving barking is a run of passion that is educative and purifying. Those who have followed so are sickened, and so in a way, perhaps, inoculated. We shall not go there. Our passions will more easily recognize the place when we begin to sail that

111. There is a vociferous debate in the literature (Mossman gives a sensible discussion of the issue; see 142–63) about the eroticisation of Polyxena's sacrifice. Let us admit that eros can be for something besides bodies and then there is no reason for the debate. Polyxena is unquestionably the most erotic figure in the play, but to limit that eros to necrophilia or even the lowest rung of Diotima's ladder is a peculiarly modern perversion. One cannot expect such creatures to give the right explication of the play, though even they may be attracted to the right through the play. Beauty is the one spiritual thing we love by instinct; it affects us mimetically, before reason becomes active. And our love for beauty includes elements a body can only dream of.

sea ourselves. We may even recognize it without reflection, through feeling, the pulling tide of which we have felt in this theater.

If Nussbaum is, unfortunately, not sufficiently attentive to the movement of our feelings because of her philosophically oriented error about tragedy's aim, other intellectualist critics run roughshod over them. For example, in *Anxiety Veiled*, Nancy Sorkin Rabinowitz analyzes *Hecuba* as "the imitation not of one action but of two, a sacrifice and a revenge."[112] In the sacrifice, the virgin is represented "as adopting the masculine value system and willingly subjecting [herself] to the male gaze" (103), while in the revenge the crone who knows "she has no value in a system where women get what value they have either through marrying and reproducing . . . or by being objects of desire, . . . tries to intervene in the masculine order" (114), and by doing so exceeds the bounds, making herself "uncanny" (116) and the source of male anxiety. Thus Polyxena affirms the system that silences her, while Hecuba, attempting to subvert it, is rendered terrible; and so the play as a whole works to strengthen the system of male hegemony and social interchange in which women are objects.

It follows that the way of experiencing the play that is required if we are to resist this patriarchal ideology and its concomitant ethos is to resist the effects of its representations. So we must feel Polyxena is piteously misled into buying the male-approved representation of courage and we must "refuse to accept the definition of [Hecuba's] revenge as double and instead revel in her success" (124). In other words, such a reading requires that we must cease to feel that Polyxena is courageous and cease to feel that Hecuba's indignation is taken too far or acted out upon an improper object (or two). All the language—Polyxena's speech, Talthybius's report, Polymestor's prophecy—and symbolism (from the statue of the goddess to the marker of the Bitch's Grave), and mimetic action of the play speak on the opposite side of such requirements. The play leads the passions otherwise than this. Were this explication of the play accurate, there seems to be no reason to consider Polymestor's killing of Polydorus a particularly heinous crime; if we are going to revel in the killing of two we should at least suffer a modicum of enjoyment at the murder of the first, who was, after all, the last male child.

To respond that all these requirements are unnatural would probably be

112. Nancy Sorkin Rabinowitz, *Anxiety Veiled: Euripides and the Traffic in Women* (Ithaca, N.Y.: Cornell University Press, 1993), 106.

put down to the heavy impress of masculine hegemony upon my feelings, or the weight between my legs, or both. Nonetheless, I would like to suggest that a play that ends with two bloody children left dead on the stage, while their father howls blindly and is bundled off, is meant to raise our indignation toward, and our terror at—not our pity for—the instigator. The effect we are led to from the excessive pity in which Hecuba begins (both for Odysseus—a captured spy in time of war, and for herself thereafter) is horror. Still less is such an ending supposed to lead us to her affirmation and approval. It is only at the end of a very bloody century that someone could get away with suggesting that such deaths should not repulse us, or that perhaps, in fact, the death of the innocent is a kind of justice and we should revel in it. But, in fact, it is unnatural to think and feel so, and so it is bad reading too. Rabinowitz suggests that the whole ship of ordinary readers who consider Polyxena courageous are like the Greek army: "she has given herself up in honor of Achilles, and they in turn bring gifts to honor her. But their praise is itself a form of lust" (59). As if Polyxena is giving herself up in honor of Achilles; as if, after death, she would really be the slave she scorned to be in life. Even if it is universally true of the Greek army that their praise is a form of lust, which I doubt, for Talthybius is a member of that army and he *weeps* again to tell the story—it is obviously false that Polyxena gives herself up in honor of Achilles. As clear as any day can be she says she goes to death in honor of fallen Troy, for she will go to the underworld a princess and never as a slave (*Hec.* 549–52). She does not go to be wived to Achilles, but "with eyes still free" (*Hec.* 367). She says so, and transforms the honor of Achilles into a funeral pyre in homage to her. Achilles' shade will not approach this light except upon his knees. To think that by suffering under the Greek ritual she has become subject to the cultic desire is to give to local and perverted practice the universal significance it pretends to have. This is precisely the deep philosophical error of such feminism; it presumes that cult and culture completely erase nature, that subjectivity is entirely a construct of culture and in accord with culture and that the *nomos* of cult and culture is fully definitive of human *phusis*. Hecuba will make the same error. Mark her. Euripides does.

Even if historical criticism could prove that the purposeful cold-blooded killing of children may not have been considered essentially evil in Greece at this time, may it not be possible for a poet (and a noted critic of his society) to feel differently and aim his audience differently than the usual corruptions of the day portend? Certainly Aristotle does not allow that just because a certain culture allows the eating of children it may be something other than barbaric. Historical criticism cannot decide this issue because it cannot touch it. In fact, to be a strict historicist is to make the work of art into a hothouse flower incapable of life in any real weather; art becomes powerless and the artist, successfully or not, is but the sycophant of his age.

But *Hecuba* is more honest; the queen herself draws the true conclusion of such premises:

> Then no man on earth is truly free. All are slaves of money or necessity. Public opinion or fear of prosecution forces each one, against his conscience, to conform. (864–68)

Hecuba sees that if subjectivity is a completely cultural construct, then there is no such thing as subjectivity—the *nomoi* of money, public opinion, and other necessities explain the animal completely. She outlines the postmodern thesis of the death of the subject in three lines.[113] There is mere convention and there is the harsh necessity of animal nature, and that is all. But neither do we construct the world nor ourselves; language reveals the world, and Hecuba's language reveals something about the world too. Hecuba is honest even in her error, for she confesses that such cultured animal slavishness is *against conscience*. What can conscience be if it is not the *nomos* of the cult and culture, if it is not the coin of the realm?

Hecuba reveals even in her despair that what we might be tempted to call subjectivity is the symptom of a deeper fact, the fact of freedom. Upon this fact morality builds her kingdom and no cult or culture, no ritual or power, not even death can remove a princess from this tower. She must surrender in order to lose, and Polyxena does not surrender. Talthybius recognizes this and weeps, for he has participated in the destruction of the good even by watching it. There is a word for Polyxena's action in every human culture and that word is both a recognition and a confession, a praise and an ecstasy. There is, therefore, a natural emotional response called forth by Polyxena's actions in this play from every soul that is not utterly ruined for virtue; that emotional reaction is not defined by the cult, culture, or economy of the audience, but by freedom's feeling recognition of its own. Any oth-

113. Hecuba's sophistry is exceedingly popular in present-day moral and literary theory: each individual is merely a preference algorithm of heteronomous feelings. For examples, see Barbara Herrnstein Smith, *Contingencies of Value*, and Gilbert Harmon, *Moral Relativism and Moral Objectivity*.

er reaction is slavery.[114] Rabinowitz would teach stars how not to sing. She commits the murder of the muses.

What happens in the play—how events turn out in response to the actions of the characters—does not directly teach us the playwright's morals (only a consequentialist could think that), nor do the results in the play necessarily point to the kind of moral judgment the poet means to criticize or embrace. It is the result in the theater that matters. So, for example, we do not need to await the judgment of Agamemnon, nor do our passions do so, when Polymestor comes out with the bodies of his children.[115] Nor does "the ultimate inefficacy of [Polyxena's] sacrifice [the winds do not change immediately after]"[116] prove that Polyxena erred, that she "play[ed] into the hands of her enemies . . . by her willing participation."[117] In fact, such a concatenation of events might just as well point out that the request for her sacrifice was not a pious religious ritual, but a demonic one, and her courage in the face of such lawlessness and sacriligious action is recognized even by the demons, who fail their worshippers in powerless homage to the good.

Nor is the unity of the play to be found in the ideology of the society in which it was produced, but in the effect of the whole upon the feelings—its catharsis. Were *Hecuba* a newly discovered play from that area around the Black Sea supposedly once ruled by Amazons would we still have to consider Polyxena mistaken? Because a nearby barbarian culture allowed not only the killing, but the eating of children (*NE* 7.5) should we feel that Hecuba—in only killing them—hits the mean in action and emotion? She is thereby teaching her culture moderation? Do we not know how to respond to human suffering, to courage in the face of death, to injustice or the murder of children—do we not even know what they are—until a sexual politics or a "properly historicized" ethic is explained to us?[118] Even without meaning, does not a human *barking* have an immediate effect: is it to draw near? Then let

114. A remark of Mossman's about the chorus, one she means literally, is morally true of everyone: "so long as Polyxena lives they cannot be carried into slavery" (79). Polyxena lives.

115. Mossman seems to think we must agree with a judge (Agamemnon) whose very reappearance should engender disgust; cf. 134–38, 190–203, 239. He has proven himself to not even be much of a man compared to Polyxena, much less a king: he is ruled, not ruler.

116. Gregory, *Euripides and the Instruction of the Athenians*, 96, cf. 98.

117. Ibid., 97.

118. Mossman suggests that the killing of children in such circumstances *might not* have been particularly problematic for historical reasons (esp. 169–77, 188–90); Rabinowitz says it *should not* be problematic for reasons of sexual politics.

> Blood and destruction be in such use
> And dreadful objects so familiar
> That mothers shall but smile when they behold
> Their infants quartered with the hands of war,
> All pity choked with custom of fell deeds. (*Julius Caesar* 3.1.265–69)

On the contrary, because virtue has a basis in human nature but is not completed by nature, it is possible, Aristotle thinks, that a culture—a system of *nomos*—that does not bring its children up rightly ruins them for the natural good of virtue, and thereby ruins any chance they might have for human happiness. No doubt such a culture would never be able to recognize itself and would crucify anyone who dared to tell it it was mistaken. But perhaps a great work of art could begin to make them *feel* differently about it. Perhaps in a properly arranged series of events they could begin to feel that the murder of children is too high a price to pay for their glorious revolution.

7. THE CASE OF THE *IPHIGENIA*

The thaumaturgic concerns laid out in the preceding sections will be exploited in this section to show that Aristotle was correct to consider the *Iphigenia in Tauris* an exemplum of the best form of tragedy.

It is the usual opinion that "the more uncompromisingly tragic effect"[119] is accomplished by the play in which the deed of suffering is accomplished rather than avoided. So, for instance, John Moles has said,

> of course it is true that the fear and pity evoked by a "tragic" tragedy are of a more profound and lasting kind, that the scheme of realization [of the error] before an action necessarily puts greater emphasis upon a single climactic scene . . . and that such a formula can hardly produce *great* tragedy.[120]

Gould, similarly, thinks the nontragic conclusion makes a play have "a weaker pathos and less pity."[121] But if the purpose of tragedy is what defines the genre, and the purpose is catharsis through pity and fear of suchlike passions—which catharsis is linked, as we have seen, with education and intel-

119. Heath, *The Poetics of Greek Tragedy*, 56.
120. "Notes," 92; Moles's emphasis.
121. *The Ancient Quarrel*, 54.

lectual recreation—then there is no need to hold to this opinion. There is also, therefore, no reason to conclude that Aristotle erred or was suffering from a jaded palate when he awarded the palm to Iphigenia.[122]

Thus Moles's double complaint that "the fear and pity evoked by a 'tragic' tragedy are of a *more profound* and *lasting* kind" (my italics), seems to be false, on the one hand, and morbid, on the other. Moles himself allowed that

> the scheme of realization before action would obviously be a highly efficient mechanism (arguably a more efficient mechanism than realization after the action) for securing tragic catharsis. In a "tragic" tragedy the emotions of pity and fear are purged away by their own excess, but in a "happy ending" tragedy the dramatist himself brings about their purgation by working them up to an almost intolerable pitch, and then relieving them by averting catastrophe at the last possible moment. (85f)

Unfortunately, Moles was convinced by Else to think such an emotional catharsis a "moot point" and not the proper aim of the poet (86). If emotional catharsis is rightly seen as the end, however, Moles's argument falls exactly into place.[123] *Iphigenia*, according to Moles' own reasoning, will be both more effective at raising the painful emotions than a tragedy like *Oedipus* and more effective at leaving the audience in an emotionally satisfying state, for there will be no hint of the disgusting since the act is not accomplished.

Despite himself, Moles provides several good reasons to consider the *Iphigenia*'s plot more effective at providing catharsis than any other kind of plot. First, more emotion is generated by a prospective act—something we see about to be done—than is generated by uncovering evidence leading to a recognition about a past act (84) as *Oedipus* does. Further, since the arousal of pity depends on undeserved misfortune, in general, danger to the more decent (ἐπιεκεῖς; 1452b34) should arouse the greater sympathy, but Aristotle calls the *fall* of such a one repugnant (μίαρον; 1452b35). As T. C. W. Stin-

122. Else considered Aristotle's choices damaging to his reputation as a critic, and held that the *Iphigenia* "cannot honestly be called much more than a good melodrama" (446). Kitto also calls it "melodrama" (218), adding the further insult "romantic" (311) later, though unlike others of that ilk he calls the plot construction "deft and elegant to a remarkable degree" (311).

123. I am not sure what he means by the passions being "purged away by their own excess"; the purging or purification must take place by the intense building up of painful passions followed by the recognition and sudden reversal that releases the pity and fear. Building passions like pity or fear up to an excessive level does not lead to release from them of their own accord, as rhetoricians like Mark Antony know. See *Julius Caesar* 3.2 and the following scene's result on poetry, figured by Cinna, the poet; I propose that Shakespeare is critiquing a certain view of catharsis here. Antony's speech does not seek its catharsis in the theater; his work is left poetically incomplete in order to accomplish its catharsis in the body politic.

ton argued, the μίαρον is avoided if there is no downfall; "before the actual disaster we shall pity [her] more than we should pity the actual downfall of a less good (and less sympathetic) character."[124] Against this Moles had contended that such an excellent character would not be enough "like us" to arouse fear (1453a6) or pity (*Rh.* 1385b13, 1386a24). This seems false, however; apparently even the suffering of the bad man can move us to philanthropy, if not to pity and fear (*Po.* 1453a1–3), since even such a one is enough like us in being human. Further down that line, we are not justly moved by the fall of the depraved, who according to *NE* 7.1 and 7.5 are as far removed from humanity (being beneath it, it seems, lacking freedom) as godlike virtue is above it. When the action of the play concerns the thoroughly good person, however, the only limitation on appropriate feeling being engendered in the audience seems to be the μίαρον—which comes from her fall. It seems it is precisely in their ability to suffer that the good are sufficiently like us to arouse pity and fear. Clearly, the main reason we can be moved by the *Prometheus* is that even the god himself can, and does, suffer—and he suffers for performing a deed for which all mankind must be grateful, a deed that he performed knowing that he would suffer for it. The deed was not one we could have managed for ourselves: our pity and fear are enhanced by the story of our need—he suffers for a good done to us. His predicted victory, through the descendants of god-burdened Io, is, then, also ours. If *Prometheus* can work as a tragedy, through fear and pity effecting its catharsis, certainly the threatened suffering and near destruction of the exceptionally good *person* or her philoi will be able to rouse pity and fear so much the more than this, since she is so much less able than a god to bear it. Iphigenia, an innocent willingly sacrificed by her father, saved by the goddess into exile among a foreign people, and made priestess overseeing the most barbaric and inhuman of their rituals—the slaughter of any visitor—about to kill, unknowingly, the one being with whom exile and sacrifice might be exchanged for human philia, is in such a position.

We may conclude that there are many reasons to consider *Iphigenia* the most effective kind of play for producing catharsis in all audiences, and better than the *Oedipus* that is valorized by Aristotle in chapter 13. First, because the fearful event is impending rather than completed, the poet is able to raise all the painful passions to a higher pitch: good and evil are still both

124. "Hamartia in Aristotle and Greek Tragedy," *Classical Quarterly* 25 (1975): 253.

possible, there is a world to lose—or save. The horror comes within a hairsbreadth—even the deficient should be raised, though not the dead. Second, because the character is unequivocally good rather than hamartemic—as Oedipus—pity, fear, and indignation can all be raised more easily and to a greater degree. Third, indignation and pity have their most proper object when aroused by a case like Iphigenia's rather than Oedipus's—for she is *thoroughly* innocent, and, as we said before, these passions increase both each other and fear in the poetic, though not the rhetorical, situation. Even those excessively given to self-pity and fear will recognize that they and theirs have never been so undeservedly and completely endangered. In addition, the resolution of the play in the happy ending frees the virtuous in the audience from any possible feeling of the μίαρον—the disgusting or polluting—which they should feel something of at the revelation of Oedipus's crimes, and must feel at the sight of Hecuba's deeds. (And in fact, this feeling of the disgusting is the correct feeling to have at these events.) And finally, while the double plot Aristotle criticizes may dissipate the emotional effect, there is no reason to think that the singular "happy ending" of the *Iphigenia* causes pity and fear to be poorly aroused or improperly purified, nor is there any reason to consider that the rousing and satisfaction of philanthropy is itself a flaw in tragedy.[125] On the contrary, it may well be that philanthropy is necessarily involved in any situation in which fear and pity are aroused, for philanthropy applies further down the ladder from perfect virtue than even pity: we may feel philanthropy (though not pity) even for the wicked falling into adversity—and we cannot easily consider that there is suffering (though there is pain) below that (among the bestial). It also seems philanthropy is aroused farther up the ladder than pity, for Prometheus wins our love even as he despises our pity. We love him insofar as he is like us human beings and can suffer, and he has done us a good for which the proper repayment is a greater affection than he may have for us (*NE* 1164a33–b6). It is at least the case that a plot like the *Iphigenia*'s which arouses all three passions is no less excellent thaumaturgy than *Oedipus*, and critical denigration of the play must cease. Aristotle supplies a reason from another, less fragmented text: "Dramatic turns of fortune and hairbreadth escapes from perils are pleasant, because we feel all such things are wonderful" (θαυμαστά; *Rh*. 1371b10–12).

Unlike the melodramas of romantic love with which it is sometimes

125. Moles makes these last two claims as part of the reason Aristotle criticizes double-issue plots in "Philanthropia" (334), but they would apply in this case as well—if they were true.

compared, the *Iphigenia* centers on the loss of philia and threatening irrevocable loss of every possibility of this most important of external goods.[126] The threat of bringing this kind of suffering on oneself, unknowingly, on a barren rock, surrounded by a barbarian people, should arouse every audience member's pity and fear to the climax—at which point Euripides places his recognition, from which salvation follows. It is not a matter of an evil power set against an innocent damsel—on which many exciting scenes may be based—but a complex and unified series of probable events, woven out of the ignorance and powerlessness of the philoi themselves, which puts themselves and all they love at risk. Such ignorance and powerlessness are plausibly extended even to the virtuous (like Iphigenia) and require no further dark-mustachioed excitements of our reason or our blood—for nothing human can matter more to us than this kind of situation, nor is anything more capable of arousing our painful emotions. Even the apathetic must have their fear and pity awakened. And here, as with Polyxena, the beauty of the girl—or in ancient Greece, the mask—plays an important emotional role. The recognition and escape of the beautiful and good allows pity and fear to be completely purified, without remainder or quibble: *the world most to be feared* (where innocent beauty is innocently involved in the destruction of all its good) *is felt to be avoided* when on the stage it is avoided. Our painful passions are properly raised about proper objects and when escape is discovered we have the experience of those passions dissolving to joy. This passional movement, through a building up and containment of fear, from which we are released to joy, is a mimesis of courage, for in acts of courage this is precisely the emotional movement that takes place. Like a good coach, the play has taken our soul through the passional movements of the courageous in act. Courage is the primary virtue in regard to painful things, the primary virtue of the irascible appetite. Let the good therefore enjoy this movement; let the excessive and deficient suffer such transformations until they are better. Such thaumaturgy has good cause to be part of the state religion.

That such a play can be profound, then, and profoundly affecting for every audience member, is clear. As to Moles's second criticism, to complain that such a play's effect is not "lasting" is either false or morbid.[127] It may be

126. Cf. Belfiore, "Aristotle and Iphigenia," 367, 370.

127. Gilbert Murray is aware of approaching this problem, if not openly admitting to it, in his introduction to the play: "Romantic plays with happy endings are almost of necessity inferior in artistic value to true tragedies. Not, one would hope, simply because they end happily; happiness in itself is certainly not less beautiful than grief; but because tragedy in its great moments can

that by "lasting" Moles means that after "*great* tragedy" (92) we carry the pity and fear, and perhaps the disgust, aroused by the play out of the theater with us, but except for the case of an originally deficient and apathetic audience member, such a result could hardly be considered good by Aristotle. Such an effect might in fact be accomplished by a bad tragedy, especially on a melancholic disposition, but it should never be the result of a fine work of art on the virtuous, or on the already excessively pitying and fearful—most especially not if *catharsis* is the end of the art. To expect or desire such an effect is morbidity: it may be that some folks expect and desire this from their plays and their music, but the weakness of the audience should not be definitive of the aims of art.

On the other hand, if he means by "lasting" that the emotional purification of the play is not lasting, there is no reason to suspect that the claim is any more true of this kind of play than of any other—the plays of the religious festival work our emotions into a more proper order, or allow the properly ordered passions a more complete satisfaction than life often does; next year we need to do it again. Perhaps in a less human life than ancient Athens such catharses are needed more frequently. The effect of any play, like that of a piece of music, can last only so long as we hold it in memory, perhaps only as long as it is playing does it really have its effect—but that effect is effective: it turns the passions out of, and away from, their ordinary unfree, or excessive, or deficient patterns, and by doing so stretches the sinews of the soul to heights and depths they are not extended in ordinary time, but which are yet human and good. Attending to the play takes us through that process, which Aristotle called catharsis. Thereafter we stand more perfectly upright, move with more grace, respond with more adequate feeling and imagination, are shaped to what more good a better proposer can burden us withal. Such exercises and effects cannot but be pleasurable to the good, and requested again; those less good, less healthy, must learn to be pleased with the medicine that is appropriate to them (if they are not pleased already),[128] and so be moved to more proper and adequate responses. Aristotle, of course,

---

generally afford to be sincere, while romantic plays live in an atmosphere of ingenuity and make-believe" (x). There is much to think about in this remark—not so much about Euripides. It implies that happiness is either impossible or insincere. Then so is love; but this thesis too is a modern corruption.

128. Consider, again, Hamlet's thoroughly philosophically accurate remark when he finds that the king is distempered by the play: "For if the king like not the comedy, / Why then, belike he likes it not, perdy" (3.2.282–83). The king's not liking it is not a remark on the worth of the play, though he might like to think it is. The feelings of the morally corrupt are corrupt judges.

thinks it is possible for whole cultures to be lost to barbarism and slavish dispositions, and for them not only can great art not accomplish its purpose, but it is plausible to think that it cannot even be recognized. On this matter Plato is more democratic, for he thinks that the cave is open along its entire length, and that we cannot fail to love beauty when we see it, though—like Phaedrus—we may not yet be capable of appropriate response to her.

8. RESOLVING THE CONTRADICTION BETWEEN *POETICS* 13 AND 14

We have seen how Aristotle's understanding of the purpose of tragedy allows not only the claim that *Iphigenia* is a tragedy, but also an argument for it being the best kind of tragedy. Before turning to the problem of comedy we should attempt to reconcile the seeming contradiction between chapter 13's claim that the finest tragedy includes a fall from prosperity to adversity, and chapter 14's choice of *Iphigenia* as best.

If we are convinced that everything in the play is there for the sake of the plot, and the plot aims at an end outside the play—in the audience—we can at least begin to make the contradiction with which we started less striking. As many critics have said, chapter 13 seems to be making the more general set of remarks about plot, marking a beginning to the consideration of "what should be aimed at and avoided in the construction of the plot and the achievement of its work" (1452b27–30). This wide-open and general question, linking structure with tragic ἔργον, is the chapter's opening. For the middle of a book these seem rather large open questions, particularly considering he has been explicitly demanding unity (beginning, middle, and end), complexity, and other plot matters for several chapters. Aristotle assumes that, since complexity will allow of greater ἔκπληξις and emotional change—and thereby more effective catharsis, as we have seen—complexity of plot is the first thing that should be aimed at (1452b30–31). Similarly, since pity and fear are the particular emotions tragedy concerns itself with, the events must raise such emotions, and so Aristotle rules out several kinds of change in which tragic emotions (or those which underlie them, like philanthropy) are impossible or less likely (1452b31–53a23), ending with the conclusion that the example of Oedipus, and the stories of several other families—those who have suffered or perpetrated terrible things (1453a21–22), are of the type to provide the right kind of feelings. These general points are the burden of chapter 13.

We should note that he says this type of story (that of Oedipus) remains, as if he has been sifting out from popular opinions and the large inventory of possibilities the kind that is most likely to achieve the end: catharsis of pity and fear. It seems that he is in fact doing exactly that, for, beginning with the entire shopping cart of ordinary opinion, he criticizes precisely the kind of stuff many people have come to expect from tragedy—as if evil characters, worse deeds, horror shows that merely multiply bodies and blood and other repugnancies are such dreams as tragedies are made on. This kind of sorting would go along with the wideness of his opening question. He gives us examples of Oedipal and Pelopid families as matching up to "what remains" of the sad and bad happenings people expect to see in a tragedy and outlines what makes them fine plots—single issue, complex plot, and so greater shifts of feeling, with changes of fortune not from misery to happiness, but the reverse, the cause being hamartia and the man being intermediate or somewhat better, thereby arousing the right passions (1453a11–17). He confirms this theory with the fact that the finest tragedies are built on the stories of a few houses—Oedipus and Orestes are both included in his summary examples (17–23). The best plot, he concludes, has this kind of structure because it gets more adequately at the correct passions and does the right sort of thing with them (where the more favored double-ending plot does not). At every turn in this chapter the argument depends on the kinds of emotions roused by the characters and action. Curiously, he says second-best structure is that called first by some, which has a double issue (1053a22f, 30f). This final reference to the inaccuracy of audience preference, as well as to a kind of play that results in an inappropriate pleasure as "second" should convince us that the whole discussion of this chapter is a rather general sorting of popular opinions the opening question invited. Nowhere in this chapter does he name specific tragedies. In fact, the only specific work he mentions is *Odyssey*—the kind of double story that *shouldn't* be constructed.

Aristotle regularly does such opinion sifting in the early parts of many discussions throughout the corpus, and usually finds that there is something in the common opinion that roughly marks an insight, and after sifting through to a conclusion against some plausible or popular opinion, he regularly tries to show how the facts line up better under his more particular dispensation and distinctions. The most well-known example is *NE* 1 where he takes up the popular list of candidates for *eudaimonia*, to which he adds his own—contemplation—out of the blue. He then sifts down to three legitimate contenders, two of which are popular. He does not only do such sifting of common opinion early, but uses it later on in as a way into discussion of particularly important matters. For example, *Physics* 4.6 begins with the opinions of others on the existence of the void; he gives a brief outline of the virtues in *NE* 2.12 before going into his own more particular analyses in 3.6–4.8. In the sifting of *Poetics* 13 he finds the fall of the relatively good man through some hamartia, but does not—before he comes to the conclusion of his sifting—either affirm or decline the type of plot and character we see in *Iphigenia*, passing over it while including its "house" along with that of Oedipus. I suggest, then, that in chapter 13 Aristotle is sifting through the mixed bag of horrors and evils people might commonly lump together as tragic. He argues that the fall of the good through hamartia is better than much more horrifying stories like Medea's—where a bad woman who commits a terrible deed with knowledge gets saved. Though Medea's act might rouse more terror, horror, or fear—as *Friday the 13th, Part V* might these days—it does not provide a very good catharsis. Tragedy's purpose is not just emotional fireworks of the darker colors, but purification. For that, the fall of the relatively good is the best story in this popular mixed bag. He concludes with a statement against the popular double-issue plot; showing that popular opinion even (at least sometimes) gets wrong what kind of catharsis and passions tragedy's ἔργον really is about.

In chapter 14, then, he seems to get more specific; it is not a matter of changing from plot to incident so much as a higher power of focus, from general rules about what kinds of thing suit tragedy's ἔργον and generic inadequacies of some kinds of character and emplotment—which effectively denigrates a number of possibilities—to specific plots. There are many things that work together to arouse pity and fear; besides those elements mentioned in chapter 13, Aristotle mentions spectacle at the opening of 14. It is, however, "the structure of the events which is the higher priority and the aim of the superior poet" (1453b1–3). He is reiterating that fireworks for their own sake are not the purpose and centering on emplotment. After this opening he gets down to the detailed examination of exactly this higher matter: plot structures, what should be built into the events (1453b13). In that examination some, but not all, of the earlier chapter's horrors are reexamined, and the new combination of character cum plot form—that of *Iphigenia*—is added. Like his own addition to the popular opinions in *NE*, it is found to be the best solution.

We see Aristotle work in this way elsewhere in *Poetics* as well. In chapter 6, his famous definition, supposedly "emerging from what has been said" (1449b22–23) adds the as-yet-unspoken-of final cause, catharsis. He follows the definition with a brief list and description of the components of tragedy—spectacle, melody, diction, thought, character, plot (1449b30–50a10)—each of which he then takes up individually in more exacting focus in later chapters—among them the chapters we have now in view. Between that first gross anatomical focus and this last fine focus he has a middle focus for some of the terms, like plot (1450a37–b8), character (1450b8–10), thought (1450b10–12), and diction (1450b12–13), but he pretty much abandons the nonlinguistic elements of music and spectacle. It is when he brings each thing up for his most focused examination that he makes his most particular points, as we see when he focuses on diction in chapter 22, providing a perfect lesson plan for a creative writing class that is attempting to work on voice and word selection. Chapter 14 is precisely this kind of detailed high-focus examination of plot structures. He logically delineates four permutations of action and knowledge; he names or alludes to the plots of ten specific plays, sorting them according to that logical division, and is clearly giving his most exacting account. *Iphigenia* wins.[129] Like the Oedipus story mentioned here and in the preceding chapter, it has a complex plot with a single resolution, containing within it the kinds of people and proceedings that arouse pity and fear.[130] The only reason Aristotle can have for picking *Iphigenia* over *Oedipus*, since both meet all the general requirements of chapter 13,

129. I agree with Stephen White that *Poetics* 13 and 14 are continuous, though I disagree that the continuities allow us to place the *Oedipus* and *Iphigenia* on the same level—both among the finest (cf. 235–37). The two chapters are continuous and 14 is conclusive. The topic in chapter 15 is the next most important element of the poem: character. I think White may be inhibited from following Aristotle's argument all the way to my conclusion due to the magnetism of the formalist fallacy—he can't believe Aristotle would really pick a smiling plot for the best tragedy; *Oedipus* must be equal to it, at least. Halliwell (*Aristotle's "Poetics,"* 216–37) also argues for the continuity of chapters 13 and 14, though it will be clear that I do not agree with his conclusion that "Aristotle attempts to set limits on tragedy against its true nature" (237n). On the contrary, Aristotle is describing tragedy's true nature, and correctly.

130. Despite Kitto, who says the "intrinsic importance of the dramatic material" of the play is not "big enough" (320), and that "intellectual profundity is as alien to this tragi-comedy as moral profundity" (316). Intellectual profundity is not tragedy's primary purpose, and the moral profundity of a play is in its work, through mimesis, on the passions, not its talking about ethics or illustration of moral problems. Plato seems to make the same distinction, in *Laws*, in differentiating the work of the laws from the recreative work of choristry upon the whole soul (cf. William Welton, "Divine Inspiration and the Origins of the Laws in Plato's *Laws*," esp. 76–80).

and their peripeties are tied closely to their recognitions (1452a31–33), is that *Iphigenia* is more effective, in his judgment, at bringing about the final cause that is the purpose of tragedy: catharsis of the painful passions. As discussed in the previous section, there is good reason to agree with him.

Since the solution we have provided, based on a clearer understanding of the final causality of tragedy, resolves the problems of both the supposed mislabeling of the *Iphigenia* as a tragedy and the seeming contradiction between the claims of chapters 13 and 14, we should suspect that a similar necessity to understand the final cause will be the key to the Aristotelian—and true—account of comedy. The recent attempts to explain catharsis as a process emphasizing intellectual clarifications and rational judgments fail utterly to explain why the *Iphigenia* might be thought a tragedy by Aristotle, and cannot attempt to explain why he would think it the best sort of tragedy. It is likely such critics will also be mistaken about comedy when they attempt to explain it.

The inadequacy of intellectualist explanations is magnified when we move to the correlative genre, comedy. It is, for example, insufficient to hold that comedy must be constructed "so that the universal insight at which all artistic mimesis aims will be evident,"[131] and it destroys the distinctiveness of the genre to argue that it is through "a sudden flash of tragic wisdom"[132] that a comedy reaches its catharsis. In order to hold any of the intellectualist theories, one must clearly distinguish comic insight from tragic insight, and then show how the *Iphigenia* fits the latter, if one is to be giving an Aristotelian explanation of tragedy—or of comedy.[133] If the particular "intellectual pleasure" of tragedy is not distinguished from that of comedy by reference to some particular nature of its insight, then we must revert to the fallacy of Aristotelian formalism to distinguish the genres, and *Iphigenia* must be a comedy or some middling form—as many have said, *Aristotle distinctly not among them*. Any argument against this position (which I take to be Aristotle's) requires, besides a deconstruction of the argument here set forth, the defense of a different final cause for tragedy together with an explanation of how the *Iphigenia* fits it; otherwise one must claim that Aristotle so thoroughly misunderstood his own ideas as to claim that the best specific example of a kind is something not even in the kind at all.

131. Golden, *Tragic and Comic Mimesis*, 73.

132. Ibid., 97, quoting Segal ("Aristophanes' Cloud-Chorus," 157) with approval.

133. It would follow from the argument here presented that *The Winter's Tale* is a tragedy of the best sort—perhaps even better than the best sort Aristotle can imagine, for it has *both* the deed of suffering *and* salvation. Suppose the statement "Behold, I make all things new again" is true.

2

THE PURPOSE OF COMEDY

Be you on your guard, nor surrender the bard;
for his art shall be righteous and true.
Rare blessings and great will he work for the state
rare happiness shower upon you;
Not fawning or bribing, nor striving to cheat
with an empty unprincipled jest;
Not seeking your favor to curry or nurse,
but teaching the things that are best.

Aristophanes, *Acharnians* 655–58 (Hadas)

Let it be said what this practice of yours is that makes the same men equally courageous before sufferings and pleasures.

Plato, *Laws* 634b

1. FORMAL, MATERIAL, AND EFFICIENT CAUSES

The question of comedy's telos, or final cause, is just one of the questions left open due to that most famous nonextant book in history, the second book of Aristotle's *Poetics*, and there have been not a few suggestions to fill the gap. Before we turn to them, let us begin by remembering the definition of tragedy, for its part the most well-known sentence in literary criticism:

A tragedy is a mimesis of action that is serious, complete, and has magnitude; in language with pleasurable accessories, each brought in in various parts; in a dramatic, not narrative form; with incidents arousing pity and fear, through which a catharsis of such emotions is accomplished. (1449b 24–28)

If we were to guess at a definition of comedy without any further investigation we could be sure of getting several things right. Since comedy is the sister art of tragedy, we should expect that its efficient cause—dramatizing not narrating—and its material causes—language and pleasurable accessories (meter, rhythm, melody, color, shape, et al.)—will be the same. In fact, we don't have to leave the extant *Poetics* to get this far, since Aristotle joins tragedy and comedy twice in his discussion: once in speaking of those forms of mimesis that combine all the means of mimesis (1447b 23–26), and later in distinguishing the dramatic method of both from the nondramatic *modus praesentandi* of epic (1448a 25–29). So, Aristotle has already told us about the material and efficient causes of comedy. It is the formal and final causes that allow for questions, and indeed that is precisely where scholars disagree.

With regard to the first question Aristotle himself is clear: where tragedy is a mimesis of an action that is σπουδαίας (serious), comedy is a μίμησις φαυλοτέρων (more vulgar, 1449a31). This distinction echoes the remark in chapter 2 that,

> [S]ince the objects of imitation are men in action, and it is necessary for these to be either σπουδαίους or φαύλους (for ἤθη aligns this way, badness [κακίᾳ] and excellence [ἀρετῇ] distinguish the ἤθη of all), it follows that they must be better, or worse, or the same as we are. (1448a1–5)

What is not clear is precisely how this should be taken. Leon Golden *(Tragic and Comic)* suggests that Aristotle considers "φαῦλος as the antonym of σπουδαῖος"—which is exactly what Aristotle says—but then Golden treats the ridiculous, τὸ γελοῖον, as the opposite of ἔλεος και φόβος" (44n), pity and fear, suggesting that this is a correction of Plato's misunderstanding of how comic mimesis works. His interpretation requires the most moralistic implication of the operative terms (σπουδαῖος/φαῦλος)—namely, good and evil. I think Aristotle is not doing that. While the large generic distinctions good and bad noted here in chapter 2 of *Poetics* may have beneath them the more specific kinds *Nicomachean Ethics* 2.3 itemizes as "the fine, the advantageous, and the pleasant, and their contraries the shameful (αἰσχροῦ), the injurious, and the painful" (1104b30–32)—namely, those things about which the good (ἀγαθοί) choose correctly and the bad (κακοί) err—neither σπουδαῖος nor φαῦλος are used in that more particularly ethical itemization in *Nicomachean Ethics.*

Furthermore, in chapter 5 of *Poetics* he seems to turn these words touching upon ethos to more poetic and less moralizing concerns than we mean by ethics when he says of the μίμησις φαυλοτέρων, that the sense of the word does not refer to the wholly bad (πᾶσαν κακίαν), but rather the ludicrous, "a species of the ugly (τοῦ αἰσχροῦ). It is an error or ugliness not productive of pain or harm," like the comic mask (1449a31–33). So it seems Aristotle here is making explicit what he means by φαῦλος in the context of poetics—τὸ γελοῖον. Φαύλος, then, which ordinarily might include the (morally) bad (κακία), or be included under it, and so contradict virtue (which would be a serious matter), is here being limited to the ridiculous—which could be neither vice nor virtue.[1] If it implies anything about fear and pity, such an analysis would not imply opposition so much as complementarity: the φαῦλος that is γελοῖος is that where fear and pity are not, though there might be some things that are φαῦλος and not γελοῖος where fear and pity can be caused.

My argument will hew to this least moralizing view of σπουδαῖος/φαῦλος, and in doing so attempt to illustrate otherwise than Golden thinks; namely, that Plato and Aristotle will agree that the ridiculous rather than the bad is opposed to σπουδαῖος in poetic contexts, and, as Plato suggested, this allows us to learn "the nature of the noble through learning the nature of its opposite, the ridiculous."[2] Learning will have to be of a rather greater scope than our usual interpretation of it as "coming to intellectual understanding"—that is, that wider scope we have been arguing for as the particular work of mimesis in its anthropological firstness; and comic mimeses, too, and their action, are directed to the emotions. The quote from Aristophanes at the head of this chapter will, then, also mean "teach" in a different way than usual as well. The teaching and learning that happens first through mimesis is a prereflective, mechanical or osmotic becoming like. From such repeated experiences we rise to universals and then, perhaps, to make distinctions.

1. Aristotle's use of the comparative (φαυλότερον) instead of simply contrasting mimeses σπουδαῖος and φαῦλος, might be a further indication of stepping away from a moralistic division; comedy is "rather vulgar" when seen next to her sister, rather more common. Certainly comedy's language is so.

2. Cf. Golden's claim, in *Tragic and Comic Mimesis.* There he says comedy is allowed only for this "narrowly moralistic and didactic purpose" and he means didactic in its most intellectualist sense (like Aesop) and where the ridiculous is the bad (43–44). The reference to Plato is to *Laws* 816e.

It is quite probable, then, that Aristotle is, here in *Poetics*, being extremely explicit in his choice of terms and wishes to signify, by the use of terms farthest from his discussion of moral choice in *NE*, that the "men in action" in tragedy and comedy are not so much distinguished by what we should call their morals, as by the kind of action the poet puts them into. Later in *NE* he does use the terms we find in *Poetics*, and precisely in sorting the kind of *activities* a life may encompass:

> The happy life is thought to be that according to virtue, but such a life concerns the serious things (μετὰ σπουδῆς) and not the amusing (ἀλλ᾽ οὐκ ἐν παιδιᾷ). We call the serious things (τὰ σπουδαῖα) better than the laughable (τῶν γελοίων) and those which concern amusement (τῶν μετὰ παιδιᾶς); and the better a part or a person is, the more serious their activities. (1177a1–5)

The use of the contraries τα σπουδαῖα and τα γελοῖα here is part of a long argument allowing that both the virtuous and the vicious may engage in both, for all make use of amusement; however, the good will engage in the amusing differently than the bad, and the laughable and amusing become a serious problem when they are made or considered the stuff of life rather than play. The happiness of life is measured in its serious activities: the political, familial, and intellectual activities, not by how often or how well one eats in fine restaurants, vacations in exotic places, or is allowed to play one's favorite game, party at the A-list clubs, or play practical jokes. The better person engages in serious activities, and in amusement for the sake of the serious (*NE* 1176b28–36).[3]

Mise en abyme: The Socrates and Phaedrus of *Phaedrus*—We can now broach a seemingly troubling question about the formal cause of comedy with more ease. We might have been tempted to ask Aristotle, of his sense of μίμησις φαυλοτέρων, "How could an error or ugliness not be produc-

3. I disagree, then, with Elder Olsen's connection of the related terms serious/ludicrous, good/bad, tragedy/comedy. In particular it is the connection of the others to the middle and moral set of terms that leads to trouble. He says "if actions are serious or ludicrous according to the degree in which they involve happiness or misery, and if happiness and misery are functions of the moral characters of the persons involved, the imitative action, or plot, cannot consist of events simply, or actions simply, but of activity of a certain moral quality, such that it produces a particular emotional effect" ("The Poetic Method," 188). This seems to mean either that we must connect moral badness to comedy and the ludicrous, in which case it would seem comic characters should always end up in misery; or that comedy cannot involve any *significant* happiness or misery at all. On the contrary, the serious and the ludicrous cross the moral boundaries of good/bad in poetry without involving us in moral judgment. One reason it is possible for poetry to do this is because we are not speaking of *making choices*, but of *looking (theōrein)*; a theater is a place for such looking.

tive of pain or harm?" The response I think correct, in the general line of the preceding discussion, can best be brought into focus by the consideration of a specific example; let us consider a comic dialogue Aristotle probably knew by heart: his teacher's *Phaedrus*. Phaedrus has the soul of a little girl, one who can be carried off by any wind that blows (229c, d). He gets so caught up in Socrates' talk as they are walking that he blows right by the tree he himself suggested they make for (230b, cf. 229a, b). He then carries himself off by reading Lysias's speech, as Socrates remarks (234d). And again, when Socrates gives a speech he says will make him ridiculous (γελοῖος, 236d)—so much so that he covers his head while giving it (237a)—Phaedrus wishes him to carry on still further (241e), perhaps exercising some extratextual compulsion to get Socrates to stay on his side of the stream (242a). Having felt the divine sign, Socrates gives a second speech about the chariot of the soul, which just barely gets Phaedrus to say Amen to Socrates' prayer for him before making off to the next topic (257bc). All this takes place after a very exciting morning in the heat of Lysias's classroom.

The repeated incidents of Phaedrus's carrying off are part of a comic action; he cannot keep his feet on the ground. The comedy of this action is explicated by the central and longest speech Socrates gives: a kind of *mise en abyme* emblematically portraying the root of the action—the speech about the chariot of the soul. It is clear that Phaedrus's horses have huge wings; he sails on a puff of Lysias's for a whole morning, but luckily he lands near Socrates instead of in Lysias's bed. Phaedrus's inability to control the chariot of his soul—as well as his ears and tongue—is ludicrous: it is an *hamartema* not productive of harm to himself—or to Lysias (whose dark horse is undoubtedly stamping its feet impatiently back in Athens). It is also clear that the incidents of the dialogue could be connected in a different and far less ludicrous action. For example, say Socrates, rising after his first speech in order to cross the stream, is hindered by Phaedrus, sitting beside him, who, grasping his thigh, pulls him back down beside him declaring there are better things to do in the heat of the day than take long walks in the sun. Say this other Socrates finds something better to do than give a speech to purify himself (243a). Let us not go into the details, for we are—after all—all teachers, we are acquainted with the phenomenon Freud will later call transference, and this is—after all—an example, not a reading of *Phaedrus* I wish to defend with the full panoply of scholarly resource. An easier way to put these events together into that less comic action would be to have Phaedrus memorize the speech in his pocket and then go running back to that shadow Socrates who goes by the name of Lysias—pleasantly (but tragically) carried off by the speech he has read to himself into the music of the night conducted by his morning teacher.

In the background of the story Plato wrote, his speech framed by Socrates' first speech (237b), is a character decidedly worse—and worse in a less ridiculous way—than either of the two actually present before us. But this kind of ethical φαυλότερος is not presented *in propria persona* in the dialogue, and his real absence makes it possible for us to consider his threat to Phaedrus as not particularly dangerous and his power to effect it as not very credible: he is a paper evil demon. The way Socrates laughingly criticizes the paper speech reinforces this feeling (234d–35d). It is probably true that Lysias' dark horse has won a large measure of control over his own chariot; the charioteer has become a very clever speaker for the sake of the dark horse of physical passion, but that kind of ugliness—in another part of the shameful than the ridiculous—is only inferred by the reflective reader, never seen active in the dialogue, and its actual ineffectiveness throughout the dialogue renders it, in any case, harmless. Such Dastard Dicks are stock characters of melodrama and comedy. For example, the evil Duke and Oliver in *As You Like It* both see their personal power and their plots defeated or flouted from their very first scenes; the great evils of the Informer and Nicarchus in *Acharnians* are expected to be held at bay by three knotted cords Dicaeopolis deposits as his market clerks, and their effect is nil even when they get past the knots. In each play what could be (and was, in Athens, and in England) a real evil—not a powerless one—is shown up to be ridiculous, converted, or disempowered in the play. Similarly, in *Phaedrus* the real evil never comes out of the background (Charlie Chaplin does the same with Hitler). Against this darker background we see the considerably lighter play of two others. The first, a charioteer who has no idea of the kind of machine he drives, and who, because of that and lack of training, is carried off by it but is hardly driving. The second figure is the more psychically adequate, but ugly, Socrates.

Socrates and Phaedrus are perfect examples of error or ugliness not productive of harm. It looks like the moral weight and power (particularly for ill) of eros are not of serious (σπουδαῖα) account *in their interaction,* even though *the dialogue* gives eros a most serious account. This is a common trope in comedy. In *Acharnians* war and Lamachus are not seriously acted, but war and the choices of generals are given some very serious words. In both cases, the shredding of the paper tiger—Lysias or Lamachus, eros or war—is a method moving us through the attachment to such things as the be-all and end-all of life. This is one way the comic playwright uses a motley action as his stalking horse for serious logos and thus engages in his sublime work upon both the passions and the intellect. The moral weight and power of an eros for the beauties of the soul *is* at stake in *the poet's interaction with us*, and the interaction of Socrates with Phaedrus is a mimesis of that stake within the play as well, though the plot looks to be a thing of nothing. The frivolous, light-hearted action of *Phaedrus*, the incidents and their connection, is in comic contrast to the growing speeches of Socrates—who becomes a mystic—and the darker background of the anchoring Lysias—who is after something more material. Lysias's (spiritual) defect is already polluting, if not harmful, but he appears only in the pocket and then the mouth of Phaedrus—he has become not a knot, but a scrap of paper, and the speech of a flighty soul. When Socrates comments on the speech, we find Lysias to be even less likely to be harmful; it's simply ridiculous for a writer of speeches to be so discombobulated as Socrates points out the speech is. We should see that Lysias's speech is a mimesis of *non compos mentis* which is meant to develop just that state in the hearer. It did so in Phaedrus (not that he needed much charming to fall under its infection), who is surprised Socrates can raise questions to it (235b–e) and might miss Socrates' rather pointed prescription for such a lover as Lysias (239c). Phaedrus's defective control, on the other hand, is not only not harmful to anyone—yet—but, in fact, it is because of his defective control (neither horse nor the charioteer being in command) that he lands, *mirabile dictu*, next to Socrates, who has the chance to begin the driving lessons (safely outside of the bustling and heat of the city) by pointing out to Phaedrus the widely divergent qualities of his steeds (which might be figures of his teachers for the day). "Oh my!" Phaedrus exclaims, "I do have two hands!" This altogether pleasant, useful, and good result makes Phaedrus' error even more comical.

Phaedrus, in his naiveté, is worse than us—or at least worse than me (as I well know)—but his defect is not productive of harm, it is ludicrous. Compare him to the ugly comic mask of the Socrates next to him. Socrates, too, is worse than us, in his way; in a materialist culture, we might consider such a mug as his a harm to Socrates, who suggests that a Lysian argument in favor of the youthful and beautiful beloved giving himself to the old, poor, and entirely ordinary would be something he (Socrates) would really like to hear (227cd). Be that as it may, his long speech in *Phaedrus* clearly has a different idea of what the beautiful really is, a spiritual ideal which is exhibited by Socrates' driving of his chariot. The famously ugly mug is the mask of the most perfect driver known to the ancient world. So this mask too is comical, as is his poverty and age—it is something worse than our own situation (mine anyway), but not productive of harm to anyone. (There is, in this comparison of Phaedrus—youthful and handsome [237b]—and Socrates, the additional irony of the difference between the inner and the outer, but that is the subject of a different dissertation. I leave irony for less handsome writers.)[4] In fact, Socrates' less than handsome condition, like Phaedrus's flightiness of soul, may even have been *productive of good*, for it aided him in becoming the superb erotist of the soul, which good looks and wealth might well hamper—as it does in Phaedrus's case. Both characters, then, are comic, each in a different way, though those defects and uglinesses agree in not being productive of harm even to themselves—as the action and speech of the dialogue allows us to see. In fact, we must *feel* that despite the ludicrous action, the characters are good—at least one of them is supremely so, not bad, and that they live happily, rather than unhappily, afterward—at least so far as we can see and judge about such serious matters under the conditions of such airy dancing.[5] If real evil were the tone of either character, or of the play's action or result, we could not be released into its humor or in such an unmitigated way love its beauties. The presence of the real and superior good (of the soul) in Socrates gives the desire of both Lysias in the play and the reader outside of it a more adequate object. More adequate, even, than life generally provides, for it is seen far more clearly in Socrates' speech and action.

So, then, the difference between comedy and tragedy is not a difference between good and evil actions done by good or evil human beings so much as the difference between an important action (Agamemnon's going off to war) and a trivial one (Phaedrus's going for a walk), a serious matter (Socrates defending himself in court) and an insignificant one (Socrates batting a geegaw of Lysias's), or, more poetically, it rests on the difference between the heaviness (men sacrificing their daughters to go to war—

4. The unsurpassed study of this topic is Kierkegaard's doctoral dissertation, *On the Concept of Irony, with Constant Reference to Socrates.*

5. Again, contrast Olsen, footnote 3 above.

Agamemnon) and the lightness (women closing their legs to keep men from war—*Lysistrata*) of being. One need not hang one's hat on rustic characters, rather than the urbane, or ordinary language rather than high and polished, for even a god might appear in a comedy, as Dionysos does in Aristophanes' *Frogs*. Similarly, high tragic language appears—but the context of action and speaker make it overblown. (Some poets do this by accident in their tragedies, which can destroy a serious mood entirely.) But the action of *Frogs*, and the god's own characterization as somewhat more cowardly than his rather cowardly human slave, is indicative of the kind of drama the poet is making.[6] I conclude that when Aristotle says "in one respect Sophocles could be classed as the same kind of mimetic artist as Homer, since both imitate the σπουδαίους, but in another the same as Aristophanes since both imitate actors and action" (1448a25–29), we should not translate σπουδαίους as "good" with the concomitant opposite implication for comedy (as Golden does, e.g., in *Tragic and Comic*, 71), for such serious moral judgments are out of place due to the lack of weight of the action. This lack of weight to the action, its holiday spirit of amusement or impossibility, lightens the real-life (serious) moral weight we know inhabits Lamachus, Socrates, Alcibiades, or even Hitler or the god Dionysos, when they are made into characters of comedy. Such a serious moral judgment as Golden makes is also false since there is often considerable lack of moral goodness in most of the characters and actions of the σπουδαῖος tragedy: Medea comes to mind, and what is good about Agamemnon is not easy to see.

To be carried a half step ahead of ourselves, we might note that though the action be unserious or ridiculous—for example, taking a walk in order to discuss a pretty absurd piece of flimflam—it is clear that comedy can evoke more serious desires in the audience (as well as in some characters—even Phaedrus, for a breath or two). This is what comedy is "about"—meaning what its work is up to—the evocation of desire, whether for the beautiful youth, Phaedrus, who himself evokes so many speeches (242b), or for the

6. M. S. Silk thinks that "the traditional Aristotelian or Aristotelian-based assumption that tragedy and comedy are opposites is false and, . . . pernicious" and considers that it requires or implies the distinctions of language, social class, or moral stature of [each art's] characters (55–56). On the contrary, while they may be usual, surely all such differences are not necessary to make Aristotle's distinction between a serious plot and action in tragedy and a ridiculous or small action in comedy. Clearly, to take Aristotle's division that far is pernicious; I also think it is false about Aristotle. Nor does the Aristotelian position imply (as Silk thinks it does for some Aristotelians) that comedy "seeks merely to amuse" (59).

girl, Rosalind, or for the beautiful, well-driven soul, or the beauties of peace and pleasures of drinking.

A critic may complain of two matters at this point. The first is that Aristotle clearly distinguishes Socratic dialogue from both tragedy and comedy in *Poetics* 1. My example of *Phaedrus* therefore is illegitimate. The second complaint is that even if the example is legitimate, I have excessively narrowed the range of comic action and not sufficiently distinguished it from the tragic, for many comic plays deal with serious matters—for example, going to war, or being driven from one's home. Regarding the first it is sufficient to point out that in chapter 1 Aristotle is distinguishing mimetic arts according to their means. Thus "color and form are used by some," "and voice is used by others," "harmony and rhythm alone is the means in flute and lyre playing"; "there is a further art which imitates by language alone," under which category falls mime and Socratic conversation; lastly there are those arts which "combine all of the means enumerated," among which are comedy and tragedy (*Po.* 1447a18–28). Socratic conversation is clearly distinguished from tragedy on the grounds of using fewer of the available *means*, but this distinction does not deny that we can link comedy or tragedy with Socratic dialogue under a different heading, for example, *mode* of presentation or formal or final cause. So, we may expect that a song may agree with drama in being a mimesis of a serious or ludicrous state of character—("rhythms and melodies . . . like the true nature of moral qualities"; *Pol.* 1340a18–22). Song and drama might agree in manner as well, being dramatically direct mimeses, not narrative or mixed, as epic (though some songs work in the narrative or epic manner). Aristotle himself allows that there are both comic and tragic epics, having first distinguished epic from drama as well. It is fairly clear that Aristotle spends most of the remainder of *Poetics* speaking of tragedy because by speaking of that most encompassing art of making he can, at least by implication and to some extent, deal with all the other arts of poesis, each of which use a single, or perhaps two, of the means of mimesis found in tragedy. So, when he picks up epic, he notes that "it is evident that it has several points in common with tragedy" (1459a17). The most notable differences—besides being diegetic (1459a16) rather than enacted (1459a14)—are in epic's length and meter (1459a17–18). Despite the differences, however, Aristotle gives Homer credit for teaching all other poets (i.e., all other makers of mimeses)—including the tragedians, as his examples show—the way to lie rightly (1460a18–

19) and the right way to be a poet: "For the poet should say as little as possible in his own voice, as it is not this which makes him a mimetic artist" (1460a7–8). It is clear that Aristotle takes drama as the central mimetic art, even though epic is its temporal precursor, because drama is the intersection of all the means of mimesis. He can thereby be outlining an entire theory of art synecdochically through a discussion of drama.[7] What he discusses regarding drama, then, applies to all those other forms—like Socratic conversation—insofar as those forms use the same means as drama and so have similar qualitative parts as drama. As his use of epic examples even invades his discussion of tragic dramatic plots (1453a32), we should be able to look for and analyze plot, character, diction, and thought in Socratic conversation or Sophronic mime in accord with the outlines he presents for drama.[8] It is also certain that if a mimetic artist is one "who says as little as possible in his own voice," Plato is a *mimētēs par excellence.*

As to the second complaint, even when the action of a play has seemingly serious content, the usually serious matter is not treated seriously.[9] For instance, *Acharnians'* ally- and peace-seeking ambassadors complain about the difficulties of being carried in litters and feted wherever they go for several years; Dicaeopolis berags himself with leftovers from Euripides before

7. I find it strange for M. S. Silk to say "comedy is accidentally dramatic, whereas tragedy is essentially dramatic" (61) or "tragedy is a dramatic genre, whereas 'comedy' . . . is evidently something wider altogether" (62) and that the distinction between comic and tragic forms cannot really be carried through in other arts than drama. He says the first because jokes, whether our own in conversation or a stand-up comedian's, are not dramatic and we have no parallel "tragic" short form; "there is no such thing as a tragic epigram or a tragic sonnet" (61). But this seems questionable if we spend some time comparing certain maxims and arrows of Nietzsche with selected aphorisms of Oscar Wilde. Further, just as we sometimes tell jokes at another's expense, we make short speeches of praise in which we retell some serious or weighty episode. As for tragic sonnets, one wonders what to make of Hopkins's "Carrion Comfort" or "No worst, there is none." Finally, Silk himself says the *Iliad* is "too discursive or too tolerant of the unheightened" (61) to allow us to think of it as tragedy. Clearly that position is un-Aristotelian, as is the suggestion that comedy seeks merely to amuse (see above note).

8. Cooper argues that Socratic conversation should be grouped with comic literature rather than tragic (*Comedy* 103; cf. 112, 122, 168f). I am not sure Socratic dialogues are "generically comic" as he says—though the idea is worth thought; I presume their filiation should be decided on a case-by-case basis. In any case we must decide upon the final cause of comedy before going so far. *Phaedo* and *Apology* are clearly about a serious (σπουδαῖος) matter for Socrates; a materialist would not think they end well. It seems plausible to think that their aim, as their content, has much to do with the pitiable and the fearful. The important question, I would argue, is whether they work more upon our fear and pity or upon our desire and sympathy.

9. As Elder Olson points out, war, rape, and incest can be subjects of comedy at least among Greeks; so he suggests that "when we say . . . that tragedy imitates a serious action, we mean that it imitates an action *which it makes serious*; and comparably, comedy imitates an action *which it makes a matter for levity*" (*Theory*, 36; emphasis in Olsen).

he goes to defend his head in court; he uses a general's crest to make himself vomit. Rosalind and Celia make a game of Rosalind's banishment and take along a clown for protection, while the banished good duke praises the life of the forest, and lacks the attendance of courtly fops like Le Beau in *As You Like It*. This lack of taking the matter seriously does not mean that comedy may not itself be important and the making of it a serious matter—the discussions of the art in itself (καθ' αὑτό) and the art in relation to the audience (πρὸς τὰ θέατρα) are two different speeches (1449a8–9). In any case, the direction in which we should take Aristotle's phrasing about the two kinds of action of which tragedy and comedy are the mimeses seems to be this—not so much noble and foul, still less good and evil—but serious and ridiculous, or the weighty and that of little account.[10] In this way we can make perfect sense of his phrase "an error or ugliness not productive of harm."

It is now clear how *Phaedrus*, like *Acharnians* or *As You Like It*, is a μίμησις φαυλοτέρων—a mimesis of an insignificant, unimportant, or worthless action. In the case of *Acharnians* we might better call it an impossible action—for since war is a political affair, it is impossible to engage in negotiating to a private peace.[11] These words—φαῦλος and σπουδαῖος—should not, then, be understood as moral evaluations so much as acknowledgments about, besides the action's importance, the relative weight of the deed of suffering that threatens or is effected. Judging about such seriousness (or its likelihood) is something even children can do fairly accurately, and it is this that is required for distinguishing comic from tragic action. The characters of comedy, then, need not be low class, or insignificant, or even behave with bad accent—as the good duke in *As You Like It* does not. Nor does the action—banishment and return, or making a private peace—need be a com-

10. On the mixture of social and ethical components of the σπουδαῖος person and σπουδαῖα action, see Belfiore, *Pleasures*, 100–107; Halliwell, rightly, pushes the interpretation of "the heroic standing of the agents in tragedy . . . principally in terms of their great esteem and prosperity not their ethical character" (*Aristotle's "Poetics,"* 179). It should be clear that Aristotle has such culturally esteemed characters in tragedy precisely because of *the action* he thinks tragedy must be a mimesis of—serious and important things. Slaves and landless men, as the disesteemed, generally have not the wherewithal to participate in such actions; the acts of a king or tyrannos cause greater effects. Euripides is original, and probably not well liked by the wealthier Athenians, because he makes his farmers' lives serious and important. The natural mimetic capacity answers to such poems just as well as to those of Aeschylus.

11. This might provide a hint to a comic poet: make your premise an impossible action; given that, you can do anything next. "Let us fly to heaven on a dung beetle." The threat of real evil (and so fear) in such a world will also be highly constrained, the world being impossible *ex origo*.

pletely worthless inanity—it may, in fact, be an impossibility greatly to be wished for—but the threats and dangers, or the reality of suffering them (and sometimes the rewards), must be minimal: In *As You Like It* the coup d'etat has led to a forest picnic among the duke and his merry men, while the sentence of banishment leads to a game between Rosalind and Celia, which is carried out under the aegis of the clown. On the other hand, in Shakespeare the rewards are usually considerable: four weddings and a return to the world and power. In Aristophanes the rewards are as insignificant as the threats: Dicaeopolis's private peace allows him the freedom to get drunk and trade for a couple of Megarian girls disguised as pigs[12] by their war-starved father. In each case the rewards accord with the ethos of the characters, and, particularly in *As You Like It,* they far exceed the risks of suffering apparently available in the action. About this Shakespearean excess we will have more to say later.

Be that as it may, from this discussion we might now describe all the parts of comedy except the one that is the burden of this part of our investigation: a comedy is a mimesis of an action that is impossible (a journey into Hades to bring back a good poet) or frivolous (a walk outside the walls of Athens), complete (there and back), and has magnitude (in the sense that it takes some time to complete), but does not have magnitude (in the sense that it is weighty or serious); in language with pleasurable accessories, each brought in in the appropriate parts; in a dramatic not narrative form; with incidents arousing x and y, through which a catharsis of such passions is accomplished.[13] We can see from the examples we have been using that it is not necessary that the speeches of the characters be frivolous or unimportant, for though the action is a comic one dramatists from Aristophanes and Plato to George Bernard Shaw and Samuel Beckett have managed to put lots of stuff in their nonsense. But before we look at the details of comedy, or infer too much from its logos, we need to finish our definition of comedy as a mimetic art.

12. The Greek of this scene would require an English-speaking director to dress the girls (preferably thinly) as pussy cats in order to bring out the *double* of the *entente*. Dicaeoplis knows what he is getting: not a cat. See Reckford *Aristophanes'* 168–70, Dover 63–65. It is plausible that these two parts would have been played by naked slave girls (cf. Sandbach, 28 and note): "a fine girl indeed!" (*Hippias* 287e).

13. Thus far I am largely in agreement with Leon Golden's earlier attempt to build up an Aristotelian theory of comedy. See "Aristotle on Comedy," 283, 285–86. As was the case with tragedy, it is also possible here that an interpretation of Aristotle gets much correct without putting one's finger on the final cause.

To set up for the solution for passions x and y, let us return to the definition of tragedy and note the relation of the painful emotions particularly aroused in it, and how they are aroused. The fearful things that happen or threaten in the tragedy rouse both fear and pity (among other painful passions) in the audience. Fear and pity are related as major and minor chords of the same key: what we directly fear if it would happen to us, we pity in other's lives. But further, fear is raised when we see destructive evils at work on those who are like ourselves. There is some debate about what Aristotle means by this matter,[14] so let us take the largest possible range his language allows: First of all, that the raising of fear in humans, or in the significantly humanlike—Chewbacca or C3PO—itself transfers by mimesis to other humans (but not to robots). I mean by this first explanation of likeness to recall Chapter 1's description of how, in the root sense of mimesis, fear is raised prior to the working of reason or perhaps even a clear distinction between self and others, certainly at times burying that distinction again in the impersonal. This too is active in works of mimesis, the poet himself perhaps the first to suffer it (1455a29–34). Further, that the vision or anticipation of destructive evils raises our fear for the characters in the play *and* for ourselves, *and* also raises our pity for the characters. (We might see something to fear or pity before they do; this fear and pity does require judgment.) I suppose that mainly our fear is for the characters, and secondarily for ourselves insofar as we are like them (at least in being human or able to suffer, if not morally like them), and the characters are objects of our pity because suffering threatens or occurs that they do not deserve. Their humanity—the possibility of moral choice and plausibility of suffering—raises our philanthropy as well, and this is probably a prerequisite for our pity and fear, for the depraved (who are beneath humanity, having neither human ends nor moral choice; *NE* 7.1, 7.5) can raise none of these emotions.[15] Now what emotions does comedy raise?

14. On "like ourselves," see Belfiore, *Pleasures*, 106–7; Golden, *Tragic and Comic*, 80; Else, *Argument*, 78–82, 372, 460–61.

15. Aristotle is not deceived by the fact that a thing looks human into thinking it is so, nor, I suppose, would he consider it illegitimate to react to something naturally unhuman—C3-PO or R2D2, or Prometheus—as a member of the community of *anthrōpos*, for all of these seem to exercise moral choice and to be able to suffer the loss of recognizably good and important elements of their and every "human" happiness. It should be noted here that I disagree with Moles's view that the philanthropic and the pity-arousing must be contradictories ("Philanthropia," 332), a view that seems to make philanthropy exactly equivalent to desire for justice.

We should notice before we go further that the central emotion of tragedy—fear—is, in a way, an unoriginal passion.[16] What we fear in the *Iphigenia*, for example, is that she will, all unknowing, carry out the horrible sacrifice of her brother. Our fear and horror depend upon a deeper passion; perhaps it is the root of our philanthropy itself. Whatever its specific nature may be, clearly that deeper passion is most broadly termed desire. *We desire* that philoi not destroy each other, *and so fear* is aroused when it looks like they may. Similarly, our pity is based upon a desire that the good or not entirely corrupted tragic hero be given (at least) not worse than he deserves (treat every man as he deserves and which of us shall escape whipping?). Love's good is a good. And in Aristotle's warning that the eminently good falling into adversity, or the man in full knowledge attempting to make a philos suffer are each repugnant or polluting, it seems we catch a glimpse of the grounding passion, the passion that underlies all our fear and pity as somehow connected to a love of justice. Plato would perhaps call it an eros for the Good. The child-eating barbarians of the *NE* (7.5) would not, then, be suitable subjects for tragedy (thus always with demons), though they might be agents in someone else's tragedy. We should recall that though philia (as Aristotle outlines in it *NE* 8 and 9) may be grounded in use, pleasure, or virtue, it is only the last form of philia that binds together truly and enduringly; it is this form of philia which is the primary significance of the term, the other two are philia by analogy to it. And this love's good is a justice in action and passion between lover and beloved.

However, even without appealing to that central moral concept, which in its most precise sense can arise only from the rational part,[17] the fact of our physical nature itself is intimately tied up with fear and anger (*DA* 403b16); before we know of anything so spiritual as justice, it is natural in the living being to love its physical being and its fears are the irascible appetite's reactions to threats against that being. Even in plants "the soul's power is to preserve what possesses it (soul) as a thing of a certain kind" for which nourishment is necessary (*DA* 416b17–20), and the addition of perception and locomotion are the *incipit* of desire. Therefore Aquinas summarizes, in

16. If Girard is correct about the mimetic nature of fear and desire, then both are unoriginal in another sense: we become infected with them by mimesis. This sense is available in Aristotle as well, since all things—from the stars and planets to the plants and stones—imitate the Prime Mover: mimesis is the mechanism by which the universe *first* moves.

17. Aristotle thinks that wild animals and young children may have "natural virtues," but virtue in the precise sense needs *nous* (intelligence); see *NE* 1144b3–17.

his *Commentary on De Anima* (book 3, lecture 16, §805), "every movement of the irascible appetite starts from and ends in a movement of the concupiscible appetite. . . . Hence some say that to overcome obstacles is the precise object of the irascible appetite"—for an obstacle is precisely what gets in the way of an already present aim, the already active eros, philia, or desire. If every kind of physical being has a similitude of desire[18] which is most truly its own because it has an end most truly its own (mere life?, perception?, but to sleep and feed?), then that passion (or similitude of passion) will be (as it were) the spine of the creature's soul and in relation to that will it live and move and keep its being (cf. *NE* 1097b33–98a3, 1102a33–b18). Since fear and pity and the other irascible passions are not the deepest passions of embodied souls, we might expect that tragedy is not the highest art for an embodied soul with the power of rational making and thought. If, as I argued in the previous part, tragedy works on and through what Aquinas here calls the irascible appetite, then another art must work on and through the concupiscible. That art is tragedy's antistrophe—comedy. Furthermore, if the irascible starts and ends in the consupiscible, comedy, then, is more basic to our being than tragedy, for each soul's fundamental passion is joy in achievement of its proper end and only by a splitting from (or of) this fundamental psychic principle can any tragic feeling be engendered. Aristophanes gives us an image of this (according to Plato, in *Symposium*). But thinking on this image aims us far past our present question. Let us return and take up in more detail that question to which we have already begun our answer: What emotions does comedy raise or of what passions does it provide a catharsis?

It has seemed to several scholars that there neither can nor should be such a thing as comic catharsis. For example, Elder Olsen argues that comedy,

> has no catharsis, since all the kinds of the comic—the ridiculous and ludicrous, for example—are naturally pleasant. Tragedy exhausts pity and fear by arousing these emotions to their utmost and by providing them with their most perfect objects. . . . Comedy, on the other hand, removes concern by showing it was absurd to think that there was ground for it. . . . We may define comedy as an imitation of valueless action, in language, performed and not narrated, effecting a *katastasis* of concern through the absurd.[19]

18. For we say, when we are learning chemistry, that the hydrogen atoms want to share their electron with oxygen and form water. For further discussion of these similitudes of desire, see *Is Hamlet a Religious Drama?*, chapter 3, the section entitled "Ecstasy?" (92–110).

19. *Theory of Comedy*, 36; cf. 25, 46f. Note that Olsen agrees with our position on comedy with regard to several of its elements, though not in final causality.

Comedy's purpose, then, is to relieve us of concern, leaving us, perhaps, in the state of an Indian sage: Om.[20]

Olsen's definition implies that the comic object be able to arouse some desire, while at the same time "it must not arouse desire or aversion or emotion to such a degree that they cannot easily be extinguished. For it is precisely by the destruction or annihilation of the *ground* of the desire or aversion or emotion that the comic operates" (23; emphasis in Olsen). It must be said in favor of Olsen's view that while this might seem on its face to be a self-contradictory modus operandi, there really is no such problem with the requirements that the comic object arouse an emotion and extinguish or release it. It is fairly well agreed upon that jokes do this,[21] and a similar sort of thing has already been explicated as the process of the best tragic catharsis. There the plot both arouses and releases the tragic emotions, and in *Iphigenia* fear and pity after being raised to their highest pitch are completely extinguished and left behind on the Taurean shore. Lesser tragedies, like *Medea,* leave us with some residual disgust, an incompletely resolved irascibility.

There is a serious problem with his view of comedy, however. Olsen seems to overlook the fact that for Aristotle the pleasant isn't always the good, although the good will always be naturally pleasant. It might, then, be necessary to purify or purge certain pleasures, and so a process of catharsis for pleasant emotions is not prima facie absurd, as he seems to think. In fact, it may be, as the Athenian hints in the first books of *Laws*, that this kind of catharsis is more difficult to achieve, and less considered by all politicians, and therefore more important (for these social and rhetorical reasons) for any political, moral, or aesthetic discussion. Further, it would seem that annihilation of the *ground* of the emotion aroused in a comedy goes too far. It can hardly have been Aristophanes' purpose, in plays like *Acharnians*, *Lysistrata*, or *Peace*, to disable or reduce to nothing the desire for peace (which is the emotional ground for the action of the play), or evaporate the grounds of our hope for the success of Dicaeopolis's or Lysistrata's project; in these matters a success-

20. I would not deny that this is one possible end and purpose of comedy, as the discussion of *As You Like It* (Chapter 3) will explore. A correlative view to Olsen's, but of tragedy's, work is that it dissolves the *principium individuationis* (cf. Nietzsche, *Birth of Tragedy*). Notice that what one says about comedy or tragedy implies a confession—one that is metaphysical and anthropological, if not best labeled religious—for it is a confession about that state of soul or being which it is good for us to be in. It is plausible to hold that one can only know such finalities by faith. Olsen and Neitzche, then, share the same faith about the end of man.

21. For example, see Kant, *KU* 332: "Laughter is an affection arising from a strained expectation being suddenly reduced to nothing."

ful climax is much to be wished for. And, in fact, the plays do not evaporate our hopes, rather, they clarify or purify and strengthen the desires that are the grounds of the action and the hope. Sometimes, in fact, a comedy may raise a passion. I will not speak of Augustine's famous and troubling case of the picture of the god committing yet another adultery (*Confessions* 1.16.26), but recall that the Athenian Stranger suggests in *Laws* that the old sometimes lack eros and need a music that will raise them into it. It is perhaps in our day a rare disease, and the little blue pill promises it henceforth will only be a problem for the poor, but it is common enough in classical comedy that the old stand inflexible before the desires of youth and call wisdom what is cold and passionless. In less youth-oriented and democratic societies (like those of Aristophanes and Shakespeare) such characters must have been both more numerous and more powerful. The music and action of the comic play might raise them from their deficiency—into eros, not out of it.

For example, the music alone of the heroine's meltingly sweet aria "O mio papino caro," from Puccini's *Gianni Schicchi* might make an old man feel the importance and value of the love the daughter both feels and pleads for. It certainly shapes a listener's desires to say "yes" to her request even without knowing Italian, or that it is a request. When the father says "no" after such love songs—especially when he says so passionately (as he usually does)—our feelings are taken from the heights of eros into the depths of his deficiency and we feel it as deficiency, even if we ourselves suffer (or have suffered) from that same lack. The music itself engenders a mimesis of this passional movement, knowledge of Italian is not required.[22] Thus such music "physics the subject, makes old hearts fresh" (*Winter's Tale* 1.1.38–39). As was the case with tragedy, this does not occur via identification with a single character, rather it is through the string of interactions which are the plot and melody that our desiring passions are raised and modified, via (often fantastic) excess and deficiency, in such a way that "the confusions, transformations and disorientations of the *processus turbarum* lead eventually to self-possession and re-formation."[23] Music seems, more than the other art forms,

22. Thomas Pangle makes a similar point (but about fear) in his essay on Plato's *Laws,* bound with his translation: "terror *can* be counteracted and overlaid—by faith in healing gods and by music. In this context the *alogon* (speechless) dimension of music is at least as beneficial as the *logos* that gives content to the songs." This is an admission of the way the body can have "a formative influence on the soul" (Pangle, *Laws*, 479)—precisely what a mechanical or infectious model of mimesis (as Girard's) presumes, but a cognitivist model does not regard.

23. Nevo, *Comic Transformations in Shakespeare*, 218.

to make the one who hears it feel the passion we often say it expresses. In this case we see (or should I say hear?) the daughter's song make the erotically deficient old man rise—perhaps not to the level of her own eros, but at least to the level of being able to allow her to follow it—as we do in the audience. Perhaps a father's refusal *is* wisdom, but the music aims to make sure that it is not from lack of appropriate affect, which the music brings us to, that thought comes to function appropriately. This is all an echo of Plato, who, playing on the double meaning of *nomoi*, claims that all laws (*nomoi*), like kitharic melodies (*nomoi*), need preludes to prepare the hearer to follow them (*Laws* 700b, 722de, 723d).

It should be clear (and become clearer) that the view I am espousing, while it centers on the emotions and not intellectual recognitions, disagrees entirely with those, like K. J. Dover, who think that the purpose of art and literature is "to compensate for the inadequacies of life."[24] So, while *Acharnians* may look like "a fantasy of total selfishness" (Dover, 40), that is not what either we or the ancient Greeks cheer for at the conclusion.[25] Reckford seems more accurate, and what he says of a single scene (the rural Dionysia in *Acharnians*) applies as well to the κῶμος at the play's end, *and* our attendance at the play itself: "*This little celebration is an end in itself*, a rite of Dionysos, an affirmation of life's goodness"[26] and through the action and experience of the play "a better taste is recovered *and* enjoyed" (32, my emphasis) so that "by a kind of prevenient grace inherent in comedy [we are supplied with] the good will, the good hope, and the good perspective on which any specific right decisions in day-to-day politics must finally depend" (11). We are infected by a joy that allows our eros and sympathy a more adequate exercise by having been granted such a well-shaped free run.[27] Our deeper understanding *follows upon* and is made possible by the more joyful perspective comedy *takes us into*: not katastasis, nor yet substitutive fantasy, but cathartic suffering is the purpose of art—a suffering that begins and allows a more perfect joy.

24. K. J. Dover, *Aristophanic Comedy*, 240.

25. Sandbach (*The Comic Theatre of Greece and Rome*) has recourse to a similar Freudian reduction in discussing Aristophanes' plays—"no more than an agreeable fantasy" (35, cf. 34, 37).

26. Kenneth Reckford, *Aristophanes' Old and New Comedy*, 107, my emphasis.

27. We should note that Reckford here is echoing Plato's Athenian Stranger who held that "Each person should spend the greatest and best part of his life in peace. One should live out one's days playing at certain games—sacrificing, singing, dancing" (803d). This will also have a result, but such games are, first of all, an end in themselves. Hence, "There shall be no fewer than 365 festival days" (*Laws* 828b).

Eliciting the same reasoning as Olsen about the pleasant passions, but with a dissimilar replacement, Dana F. Sutton recently suggested that the purpose of comedy is through "pleasure and laughter to achieve a catharsis of . . . pity and fear" (14). Like Olsen, he argues that it is only painful—unpleasant or uncomfortable—emotions that would need a catharsis, and that catharsis "is pre-eminently an entropy-achieving event, and so produces pleasure" (10); no one, he presumes, would find a reduction of pleasure to entropy pleasant. So while Sutton considers comic catharsis a possibility, he makes it essentially indistinguishable from tragic catharsis. What is different about the art forms according to him is that through which catharsis is achieved: ridiculous acts, not fearful ones.

Let us note first that this "entropy-achieving" idea presumes the translation of catharsis as purgation—the physical form of reduction to entropy. Secondly, whatever other uses his theory might offer, it is likely to lead us in ways even less Aristotelian than Olsen's. Aristotle considers it quite possible that a person feel pleasure in the wrong way, about the wrong things, at the wrong time, and to the wrong degree, and he pretty clearly thinks that pleasure, since we have grown up with it from childhood, is what is most likely to lead us astray (cf. *NE* 1109b7–10, 1119b3–15). Speaking entirely from the point of view of my own anecdotal experience, Aristotle seems to be correct about this, and so it is not at all absurd to consider that even pleasant feelings will need a catharsis and that a reduction of certain excessive, inappropriate, or disordered pleasures to entropy *will* be naturally pleasant. It will be pleasant, at least, to all those audience members whose capacity for virtue is not entirely destroyed. Alternatively, in those rare circumstances where a person does not feel sufficient pleasure—as the old may not, being highly constrained by life—comedy must be able to raise them to the mean.

Further, if the final cause of both comedy and tragedy is the same—as Sutton has it—the difference in formal causes will become problematic. It would be very surprising, to say the least, for an Aristotelian to discover that contrary forms could be equally well related to the same function.[28] Finally,

28. Cooper argued against a catharsis of pity and fear being the purpose of comedy on the basis of this point (*Comedy*, 60, see also 42f); his argument is not dealt with by Sutton. Ruth Nevo also overlooks this issue in her discussion of "Comic Remedies" (*Comic Transformations*, 216–27), holding that comedy "removes *these same* fearful emotions through pleasure and laughter" (221, italics original). The failure to recognize the connection between form and function in this matter is the signal weakness of her otherwise fine discussion of comic catharsis and transformation. Everything else in her book argues against comedy working on the fearful emotions, but working instead on desire and sympathy.

this proposed agreement in telos would require a rating of the two forms regarding their variable success at achieving that one telos, as both Plato and Aristotle rate constitutions according to their achievement of the single final end of politics, no matter that they differ in form. Such a rating regarding the two kinds of poetry neither author ever proposes. Quite the contrary, it is clear from what Aristotle has said about these two arts in *Poetics*, that he does not consider comedy and tragedy to be competitors in the same arena, as indeed they were not historically. Comedy and Tragedy are distinct portfolios in the federal government of Mimesis: they have different aims, and these aims require their distinctive constructions and content. It is highly likely that an art form directed to involving the painful and fearful passions will end up badly (as most tragic plots do); so, too, it is highly likely that an art form directed at involving eros and sympathy will end "happily." The usual shape of each art form's plot is due to its telos; it is the telos that is definitive, however, not the shape of the plot. The formal construction of a smiling plot is neither necessarily comic nor necessary for comedy; as Chapter 1 showed, form alone cannot be used to distinguish comedy from tragedy for Aristotle.

Professor Sutton developed his thesis from a well-known epitome on comedy called the *Tractatus Coislinianus*, interpreting a phrase we discussed in Chapter 1 which the tract reiterates—"to achieve a catharsis of such emotions"—as referring to the same emotions as those referred to in the extant definition of tragedy. Such an interpretation of the document is all but impossible, and given the falsity of his extratextual supporting arguments there is no reason to consider his suggestion further, but the *Tractatus* itself has quite a bit to be said for it, as efforts to reconstruct an Aristotelian poetics of comedy from it by Lane Cooper and Richard Janko have shown.

Before we take up their suggestions, however, we should return to the intellectualist interpretation of catharsis as seen from the comic side of dramatic art. In the discussion of tragedy of the previous part, we took up several versions of intellectual catharsis in detail. Leon Golden's arguments on behalf of this interpretation are the most widely accepted ones, and he is the only scholar taking this view who has written extensively on comedy. Golden holds that since mimesis "*necessarily* involves intellectual pleasure" and Aristotle, in *Politics*, identifies "διαγωγή as the highest goal, the end in itself of music, and of art in general," he is clearly implying "that the *katharsis* associated with this essential goal must be intellectual and not purgative."[29] It follows that,

> the action must unfold with intellectual clarity so that the universal insight at which all artistic *mimēsis* aims will be evident. If the beginning, middle and end of an action are persuasively motivated, and if the action unfolds with its requisite clarity, then its salient details will be held in the memory of the audience and the conditions will be present that make possible the experience of learning and inference, which, for Aristotle, is the fundamental goal and pleasure of all *mimēsis* both tragic and comic. (*Tragic and Comic*, 73)

Golden further invokes "the antonymic relationship established by Aristotle at *Rhetoric* 1386b8–12 between the fundamental tragic emotion of pity, a feeling of pain at *undeserved bad fortune*, and indignation, a feeling of pain at *undeserved good fortune*," (95, emphasis in Golden), as the source which explains (a) "the double plot of comedy, with its appropriately and necessarily antithetical destinies for good and bad characters" (94), (b) the fact that the characters must be "ignoble (φαῦλος)," and so rather than like ourselves, "inferior to us" (91), and (c) the kathartic conclusion in which "the comic framework of 'success without merit' comes crashing down to the ground through what Charles Segal has aptly called a 'sudden flash of tragic wisdom.'"[30]

Against this I have argued that Aristotle's explanation of our natural delight in mimesis (*Po.* 4) leads to and is strongly connected with our delight in learning, but that this does not *necessarily* involve intellectual discovery and inference, as delight in mimeses operates in the youngest children, well before Aristotle would consider the higher powers of the soul to be operative.[31] Further, we see in the discussion of music (*Pol.* 8) that catharsis is separated as an effect from διαγωγή (1341b39–41), and while the highest aim of music (and by analogy the other arts) is to allow for διαγωγή (for all the powers of the soul exist for the sake of what is best and highest in the soul), the diagogic and cathartic effects are not the same thing, and their accom-

29. *Tragic and Comic Mimesis*, 37. We should note that besides arguing against emotivism, this phrasing presumes the purgative translation of catharsis.

30. *Tragic and Comic Mimesis*, 97; Golden is quoting Charles Segal, "Aristophanes' Cloud-Chorus," *Arethusa* 2 (1969): 175.

31. See Propylaia, pages 4–7 and Chapter 1 above, pages 19, 34, 43–44. Else also considered Aristotle's use of μανθάνειν in this context in a much more intellectualist way than it need be taken. Against this view, see Halliwell in *Making Sense of Aristotle: Essays in Poetics*.

plishment in any particular case may well depend on the capacity of the soul in question. Most people never achieve a very high level of διαγωγή in music or the other arts. In the mirror image of this argument (with the object rather than the subject being in question), Aristotle rules out use of the aulos in education, saying its proper use is not instruction (μάθησις) but catharsis (*Pol.* 1341a23–24). Clearly, then, Aristotle thinks these effects are distinct. One effect is of the rational part, for mimesis does develop understanding; another effect is of the part that suffers, being a purification or catharsis. One may say with Aristophanes' claim in this chapter's epigram that comedy is teaching or directing in both cases. Later Aristotle claims that *all* get some cathartic benefit from music (1342a7, 15), but it is equally clear that not all achieve the diagogic pleasure Aristotle considers to be the best. Children, animals, and slaves, for example, do not. The relationships between these two ends are involved but clear. Catharsis is the universal end of drama and music; διαγωγή is these arts' highest end.

Consider the political analogy: the aim in politics is to make the citizens happy, which requires both moral and intellectual upbringing; these two purposes are linked—moral virtue is required for intellectual virtue, for example. Aristotle clearly thinks that the first of these ends is available to all who are not morbidly diseased or barbaric; the second—intellectual virtue—seems not to be so universally achievable. In any case it is not necessarily produced when the first one is. The aim of the state is to make the citizens good because this *will allow* them to be happy. That aim requires laws that train all into moral virtue; it does not require everyone to be given a sabbatical to do philosophy (though the morally good—generous—state will support this as well for those who are capable). Similarly with art: there are two linked purposes; one of them is universally attainable; that must be the first and universal aim of art, though it need not be the only aim, or even the highest. The mimetic arts prepare us, and re-create our ability, to participate in a life that exceeds what they themselves create, as the political and moral virtues create the kind of life and state in which the intellectual virtues may be developed and practiced. The universal is, in each case, what must be achieved; the universal end of art is catharsis.

We should be wary of discovering the passions with which comedy concerns itself directly through reading about the opposition of passions in *Rhetoric*, as Golden does. We have already noted (in Chapter 1) that in a rhetorical situation (a situation in which a decision must be rendered or an action taken) fear can drive out pity (1385b33), but that these passions may work together to heighten each other in tragic poetry. Similarly, the opposition of pity and indignation (1386b9) is also clearly the case in a rhetorical situation, but just as clearly not the case in poetry. In *Hecuba* we saw how the disgusting acts and speeches of Odysseus aroused our indignation against his undeserved letting off and that this indignation served to increase our pity for Hecuba, as well as our respect for Polyxena and the concomitant grief at her loss. In the poetic situation this increasing of both fear *and* pity, and the increasing of pity *by rousing* indignation against an antagonist is rather the rule than the exception. We must find a deeper opposition of emotions than the ones Aristotle sets up in rhetorical situations in order to find the opposing emotions at which comedy and tragedy aim. The opposition we are looking for is one in the nature of *the being*, not one limited to or varying with the rhetorical or political *situation* which, in any case, *we are not in* while watching a play—which presents us with an entirely distinct cosmos. The mimetic, as Aristotle said, is natural to man; it is working in and on us in all situations; it originally broke into two forms depending on the character of the maker of the mimesis: the φαῦλος and the more buffoonish turning to comedy.

Turning to the more specific application of his ideas to comedy (a, b, c on page 129 above) and starting with the last, we see that Golden's intellectualist interpretation of catharsis requires an action with "intellectual clarity" leading to a "universal insight" and the pleasure of "learning and inference," but the action of comedy presumably revolves around events of undeserved good fortune or other events that evoke indignation (raised by success without merit) rather than pity. The comic catharsis (c) is apparently the "sudden flash of tragic wisdom" we achieve when we see the "comic framework of success without merit" come crashing down into "antithetical destinies for the good and bad characters."

There are several and considerable difficulties in this attempted elucidation. The elements of the intellectualist's view which are common to his explication of both tragedy and comedy—intellectual clarity of action leading to a universal insight and the pleasure of learning and inference—require that the difference between comedy and tragedy be played out on the question of what the insight involves. Golden answers by claiming that comedy gives us insight about indignation causing events, or about indignation, rather than, as in tragedy, pity or pitiable events. It seems that requiring the action to have intellectual clarity and lead to insight about indignation or indignation-causing events leaves much—even of ancient comedy—out of account. Dicaeopolis gets as indignant with his failed knotty market clerks as he had with the failed ambassadors earlier, and seems not to be indignant with Lamachus; Lamachus gets by far the worse treatment in the action of the play. Further, it is not clear that Dicaeopolis is any more deserving of success than Lamachus, as he makes clear by spending his peace in drunkenness. Indeed Dicaeopolis himself might be a good example of success without merit—he is clearly not a particularly intelligent businessman—as his buying not one, but two starving pigs in a poke bears out—and that's the nonscandalous way of putting his poking. If the comedy actually included (or threatened to include) the scandalous action his language bandies, we would be in another art form, and probably a polluting version of that (since we have a father knowingly selling his daughters into sluttish uses). But the important thing is, Dicaeopolis doesn't have to be intelligent; he has the most important thing—peace; therefore the world is made of gravy. Finally, his world does not come crashing down. Further examples abound: there seems to be little of indignation or indignation-causing events in *Phaedrus*, and I suppose what Orlando learns of it in the forest of Arden can be reduced to "let it go." This is perhaps a good thing to learn, but its a rather long play for such a short lesson, and wouldn't bear much repetition. The comedies of Aristophanes, Plato, and Shakespeare do bear repetition, but with the exception of Plato I am not at all convinced that what we get out of repetition is further inferences regarding universal insights. Rather, in fact, "they work" is shorthand for they work on one's passions; providing in that work less intellectual insight than emotional recreation through an unconstrained exercise. Precisely because their work is on the passions in this way is why and how their repetition is always a "learning" experience.

In addition, comic *action* seems to have a very loose idea of intellectual clarity. Dicaeopolis's knot-clerks may signify the administrative uselessness of Athenian market-clerks, but it is hard to clarify what significance the action of flying to heaven on a dung beetle—as Trygaeus in *Peace*—could have. Perhaps it would be hazardous to attempt such a clarification in a city where people are put to death for saying novel things about the gods, but in any case it is not at all necessary to get clear on any of this for the play to work. As in this case, much of comedy proceeds by impossibility and absurdity, and to attempt to become intellectually clear about such action seems a misplaced effort, if not an impossible or absurd one. No doubt there is a Monty Python skit about a group of professors trying to do just this. Even comic *language* sometimes lacks this modicum of clarity (as in nonsense poems like "Jabberwocky"), and if even the language may lack such intellectual clarity—which might seem a minimal requirement of any art form using language—to require intellectual clarification to be the single and most final end of an art form which includes every other means of mimesis as well as that most intellectual one seems peculiarly restrictive.

Finally, we have to consider the problematic description that "the comic framework" comes crashing down "through a sudden flash of tragic wisdom." I am not sure whether this means that the sudden flash of tragic wisdom belongs to the comic hero who through it brings the play to its conclusion, or to the audience which suddenly grasps the tragically wise point as the play concludes. In *As You Like It*, it is clearly Rosalind's wit and wisdom that brings about the concluding marriage dance—but why this wisdom should be called tragic—or how it brings things crashing down—is beyond me. On the other hand, we might see that drunkenness is better—at least more pleasant—than woundings at the close of *Acharnians*, but this seems to be rather thin beer for wisdom, and not particularly definable as a libation of either the tragic or the comic kind. It is not Dicaeopolis's project that crashes, but Lamachus's. Whatever the Segal-Golden phraseology means, one loses track of what kind of insight it must be at which comedy *distinctively* aims. If it were true (and I am not sure that it is even understandable) that comedy's catharsis is (or results from) a sudden flash of tragic wisdom, it seems, as was the case with Sutton, to make comedy a dependent rather than a correlative art form, with all the problems thereby entailed and already raised to Sutton's view. Aristotle's extant text can only begin to be interpreted this way because of its silence about comedy. This silence may not be taken as an argument for anything, however, certainly not for collapsing comedy's end into tragedy.

There remain two minor quibbles (a, b), and a more far-reaching problem as well. About the quibbles I will be brief. It is true that Aristotle says that the double-issue plot "is more appropriate to comedy" (1453a35–40), but he does not hint that this ending is required for it, as Golden says. In fact, the remainder of Aristotle's phrase seems to suggest an (even better?) single issue for comedy—"where those who are deadliest enemies in the plot, such as Orestes and Aegisthus, exit at the end as friends." This sounds like utter foolishness, but it need not be. Shakespeare achieves such miracles regularly. It is his "problem comedies," like *Measure for Measure*, which have the double ending; that they are called problem comedies is indicative: it is perhaps not the best ending even for comedy to exit in two different directions (as Lamachus and Dicaeopolis). And it is not the best because the catharsis is not as effective as in the single ending (or single ending multiplied by four: *As You Like It*), but is, rather, emotionally problematic. The "problem comedies" are the comic correlate of tragedies with a significant remainder of the disgusting.

Regarding (b), if Golden is correct about the strongly moral qualification of the φαῦλος comic characters—that they distinguish themselves from us by being morally inferior—then it follows that Socrates could never be a comic hero, nor could Rosalind or a legion of others be so either. Many of that more noble legion, admittedly, were invented after Aristotle wrote, but as poetry is more philosophical than history, philosophy is more true than the history of poetry, and if the phaul word can be charitably interpreted in the way I have above—a way which allows both Socrates and Rosalind their status (φαῦλος without being morally lower) as protagonists in a comic action—then it should be so interpreted: it lines Aristotle up with the truth of things. There is no reason to think Aristotle was unaware of how things could or should go just because we have no extant example of things at his time going that way—though Plato is extant, and *Republic* and *Symposium* end as you like it, the main chacter being "lower" only in looks and economic status. To say *Poetics* is prescriptive as well as descriptive might just be to say Aristotle is a scientist about things and predicts, based upon his knowledge of the passions, what the most effective form of the art will be, and so what one should do to achieve those effects—Aristophanes perhaps having not quite achieved it.[32]

More far reaching is the question Golden makes us raise of art taking good and bad fortune as its particular objects—or, more precisely, undeserved bad fortune and undeserved good fortune. Martha Nussbaum has argued at great length and with considerable force that Aristotle, unlike Plato, considers happiness to be bound up with fortune to a quite significant degree.[33] It is this difference, she holds, that allows Aristotle to defend poetry

32. I think Plato's *Symposium* suggests a lack in Aristophanic comedy as well, and will discuss this matter in the Epilogue.

33. From *Fragility* through *Love's Knowledge* and *Therapy of Desire* to *Upheavals of Thought*

against its cultured despiser, and leads her, in agreement with Golden, to rehabilitate literature as philosophically significant. Poetry enlightens us about the fragility of goodness, and denies that virtue is sufficient for happiness.

We defy augury. It is not that I think Plato is right about the arguments against poetry long linked to his name; on the contrary, I do not think he even believes them.[34] It is not that I think literature is philosophically insignificant, or incapable of providing diagogic pleasure to those who are capable of it, for it clearly does that, as does music. It is simply not necessary either to make the moral claim linking happiness to fortune, or to transform artistic work or catharsis into primarily intellectual matters in which we learn about these connections, in order to make the argument in favor of poetry, as Nussbaum does. This is Aristotle's great contribution to the discussion at which Glaucon failed. In fact, an intellectualist view of catharsis is, in a paradoxical way, a "Platonizing" or Stoicising game. Nussbaum's conversion to a latter day Stoicism proves the point. By making the value of art depend upon its intellectual effects and reducing art's influence on the passions or making that of secondary importance (or making the passions themselves into propositional judgments), it links the value of art (or of anything else) to matters intellectual while associating lesser value with the passions or the body, which is the first and final locus of our suffering.

By the emotional or passional, then, I mean not things that are necessarily antirational,[35] but those things that arise out of our inevitable suffering of pleasure and pain, which do not care how we think. From this grows the natural desire for one and avoidance of/fear of the other; these should be called arational, or, as mimesis, prerational, though naturally reason comes to give us much more power to see such things coming. This capability (passion or emotion) is not ours either because of reason or despite it, but because we are finite in both power and knowledge. Because we are "the most mimetic" as well as "animal," these passions can be aroused in us through mimesis as well as by directly suffering pleasure or pain. The contradiction between our power and desire or knowledge which, taken in one direction is comic, taken in another is tragic. Similarly the contradiction between our finite power

two common themes of Nussbaum's work are an anti-Platonic bias and an interpretation of Aristotle as a strong inclusivist regarding happiness (against which see Chapter 4, § 1 below).

34. For argument that he does not believe them, see my "*Ion*: Plato's Defense of Poetry," in *Platonic Errors*.

35. As, for example, W. F. Otto. *Dionysos: Myth and Cult*, Morton Gurewitch, *The Irrational Vision*, and Nietzsche, *The Birth of Tragedy*; against their excesses see Karl Kerenyi, *Dionysus*.

and knowledge and the world taken in one way is comic and in another is tragic. Nussbaum's attempts to avoid the Platonizing effect (the denigration of the emotions as such in favor of reason) of intellectualist interpretations of literature are perhaps more effective than Golden's, but an emotivist interpretation of catharsis avoids the problem entirely and overthrows in one fell swoop the problems foisted on poetics by the Socrates of *Republic*. Plato *shows*, in his construction of that dialogue, exactly *what is going on* that requires the false argument: the young men are all too mimetically moved and passionate: the merest suggestion of courtesans and cakes by one of them leads all to abandon the search for a healthy city; a desire for some detail about the sharing of women leads them to vote unanimously for a sex talk rather than a discussion of forms of constitution. And talk of coed naked wrestling leads to an animal agreement about human coupling. Even persons not ordinarily so erotic (or erotic in that direction) rise up into excited demands. Even so is adolescent reason carried wherever mimetically inspired desire takes it. (Actually, mimesis takes the whole person along, as passions are of the individual; see *DA* 408b27–30). In his art, Plato shows how art works. Art aims at the emotions directly, it is not a third-rate copy of something we know or can know; epistemological questions are not to the point. The traditional interpretation of *Poetics*, as supplying the defense Socrates almost begged Glaucon to give in *Republic* 10—thereby making love speak up in its own defense—is the right way to go. But it is love that must speak, not knowledge. To bring the passions into language is a power only mimesis has. Perhaps, as Mendelssohn said, mimesis (music, to quote him exactly) is more precise than language.[36] Philosophy begins its work thereafter. Mimeses conjure the passions to speak that we may know them; to speak in their own manner, to be known as they really are: as emotions suffered. Such conjuring is not Philosophy's aim—but she requires it. Poetry is her other half. They wish to be united.

We may now turn to a final group of critics who all agree there must be a distinctive and emotional comic catharsis, and move us incrementally closer to the position I have been defending. Northrop Frye, in *The Anatomy of Criticism*, says that comedy "seems to raise . . . the emotions sympathy and ridicule, and cast them out," (177, cf. 43) and such is the catharsis it pro-

36. Actually, I think Mendelssohn's romanticism extreme. By contrast, the Aristotelian position, that art's first (but not highest) aim is catharsis of the passions and that it can do this for all (not just the exacting intellects in the audience) hits the mean.

vides. Being an anatomist, Frye does not much explicate this physiology or attempt to show how these emotions and this catharsis are connected to the various characters in the audience, or to the structures of comedy. However, his own emphasis on the comic theme as "the integration of society" (43) and its preferred mythos, the "drama of the green world" of desire (182–85), seems to militate against ridicule as a primary emotion the comic play aims to act upon or raise up and rather suggests that since "the presiding genius of comedy is Eros" (181), the primary emotion raised and catharsized will be just that.[37] It would be no surprise to Shakespeare if the spirit of comedy would be found to cry out:

> I conjure thee by Rosaline's bright eyes,
> By her high forehead and her scarlet lip,
> By her fine foot, straight leg, and quivering thigh,
> And the demesnes that there adjacent lie,
> That in thy likeness thou appear to us!
>
> (*Romeo and Juliet* 2.1.17–21)

But let that be. As a way of beginning our defense of this erotic position, let us take note of several problems in Frye's idea. First of all, phrasing catharsis as a process of "raising and casting out" makes catharsis a homeopathic purgation of excess. This is Bernays's interpretation of catharsis, and subject to the same problems as his theory about tragic catharsis. Most importantly, it seems to consider the emotion itself a bad thing that must be got rid of. Then, as with tragedy, comedy's offers of such purgation would only be needed by some people, and those not among the best, but rather the excessive. What good such catharsis would do for the moderate or the deficient—or how it would be possible for them—is left out of the account.

37. D. W. Lucas very briefly suggests that "the emotions purged by comedy . . . would be scorn and over-confidence" (287); he then replaces this suggestion with "a more interesting possibility. . . . There is more sexual licence in comedy than in most life. Many societies have allowed occasions when there was a communal kicking over of the traces, like the Roman Saturnalia. . . . No doubt they gave relief to the tensions caused by the restraint, internal and external, on which the society depends. . . . A *katharsis* of the impulses which lead to defiance of convention and contempt of authority would make good sense in the light of modern ideas, and Aristotle might have reserved his full treatment of *katharsis* for the section on comedy because it provided the more important illustration" (288). Certainly eros, from of old called a tyrant, frequently drives such defiance (*Rep.* 573b). Like Frye and Bernays, Lucas seems to make catharsis a purge for excessive passions, but his "more interesting" suggestion does suggest that the erotic passions are at the center of comic poetry and this seems to me to be correct—though I would not be so eager to tread the Freudian road of substitutive satisfaction as he seems to be. The "modern idea" here seems rather childish. It is certainly reductive. Regularly "kicking over the traces" does not seem particularly curative for a tyrannical passion, rather the opposite.

The problem with such medical analogies is that they take up the flavor of their analogate—in this case comedy begins to taste like medicine for people of particularly excessive humours. Perhaps it can be this; but it must be more. For *pathē* (passion) is natural to man. There is a natural goodness in certain runnings of the passions. Such runnings must be pleasant to the virtuous as well as to all who are still capable of it.

We must also (a) raise the question of whether or not ridicule is an emotion, (b) consider whether it or sympathy need to be cast out, and then (c) notice that the two "emotions" Frye suggests as those comedy works upon are not related in the way in which fear and pity are, for sympathy and ridicule seem opposed in many ways in which fear and pity are not. As to the first matter: ridicule is not so much an emotion as an act, and its action may be driven by any of a number of emotions—ranging from hatred to love, from fear to confidence, and including anger, jealousy, envy, pride, and disgust. Ridicule will have a different tone, and be applied to different acts or people in each case. Regarding (b), we saw in the case of the tragic emotions that it is not proper to cast out fear and pity entirely, for the passions themselves are not the problem, and they cannot be got rid of in any case, for they are the moving causes of the animal. Similarly here, sympathy is not something that must be cast out, though it may need to be purified in one of several ways; and ridicule is likewise not, *eo ipso*, a morally bad activity that must be got rid of—nor are all of the desires known to drive it problematic even when they result in ridicule. Like the tragic emotions, sympathy and ridicule both have times and places when they are appropriate.

As to the last point, (c), while in bad tragedies and real life or rhetorical situations fear may be aroused without pity, or drive it out—for the tragedy may be merely horrifying and in real life perceptible danger to ourselves drives out pity—such monstrosities are not the effects at which tragedy aims (*Po.* 1453b8–10). Far more fitting is Frye's description of tragic fictions as those "in which the hero becomes isolated from his society,"[38] for these are the kind of events or threatening events—the destruction of all relations of philia—that rouse pity and fear. If we both fear regarding the tragic action (and characters) and pity them at the loss or threatened loss of their philoi, it seems sensible to think that in comedy we would both desire with, and have sympathy for, those in the comic action. Indeed, this is one of Frye's conclusions: "The final cause is the audience, which is expected by its applause to

38. *Anatomy of Criticism*, 35, cf. 218.

take part in the comic resolution."[39] Perhaps we also have some desire as well as sympathy for the comic heroine, as we might have had some admiration or attraction for the σπουδαῖος tragic hero. But where fear and pity can be seen to work hand in hand and are aroused by the same kinds of action in tragedy, sympathy and ridicule are not generally aroused together, and even if one act may embody both, it is hard to see how in such an act either one could increase the others' power, as increased fear (in a play) increases pity. So while we may well acknowledge Socrates' ridicule of Phaedrus as sympathetic, if increased ridicule increased our sympathy we should, at the end of *Acharnians*, march out with Lamachus rather than dance with Dicaeopolis.

There is, despite these problems, something right about Frye's connection of sympathy and ridicule, as we can see by returning to *Phaedrus*. Clearly Socrates (and Plato) have quite a bit of sympathy for the young, handsome, flighty, and not entirely brainless Phaedrus. They are also sympathetic to Phaedrus's desire for knowledge and verbal skill, which desire leads to and drives the action of the dialogue, as it was the cause of his approach to Lysias earlier in the day. Socrates' sympathy inspires him to give that ridiculous first speech (237a–38c), which both follows upon and continues his ridicule of Phaedrus (234d–37) for being so inspired while repeating Lysias's speech. Phaedrus doesn't get the point of the ridicule, but is carried even further—perhaps going so far later as to grab Socrates as he tries to escape across the stream (242a). The purpose of the ridicule is to cure Phaedrus of his about to be (if not already) misplaced eros, his excessive and fetishistic desire, and by so doing to transform it to a more proper eros, an eros more capable of adequate objects, or perhaps simply more capable.[40] Not the death of eros nor its expulsion, but its catharsis—its purification—is the aim of the Socratic ridicule, and of the Platonic dialogue.[41] It may be that this purification can not be once and for all completed by human art, for there is, according to the wise and sympathetic Diotima, a ladder of eros the top of which is not entirely within our power. This only shows there is all the more reason, and a permanent need, for comic art—to prepare us for the happy conclusion that

39. "The Argument of Comedy," 60.

40. A fine discussion of Phaedrus's erotic failure may be found in Catherine Pickstock's *After Writing*, 3–46.

41. The Eleatic Stranger openly suggests this use of ridicule at *Sophist* 230b–d, and the Platonic Socrates is known to have embarrassed several other interlocutors—Thrasymachus, Anytus, and Alcibiades come to mind. These embarrassments all have distinct flavors (depending on the character of the character's passions), but the same generic purpose: purification of eros. It doesn't work with Callicles; cf. McKim, "Shame and Truth in Plato's *Gorgias*."

can only be given by a different power. All too frequently, like Phaedrus, we imagine our eros has found its perfect term—and so we fall.

Plato clearly has sympathy (and his text builds up sympathy in us) for that beautiful and flighty Phaedrus, a Phaedrus who suffers from a defect that is not allowed to cause him pain or harm in the dialogue, and who, through the course of incidents and speeches in the dialogue, comes to a resolution about his eros that allows us to keep our sympathy for him without fearing that he will be quickly led into painful or harmful abuse by his original defect. Perhaps Plato (or Socrates) also had an eros for the historical Phaedrus, as Lysias did, but if so it is clearly a purified eros, one that aims at Phaedrus's well-running chariot—that is, it aims at Phaedrus running his chariot in the circle of the gods, rather than aiming at a chariot that runs Socrates' way. Let us not speak of ruts. What is right about Frye's connection between sympathy and ridicule, then, is that ridicule is one primary *means* that sympathy uses to bring the horses of eros under control. We might more accurately adapt Frye by saying that in *Phaedrus* eros rouses and purifies eros through an action of sympathy and ridicule.[42] Such a story about comedy has the additional advantage of uniting what history and criticism divide under the rubrics "old" and "new" comedy or "satiric" and "romantic," "Jonsonian" and "Shakespearian," or "renaissance" and "medieval": the aim of the derisive Aristophanes and gentle Shakespeare—as all the others—is the same catharsis through the different means of ridicule or sympathy. It is only after knowing the principle of the whole that we may therafter distinguish the kinds and their methods, as these terms do.

3. COMIC CATHARSIS

The most finely detailed and cogent explications of comic catharsis in the last century, those of Cooper and Janko, are each less and more closely tied to a short document that Janko defends as an accurate extract of

42. "Comedy is designed not to condemn evil, but to ridicule a lack of self-knowledge" (Frye, "Argument," 61). Much of comedy clearly involves just that kind of *action*: ridicule of lack of self-knowledge; the recognition of this lack (its cure) generally leads to the peripety of the play and this is another way in which comedy may be described as "a comic Oedipus situation" (ibid., 58). But the purpose of dramatic *action*, according to Aristotle, is to work on the passions; in this case, the inadequacies of one's *love*, which might well be purified through the re-creation of the wholly adequate eros of the virtuous.

Aristotle's second book of *Poetics*: the *Tractatus Coislinianus.* Let us begin with Cooper. He begins by suggesting "anger and envy might be said to be purged away by comedy."[43] This cure being allopathic, he considers further that these emotions arise from a sense of disproportion and suggests that comedy's aim is to relieve us "of the sense of disproportion—and by a homeopathic means," namely, the exaggeration of disproportion in the comic play (68). Perhaps troubled by the fact that disproportions of justice, of evil, of error and punishment, or of worth and fate are the emotional stuff of tragedy as well—and in the best tragedy, *Iphigenia*, these disproportions are relieved entirely rather than left in place or intensified—he takes up the suggestion of the *Tractatus* that it is "through pleasure and laughter [that comedy achieves] the catharsis of such emotions" (69, 71–76). He considers this phrasing as signifying that beauty (which brings pleasure) and ridicule (which brings laughter) are joined together in comedy to bring the audience to a symmetry, "a due proportion of laughter. . . . The combination of beauty with the lower forms of the ludicrous gives rise to a catharsis differing from the effect of the obscene when unalloyed" (76).

In his review of Cooper's effort, Kendall Smith is largely in agreement about the emotions involved in comedy, though he thinks such plays work to release the pleasurable emotion of superiority.

> Neither "Derision" nor "Ridicule" is an accurate description of the emotion. The emotion is a composite of two kinds of satisfaction, one malicious, the other innocent. Anger and envy enter into the situation as the background of the most comic situations. . . . I know of no two words [other than the *Tractate*'s pleasure and laughter] which Aristotle would more probably have used.[44]

So, according to Smith, while anger and envy and the disproportions that arouse them are somehow "behind" comedy, these irascible passions are worked out through pleasure and laughter, bringing the audience to either a "due proportion" of laughter at disproportion, or to a pleasurable feeling of superiority.

In his reconstruction, Janko represents Aristotle as coming to a similar conclusion as Cooper: comedy has "the beneficial effect of reducing the

43. *An Aristotelian Theory of Comedy*, 67.

44. Smith, 155. Dover agrees with him that one of the elements of greatest importance to Aristophanic comedy is "the fulfillment of a grandiose ambition by a character with whom the average member of the audience can identify himself" (30); this allows the audience to experience the pleasure of superiority substitutively. As Janko notes (*On Comedy*, 145), Bernays considered the balancing of a ludicrous and an innocent delight a likely Aristotelian element in comedy.

human propensity to excessive buffoonery and impropriety."[45] He takes up, but opposes, Smith's emotive result, saying, "in the narrow interpretation, the emotions *to be purged* would be scorn and over-confidence" (143), and approvingly quotes Lucas's statement that "as the unstable man might be helped by tragedy to maintain his composure in time of trouble, so comedy might help him maintain his dignity and refrain from contempt in prosperity."[46] So comedy controls by mocking—or it purges—the emotion of superiority, rather than allowing us its simple pleasurable release.[47]

There is much to consider in these suggestions, and much of it touches what is true. As Cooper points out, the modern judgment against the seeming obscenity of Aristophanic comedy, while perhaps partly due to the Puritan strand of our heritage, is more likely the result of not being able to translate the beauty of Aristophanes' lyrics or being unwilling to stage the play as beautifully as the plot seems to require (71–73). This leaves us a half of the comedy that is considerably less than the half, and so less fully comic. For without the beauty, eros may be mocked as excessive or badly directed, but it has nothing to come home to, and soon it no longer plays. To mock an excessive eros that is unbelievable as eros touches us at no point. There must be something in the impossible or frivolous action that calls up our eros, or we have mere farce. We might consider the balance between the ludicrous and the beautiful in the play as what allows an artist to avoid the crass obscenity that shouts at one end and the romanticizing pornography that lies undressed at the other end of a merely materialist and utilitarian spectrum. A combination of character traits labeled excessive and deficient by the *NE* cause various members of a society to misdraw these lines: the self-indulgent,

45. R. Janko, *On Comedy*, 96.

46. D. W. Lucas, 288, quoted in Janko, *On Comedy*, 143.

47. Though he argues that this is a flaw in poetry, Stanley Rosen suggests something similar in his remarks on Aristophanes: "[A]lthough sexuality is in principle the domain of human preservation and contentment, it must not be allowed to follow its natural bent toward hybris. . . . Aristophanes must therefore find a way either to restrict Eros through the body or to turn Eros against itself. If I am not mistaken, this need accounts for Aristophanic obscenity (and perhaps for that of later moralists like Rabelais and Swift as well)" (*Sym.* 125). See also Reckford, who says of the comic shenanigans "if our educated and civilized laughter includes a happy sense of superiority to human folly in its various manifestations, it is at the same time our own potential folly that we laugh at and, *in laughing, decisively reject*" (371; my italics). This strikes me as the right evaluation of the comic poet's project. What we are laughing at is not our potential to act that way (e.g., feeding shitcakes to a dung beetle), but our potential to be driven by the same excessive, deficient, or crooked desires that lead to feeding the dung beetle or following an ever enlarging phallus to negotiations with Lysistrata. These passions are called into play by the play, and the passions make all men equal. Reckford, too, compares Aristophanes' method with the passions to that of Rabelais (*Aristophanes*, 383–87).

soft, and prodigal will tend in the latter direction—romanticism—while the irascible and buffoonish tend in the other; the examples are well-known in every society and time, there is no need to name names. According to Aristotle, art too must hit a mean; it is not the shock troop of a culture—decadent or imperialist—nor is it the easy pleasure of a lower class hetaira.

I agree, then, that the combination of a derisive and an innocent delight seems to be accurate about much of the action *that goes on within* the comic play. We have already noted Socrates' mockery of Phaedrus, which seems itself to partake of both; there is also the somewhat more pointed ridicule of Lysias, and the whole is certainly shot through with beauties of no ordinary poetic language or fancy. In *As You Like It* we see Rosalind mock the romantic fantasies of Phebe, the shepherdess who loves her, and less bitingly, her own Orlando, while Touchstone (a name Aristophanes would wish to have invented) reduces love entirely to its animal impetus, and Jacques mocks the entire circle as fools. All these various forms and degrees of mockery, however, subsist within the green world of Arden, a world of song, pleasant picnicking, miraculous escapes, and love at first sight for Oliver and Celia among others. It need not be added that the language that creates the whole cosmos is of unsurpassed beauty. Cooper's defense of Aristophanes speaks similarly for the ancient version of the art.

For as accurate as the view of the *Tractatus*, thus explicated, is about what happens within the play itself (καθ' αὑτό), I am not convinced that the Cooper-Smith-Janko explication has the correct analysis of the play's relation to the audience (πρὸς τὰ θέατρα). This latter is the category in which catharsis belongs and to it we must turn to find the art's final cause. It does, on the other hand, seem the *Tractatus* may be more accurate than Cooper et al. give it credit for when it says that "laughter is the mother" of comedy (or of the comic catharsis) as painful feelings are the "mother" of tragedy (or the tragic catharsis).[48] The mother is, in Aristotle's biology, the incubator and supplier of the matter for the developing being, while the course of development and the end result are dictated by the activity of the form—the ensouled homunculus—introduced by the father. In Chapter 1 I argued that tragedy works on the painful feelings—pity, fear, anger, and the like (all of

48. See Janko's text and translation, *On Comedy*, 22, 23; cf. Cooper, *Comedy*, 228. Janko dislikes this pair of "mothering" phrases, citing Bernays, who called it "a tasteless metaphor and the opposite of Aristotelian teaching" and Guthrie, who notes Aristotle's use of "imperfect" analogies (Janko, 137), considering it "vague and unsatisfactory" (138, cf. 160f). Cooper says it seems "very un-Aristotelian" (12).

which are defined by Aristotle as first of all "feelings of pain")—it works on them through the plot, "the soul of tragedy" and it makes sense that tragedy brings to birth somewhat different children—different individual catharses—depending on the differences of plot, though in all cases the plot, as *psuchē* and *archē*, shapes, in a fathering way, painful feelings. In our attending to the play, the plot develops and leads us through these painful feelings, and what is brought to birth is a particularly shaped catharsis of such feelings in the audience: our own passions (painful in tragedy, pleasant in comedy) are the mother, the poem (particularly through its movement—the plot) gives them form and moving. Our passions are shaped by the *psuchē* of plot (or in music the connection of tones and rhythms). As in Aristotle's biology, the ordering principle, or the fathering *psuchē*, is introduced directly into the mothering being: our passions. Because the fathers are different, the *Oedipus* provides a somewhat different catharsis from the *Iphigenia* (which latter Aristotle considers the better child), though since the children have the same mother (our painful feelings) and fathers who are quite similar (being plots of serious matters threatening a suffering treated seriously), they are obviously siblings. In one sense (καθ' αὑτό), then, the child is the play: in which serious matters of painful suffering are arranged according to the necessities and probabilities of a particular plot (as *archē*); and in another sense (πρὸς τὰ θέατρα) the child is the catharsis born *of* the painful feelings drawn out by the serious actions of the plot (as *psuchē*) together with the diction, thought, rhythms, and spectacle. In both cases, painful feelings are the mother. The metaphor is excellent and very Aristotelian.

If the distinction between the "mothers" of the arts according to the *Tractatus*—laughter or painful feelings—provides an appropriately Aristotelian clue to distinguish comedy from tragedy, we should recall further the way Aristotle talks about the virtues. Virtue is a characteristic that hits the mean with regard to feelings and actions (περὶ πάθη καὶ πράξεις; *NE* 1106b24). When Aristotle begins his analysis of particular virtues, both in the brief description (NE 2.7) and in the more extensive version (3.6–4.9), he first of all speaks of courage—the mean with regard to feelings of fear and confidence in facing danger. Second, he considers σωφροσύνη, the virtue that hits the mean with regard to desire for pleasure (concerned in a lesser degree and in a different way with pains; 1117b25–27). He considers these virtues first "for these appear to be the virtues of the irrational parts (τῶν ἀλόγων μέρων) of the soul" (1117b24–25). If our discussion of the prerational or arational anthropological fundamentality of mimesis in Chapter 1 and the Propylaia has been convincing, then it is these two virtues, the passions and feelings with which they are concerned, that will be most influenced by mimesis, and the ones which the early use of music and other mimetic arts (as well as simply the way the neighborhood acts) will be most able to effect before reason begins its work.[49] Appropriate fear and appropriate desire for pleasure are exactly the emotions Plato aims at through his criticisms of art in raising the children of *Republic*. Similarly, in *Laws*, the Athenian Stranger makes clear that the laws need to bring up children into the appropriate feelings and actions not only regarding fears and pains, but also against desires and pleasure. Mimesis is that through which we first are affected by and "learn" these things—for melodies charm both children and Bacchic revelers, and the rocking of infants, "brought from without, overpowers the fear and mad emotion within, and having overpowered it, makes a calm stillness appear in the soul" (*Laws* 790de). Again we note the mechanical metaphor underlying mimetic work, the clear nonnecessity of *logos* or judgment. Plato expects that if they are fine "the young, dwelling as it were in a healthy place, will be benefitted by everything . . . [which] without their awareness will lead them" to love of the beautiful (*Rep.* 410cd). Though he is not quite so poetic, Aristotle's remarks about the educative effect of music which "accustoms human beings to be able to rejoice rightly" at *Politics* 1339a24–25 clearly agree in this general view, if not in the specific laws proposed by *Republic*.[50]

As pain and pleasure are what move the animal, the fear of pain and desire of pleasure are natural; what culture can shape to a large extent is their strength, their degree of influence, and their objects—even before judgment, "without their awareness," the work "τῶν ἀλόγων μέρων." The purpose of Plato's upbringing amid appropriate objects (mimesis being natural) is what Aristotle says is *also* true of the man who has a rational principle: to do and desire the right thing, at the right time, in the right way . . . which is what principle (*logos*) ordains (*NE* 1119b15–19). What works *on* the irrational part of the soul, however, is not rational principle—which requires an already habituated and reflective agent—but mimesis.[51]

49. The mimetic continues to work directly on this irrational—or perhaps better, arational—part of the soul after reason and judgment begin their work as well. We can be taken up by the mimetic arts (as Bacchic revelers) or the mimetic infection of a crowd, even much later in life.

50. At *NE* 1104b12–14 Aristotle also explicitly notes his agreement with Plato.

51. On mimesis as the way we become ready for the principled actions of the ethical, see Fossheim, "Mimesis and Aristotle's Ethics," in *Making Sense of Aristotle: Essays in Poetics*.

With this in mind, let us return to comedy's relation to the audience. A critic might have complained that the *Tractate*'s idea of catharsis suffers both from the error of calling laughter and pleasure emotions, as well as the flaw of choosing "emotions" that are not related to each other in the fashion that the emotions of tragedy are.[52] Janko agrees that Smith's specification of the *Tractate*'s terms as referring to "malicious fun or ridicule" and "innocent mirth and delight" is both accurate and a philologically adequate translation and description of the pleasures comedy brings about. We have also seen that these two opposing pleasures are a large part of the action, *melis* and diction, as well as spectacle, of comedy. What remains to be pointed out is (i) why these particular pleasures are pleasures, (ii) what it means to catharsize them, and (iii) why this catharsis is a good thing.

Let us first recall the tragic cathartic process we have argued for. The pleasure peculiar to tragedy was not due to suffering fear and pity per se, but came through the catharsis of such passions. Catharsis is the process of leading us through extremities of painful emotions plausibly linked, shaping us into or allowing us access to the passions of the virtuous in such situations. On the other side, in comedy it seems we may very well enjoy the malicious and the innocent fun, but still it is the catharsis of these "sufferings"[53] at which the comedy aims. So the emotions or sufferings of which the play is a mimesis (those *in* the play) are a combination of the malicious and innocent pleasures, but the catharsis is of what those "sufferings" raise in us. The distinction between the play καθ' αὑτό and the play πρὸς τὰ θέατρα (1449a7–8) must be kept clear here as elsewhere. What the fearful and pitiable things suffered in the tragic play raise in us are fear and pity as well as other painful emotions. What the malicious fun and innocent mirth of comedy raise and lower in us is not so much malice and pleasure, but desire (eros and philia) and sympathy. Unlike the old iambic poets Aristotle criticizes in *Poetics* 4 (1148b33–49a6), real comedy is not mere invective, nor a dramatization thereof; though even to enjoy this we must have some desire for a good whose enemy is ridiculed in the invective. Comedy's real form is glimpsed in the *Margites*, and is aiming at something else than mere mockery or malicious pleasure. Clearly malicious iambization and innocent lyric

52. These problems are taken up in philologically exact terms by Janko, *On Comedy*, 156–60.

53. The *pathēmata* or *pathē* of comedy may be understood either as the stuff that happens in, or the stuff that happens to us in watching, a comedy. In this latter sense, laughter could be something we suffer, as the characters suffer ridicule (cf. Janko, *On Comedy*, 156f).

are an insufficient actualization of the form, although, just as clearly, Aristotle thinks such are the seeds with which comedy began, and these elements clearly play a continuing part in much comic drama. Comedy's mother is laughter (pleasures innocent and malicious), but what it seeks to bring to birth is a catharsis.

How do, and of what passions is it that, the *activities* of malicious and innocent pleasure—of which comedy is the mimesis—raise (and lower) and, through doing so, provide a catharsis? Smith considered that "the peculiar function of comedy is to make us laugh at follies and vices" (155). The intensification of the natural antagonism between moral opposites like "pacifist vs. bellicose (*Acharnians*), miser vs. spendthrift (*Clouds*)" will "both in the spectators and in the actors of the drama . . . give relish to the comedy . . . [and] demolish the superiority of those we envy, and establish in ourselves a sense of superiority over those with whom we are angry" (155). But this is not exact enough: Dicaeopolis is hardly a pacifist and vice is always excessive or deficient (so foolish) though not laughable (because causing harm). Smith's view is also not quite sufficient, for sometimes our envy or anger are misdirected, and the wish to feel superior is not always to be fulfilled, nor should we wish it to be fulfilled. Innocent laughter, if we can believe in such a thing in these dark days, must arise from a naturally good desire on its holiday. Malicious laughter—for example, at the beating of Lamachus—arises from a sympathy for the opposing power, by which I mean the power opposite to the character rousing the malicious laughter. The mean is opposed to both extremes. So, for example, we laugh at the beating of Lamachus because of our sympathy for the cause of peace (or wine, women, song, and garlic), opposed to which and in which contrary's service he is beaten (the war that denies these goods to all—except the absent ambassadors). We also laugh at Dicaeopolis, who spells peace as phallic celebration. What that malicious laughter demolishes, then, is not the superiority of a person (the much honored Lamachus), but *the rule of a set of passions*, a binding and self-blinded love for war and honor. It is the superiority of these passions as rulers in our lives that is mocked, and over which we enjoy a proleptic (for the less than virtuous) or ideal and uninhibited (for the virtuous) victory. The passions themselves are not thereby demolished; they can't be, and should not be. So comedy and carneval set up lords of misrule to let us feel and see the foolishness of the regime of the many-headed beast (*Rep.* 588b–89b)—which frequently, in a democracy, is precisely the regime we live under. (And those with democratic souls live under it all the time.) In less democratic regimes the head of passion might be more singular. To laugh at the beast is to begin and proleptically celebrate the victory of the revolution in the soul. So, in Athens, it happened that one of the casualties of war was comedy, outlawed from 440 to 437 B.C. A tyrant Eros does not suffer mockery; only tragedy may approach him.

Virtue is what is naturally pleasant, as Smith's "laughter at vice" indicates without saying; the problem is that most of us miss the mark, both in theory and in practice. And, as with tragedy and its emotions, life frequently stands in the way of even the most perfect soul's desires and sympathies. A constant state of war, for example, might do much to inhibit or slacken "the education which consists in correctly trained pleasures and pains"—it would certainly inhibit their perfect enjoyment.

> Taking pity on this suffering that is natural to the human race, the gods have ordained the change of holidays. . . . They have given as fellow celebrants the Muses, with their leader Apollo, and Dionysus in order that these divinities might set humans right again. (*Laws* 653cd)

So, as was the case with tragedy and its catharsis for the good, comedy too will allow a run of the desiring passions that is unimpeded by the limitations of the quotidian and so be a purification also for the good.

The comic intensification of opposition between vices is pleasant to us and can only be pleasant to all *because* it makes that good we all naturally desire appear more clearly and obviously—many times precisely by not appearing. *Acharnians* raises our desire for the good thing—a peaceful political situation—by placing before us the bellicose Lamachus and the war-disgusted but foolish (indeed, impossible) Dicaeopolis, whose idea of a good life amounts to eating, drinking, and wenching. Those members of the audience who may have been made "insensitive" to desire by the war (*NE* 1119a5–7) will find, in Dicaeopolis's enjoyment of the country Dionysia, their desires for such familiar and familial pleasures both aroused and mimetically satisfied. The limitations on desire dictated by the war are abandoned in the theater. At the same time, those who have exceeded in love for honor—finding it at the stake in every bag of charcoal—or for total victory at any cost find their particular eros embodied in characters who fail ridiculously, and are mocked by an action that desires past them into a rejoicing *kōmos*. The excessive and deficient, too, enjoy their catharsis.

What is missing between the extremely drawn characters of Aristophanes—and what was missing in Athens at the time of the play's presentation—speaks to our desire. In fact, what is missing elicits a desire of a particular shape.[54] This is why comedy's pleasure—in answer to (i) above (pp. 146)—can be called true. Comedy is the truing of desire and sympathy.[55] The worthwhile work of comic mimesis calls forth their true running: as the love of a real peace is aroused and given its run under the impossible and ludicrous Dicaeopolis. Aristophanes points out this true love by giving the ridiculous leader of the comedy the name of the truest peace: Just City. Under the cover of this motley clothing desire is given its proper object (which is not enacted in the play). That Dicaeopolis is the just city is itself a piece of comedy—since he abrogates polity entirely from the beginning of the play, where he begins to negotiate for his private peace. Nonetheless, through the play we are moved to enjoy some part of a real peace's pleasures. Not the least of these is that for two hours we are not worried about anything except the success of his nonsense. This truing of desire gives anger, envy and superiority—the passions involved in Smith's and Cooper's "malicious laughter"—their proper orientation in the soul, for the irascible passions find their end in the concupiscible good. This truing of desire under the aegis of laughter means the laughter is not merely an excused release on a straw man. That is to say, comedy's central purpose is not a substitutive satisfaction for the malice society does not allow. About such substitutive satisfactions Plato is undoubtedly right against Freud: such practices will corrupt even the better sort of men (*Rep.* 605c). Pornography is said to function as a substitutive satisfaction; art certainly does not. Comedy is more a release *from* malicious desire and a breaking away from luxury through mockery of it which at the same time attaches us to a desire that is more proper than it is a release *of* malicious pleasure upon an imaginary object. This, at least, is far the better way, though in a low mimetic age it is, perhaps, not often practiced. Our malicious laughter disconnects us from the passion involving the figure or events that raise it. At the same time, our innocent pleasure is al-

54. Freud is comical because he takes such language as this (desire of a particular shape) literally. Plato uses this poetic technique, carving out an empty space for the right response to fill, in an intellectual way when he constructs *Ion* and *Meno*; see the relevant chapters in my *Platonic Errors*.

55. As one of my critics finds this phrasing a pretentious neologism, I should perhaps say I chose it because it embodies the kind of mechanical metaphor—as in truing a wheel or an arrow—that I think is at the root of mimesis. Truing in a first, descriptive sense means running in accord with the neighborhood, but it aims at the prescriptive purpose both Aristotle and Plato indicate for the mimetic arts and the polis. Any culture's truing may be a warping that disables one for virtue. It also fits with Aristotle's own metaphor of the changing size of the soul's passional wheels in *De Motu* 701b, which is what makes the animal turn one way rather than another.

lowed a greater freedom and passional completion than life generally offers, particularly in time of war.

For example, consider again *Acharnians*, where, despite his ridiculous activities, Dicaeoplis makes some sound remarks against the Acharnian charcoal-lovers when he "dares to speak before the Athenian people / About the city in a comic play" (497–501, *Plays* 29). It is relatively early in the Peloponnesian War and likely that the audience contains a large number of men made after the mold Aristophanes' Aeschylus prides himself on in *Frogs* twenty years later, a year before the fall of Athens:

> But many another, like masterful Lamachus
> learned what Homer imparted;
> And his was the matrix from which I have molded
> the forms of my own lion-hearted
> Patroclus and Teucer, whose valor I trusted,
> would arouse Athenian yeomen
> To rival their deeds at the sound of the trumpet
> and vanquish the finest of foemen.
>
> (*Frogs* 1039–42, *Plays* 402)

But the fight is no longer with the Persian Aeschylus had battled and, early in *Acharnians*, the audience's excessive desire for fame and martial glory is already somewhat diminished by presenting the political powers working at war as foolish, vain, and money-loving, while the desire for the simpler pleasures of peace are mimetically rekindled and enjoyed by the open-heartedly good pleasure of a family celebration of the rural Dionysia, which the Acharnians interrupt. The less appropriate desires are mocked, the more proper attachments have already begun to be made and strengthened even while Dicaeopolis is being robbed of his garlic. It is because the extreme desires of the audience (whether excessive for glory or Spartanly diminished for simple pleasures disallowed by the exigencies of war) have been exhibited as empty on the one hand or developed into a festival by our hero's open desire, practice, and enjoyment on the other that Dicaeopolis can dare to say "that in many ways the Spartans at our hands have suffered wrong" (*Acharnians* 314, *Plays* 24) and suggest that the Spartan offer of peace should be accepted so long as they don't ask Athens to give up the home of their poet (*Acharnians* 652–54, *Plays* 34).

The poet is, in his play, granting us—for the length of the play—exactly the private peace his hero enjoys, with its already felt joys and vision of unconstrained continuance. Desire's freedom from the constraint of the war for two hours is passion's real participation in that which is most to be wished for: the peace of a just city. Were we still in a mood funded by malice such midplay words would be dangerous. But we are in a different world from the ordinary one, and our passions are being moved in accord with that world. It is because the passions of martial excess and erotic deficiency are undergoing their catharsis, it is because the reborn desire has disarmed the twists of malice, that reason can sit at an even enough keel for Aristophanes to get away with such remarks. The truing of our passions which is catharsis—and is the answer to (ii) above—is *feeling's arousal to the good*, and release from the sticking points ordinarily inhibiting that, both in the external world (for all) and in our own excesses and deficiencies (for the less than virtuous). The cathartic process the play takes us through begins, allows, and makes us more ardently aim to achieve the good in life. Feeling's manner of arousal to the good is by *mimetically participating* in the innocent pleasures and laughing at the mockery of what embodies opposing desires. We mimetically enjoy the passions of the rural Dionysia; we suffer real laughter at the hubris of the imaginary general, real pleasure at the imaginary party. In raising or ridiculing such desires, the play also raises our sympathy for the characters in the action: for Dicaeopolis because there is something right about both his desire and his ridicule, for Lamachus because there is something right about his actions—he takes life (albeit life in a comedy) more seriously than his counterpart. It is not so much that comedy *represents* the passions as it *draws them out* to the extreme objects—constituting those objects—and it constitutes them at such extremes that we laugh at them. The comic hero comes in walking crooked, but we like to see the thieves, lawyers, and city administrators (I repeat myself) he aims at ridiculed *because of their excessive or deficient desires*—which are in fact exhibited on meeting them (I speak of the play). On the one hand, the hero's antagonist is overblown and suffers, but, on the other hand, he has a name we honor in life; between the overblown and the name of honor the more proper passion finds its path. It is not a matter of the persons represented (farmers or clerks) and the position of *our own* superiority regarding them that must be affirmed; rather, comic catharsis charms forth the superiority of the naturally better passions to which we find our way through comic exaggeration of the opposites at which we laugh.

Smith is right that comedy makes us laugh at folly and vice, but we laugh *because* while attending it we can feel and see more clearly and correctly how foolish or vicious the actions, characters, language, and so on are. Comedy's aim is to purify our desire and sympathy, which it does by raising it rightly between the legs of folly and excessive desire. In Shakespeare, unlike in Aristophanes, the node of truth becomes visible in the play (and so the feelings of the characters come to a resolution as the feelings of the audience come to their catharsis) when Hymen drops in on four weddings at the close of *As You Like It*. Far from leaving the audience with a feeling of superiority over others, both Aristophanes and Shakespeare leave the audience with a feeling of united hope for and desire of the real good, a good not arrived at by political backstabbing and compromise, humourous bodily secretions, stupidity, folly, laziness, or the momentary fluctations of fashionable whim and demogogic popularity. The comic catharsis makes these real but harmful and ignoble motives dissolve in the laughter that sets us free from subjection to them. Laughing at such things as comedy presents is an outward sign of that inward grace of passion's loving recognition of the good that is absent or incomplete within many of this muse's plays. Mockery of extemes does not lead to a catastasis or entropy of desire, but to the chaff-free grain of the good, which is what must be growing for us to laugh at both sides. The ability to laugh with and at the crooked comic hero is tied up with a recognition of that part of the straightforward good he aims at—and the part that he avoids. Comedy depends as much upon a sustaining of difference from, as an identification with, the hero.

That Aristotle would consider such a catharsis both pleasant and good (problem iii, page 146), and the occupation of providing such to the state both noble and beneficial, now goes without saying. It should be quite clear that it is a liturgical act. First of all it is liturgical in the original Greek sense of a state service paid for by an individual—in this case the poet, who spends his time and effort in making it (though perhaps not paying the chorus). Comedy also approaches the liturgical in our more common religious meaning, in which connection we should remember Plato's remark about our need for constant recreation with the gods (*Laws* 653d) and also that one of the original uses of the word *catharsis* in Greek refers to religious purifications. The festivals of which comedy was a signal part are not accidentally religious. I conclude that it is far more in keeping with the pattern of relations set up in Aristotle's definition of tragedy and his teaching about the passions to say that comedy is an imitation of a small (or ridiculous) action (maliciously) laughable and (innocently) pleasant; in language with pleasurable accessories; dramatizing, not narrating incidents *arousing desire and sympathy*; through which it accomplishes a catharsis of such emotions. Perhaps this is even how the original source, of which the *Tractatus Coislinianus* is considered a (somewhat botched) epitome, ran. As the art's educational use is "to draw the soul of the child at play toward an erotic attachment to what he must do when he becomes a man" (*Laws* 643d), so its cathartic effect is to revivfy and correct through pleasure those erotic attachments.

There are more detailed reasons to consider desire and sympathy the emotions comedy aims at and, although I think his view of comedy's final cause is false, what Janko's suggested reconstruction hints at is important as a starting point. What "through pleasure and laughter achieving the purgation of like emotions" (*On Comedy*, 93, 156–60) approaches is the idea that as tragedy aims at a catharsis of the painful and the irascible passions, comedy aims at the purification of pleasure and the concupiscible passions. Aristotle's theory of the arts, then, can again be seen as having important links to the ethical life of the individual (both as a youth and as an adult) and to the social life of the polis, for it is the passions—and first of all fear and desire—that cause both the binding and the loosing of the social realm—and the beginning and end of states and families.

This passional application of comedy and her sister, tragedy, ties in with a number of important elements of Aristotle's philosophy elsewhere. For example, we have already pointed out that *Nicomachean Ethics* discusses first courage (which deals with facing pain) and then self-control (which deals with the desire for pleasure) as the passions of the specifically appetitive part of the soul. The appetitive part, while it can be *trained* up by reason, seems not as *educable* to reason's directions as those emotions and actions that have to do with giving and taking of money, social interaction, honor seeking, and so on. Aristotle, at any rate, suggests the virtues having to do with fear of death and desire for bodily pleasure are structurally distinct from the virtues having to do with other desires in that the former two are more completely virtues of the irrational part than the latter (see *NE* 1117b22f). It makes sense to consider, then, that the virtues which have to do with fear (φόβος) and desire (ἐπιθυμία), more than any other virtues, must be learned and purified by mimesis rather than through more rational and diagogic iconic representation. The more intellectual type of teaching and learning seem less the object of the mimetic arts precisely because the passions raised are the most closely tied to natural animal and physiological reaction: pleasure and pain, desire and fear. One does not have to have an opinion, belief, or knowledge to suffer pain or pleasure, one only needs to have a belly button. Clearly wit and generosity as well as those other virtues discussed later in *NE* than courage and self-control do require the use of intellectual processes; they might be, then, somewhat less susceptible to mimesis, or the form of mimesis required to work on them might be more easily connected to *logos*.

We should also recall that the character easiest to bring to real courage is the one who *doesn't think*, but responds spiritedly: he has the right passional response (which can apparently be achieved without thought) and "needs only that choice and purpose be added" (*NE* 1117a4); this person is, however, more like the beast who fights not out of courage, but because he is in pain (1116b30–37). As that through which we first learn, mimesis is clearly able to bring us to these right responses (or the wrong ones). Aristotle clearly thinks it is much easier to add deliberate thought to rightly oriented passions than it is for thought to change the habitual orientation of fear or desire by law (*nomos*) or reason (*logos*).[56] And since some mimeses are even effective in animals, and are explicitly advised for ethical education of the young, it is clearly through mimesis that the "learning" of such habitual orientations (whether for vice or virtue) begins, or their re-creation is enabled. Plato makes the same point: music is the "antistrophe to gymnastic, . . . [which] educates through habits, transmitting by harmony a certain harmoniousness, not knowledge, . . . and connected with it were certain other habits, akin to these, conveyed by speeches" (*Rep.* 522a). Since learning by mimesis is thought by Aristotle to be one of the natural root causes of poetry, we may reaffirm that the mimetic arts are necessary for man to become human. So then, art's aim is through mimesis to lead to a purification of our painful feelings of fear, anger, pity, and so on in tragedy, and of the pleasant feelings of desire, sympathy, and the like in comedy. Both arts reach all the way down into our animal nature, which may not remain merely animal.

Further, we can see how what Aristotle says about music in the last book of the *Politics* fits with what I conjecture he said, but which we have lost, about comedy. For while music has as its purposes relaxation, catharsis/moral

56. Nussbaum thinks that because Aristotle says the passions are educable by reason he might be able to go along with her idea that the emotions just are judgments or beliefs. See her Gifford lectures (*Upheavals of Thought*). She does not pay attention there to the fact that Aristotle distinguishes courage and temperance from all the other virtues precisely in their being "of the irrational part."

improvement, and intellectual pleasure, comedy too provides all three ends. The comic dialogue *Phaedrus* is a good example. Phaedrus himself *illustrates* the point: he walks out to have a trivial conversation with Socrates, is carried away and laughs at various points (relaxation), participates in or affirms the ridicule of Lysias, whom his passions had identified as their proper object earlier in the day, is (finally) released by the last of Socrates' stories from confusing his excitement with merely sexual attraction (this marks the completion of his catharsis), and perhaps begins to have an inkling of why that passional mistake was plausible (a moral improvement, linked with rational investigation and clarification); at any rate he certainly *feels* different about Lysias's desirability (also a moral improvement). He is, in addition, left with a more intellectual problem about the paper that he has brought with him: does writing help or disable the mind?—an interesting puzzle with which the reader of Plato's dialogue is also left, but which, if he has read carefully, he has begun to answer, having been educated through both the mimesis and logos of the dialogue to a point beyond that attained by any figure within the dialogue; thus the reader attains what Phaedrus now has an inkling of: *intellectual pleasure* at coming to know the truth.

We, too, have, in fact, been taking part in that peculiar pleasure since we began reading the dialogue: even when it seems unclear, the dialogue involves us in that pleasure. The dialogue has provoked us into its peculiar activity—philosophizing—and has built up our pleasure in, and by doing so, our love for, that activity. The three interacting effects Aristotle mentions for music are clearly accomplished in the comic dialogue upon Phaedrus *through Socrates' poetry*. But they are accomplished by the dialogue upon the reader, too, *through Plato's poetry*. For between the ridiculous Socrates and the excessive Phaedrus readers laugh as well. That laughter at the ridiculous or excessive can only be the mark of feeling's recognition of, and love for, the more medial way. Students will always be erotically attracted to good teachers, but that this attraction can be answered by a sexual relation ought to strike us as funny. When it happens between Phaedrus and Socrates it is hilarious. That it does not appear so to us in the real situation perhaps tells us something about our desire and what we prefer to treat seriously, about where our eros is excessive and where it is deficient. But laughing at Phaedrus' excessive and flighty eros is already laughing at our own, and this laughter is what allows us to begin to feel our own excess as excess, for passions never feel so to themselves. In addition, the sheer beauty of Socrates' speeches attracts us to something beyond the Lysian reduction. Our very bodies might remember, after the play, that we have followed a particular excess into laughter before; is there not something humorous here?

One further argument might help make this case convincing and bring us full circle. If we consider that the greatest difference between comedy and tragedy must be in their final causes—the *pathē* for which each attempts to provide a catharsis—then it is possible to explain why Aristotle makes the strange claim that the best tragic action is one in which the philoi do not know who it is they are acting against, and, discovering who it is, they stop before the deed of suffering takes place, as in *Iphigenia in Tauris*. If the aim of tragedy is to raise and purify the emotions of pity and fear, we can see why Aristotle would say this, for we see a sister about to kill her only brother, but then this steadily increasing fear in us is suddenly released when she discovers his identity. Thereafter our fear is that they may not escape together, and this fear too is released in the course of the incidents of the plot. If Leon Golden and other critics were correct to think that the purpose of tragedy is intellectual clarification, we should be able to think of no reason for Aristotle to consider this the best form a tragedy can take. We could think of no reason even to consider this a tragedy, and such critics must think that here Aristotle nods, falls off his stool, hits his head on the way down, and continues sleeping. Tragedy can, under such a theory, hardly fail to become a structural category—the label depends upon the movement of the hero from happiness to misery. And our "catharsis" is at the recognition of how this tragic state of affairs can come to be in life. In just this way, the denial of importance of final causality in the arts, or the misapprehension of what that final cause is, has led to the various structuralisms aesthetics currently suffers under. Perhaps this is an effect of the continuing effort to make philosophy scientific, which venture in modern times requires the rejection of finality.

But Aristotle clearly says that the incidents of tragedy can have a shape other than the simple downhill slide or the more complex upside-down U or inverted J of the protagonist raised to a great height only to fall by hamartia to a situation worse than his beginning. *Iphigenia* is his example of the best tragedy, and the only possible reason for this choice must be because this play, despite its J- or U-shaped smiling structure, provides a catharsis of the appropriate passions: pity and fear rather than eros and sympathy. Further, it supplies the best catharsis of those passions as has been shown in the previous chapter.

3.1. The Example of a Falling Comedy: *Hippias Major*

We should suspect that the book on comedy might have had a comparably troubling example to the *Iphigenia*: Aristotle would have named as a comedy, perhaps even the best, one in which the structure of the incidents is what we today mistakenly call tragic: the protagonist is raised above the usual state only to fall of his own hamartia. Shakespeare does it by fours in *Love's Labour's Lost*, a comedy that ends in "tragic" dispersal. The existence of that comedy shows us that Shakespeare knows how the concepts work, that a comedy is not defined by its form, but by the catharsis of the passions it engenders and purifies. In this play we see lovers who fail to treat love seriously—riding its effervescent feeling into high-spirited games and mockery; they are shocked when they do not win; the flighty tendencies of our own eros are purified by this loss. We cannot really desire love to be mere bubbly washes of feeling; to be purified of this popular intoxication through the mimetic action of the play upon our desire and sympathy is not to cure us *of* eros, but to cure us *for* it. We have ridden the pleasant effervescence of eros into the shadow of death, and felt all its bubbles collapse; we are led to want the boys to succeed in the tasks their beloveds have set, but we do not see that success. In the course of the play our feelings have been led from the pleasant effervescence of desire, through collapse, to steadfastness; exactly the kind of transformation erotic feeling must go through if its easy and delightful pleasures are to become anything approaching marital bliss—or actually even friendship.

My less brief suggestion for an example Aristotle would have known well is Plato's *Hippias Major*. *Hippias Major* is structured as a chiasmus on its opening sentence: "Here comes Hippias *fine* and *wise*" (281a). The dialogue breaks into two unequal halves—the first being a comparison of modern Hippiate *wisdom* with that of the ancients and the uneducated Spartans, and the second being the discussion of the *fine* (286a3–304e), which is usually taken as the philosophical meat of the work—such as it is.[57] This structural point has not been noticed in scholarly discussions of the dialogue, and

57. While *Hippias* is frequently mined for insight into Plato's aesthetic theory, and not always treated as a serious effort in that regard, I have been able to find no secondary literature at all on the dialogue's discussion of wisdom, or wisdom's relation to the Spartan laws: the first structural half of the dialogue. Woodruff, in fact, in his recent translation and commentary, *Hippias Major* (Hackett, 1982), calls this part—one structural half of the dialogue on my reading—"Preliminary Skirmish" (pp. xiii, 35–42), and does not include it in his analysis of "The Argument," which starts thereafter. Such a treatment of the dialogue seems universal.

noticing it opens up some interesting literary as well as philosophical issues, and raises a number of questions to the usual interpretation. Socratic dialogues share with comedy and tragedy that they have a structure of events as well as thought, character, and diction; to read such mimetic works as merely decorated presentations of philosophical arguments is clearly not Aristotle's understanding of what they are or how they work. They are not ostracized from the mimetic, as are the poems of Empedocles. Nonetheless, it remains the most popular approach. Woodruff, for instance, considers that 281a–286c3 is given over to the "exiguous subject" of "discussion and display of Hippias' talents" (35) and, like previous commentators, considers its main task to be the presentation of Hippias' arrogant stupidity.[58] While Socrates is being ironic, it is perfectly clear that the wit and subtlety of his irony largely goes right by most commentators, as its more blunt passes go by Hippias.

Hippias, at least, sees that he and Socrates have come to some large areas of unanimity on the dialogue's first half set of issues: Spartan ignorance, the progress of wisdom, the worth and importance of his teaching. He reasonably expects, then, that they will quickly come to agreement in the matter of the fine as well. Instead, the wise Hippias slips on banana peel after banana peel in that discussion. So the dialogue, while extremely funny, exhibits the parabolic structure we have come to associate with tragedy, in which the hero at the zenith of his fame, power, wisdom, and communal recognition and fulfillment begins the slide that will take him under those he presently lords it over (the ancients and the Spartans), and break the previous amity into oppositions. That it happens to someone as full of himself as Hippias—a *miles gloriosus* of dialectics—is the main reason everyone calls the dialogue comic despite a plot structure more familiar to the opposite form of literature. But it also works on different passions, and that is the real reason behind our agreement that it is comic. While I do not disagree that the discussion of the fine in the second half of the dialogue possesses its interest, and while I do not at all want to imply that the two paths of the chiasmus are philosophically independent, I think that the particularly comic aspect of the dialogue is best brought out by examining the question of wisdom raised by the second epithet and brought to the bar in the opening half of the discussion.

58. Woodruff notes Schleiermacher, Ast, Horneffer, and Tarrant questioning why Plato would spend so much time doing this (94–103); that it has been read as a personal attack is one of the main reasons for thinking the dialogue is not Platonic (by Schleiermacher, Thesleff, Wilamowitz; cf. Woodruff, 97 and notes).

In that opening discussion the wisdom of the ancient sages and of Spartan law are called into question by the modern wisdom of the visitor from Elis. And it is Socrates, regarding both topics, who sets up Hippias to make the judgment upon his competitors for the title of wise. Early on he praises Hippias:

> In private you are able to make a lot of money from young people (and to give still greater benefits to those from whom you take it); while in public you are able to provide your own city with good service (as is proper for one who expects not to be despised, but admired by ordinary people).

But that praise leads immediately to the question,

> how in the world do you explain this: in the old days people who are still famous for wisdom—Pittacus and Bias . . . down to Anaxagoras—all or most of those people, we see, kept away from affairs of state? (281b6–c7)

Hippias's judgment is quick and sure:

> Isn't it that they were weak and unable to carry their good sense successfully into both areas, the public and private (281d).

Socrates seconds him, affirming that the improvements in the *technē* of wisdom (σοφιστῶν τέχνην; 281d5) by Hippias and his ilk are just like the improvements in other skills, where the ancient *technai* have been far surpassed by our modern technological and artistic feats.

Though they agree there was a lot of ignorance back then, particularly with regards to the value of money (282d, 283a), Hippias says that he usually praises the ancients, "for while I take care to avoid the envy of the living, I fear the wrath of the dead" (282c8–10). Now, if this dialogue (or this part of it) is mere malicious mockery of Hippias, we might wonder why such a proper and sensible sentiment is put so early into his mouth. Perhaps his conscience is not entirely clear on this matter of ancient wisdom, or perhaps Plato has here come across Polonius's great great grandfather—a man who can mouth the appropriate moral sentiment, being full of wise maxim but devoid of truth. The case is not entirely clear.

According to Hippias and Socrates the case for the new wisdom against that of the ancient sages rests on the following points:

1. None of the early thinkers saw fit to charge a monetary fee or give displays of wisdom for all comers (282d1).

2. They did not know that one needs to be wise primarily for one's own sake, the measure of which is making money (283b3).

3. They kept away from the affairs of state (281c8).

The first point seems to claim a kind of shyness in those ancients—as if display were a kind of vice. The first two points show the ancients did not know much about money; that is to say they didn't make much of their wisdom (282b2, 283b3). The third would seem to indicate they did not know much about politics, and that Hippias's evaluation of them not being able to turn personal wisdom into public benefit is correct. If all three are the case, we might wonder why Hippias is willing to give them the credit of having any good sense in either the public or the private area to carry over into the other. Anaxagoras, for example, lost a large sum of money he had inherited—so did other wise men (283a8)—and since he kept away from affairs of state he could have had no political impact. Why does Hippias call such a man wise at all, what could his private wisdom amount to (if not money) and why does he fear the postmortem wrath of such idiots savant?

As Paul Woodruff notes,[59] history tells us that the evidence appealed to here is false of Pittacus and Bias, and probably of Anaxagoras as well. Hippias, who is only allowed to talk of ancient history at Sparta and so has become quite well versed in it (285e), does not see fit to correct Socrates on the matter. So besides the fact that Hippias's "marks of the ancient lack of wisdom" exactly indict the well-known practices of Plato's protagonist (Socrates), the poet also shows the antagonist—Hippias—the historian, and Socrates—the presumably wiser—agreeing on blatant historical falsities. The only sensible reason for an author to do this is in order to signal the reader that we should try to figure out exactly how foolish Hippias is, and in the course of that, *in what his foolishness consists.* I do not think it consists in making mistakes about ancient history; foolishness, like wisdom, is always deeper than historical fact. Further, if Socrates is fooling him to the top of his bent, rather than merely equally stupid, what is the purpose of that

59. *Hippias Major*, page 37, note 6, page 39, note 23. Woodruff makes much of the fact that Socrates gets Hippias to agree to an outrageous historical falsehood (i.e., the political incapacity of the ancients) and then "pretends (with a quibble) to accept a theory of law that must have been anathema to him" (36, also 41)—that is, a theory of law that is more than the mere positivism associated with the Sophists. But besides exhibiting the versatility of Hippias's backbone (his ability to bend to whatever wind he is talking to—despite his knowledge), the introduction of the historical error by Socrates doesn't make Socrates look very intelligent either. In a fencing match we should count this as nothing either way.

action? Mere mockery for its own sake is as thoughtless a solution as it is pointless an activity.

Perhaps then, as in Aristophanes, there is a serious point in the clever servant (Socrates) making the braggart (Hippias) walk through the particular cloud castles the first half tours. Perhaps it is not just a "preliminary skirmish" or an "exiguous" subject. As an experiment in taking this part of the dialogue seriously, let us hypothesize that the case against the ancients is turned on its head (just as the first sentence of the dialogue—fine and wise—is inverted by the course of the discussion—wise, then fine). Each of the three points marked against the ancients is, then, a sign of their wisdom, and since Hippias does the opposite, they are marks of his lack of wisdom. Preliminarily, then, let the following stand for us as marks of wisdom:

1. Not to charge a monetary fee or give displays of wisdom for all comers.

2. To know one does not need to be wise primarily for one's own sake (when "one's own sake" is measured by making the most money).

3. To keep away from the affairs of state.

Being (or playing) fools, the two dialogees turn to affairs of state—and affairs of a state in which neither of them has either power or citizenship. Aristotle thought that matters of other states' laws were not deliberable (*NE* 1112a 29–30), but Hippias and Socrates are more liberal. In Sparta, where Hippias spends most of his public time, he unfortunately makes no money from his usual teaching because the Spartans have a law against foreign education. With regard to Sparta's law and the application thereof, Socrates gets Hippias to agree to the following argument:

(P 1) Lawmakers make the law to be the greatest good to the city (284d5).

(P 2) When people who are trying to make laws fail to make them good, they have failed to make them lawful (284d8–10).

(P 3) What is more beneficial is more lawful in truth for all men (284e5).

(P 4) It would be more beneficial for the Spartans to be educated by Hippias's teaching, even though it is foreign (285a).

(C) Then the Spartans are breaking the law by not giving Hippias money and entrusting their sons to him (285b2).

Perhaps fearing that we are likely not to believe the premise (P 4) about Hippias's teaching being beneficial, and thereby skip through this entire section as being such froth Aristophanic jokes are made of, Plato immediately lets us hear that the Spartans can't stand to hear about either astronomy, or harmonies and rhythms, and that most of them can't even count (285c–285d), so Hippias's skills in mathematics and geometry go unenjoyed—and unlearned—by the youth. Whether Plato's story about Sparta's niggardly provision for the education of its citizens is true or not, it seems clear that under any usual workaday idea of benefit Hippias would indeed be quite a benefit; arithmetic, geometry, and astronomy are useful skills for businessmen, farmers, or soldiers to have. The ordinary duties of citizenship and household economy seem impossible without them. And both Aristotle (in *Pol.* 8) and Plato (in *Rep.* 4, and throughout *Laws*) make music an important element of education. Arithmetic, geometry, and astronomy are central to the education of the philosopher-kings. The *amicus curiae* brief Socrates gives on Hippias's behalf, then, is sound (and is Plato's) unless we can discover that there is a greater benefit than that deliverable by mathematics and astronomy (or other sciences) delivered by the Spartan law against fornication of young minds with educators from Elis et al. If we cannot find such an argument, then Socrates must be serious in this first half of the dialogue in the matter of his praise of Hippias and it must be true that Hippias is wise, or at least wiser than xenophobic Sparta. We might upgrade the argument here using Hippias as a figure of a permanent question in education: is there a greater benefit to be found in education than the worldwide dissemination of scientific knowledge? Scientific information is something Hippias can provide; if that is the greatest benefit of education, then Sparta is foolish and Hippias and Socrates her legitimate (though distant and powerless) lawmakers.

Prima facie, the Spartan law looks silly,[60] for it keeps the culture behind the times and without the advantages of the more cosmopolitan Elis and Athens; after Socrates' argument it looks considerably worse. It is not only

60. That Socrates is supposed to have had Spartan sympathies (e.g., Woodruff, 39, note 27) and so cannot be serious about the argument he gives is to think an opinion about historical fact can negate a deductive argument's necessary conclusion. This is a frequently reiterated flaw in historical scholarship. That "Socrates probably approved of Sparta's restrictions in teaching" (Woodruff, 39) is a matter of no importance and for two reasons: (1) it is at best only Socrates' opinion, and (2) such historical knowledge about Socrates, Hippias, or Plato is itself only a matter of plausible *pistis*. Socrates here gives an argument against the validity of Spartan laws, and the argument looks deductive. One is not allowed to have opinions in the face of such arguments, nor is history a court of appeal; one must find the flaw in the argument or submit to its truth. Still, that there is much wit and irony in Plato's construction here if the alleged historical facts about the characters are true (which I am perfectly willing to admit) is a valid conclusion.

contrary to utility, it is also moral corruption. The argument which raises Hippias looks entirely valid and shows that the law itself (not just its application as in *Crito*) can be (and, according to this argument, is) unjust. However, there are several possible reasons for considering it worthwhile rather than merely senseless and unjust. I present them in the manner of the schools:

1. Sparta is a traditionalist society; any change in the traditions is likely to be devastating for the unity of communal life; any technological gains in various newly introduced fields would be more than offset by losses in authoritative organization and smoothly ordered social interaction (the historical-critical sociological reason). The coherence of the society across generations is clearly broken; not only the cohesion of the present generation with its distant ancestors, but also the agreement and unity of the present generation with its childen enthralled to the newer math. A new historicist might offer this explanation; such a one would probably add that this partly explains why Plato has Spartan sympathies: he is a traditionalist.[61]

2. Sparta is a militaristic society; to entrust education to foreigners is dangerous since if they do have any new and useful knowledge they are unlikely to teach the whole truth of the matter, which thereby leaves Sparta at their mercy; further, the state cannot depend on a constant influx of honest teachers and technicians to keep the new science up and running (the paranoid militarist reason).

3. The Spartans know that wisdom is only achieved through one's own efforts and practice at the tasks that one must learn to assign oneself, not through the passing on of information. Science is a habit, not a consumable acquisition. Technical knowledge necessary and helpful for the tasks at hand will be worked up and improved upon by the persons who are involved in the tasks, for purposes which the whole community involved in those tasks can ascertain. The knowledge gained in that way will be neither esoteric, nor create unnecessary luxury or hardship, for it will be invented only by someone strong enough to invent it, in circumstances capable of supporting its practice, and also invented because someone thoughtfully involved in the task had need of it. Science is (on this view) not only taken up as a part of the moral purpose of the community as a whole, it itself is a moral practice

61. That Plato has Spartan sympathies is a familiar scholarly claim. I think, however, that Megillus—the Spartan in *Laws*—would probably not think so given the very serious difficulties the Athenian Stranger exhibits to be the case with Spartan society and its laws.

for each individual in the community—or else *the community* has no science (and deserves none); it is also probably not a community and deserves a larger name (cf. *Rep.* 422e). In this way the community's technical skill will never overreach the moral growth or economic and intellectual capacity of its citizenry (the true philosophical reason). It should be clear that this reasoning will lead to actions that also produce benefits like those sought under the first two dispensations, but historicism and xenophobic militarism offer only partial understandings (more adequately, large misunderstandings) of what a society's purposes are, and how education engenders culture.

Socrates had said that the law is made to be the greatest good to the city and that "without that, law-abiding civilized life is impossible" (284d5). It is clear that if the third and most philosophical reason is the real reason for the Spartan law, that law is trying to make the continuing life of the Spartan community not only possible, but *the necessary and sufficient impetus* behind and within scientific, industrial, or artistic improvements and all education. Values are not put into the curriculum, the curriculum is the practice of the communal values. This argument would agree with that of the Athenian Stranger, who says that only "education from childhood in virtue" should be called education. "As for an upbringing that aims at money, or some sort of strength, or some other sort of wisdom without intelligence and justice, the argument proclaims it to be vulgar, illiberal, and wholly unworthy to be called education" (*Laws* 644a). Socrates' fooling of Hippias into admitted falsehoods plainly exhibits how that other view of education and politics works: if the aim is money or popularity, one must say what one's interlocutors find agreeable and will pay for. Let Aristophanes suggest a suitable posture for such a one. The virtues, and the upbringing that aims at them, have an intrinsic, necessary, and inescapable social reference—they make the society what it is; money, strength, and intelligence without justice will do the same thing—if the society allows their pursuit. Education aiming at those latter things is not worthy of the name, for it provides the impetus to the two greatest dangers of a society: poverty and wealth.

It is clear under this explanation that although Hippias does have knowledge of many things Spartans apparently are ignorant of, he is utterly incorrect when he claims that his wisdom is "the sort that makes those who study and learn it stronger in virtue" (283c5). In fact, insofar as he takes money for telling them things, Hippias is robbing his students of practicing the virtues required in investigation and discovery, and polluting the society with luxury by providing it with *technai* and information which its own activities are not obviously in need of for success, which do not arise out of the society's own perception of its needs or desires, and which are not likely to be able to be supported on the society's terms; besides that he is quite literally taking their money out of town. Under such conditions the society and its individual members are more likely to be "overstepping the bounds of the necessary," which *Republic* (373e) argues is the beginning of injustice, and leads necessarily to war. It is hard to tell if Hippias is a ridiculous friend or a clever enemy (*Phaedrus* 260c). That Hippias agrees with the Socrates who mocks him shows that Hippias can't tell who is what either.

Medicine teaches that an influx of foreigners may bring diverse strains of disease for which the native immune systems may not be prepared, but foreign education necessarily brings new and more serious diseases into the body politic. Whoever makes the most money at such endeavors is therefore least virtuous—and most virulent to the society. The mockery (whether malicious or innocent) in this section runs far deeper than the fact that Socrates gets Hippias to agree to historical falsehoods (about the ancient sages) or mouth agreement to arguments the historical Hippias would have disdained. The irony is personal only by accident; Hippias is the figure of a type of educational fish—and that's what Plato is frying. Far from "lacking the Socratic ethos" (Wilamowitz), the irony of this dialogue is exactly on ethos. It is not personal, but universally directed toward a certain ethos actually embodied by Hippias—and other famous lecturers past, present, and to come. Plato is also exhibiting something ironic about the human situation, for who would think that knowledge itself could be dangerous—destructive of an entire civilization when not developed by and in that civilization?[62]

This is a very serious philosophical and political problem, and it ought at least to be raised by a colonizing power (Athens or us), which considers its own life that which is to be emulated, or unquestioningly accepts multicultural education as an unconditional good. A nation's labor is not just the expression of, but the actualization of, its way of humanizing nature. Therefore, insofar as the culture merely takes up or is given technology of other peoples and cultures its labor is alienated—en masse. The culture is thereby permanently colonized even if the foreign teachers are perfectly willing to tell their native students everything and don't hide the firing pin, or fail to

62. For a contemporary philosopher who considers this argument quite favorably, see Wendell Berry; esp. "Conservation and Local Economy" in *Sex, Economy, Freedom and Community.*

explain the intricacies of carburation: there is no need for an army of occupation. The "less advanced" Spartan culture is now exactly like the visiting Elisian, and incapable of thinking otherwise since its way of dealing with (= working on) reality is exactly the same. Hollywood, Wal-Mart, and McDonald's are everywhere. The idea that we are in a postcolonial age is a great lie, and Plato knew it. In the information age Hippias is the universal colonizer. His connection with capital is his self-advertisement, his fetishization of wisdom (making it an ownable and alienable thing) is his method's *conditio sine qua non.*

Having investigated the details of what might lie behind the Spartan case, we can now see that our hypothesis about the ancients being more virtuous than Hippias, and in particular more wise, has good grounds.

1. They never took money for their displays of wisdom, probably because they never gave displays of wisdom for all comers. They knew that such *displays* could cause the ordinary folk to wonder at them, but by doing so it would take those folk (as well as the wise?) away from working out for themselves whatever they were capable of working out. Showmanship is not an intellectual virtue, and display is not teaching. In fact, to use the Newspeak of postcolonial postmodernism, such displays disempower the audience: under this condition the students (at best) watch, rather than practice, virtue. This is the aestheticization of education. It is a form of softness (*NE* 1150b16–19). One might wonder if such a creature as Hippias might not do better service to his city by being *away* from it—which he is, constantly.[63]

2. The ancient sages were probably well aware that such a disempowering would be detrimental to the growth and practice of virtue in any community, and no wise man would consent to take part in such a task or practice it upon his own or another city. In fact, he would make a law against it. He would refrain from such a thing both for his own sake (which does not mean in order "to make more money"—but does mean in order to practice virtue) and for the sake of the whole community. By so refraining from making money in this way the ancient sage exhibits his virtue, and it is a quite democratic virtue: he refuses the practices of tyranny and colonization. It is hard to say which of these aspects (communal or individual) is more important,

63. Since Hippias is "often on missions to other cities" (281b), perhaps Elis is wiser than its supposed leading citizen; this would also explain why Hippias is sent so frequently to Sparta—they keep on hoping it will lead to his reformation: that he will think about the purpose of the Spartan law and its implications. Or perhaps Elis hopes he will win—and soften up Sparta's youth.

since there is no individual life apart from a community, and the only lasting as well as the most worthwhile community is the community of virtue.[64]

3. The wise man would, in addition, stay out of politics in the sense that he knows that the most important thing is to become perfect in virtue himself, and that he recognizes that he cannot make any one else become more perfect in virtue in any case,[65] and that he himself is not yet perfect enough in virtue to have time to spend on such a vanity and chase after wind as making someone else so. At least these wise men would have the sense to stay out of politics *outside* their own state, though some of them, as was well known in Plato's day, were very important figures in the framing of *their own* cities' laws. No doubt these laws aimed at requiring the practice of virtue by the citizens. Plato may in fact be lying about some of those famous sages just in order to get his students to see the difference between the way jet-setting busybodies like Hippias are involved in politics (in every other state but their own, from which they are invariably absent) and the way in which the ancient sages—less well traveled—engaged in lawmaking for their own country, where their own practices and virtue were at stake, but did not attempt to tell the Spartans what to do in theirs.

It is now possible to expand on my suggestion about interpreting such open falsities as Socrates' remark about Pittacus and Bias not being involved in politics. The Hippiate position—which presumes that wisdom is a commodity and therefore has a price, that it both can and ought to be used to enrich oneself, and that applying it in private is an entirely different skill than applying it in public—provide the only conditions, and the sufficient conditions, to logically ground Hippias's claim to possession of the quality in question on the facts of his exceptional wealth and busyness. If these grounds are false, then both the title truly wise, which Hippias claims, *and* the alleged historical disconnection between public and private wisdom are false. But the alleged historical conclusion is false, therefore (by *modus tollens*) the premises must be incorrect. Rather than being a personal commodity, wisdom has an intrinsic connection to the continuing life of the community; we might say that wisdom is the knowledge of what is good for the whole city (*Rep*. 428d). Such wisdom is both private (for each must practice

64. This matter is familiar to Aristotelians—"for bad men cannot be unanimous (i.e., form a community) except to a small extent . . . and if people do not watch it carefully the common weal is soon destroyed" (*NE* 1167b9–11).

65. Again Aristotle: "For justice exists only between men whose mutual relations are governed by law; and law exists for men between whom there is injustice" (*NE* 1134a30).

it) and public (for the practices unite the generations of the city), and while such wisdom enriches both realms, it will never produce the wealth (much less wealth for its own sake), which is what Hippias understands as the mark of success. The ancient sages knew all this and Hippias does not. Hippias is never at home because it is impossible for him to have one. He is the original Nowhere Man. Hippias's later (utterly incapable) attempts to define the fine apart from all connection to workaday, social, moral, and political contexts is a merely a symptom of the social disease he exhibits in this first half of the dialogue. It fits perfectly with the person who exists under the arguments of the first half, which is "exiguous" only in the sense that it exhibits Hippias to be the Platonic Idea of the Exiguous. He prefers the view from nowhere—which exists wherever he is. He carries this negative along with him and it infects everything he casts his eye upon. *Plato's* argument against Hippias (for Socrates makes none, Socrates speaks in his favor) in this first half is the strongest possible argument for the unity of virtue and that it must be learned by practice.[66] Without it one cannot even tell whether a soup spoon is fine.

But that is all too intellectual a discussion to prove a point about comedy as emotional catharsis. The intellectual movement required by a Platonic dialogue will, however, have its emotional concomitants. For instance, the argument against Sparta's laws ought to raise our indignation at their injustice, while also evoking our love for good laws made on the principle Socrates spells out. As we are carried on by our love for good laws and correcting the foolishness of others to agree wholeheartedly with Socrates' argument in the first half, we then are suddenly stumped and left in aporetic inconcinnity in the second half. If this love (and our vexation) is strong enough, we may be inspired to attempt to discover in what way the wisdom the Spartans obviously lack might be considered fine by them (or we might try to show why their wisdom is not fine). Our desire and vexation together will lead us to attempt to tie the halves of the chiasmus together (as we have been doing), and doing so exhibits why such a good argument (about education) is hidden in a piece of dialogue so obviously full of mockery for the person who agrees with it. The mockery spurs on a love for the truth about justice to discover whether the mockery is just or the argument is true, and how. Philosophising follows from the aroused desire and vexation. One con-

66. That virtue is learned by practice is also Plato's argument in *Meno*; he makes his argument without Socrates ever giving an argument for it. See my essay on *Meno* in *Platonic Errors*.

siders the Spartan laws in the light of the good that they might see developing from them, a point of view which requires a certain cultural and personal humility (which Hippias fails to exercise). Having discovered the true argument under the mockery, the turn in the second half of the dialogue allows our love for justice a healthy run. For, the recently divinized—above the law—Hippias slips on one banana peel after another on the way down to a conclusion that is a gaping aporia not likely to be filled in soon by the man who seemed wiser than the very laws themselves. That he should be left, like a fish, gaping and empty on the sand, that Socrates should ironize him by mocking the ignorance of the son of Phroniscus, is an act of perfect justice, exhibiting, quite finely, the emptiness of the person who made the first half's empty claims.

In case we didn't get so far so fast, his failure in the second half should make us reflect back on Hippias's earlier success, or claim of success, as we already have, but more important than that—or at least the first order of business—might be to pay attention to the emotional changes that are wrung by the dialogue. Though he is overblown and vain, the dialogue builds up a kind of sympathy for Hippias. First of all, it does so by that early mark of respect for the ancients, but then more largely and fully as we see that he obviously knows a lot of stuff, but can't get the Spartans (some of whom can't even count) to allow him to teach it to them (not even mathematics). Any faculty member who has had to dance through the hoops of several administrators who, in the end, won't accept the result anyway must have some sympathy for him. Certainly readers who know of Socrates' own conviction under the laws of Athens must consider the question of the ground of justice of the Spartan laws with interest and sympathy. We see in Hippias a similar kind of eros for education (as well as, let it be said, for money), and a similar high evaluation of its importance as we ourselves have—teaching more than one student at a time and generally by more Hippiate than Socratic methods.

If we follow his fall, our erotic passion for the improvement of education in the state (under our bright aegis) should be purified as we lose our sympathy for someone who seems not to be able to do as finely as he says, or as well as he thinks ought to be done—though he has lectured often enough about it and perhaps even written a book or two. Hippias, had he been allowed to change the laws of Sparta, would have been as Oedipus—raised high, but in that position unknowingly screwing his own—those for whom he, as lawmaker, should have most care. Since the dialogue is a comedy, our passion—an overextended eros (the nonintellectual version of which is the main prop in *Lysistrata*)—is cured through ridicule rather than through the fearful and piteous suffering of a man too much like us. Perhaps we too are insufficiently aware of what our own loving laws would aim at or accomplish had we power and will and time to change them in, and I, for one, am less desirous of being in a position to do so after reading the dialogue. (Would that adminstrators had time to be similarly affected, but they are off at an important meeting somewhere else.)

Aristotle, I conclude, was not a formalist: the structure of the poem, the formal connection of its incidents (rising to community in comedy, falling to the destruction of philic relations in tragedy), while usual, is not the essential or definitive element for either genre; neither is the combination of plot and character in itself definitive. Though the largest portion of *Poetics* is about aspects of plot and there is no extant discussion of catharsis, this is due to Aristotle limiting the discussion (as he says in his opening words) to περὶ ποιετικῆς αὐτῆς, leaving the final cause—poetry's effect in the theater—as another speech (ἄλλος λόγος; 1149a8). In *Poetics*, as elsewhere in Aristotle's work, the nature of the thing is defined by its final cause; in poetics the final cause is a catharsis of the passions. In tragedy, the operative passions are pity and fear and their related painful passions, in comedy they are sympathy and eros and their related pleasant passions. It is for these passions that the poet aims to provide a catharsis, and if he does not achieve it his poem is a failure.

4. WHAT ART IS NOT FOR

The idea that art is for its own sake (*l'art pour l'art*) or its near correlative that comedy is mere festivity and foolishness, then, is false, and credits art with a power that is either beyond it—the creation of free value, a gravityless good—or beneath it—a pleasurable nothing. But as one would not undertake a journey through hell and purgatory merely for its own sake and for no further end, so the work of art, as Virgil says just before that long concluding *kōmos* of the great comedy, has its final cause outside itself: by calling the passions forth mimetically and making them work, art aims to bring us to the point where we may let our passions be our guide:

> Await no further sign from me:
> your will is free, erect, and whole—to act
> against that will would be to err: therefore
> I crown and miter you over yourself.
>
> (*Purgatorio* 27.139–42)

One would not think that a creature whose only possible error was a lack of understanding would need such art, and he wouldn't—philosophy would be sufficient for him. But because our passions are also disordered—our fear not of the right things, or at the right time, or to the right degree, our desire not sufficiently strengthened or directed to the sweet center of the good, but variable and polymorphous and easily seduced—we do need art, we need it to make us free and erect and whole. And where our passions are not disordered, it is likely the world is—we are not "past the steep, or past the narrow paths," and so our passions are hindered and prevented or pushed and tempted by a thousand natural shocks and more arising every day from nature—our own or the world's—or our unsocial sociability. Would that we could escape them for an hour. And so we need the world of art to allow our perfect passions—if we have them—their unhindered play. We need to be re-created in joy; the Athenian Stranger thinks we need it daily. Mimetic art is a necessary part of the human liberating process, for mimeses call the passions out to exercise, and that exercise is as necessary for the health of the soul as philosophy is for the health of the mind that is one of soul's powers, or as gymnastic is for the continued flexibility of even the healthiest body. It is because of *the exercises he takes our passions through*, not what any (or all) of his characters *say*, that Aristophanes makes the claim that he teaches the things that are best. He teaches them first through mimesis, though there is also thought expressed in his play. The play works most basically through sense and imagination (through our receptivity) rather than through reason and imagination (through our own activity). Whether or not he is right about his claim that what he teaches is the best is not, however, a judgment over which poetry itself may sit. To speak in a more modern tone: it may be true that "in music the passions enjoy themselves" (*Beyond Good and Evil* §106), but then to judge of the worth of music or to know what music is best one must know and judge what passions are so or how they all play best: one must know the enjoyment to judge of the music truly. Such judgments are the task of the one Aristotle called the man of practical wisdom, and it is most definitely not a matter that does not matter. The choruses appropriate for children are not decided upon by the children, nor are the catharses necessary for the adults matters of mere popular opinion, but each "must have the music that is fitting for them" (*Laws* 666d)—something divine is required, something that has a reference to *nous* and to the activity of the divine.

As Nietzsche himself points out in his criticism of "*l'art pour l'art*,"[67] the idea of art for art's sake is itself a comic overreaction to a simplifying moralism. That Nietzsche, like many others, lays this moralizing purpose upon Plato and Aristotle is either an indication of his incapacity to read or an act of willful re-creation of his superiors into men of straw for tilting purposes. We find, however, that Aristotle and Plato agree with the rhetorical conclusion of Nietzsche's own critique of the aesthetic movement; that is, in fact, why they both consider it so politically important (as does Nietzsche):

> what does all art do? does it not praise? glorify? choose? prefer? With all this it strengthens or weakens certain valuations. Is this merely a "moreover"? an accident? something in which the artist's instinct had no share? Or is it not the very presupposition of the artist's ability?

Perhaps all art is an attempt at liturgy—a Greek tragedian might understand that—even in its contemporary religious sense; so, too, would Aristophanes, Plato, and Aristotle—for whom all things imitate the first mover so far as they are able. The question of art then becomes the question of the proper and necessary liturgy for man. Plato's *Laws* returns to this question again and again in many ways.

On the other hand, the degree to which Nietzsche agrees with the aesthetic movement, that is, in its "fight against the moralizing tendency in art, against its subordination to morality," is also discoverable in the Platonic-Aristotelian emphasis on art's *mimetic* emotional effect, and would be more exactly directed against their less finely nuanced and more didactic followers.[68] Though Aesop might not agree, this is not how art teaches. Foremost

67. See his *Twilight of the Idols*, "Skirmishes of An Untimely Man," §24. In the Penguin *Portable Nietzsche*, translated by Walter Kaufmann (New York, 1968), it may be found on 529; all further quotations of Nietzsche in this paragraph and the next are from that page.

68. Among such followers I include (besides the majority of Platonist professors) Evanthius, Diomedes, Donatus (quoted in Coghill, 2–3), as well as Longinus, "On the Sublime," Horace, "Ars Poetica," Sidney, "Defence of Poesie." My explication here of how the aesthetic movement comes about—as a dialectical drama in which one simplifying tendency (direct moralizing) calls up an equal and opposite character (atelic uselessness) is purposely dramatic; cf. Harbage, who gives it a political causation: aestheticism "was an exclusive movement, calculated to wrest art

among those didactic followers we find those who take the Socrates of *Republic* as telling the real truth about art, or, as Nietzsche (pretends?), telling what Plato really thinks about it. To avoid both the moralizing that Nietzsche distrusts and the aestheticism that he recognizes as a foolish impossibility (though it has become more popular since Nietzsche's day), we can perhaps best begin by saying what our art is not and does not: Comedy does not (1) merely teach morals directly by what a character says (lecture and prohibition), nor does it (2) merely teach it "indirectly" by showing us a vice or folly and mocking it or leading it to a bad end. It *may* do one or both of those things, but that is not what gives art its value, for it is not art's primary way of working. To think that an art that began as a religious and festive ritual depends upon Shavian discussion or the "talking pictures" of *Hard Times* to work its magic is to misunderstand religion, festivity, ritual, tragedy, and comedy.[69] Socrates, as is well known, pretends to take art in just this way while setting up Glaucon's city in *Republic*. That the boys do not contest the issue means they have not considered what hearing the *Iliad* has done for them, or *how* it has done its work on them. For Glaucon and Adeimantus have the right feeling about justice in book 2, without having the right opinions or judgments—or even the right education if Socrates' laws and bowdlerizing of *Iliad* were true. Then again, like a certain hero, they seem to spend an inordinate amount of time and discussion worrying about the getting and dividing of women. To not find something utterly humorous in that discussion is to confess a similar lack of freedom: an eros too tyrannical to allow clear thought on many topics. Thus much for Dr. Johnson's "proper instruction required in drama": it is not *instruction*. Aesop is not great art.

To touch on a more important issue: that the boys in *Republic* do not contest Socrates' dismissal of the tragedians and comic poets means that the true festivity of their own religious practices has passed them by. They have missed it, at least they have *misunderstood* it—despite growing up during

away from the ordinary man and to make it the sole property of the virtuoso" (22). His hopeful belief in its death was greatly exaggerated. For a more philosophical discussion of this issue see the concluding sections of the next chapter.

69. The phrase "talking picture" is Sidney's ("Defence of Poesie," 3.9); the reference to a famous novel by Dickens is to conjure up the discussion of a type of literature (the realist novel) and a defense of the art favored by Martha Nussbaum; *Hard Times* is the central text of her *Poetic Justice*. A famous criticism of Shaw is that he took the passion out of theater and replaced it with philosophy. I think that criticism is largely false; what makes Shaw's plays great is what makes Shakespeare so; what makes them bad (and some are bad) is Shaw himself, in particular his didactic nature.

that age in which the tragic and comic religious festivals were at, or near, their highest point. I lean toward that being a confession not of the art's incapacity, but of their own. Socrates gives the god another chance at moving them to knowledge of him by *reintroducing all the major festivals* just before he announces that Glaucon's city is finished (427b–d). They do not notice. Similarly, they did not notice he allowed imitation of the bad back into the city "for the sake of play" at the end of a series of laws that ruled it out for the sake of the children (396e). But Socrates had noticed that something divine must have happened to Glaucon and Adiemantus (368a), something for which they themselves cannot yet give the explanation: they are in the strange position of having the right passion about justice in spite of all the wrong beliefs. As if the purifications of tragedy, comedy, and epic had affected them without their knowing, like a wind from a salubrious place (401c)—perhaps even from heaven. They are ready for philosophy, and their love has an inkling of its proper direction, but they are not yet very good at it. It is easy for Thraymachus and his kind to lead them astray because of their present lack of intellectual discipline, but their passions (rightly) resist following (as if grace prevents us everywhere).

I conclude, then, that comedy "teaches the things that are best" by taking our desiring passions through a set of movements that leaves them less constricted—as they undoubtedly are by the world, less fixated, less bound to inadequate objects and partial truths. Such recreations also make us more capable of joy by giving us joy in something like our proper loves and sympathies, as tragedy allowed an uninhibited run through the appropriate fearful and pitying passions. The first way of teaching what is best (lecture and prohibition, e.g., by a character in the drama) has exhibited its singular unsuccess since Eden, and the second (picture of evil, ridiculed) is insufficient. If the passions of the person in the audience are turned the wrong way, both example and direct catechization are as rainwater to the duck's back. All the laws need preludes. The real trick, and the only real cure, is to help the passions turn around by tempting them out of their cave and letting them run and be suffered in a world without existential import. (It is not just the mind—*nous*—that must be turned to the light.) When Dicaeopolis berates the Prytanes and ambassadors, prepares for the country Dionysia, makes a great deal for some pussy (cats), and wins a drinking contest, our own desires for the same things are raised. But the comic hero walks crooked, and so while his activity raises all our desires for peace and its pleasures, his extremity makes us laugh at the extremity of many of those very same desires and so we are laughing, too, at our own desires for a life of wine, sweet cutlets of the loin, and scurvy song. The desire for peace is not being laughed at or reduced to nothing, but is being enjoyed; the laughter at Dicaeopolis' sweet peace is an admission of love for something better. This laughter and pleasure does not *teach* us freedom, *it is the beginning of it.* The desiring passions are also practicing laughing at their own excesses and improprieties, and considering that pleasure is the one thing we are all most likely to be too attracted to (*NE* 1109b5–13), this exercise is purifying, or cathartic, for it is the beginning of freedom from such fetishism. It is not a simple matter of identifying with the protagonist, for there is here both identity and distinction. In any case it is the *action of the play,* not just the character of the protagonist, which brings the passions into play in the particular way it does.

That the arts are mimetic is what brings the passions into play. We should not think of mimesis as representation of, or telling, or showing some truth functional proposition, for all of those activities are much too intellectualizing; they do not particularly call up or charm forth the passions (though, of course, they can—in a scholarly book perhaps). Further, that view leads us inevitably toward an idea of catharsis as intellectual clarification. A work of mimesis conjures the passions—it is a work of *psychagōgia* (*Po.* 1450a33, b16). It is possible under this mimetic conception of art to think that music embodies character (though it does not embody thought) as well as a character on stage or in a realist novel does; that it can do so is a belief common to Aristotle and Plato (among others).[70] When understood mimetically and as conjuring the passions, the distinction between representational art and nonrepresentational art dissolves, for both will conjure mimetically.[71] That distinction can return as a secondary distinction, much as thought and diction are secondary to action in drama. It is perfectly plausible, given this un-

70. For a modern version of this view, see Aaron Ridley, *Music, Value and the Passions* (Ithaca, N.Y.: Cornell University Press, 1995). He argues that when we listen to the *marcia funebre* of Beethoven's *Eroica* or look at a weeping willow we "apprehend its melancholy through a kind of mirroring response"; he argues that "this kind of sympathetic response is *essential* to the experience of at least one kind of expressiveness" and "that our experience of *human* expressiveness involves, and involves essentially, our capacity for sympathetic response" (128, 129, italics in original).

71. I should point out that this magical-sounding language is used frequently by Plato: charms, spells, incantations . . . , for example, in *Laws* 659e, 933a, and 837e. The Stranger needs a binding spell to win Kleinias's assent, having already won the harmonious assent of Megillus. Unfortunately, the Spartan does not have much music in his education and so has grown rather hard of hearing and inflexible.

derstanding, to think that such remarks as Aristotle's and Plato's about character in music can apply to abstract painting and sculpture even though the Greeks did not have them; so, to consider that Rothko's *Four Darks on Red* or Brancusi's *Bird in Space* are not mimeses of character is to miss the point of them entirely; it is as if a Greek would say the same of the Parthenon because they see no person—a complaint Plato assuredly did not make (*Rep.* 401a,b).

A mimesis of character may not,[72] by itself, lead to catharsis (though it still calls forth a certain character from the audience); for catharis the mimesis of *action* is needed—at least *movement* of the passions, as in music. Mimeses conjure the passions; the particularities of the mimesis makes the passion have a certain character; comedy and tragedy as mimeses of action produce a catharsis of the passions by bringing different passions to bear on each other in various ways, through various syntheses of events. Whether the art (like architecture or most cases of lyric poetry) merely conjures a passion of a particular *ethos* or attempts the more complex and difficult task of catharsis of the fearful (tragedy) or desiring (comedy) passions, we should not consider as good art any set of practices that makes the object of those practices (our passions and *ethos*, since *ethos* includes these) worse. Given that mimesis is a *natural* way in which our passions are called forth, poetry, like politics, "is an art / That nature makes," and we can further agree that "Nature is made better by no mean / But Nature makes that mean" (*Winter's Tale* 4.4.89–92).[73] The aim of poetry, like that of politics, is that through the (natural mimetic or natural social) means our naturally mimetic and social state finds its improvement and well-being (*eudaimonia*). *Eudaimonia* is the universal end of all constitutions and poetry, at which both the communities formed among citizens and that formed between artist and audience aim. Unlike some other arts—like gardening, in which both the presence and the arrangement of the objects are matters of human choice and action, and the practice of the particular art itself is a matter to which we can say yes or no—mimeses and political arrangements are constitutive elements of our existence, over the presence and practice of which we have no power: we must practice them. Our power is only in their arrangement and interplay,

72. I say "may not" rather than "cannot" because I wonder whether the constant visible presence of a Parthenon might not, in fact, be purifying—at least to those better than ourselves.

73. Again contrast Shakespeare's classicist thought with Hobbes's that art is an imitation, as *un*natural as a civitas (*Leviathan*, section 1, §1).

and not all arrangements are created equal. Only by knowing the target can we pick out the victor.

About this last necessity even Nietzsche agrees, and his criticism of the pointlessness of aestheticism is at one with his recommendations for education:

> Rationality in education would require that under iron pressure at least one of these instinct systems be paralyzed to permit another to become strong, to become master. Today the individual still has to be made possible by being pruned: possible here means *whole*. The reverse is what happens: the claim for independence, for free development, for *laisser aller* is pressed most hotly by the very people for whom no reins would be too strict. This is true in *politics*, this is true in art. (*Twilight*, 545f.; emphases in original)

It is only the passions in a proper balance that can be let free, for art or artist, or politician; to demand anything else is a symptom of degeneration and will lead to further ills. It may be that Aristotle, Dante, and Nietzsche have a deeper than prima facie disagreement about what that more particular aim of the work of art is—some may say happiness, and another health or freedom, but that art has an aim and a purpose, and that that purpose is not merely pleasure or even merely (or primarily) intellectual recognition and its pleasure they all share. The argument about the target we will take up more exactly later, but now Aristotle's view should be perfectly clear: the target is happiness, art's way to it is catharsis of the passions, and the purpose of art is to rouse us to love and strive toward, to fear the destruction of and pity mistakes about, those glad and lovely eyes.

3

THE EXEMPLARY COMIC FICTION

Resolution, Catharsis, and Culture in *As You Like It*

Happiness does not lie in amusement; indeed it would be strange . . . if one were to take trouble and suffer hardship all one's life in order to amuse oneself. Relaxation, then, is not an end; for it is taken for the sake of activity.

Aristotle (*NE* 1176b30–35)

Comedy is a vision of dianoia, a significance which is ultimately social significance.

Anatomy of Criticism, 286

1. RESOLUTION AND CATHARSIS

Having provided an answer to the question of *what* comedy does, we may now attempt a more exacting answer to the question of *how* comedy effects a catharsis of desire (eros) and sympathy. Aristotle is clear in the extant *Poetics* that plot is that through which the play does its work—it is the play's *archē* and *psuchē*. It is particularly through recognitions and peripeties that tragic plots are made most emotionally effective, and this is especially so when they occur together (1450a32–34). Since all drama is a mimesis of action, and plot is the unitary action of the poem (1451a25–35), the structure (including peripeties and recognitions) and resolution of the plot will also be the *psychē* and *archē* of comedy. In order to examine how the comic plot effects its catharsis, we will have to take specific examples. But before we turn to a careful reading of *As You Like It* to see the kinds of resolution and catharsis that it brings about, we should consider what to expect.

We have already discussed Aristotle's statement that the catharsis resulting from sacred songs is different depending on the character of the worshipper, but that some kind of catharsis occurs in all (*Pol.* 1342a5–16); we have connected this complex idea of catharsis with music's two other benefits: education (παιδεία) and intellectual recreation (διαγωγή; 1341b33–40). If we read his discussion of music as synecdochic for all the arts of the muses, as both the Greek language and many scholars allow,[1] then these same distinctions among audience members and effects will be applicable to tragedy and comedy as well. So, we should expect that for any given play there can be several different sorts of catharsis, depending on whether the character of the audience member is better or worse. The ways of being better and worse vary (though mean, excess, and deficiency are always the range) because at times the excess (e.g., prodigality) and at other times the deficiency (e.g., insensitivity) are "considerably superior" (1121a19–27, cf. 1119a25–27, b6–11), being easier passions to move toward the mean, or passions more likely to lead one to act beneficially.

Across these distinctions of better and worse we should also remember that some audience members will enjoy other benefits as well—education and intellectual recreation—though some catharsis is enjoyed by all (*Pol.* 1342a15–16). We have already illustrated how the deficient, excessive, or virtuous may each have their own catharsis in *Hecuba*. It is more than likely that an inferior artist is less successful, or that a morally bad one can only provide a catharsis for an inferior sort of character (at best), but a great artist should be able to provide a catharsis for all. On many occasions we might have to expect the morally corrupt artist to be pandering to the *satisfaction* of a certain passion—as is the case with the gladiatorial contests Augustine castigates (*Confessions* 6.8) or any of a number of salacious entertainments available in the bars and shops behind the railway station of Copenhagen or Amsterdam—rather than providing a *catharsis* for them. The latter must be considered mimetic arts, for whether cinema or small stage, they do portray people (of various character) in action, and they are intended to rouse certain passions (and are continued because of their popular success at doing so). The medical use of and analogy for catharsis here shows its force: what

1. See, e.g., Janko, "From Catharsis," 343; he also mentions Bernays. The Socrates of *Republic* and the Athenian Stranger of *Laws* both use the term "music" in this generic way as well.

can purify or bring to health can also poison or sicken. Art, generically, mimesis, universally, is a pharmakon.[2] Further, as there are pretenders in medicine, so too in art. As a state might have an interest in legislating about the safety of drugs or the requirements of education, it must also have an interest in the arts.

Let us therefore use the good as our touchstone. In the archetypal comic plot, "a society forms around the hero" (*Anatomy*, 218). Although the generic action Frye outlines is one he explicitly derives from New Comedy, we can see what he means even in the oldest complete comedy we have.[3] Aristophanes' *Acharnians* begins with Dicaeopolis complaining about the state of Athenian affairs: the incapacity of the judges at the tragic festival, the preference for chatting and selling in the Agora when enterprises of great pitch and moment are to be debated in the assembly. He employs the silenced Ampitheus to conclude a private peace with Sparta, and after having his garlic stolen by the new mercenary protectors of the state, he meets Ampitheus coming back, chased by the veteran Acharnians who smell his treaties. The chorus threatens to stone Dicaeopolis to death until he likewise threatens to skewer a hostage coal scuttle carrying good Acharnian coal. Under this terrible threat the chorus retreats and agrees to hear his argument; then, after a visit to Euripides for tragic props, Dicaeopolis converts half of the chorus to his point of view. A scuffle breaks out and the losing "no treaty with Sparta" semichorus calls on their champion, the general Lamachus. The agon shifts to one between Lamachus and Dicaeopolis in which Lamachus comes back wounded and beaten and Dicaeopolis surrounded by flute girls, having won the prize for deep drinking. The chorus sings a victory ditty and follows Dicaeopolis and his wineskins out.

The action of *Acharnians* is quite similar to that outlined by Frye, which begins with a straitened or repressive "normal" society threatening the life,

2. At this point it is de rigueur to invoke the discussion of *Phaedrus* in Derrida's *Dissemination.*

3. In recent decades it has become possible to question the old truism that Aristophanes is what Aristotle would consider "Old Comedy," as Frye (e.g.) assumed ("Argument"). See, e.g., Reckford, *Aristophanes' Old-and-New Comedy.* My own view is that by "Old Comedy" Aristotle means the kind of thing that makes its resurgence in night-show monologues and some performance art: a string of lyric and invective unconnected by unified action. (This is about all Aristotle himself says of the "older [pre-Homeric] poets" [1448b33]; the more detailed distinction between Old and New Comedy depends on later Peripatetic philosophers and is read back into this phrase.) In contrast to such (old comic) poetry (connected perhaps only by the fact that the poet names real persons who are mocked, not by its action), *Acharnians* is already at least Middle Comedy (the idea of its disunity of action is highly overstated) and *Plutus* is New Comedy.

livelihood, happiness, and garlic of the comic protagonist(s). The democratic powers that be—the Ambassadors, Prytanes, and assembly, who are the normal society of the play, if not the normal society of Athens—are incapable of achieving (or refuse to attempt achieving) a peace treaty; their allies are garlic thieves; and informers threaten the private peace Dicaeopolis manages to achieve. Dicaeopolis—without the help (or confusion) of the tricky/wise servant of New Comedy, prefigured if not actualized in Aristophanes' own Cario of *Plutus*—sets the old order on its head, and the wine-filled chorus of the new and more festive society closes ranks behind him in the victory revel that ends the play. Dicaeopolis is in fact his own tricky/wise servant—which is to say that he is the tricky/wise servant of Aristophanes, who brings not just the chorus, but the whole assembly of the audience over to his side in a pleasant *kōmos* that accomplishes for two hours what politics has failed at for years. In his much later *Plutus*, too, all the nemeses of the new festive order—Hermes, the rich old dowager, even the priest of Zeus (who did well when Wealth was blind)—find themselves hungry, cold, and sleeping alone when he is cured. When Plutus can see, and chooses to share his largess with honesty, goodness, beauty and youth, the former sycophants become pilgrims to Chremylus's door—and the power of the Informer does not prevail against it. Our passions are allowed to rejoice over and with the victory of such psychic and physical beauties—even if the beings bearing their names are imperfect representatives.

Given this archetypal relation between the opening repressive and threatening "normal" society and the more festive comic order with which such plays conclude, it would seem that *As You Like It* is about as perfect an example of the art form as is possible. The several members of the comic community provide more definition and specificity to the comic *kōmos* than Aristophanes' single protagonist plus undifferentiated chorus allows, and this dramatic enrichment of character allows Shakespeare a variety of kinds of comic agon within a single play—for a character can only engage in those kinds of agon in which his kind of character is likely to engage. The varieties of characters in the play can thereby arouse (and mock) distinctive loves and sympathies in the audience: the heavenly and the common Aphrodite, for example. The diversities among the characters' passions, by mimesis, arouse diverse audience members (or diverse passions in any one audience member). By contrast, we aren't going to find Dicaeopolis using his peace to write a philosophical dialogue or study the movements of heaven. There is a more complete mimesis of comic (erotic and sympathetic) possibilities for the later dramatist, who has more actors at his simultaneous disposal; he can, therefore, provide mimeses of more steps on Diotima's ladder, or, more generally, diversities of desire. Each of those diverse desires defines a distinctive eros in relation to which a character can be deficient, excessive, or otherwise, and to which the various kinds of character in the audience will have closer or more distant sympathies, more or less easily charmed forth into mockery or arousal. Further, in *As You Like It*, the originally outcast younger brother not only finds true love and happiness in the green world of Arden, but the evil duke and the elder brother are converted and at the end of the drama he and the whole comic community are invited back to the "normal world" where their happiness will be assured by the assumption of power. There is no residual scapegoat or Lamachus-Cloud that might leave us feeling a bit disgusted—not even the "normal" society from which the play took its life. There is no double-issue ending, but the bitterest enemies walk off good friends (*Po.* 1453a 30–38), and the society is entirely remade. The god (Hymen) comes down to join the dancing, and all is right with the world.

The reason this plot is archetypically comic is not merely anatomical, however,[4] for its anatomical correctness allows the play to provide every type of comic resolution and catharsis. In the last scene, Rosalind, whom we see through most of the play as both being in love (as a woman) and mocking romantic love's excesses (as a man), becomes a unified being, loving and sensible; so there is a personal integration or resolution. There is, as well, an interpersonal integration: each member of the pairs of country copulatives is united with what it really desires: Orlando with Rosalind, Oliver with Celia, Sylvius with Phebe, Touchstone with Audrey. And, further, there is the already mentioned larger social *redintigratio in statuum pristinum*: the duke is returned to his lands, Oliver to his, and the whole green world society that has turned around Rosalind and Orlando is set to take its place in the normal world outside (and inside) of the forest of Arden.

Similarly, the audience members, who have gone into the golden world of the theater and who have likewise suffered the perturbations of sympathy and desire, and may have come to some recognitions of their own, are about to go out into the normal world, which is their true inheritance. Let us now

4. It is also festive and liturgical; cf. Barber, chapter 9, and Hassel, 17–27, 144–48. These words underline the cathartic effect of the drama—or else drama would not ever have been a part of the festive ceremonies of Athens or the liturgical celebrations of medieval societies.

explore in more detail those resolutions, their accompanying recognitions, and their plausible accompanying catharses. We will find two major kinds of comic resolution and catharsis, and within each kind two subtypes. We will then read through the figures of the play, and the catharses available through its playing, to the kinds of culture that need or can use each type of catharsis provided through play, ritual, liturgy. We should recall that Plato suggests that differing age groups will require diverse choruses because of the diversity in the nature and power of their passions. He makes this argument in *Laws* (666a–d), and it suggests that the proper interpretative tool for reading the dialogues is to keep in mind the kind of person Socrates is plying his music with. The difference in the laws between *Republic* and *Laws* is best explicated not as a development in Plato's thought, but rather as a difference in what kind of souls need tuning in each, and the kind of tuning they need. Aristotle also suggests that different kinds of people must have different musics (*Pol.* 1342a18–22). Insofar as choral performances are imitations of characters in all sorts of action and fortune, and each audience member brings to bear both his habitual dispositions and his capacity to imitate, we should expect that a drama (with song) that has such variety of character will evoke the passions of all types of audience member most marvelously. Shakespeare's larger number of fully drawn characters is an artistic advance over Aristophanes—as Sophocles' third actor was over Aeschylus (*Po.* 1449a18–19), because it allows a finer effect in the audience.

There is an obvious parallelism between the audience—who are taken into the green world of the comic play—and the characters of the play—who are taken into the forest of Arden (or into the festive *kōmos* building around Dicaeopolis). That parallelism no doubt includes a similarity in emotional effect, on the one due to being in Arden (where the effect on the characters is the *play's* resolution), on the other due to being in the theater (where the effect on the *audience* is the comic catharsis). This parallelism is visible under several Aristotelian statements, which we have noted frequently in previous sections. The first is his distinction between the tragedy καθ' αὑτό and the tragedy πρὸς τὰ θέατρα (1449a7–8); the second is his requirement that the final cause of tragedy be a catharsis *of* the audience's emotions of fear and pity raised by the fearful and pitiable events *in* the tragedy (1449b26–28). His further comment on those emotions in *Rhetoric*—that we pity when we see in others what we would fear were it approaching us

(1386a25)—reiterates the analogy. Hecuba, for example, not only has fears, what happens to her is fearful, and what she does is fearful too. We should naturally fear accomplishing certain acts: killing children or a brother, or marrying our mother. Disgust is roused when we see them accomplished, and avoided when the acts are avoided. Similarly, those things that we would fear if they threatened us, arouse pity when we see them happen to others: the object of pity and fear is the same, the subject's relation to that object (direct in fear, and indirect, or distant, in pity) seems to make up the largest part of the difference between the two emotions. The fearfulness of the tragic events evokes the pity of the spectators, the resolution of the plot provides the catharsis of those emotions. Catharsis of pity and fear is not the same as the resolution of the pitiable and fearful events of the plot, but the resolution of the plot (the peripeties and recognitions that lead out of the complexity that roused those passions) is the prime mover of the catharsis of the passions in the audience.

Let us play out the analogous relationship between actors and audience, between the play itself and the play in theater, for *As You Like It*. The characters in the play are embued with eros, desire. I suppose it is not unusual for some members of the audience to become directly embued with that same passion for Rosalind or Orlando, or perhaps Touchstone or Audrey. Less directly, the audience will have more or less sympathy for those erotic characters, for we all have experience of what it is to desire and to be separated from what we desire. Perhaps our desire for Rosalind or Orlando, separated from us by the curtain of art, calls that experience and those feelings up again. And even if we don't have that experience of desire and separation, desire calls up desire mimetically. It is most likely that audience members will feel something of both emotions (as we do in tragedy): an immediate *attraction* for the hero and the heroine, and the more mediated feeling, *sympathy*, for their plight. At the same time that it arouses such passions, the immediate head-over-heels nature of eros is mocked (in and by Rosalind as well as others) and in doing this the play also makes our laughter include our immediate sympathy and mimetically induced desire for the characters—for what is Rosalind that I should care for her, or Orlando that I should take thought of him? Our desire for an object is aroused by seeing the object being desired. Freud, like Shakespeare, will later make a lot of money out of these transference relations, but comedy is the better doctor, for it takes up the cure of the transference relation simultaneously with the catharsis of the other desires. A discursive method like Freud's and philosophy's can rarely accomplish such a thing, if it can find a way of attempting it.

It is important to keep in mind that the story I give here for *As You Like It* is meant to be exemplary; very few comedies work on so many levels at once as Shakespeare's, but the common elements should be easily discovered. For example, we are supposed to have an immediate attraction for Lysistrata and her girls;[5] we are also immediately attracted to Dicaeopolis—if not because of his looks, then because of his open vexation with the same unquestionably absurd "public servants" who vex us. We also desire the protagonist's project (however impossible)—in *Acharnians*, *Lysistrata*, *Plutus*, and other plays—to succeed. Our desires that the suckling pig, the wine, the flute-girls, and the wives with loose gowns and open legs come to our couch and table requires that the old inhibited and inhibiting order be thrown off, and the fact that the *kōmos* of an Aristophanic play exits so frequently with drinking and randy song over the beaten (*Acharnians*) and burning (*Clouds*) old world order makes it perfectly clear that if the world we are marching into is not exactly that of Eros perfected, it is certainly one that is very friendly to Id. But the task of the comedy, I am arguing, its final cause, is not merely to provide a substitutive wish fulfillment, but to bring about a catharsis of the emotions of desire and sympathy. How does it do this?

One reasonable story goes like this: Like the characters in the play, the audience takes part in and identifies with the green world, for that world is closer to the heart's desire, and the audience is *in fact* in that world (and wishes to be so) insofar as they have come to a comic play. As an element of what was, in many societies—ancient and medieval—part of a religious festival, the audience is already participating in something set apart from the usual society and workaday world. Even in our day a fragment of this festivity remains. The characters enter (or create) the green world in the course of the play, and within it their humorous excesses are purged by mockery or purified by being allowed arousal and enjoyment so that the personal, interpersonal, and social reintegrations can occur in the last scene. The green world is the world of desire; it is, as Northrop Frye says, not a world that judges moral worth, but one that wants to see the unity of desire with desired: it sets aside judgments of moral worth to a significant degree. "Its opposite is not the villainous but the absurd" (*Anatomy*, 167) and the absurd

5. Cf. Cooper, *An Aristotelian Theory of Comedy*, 76.

is (in the world of desire) whatever blocks desire. What happens in the audience in this case, if parallel, might quite easily seem to be of questionable worth, perhaps just because of the freedom from moral judgment that the comic play generally creates for itself. That, at least, would go far to explaining the negative view of comedy attributed to Plato and Augustine, among others: the free play of the imagination with a faculty of desire unfettered by moral judgment is not a way of thinking and feeling one should practice too often—if at all.[6]

That so-called Platonic view of comedy is a little too simplistically moralizing.[7] Generally moral questions are put off—our moral judgment is, as it were, disabled—in comedy by making the "normal" society of the play's beginning highly questionable. In *As You Like It* we see a brother plot against his brother's life and limb, and hear that the new duke has just driven his brother off the throne and out to Arden. In *Acharnians* the late-arriving Prytanes preemptive dismissal of Amphitheus's (meaning god on both sides, perhaps suggesting the god's portion in all wars) peace-seeking followed by their long, empty questioning of the debauched ambassadors and eunuch pseudo-Artabas, as well as their lightning adjournment at the first (god-sent) drop of pseudorain marks the "normal" out for ridicule. Other plays of Aristophanes begin in the ridiculous or impossible—two servants kneading dung-cakes (*Peace*), two men taking direction from a jackdaw and a crow to find a peaceful city (*Birds*)—and in this way place themselves well outside the realism of serious moral judgment from the beginning. In other plays of newer comedy the stupidity of one or another law, usually about sexual relations (*Love's Labour's Lost*) or marriage (*A Midsummer Night's Dream*), disables our moral judgment from taking the side of the "normal" society. We have seen how the real immoral was similarly backgrounded in *Phaedrus*. Such beginnings do not allow us to take the "normal" or background society as wholly serious (σπουδαῖος) or worthwhile. While such opening tropes may not be enough to make desire's world the world of moral virtue, the ridiculous law or obvious injustice, stupidity, or politic incapacity of the "normal" society is enough to give the green world freedom under a presumption of charity:

6. Not even just "for the sake of play" (*Rep.* 396e), a phrase that makes no sense at all if we take the argument preceding it seriously. For a discussion of Shakespeare's awareness of this problem as the problem of comedy, and his resolution of it, see Laura Rotunno and Gene Fendt, "'I have had a most rare vision': The Unity and Sublimity of *Midsummer Night's Dream*."

7. Probably too simplistic even for Plato, who died, so they say, with a copy of Aristophanes under his pillow. Cf. my "*Ion*: Plato's Defense of Poetry."

it can't be as stupid or immoral as that original world. I might add that in Shakespeare it never is, except in the nightmarishly animal but eventually humanized center of *Midsummer Night's Dream*—and in that case the nightmare is quickly recognized by its tricky/wise perpetrator(s) as an error, which they immediately set out to cure. That play's magical mix-ups might well be read as Shakespeare's acknowledgment that the dreams art puts on our eyes can as equally plausibly go far astray as be cathartic if the master of the revels is not very careful about both his pharmacy and the one upon whom its ointments work.

What goes on in the audience, in this case, is much more complex than morally questionable fantasizing about a world operating on laws invented by Id. Comic catharses fall into a range of possibilities, only the first of which seems entirely questionable. First, it is possible that an audience member could go into the green world of the theater as into a fantasy. And when he comes out, eyes blinking, the real world and all its moral claims and political difficulties slaps him like sunlight across the face. To take up the case of the original audience of *As You Like It*, there is still the very real law of primogeniture, I am still a younger brother with few property rights, and no hope of getting my desire for a duke's only daughter; or, I am still an older brother with all these young ones eating up my estate, nickeling and diming me to death with their requests for schooling and funds, and so on.[8] Comedy, under this dispensation, has a cathartic effect just as circling a track for an hour does: it's hypnotic; we forget our problems; but then the hypnotic or incantatory effect ends and we wake to the world going on apace. In this particular case catharsis might most adequately be translated as a purgation: for a moment it relieves our troubles. This is the best explanation of comic catharsis defensible by all those who think of art as mere entertainment. It may be true; but if it is the whole truth, there is no reason to study the humanities rather than watch football (or a tape thereof when one knows the home team will win). Further, far from providing a "vicarious benefit," or "facilitat[ing] pacification and escape" (Montrose, 53), it would seem to face the audience of such younger brothers of less than lordly families with the complete inadequacy of their own daylight world, and such comedy is likely to be as socially upsetting as Plato is said to have feared. We might call this

8. For many more details on the social import of the enmities played out in *As You Like It*, see Louis A. Montrose, "The Place of a Brother in *As You Like It*: Social Process and Comic Form," in *Shakespeare Quarterly* 32 (1981): 40–54.

version of catharsis the merely physiological catharsis, though whether it discharges itself in the theater (as Freud's theory of substitutive satisfaction posits), or on the body of the older brother (as Plato fears and Marx hopes), is left open.

An advance along this line is marked by the idea that fantasy is not *mere* fantasy for human beings, that just as we expect the new world that will form outside of Arden will be one in which the characters act in accord with what their hearts have learned within it, so too the audience of the comedy can go forth into its own world, carrying the green world's heart within them. And so younger and older brothers, knowing their legal rights, and without abrogating such law as society has, will treat each other more in accord with the happy spirit of the green world than the murderous spirit of the original dukedom. A *desire* to achieve greater equity, if not to overturn entirely the social, political, and economic inequities of normal society, has begun to take root during the play; sympathy for the desire of others has been *practiced* mimetically; and both that desire and that sympathy have received the sun and water of joy and satisfaction while at the play. Because we have felt these passions move through to their joyous conclusion, the desire for and the enactment of the personal, interpersonal, and social integration on stage will be further imitated so far as possible in the world outside the theater where it will cost us more. But we are aided to begin (or continue) because the mimetic art has already brought us through it once in a world that costs only the tuppence of admission. This more sympathetic constitution formed by the action of the play in our hearts and minds is carried out of the theater. Without yet speaking of a more intellectual vision, these emotional practices provide a version of comic catharsis *in line with* Frye's remark about *dianoia* at the head of this chapter. Comedy's vision of dianoia rouses our love. It rouses our love first, then the comedy gives us the vision we rightly desire. It is not just that the comic vision is of a society re-created in line with eros, but that the vision appears before an audience united in desire and vision. The liturgy of comedy is a practice of shared eros and shared vision, in and through which sharing we rejoice together. Even the real political world is improved by this shared eros and joy in the shared object of the play. These results are sufficient to defend comedy against its cultured despisers, for according to this explication comedy has a quite beneficent social and moral effect. Most obviously, it begins the practice of charity by its work on the community's desires and moral imagination. The effect of the comedy is to purify our desires of their murderous deficiencies or ridiculous excesses in eros and sympathy and to enlarge the field of our desire and sympathy to include our brother and the fool, the Megarian and the Boeotian, and the stiff-phallused Spartan too. Second, the comedy's mimesis of the communal *redintigratio* brings the desire for such communal action home to joy. Finally, comedy rouses our love for the infinitely sharable, universally inclusive *dianoia* by charming forth the practice of it from our all but unwitting souls. The play effects the re-creation of the erotic and sympathetic passions appropriate to our kind of being.[9]

What both of these first two views—the physiological and the social—have in common is that in them the world that answers desire, the world represented by Arden or Lysistrata's victory, is seen and felt as absolute, as that-than-which-nothing-greater-can-be-conceived, that which is to be loved with all one's heart and soul and mind (the body is already there). In the first version, that loved world is mere, or dangerous, fantasy; in the second view, it is more than that and so can be a source of "social conciliation."[10] We will find, no doubt, that the difficulties of real life far surpass the difficulties of supporting propertyless siblings (or being kept by a lordly one) in the play, but the play shapes our desire to include the good of others, and, indeed, our sympathetic reaction to the characters begins the practice of that virtue, even if the play itself accomplishes nothing further in the so-called real world. If we do not have this right desire, or if it is not sufficiently strong or active—if we do not take joy in its success—we will never act to achieve that good except via force of law. As the citizen soldier or those forced by their generals do not have true courage, and in fact only with the greatest difficulty will be led into having it (*NE* 3.8), so a state with adequate and enforced laws but inadequate poetry may have the best-behaved citizens, but not tru-

9. That this kind of feeling could be brought about by music alone seems to me undeniable, though I have no capacity here to explain it. Beethoven's "Pastoral" Symphony comes to mind. Plato derives chorus (χορός) from joy (χαρά) at *Laws* 654a. To be ἀχόρευτος is, then, to be untrained in joy as well as untrained in song and dance. I regard this argument as deductively certain, though historically minded lexicographers will say it is foolishness.

10. Montrose uses this phrase (54), but seems to have in mind a rather sanguine physiological account (facilitating pacification and escape), or a bootstrapping economic one "fostering strength and perseverance" in one's effort to achieve, as Orlando does, what birth denies (53). But those younger brothers (and Montrose mentions some historical examples) who can bootstrap out of their oppressed condition in Elizabethan society (or any other) are few, and far between, and very, very lucky. The *whole society* must change, and change its passions—that is the point the comic *kōmos* makes clear: we are all responsible for the whole. Comedy makes us feel this, and begins our re-creation into it: we are already sharing a proper eros and sympathy here at the play. See, it has been done!

ly virtuous or happy ones. If it is as necessary for our happiness to feel correctly about our actions as it is to act correctly, then the theater—whether of Dionysus or some greater unknown god—is a requirement for every human city—or every city that is to have human beings as citizens.

At Shakespeare's play those who are excessive in desire or sympathy see such excesses variously played out and mocked in Orlando, Rosalind, and Touchstone. Each character's excess is quite distinct, and thereby calls forth distinctive audience members, or, more likely, distinctive desires in each audience member—and they laugh at this excess (which is also their own). Those deficient in philia and philanthropy, to say nothing of eros, see Oliver and Jaques happily converted, their lack of desire for an equitable community (which death plots for younger brothers and strict equality for deer indicate) having led them into danger or bitterness; this peripety in the plot, as well as their change of feeling, and the sheer song of the play rousing the eros of the inadequate. Our feelings are drawn thereby toward the mean, purified of their excesses or deficiencies, and the desire for redress of the normal inequities is given a space for flourishing—a space so satisfying that we might be more tempted to make it actual. And this last element explains the catharsis of the virtuous whose proper desires flourish and rejoice in the course of the play, such as they are not often allowed in the world, hindered by inadequate laws and worse administrators.

But besides kinds of catharsis that begin from the point of taking desire's world as absolute, we must consider that there is another, entirely distinct, kind. This last kind of catharsis seems not to be operative in any Aristophanic comedy. Perhaps we should not expect anything other than worldly (physical and social) catharses and enjoyment from plays in honor of Dionysus. But because a certain kind of character is not *represented* does not mean the audience cannot *enjoy* another kind of catharsis. To state it baldly, comedy rouses and purifies our love not only for the community, but for that more singular good, *dianoia* itself, through inspiring and driving on the pleasant practice of that activity. It is *shown* to us in Shakespeare, though it is (at least minimally) *practiced* in every act of attention to a visible cosmos. In *As You Like It*, for example, there is at least one character who, seeing the green world's perfection, leaves it. And so, another type of comic catharsis than those we see in that world—one in line with the character of Jaques—must be possible. It may be, of course, that Jaques, preferring solitude and his melancholy, really never enters the green world (not seeing it as green), or if he does, does not change.[11] Early on he claims that the green world "more usurps" (2.1.27) from the natural good than the normal world from which his duke is but recently banished. His extremity is self-destructive, for it would require starvation out of "justice" for the deer. In this he would be even more humourous than Touchstone, who at least takes part in the festive couplings of the country, though he is not much pleased with Arden and reduces festivity to sex. Under this reading Jaques is simply an irrecoverable surd in the comic movement, and has to be got off stage (as Lamachus in *Acharnians*) before the ritual concluding *kōmos* can begin. It should be clear already that if the *kōmos* is "the sensible rendering of the moral idea" (*KU* 356) of the community of mankind, this ending is not fully adequate, for the community, in such a case, would not include all of mankind.

Although Frye joins many others in suggesting that Jaques must be removed (as Lamachus is) for the comedy to succeed completely, since he is the "tragic germ" in the comedy and the "refuser of festivity" (*Anatomy*, 218), it is possible to read, to see, and to play and experience Jaques as a character who comes to his own kind of recognition, and changes because of it.[12] If he does so change, he will mark a different kind of catharsis that is possible for an audience member as well. Jaques, at the end, loves the green world and sees its goodness—its happiness—but he loves it not in the way we ordinarily think of that word—as a synonym for eros, desire—he loves the world of the heart's desire seemingly without desiring it, and so he leaves it, and leaving it, he blesses it:

> You to your former honor I bequeath;
> your patience and your virtue well deserve it.
> You to a love that your true faith doth merit;
> You to your land and love and great allies;
> You to a long and well-deserved bed;
> and you to wrangling, for thy loving voyage
> is but for two months victualed. So, to your pleasures;
> I am for other than dancing measures.
>
> (5.4.178–85)

In giving this speech Jaques repeats the "ducdame" which called the forest dwellers into a circle around him in 2.5; but he is now on the outside of

11. This view still has strong adherents; see, e.g., A. D. Nuttall, "Two Unassimilable Men," and Hassell, chapter 5.

12. See Robert B. Bennett, "Reform of a Malcontent: Jaques and the Meaning of *As You Like It*," *Shakespeare Studies* (1976): 201f.

the circle of the Ardent, rather than in their midst, and seeing erotic love in its place he no longer calls them a circle of fools. There is none of his earlier melancholic bile in this speech; and of Touchstone, the one person who is not so highly blessed, he seems to be merely speaking the plain truth, one that Touchstone himself would be unlikely to deny or find fault with. Touchstone had, in fact, predicted a similar result before the marriage presided over by the hedge-priest:

> I am not in the mind but I were better to be married of him than of another; for he is not like to marry me well; and not being well married, it will be a good excuse for me hereafter to leave my wife. (3.3.77–83)

As Jaques in the play, then, may there not be one or two in the audience of the comedy, who, leaving the play, admit that all the heart's desires are satisfied in the green world, and bless that world, but are cured of desiring it? If so, they must have an inkling, as Jaques does, that desire's world is not absolute, even when it is fulfilled. I suppose Schopenhauer would like to say this: that we first feel and so learn, in comedy—and the comic catharsis makes us feel the good of—resignation of desire. But I think that the parting speech of Jaques bespeaks something other than Schopenhauerian resignation, for Schopenhauer could not bless the happy couples of the green world, as Jaques, most heartfeltly and most accurately, does.

The kind of comic catharsis I have in mind does not work just by showing us, and letting us identify with, the satisfaction of desire, or by showing it to us and excising or denying our feeling for it, but it shows the world of eros as a whole, and, as every whole that we can see *as* a whole, the world of eros is a limited whole, and all its perfected satisfactions are but the figure of something greater than that whole world, to which Jaques goes, at the edge of the forest of Arden. *What* that is he has yet to discover, but *that* it is he must already believe. This we should call a sublime comic catharsis, for it raises us entirely above thralldom to desire since it raises us above even the whole world of desire satisfied. So, of course, does Schopenhauer, in his fashion. The difference in fashion makes all the difference.

The first two, worldly, versions of catharsis are the ones most commonly attributed to comedy—we have mentioned how Freudian, Marxist, and Platonic critics can be found among the first of them, but the more Aristotelian explication of art opens the door to the second of them. Those two worldly catharses would be in line with the ethos of Aristotle's bifurcated audience—the φαῦλοι and the σπουδαῖοι—for these audience members desire (and discover) different things by definition. Each subtype of that catharsis has its figure in *As You Like It.* The purely physiological catharsis is figured in Touchstone, the "material fool" (3.3.28) who, crowding in amongst all the other country copulatives, gives away the fact that he really thinks all the other marriages are as simply physiological as his. For a taste:

As the ox hath his bow, sir, the horse his curb, and the falcon her bells, so man hath his desires; and as pigeons bill, so wedlock would be nibbling. (3.3.69–71)

and

If a hart do lack a hind
Let him seek out Rosalind.

(3.2.95–97)

and similar false gallop of verses. One sees here the thoroughly modern figure, who considers sexual desire and its act as purely consumptive.[13]

Touchstone takes his satisfaction as some audience members come to a play for entertainment or titillation; he comes to his resolution in the last scene—or shortly thereafter. He accomplishes his satisfaction upon the body of Audrey, as a younger brother in the audience might achieve some substitutive satisfaction for his real desires by seeing the play. It is "a poor virgin" (ergo, unfruitful), "an ill favored thing" (because fruitless), but his own (5.4.53–56). No doubt such play will titillate and satisfy such a one for two months or so, but then the wrangling will begin, and Audrey—fantasy fulfillment—will be put away for more suitable meat—or a different fantasy. In such a world and among such natural slaves novelty will be the prime requisite both for music and for marriage.[14] The merely physiological catharsis of art wears thin; one needs more opium, more flowers to hide the chains, or else the very thing that hid the chains makes one become more aware of the chains.[15] In short, it would seem, contra Freud,[16] that art is *less* likely than religion to provide substitutive satisfaction to the demands of a raging Id,

13. E.g., Bataille, "the sexual act is in time what the tiger is in space"; *The Accursed Share,* 1:12.

14. The corruption of music and society go hand in hand according to the argument Socrates gives in *Republic,* where, speaking of that complicitous corruption he *misquotes* the *Odyssey,* saying that "human beings most esteem the newest song the singer sings" (424b). No doubt that corrupt quotation was merely an accident.

15. Even 276 channels might not be enough. The culminating point of this type of culture, "where devotion to what is superfluous begins to be prejudicial to what is indispensable, is called luxury" (*KU* 432).

16. See Sigmund Freud, *The Future of an Illusion,* chapter 2.

for the satisfactions presented to fantasy in dramatic art are manufactured out of things that some people accomplish in the real world, religion's are not. Id is, in this one regard, a realist: it doesn't want the picture of a cigar, it wants the real cigar. Touchstone becomes an incendiary.

All this is not to say that the catharsis signified by Touchstone and accomplished in the groundling—or φαῦλος—crowd is not a catharsis, nor is it to deny that the other kinds of catharsis—those symbolized by the lovers and Jaques—are *also* physiological or accomplishable to some extent in the groundlings as well. As that poor mild virgin, Emily Dickinson, said, "When I feel physically as if the top of my head were taken off, I know this is poetry."[17] I *am* saying that this kind of reductive explication of art, long and often popular, is indicative of an inadequate understanding of the nature, purpose, and justification of art. All the arguments of *Republic*'s Socrates haunt it, and against it they hold the field. If that is all art is, then it is generally more bad than good.

The second subtype of worldly catharsis is figured variously by the other lovers, who undergo the trials and purifications of desire—the ridicule of their excessive eros (Orlando) and the arousal of their inadequate philia and eros (Oliver)—suffer the recognitions those trials lead to, and embrace the personal, interpersonal, and social *redintigratio* that the forest offers, and we, the audience, cheer—recognizing our own, and feelingly. Without extending our analysis too far afield we might see that the lower of these catharses—if it were thoroughly separated from the second—is pornography, which neither purifies desire nor satisfies the judicious. Touchstone is a perfect name for this, and his very being ridicules this motive in us. On the other hand, the scatological kissing (*Midsummer Night's Dream*) and touching (*As You Like It*) of stones is part of, and intrinsically connected to, the more beautiful (because more completely human) and more socially significant celebration of desire in the lovers' resolution and marriages and the catharsis that resolution of the play evokes in the audience. This interpersonal and more broadly social resolution brings the audience to a catharsis that fits with the ethos of the virtuous. It does not deny the physiological, but the higher takes the lower up into itself. A similar balance between the aischrological and the beautiful was discussed in the previous chapter as required in the proper understanding of Aristophanic comedy. That is to say, comic art takes up the reductively physiological as a constituent part, thereby

17. Miss Emily is quoted by Frye (*Anatomy*, 27).

shaping it to a higher end than sense alone allows; mere pornography aims to take physiology to its reductive satisfaction. Comic art must take up the physiological; justice and equity demand it, for our physiological pleasures and desires, even more naturally than bad laws and foolish administrators, are part of the normal and demanding state of affairs comedy sublates. The comic spirit does not take up the physiological merely of its own nature as comedy (as if it is just something to mock); it must take it up because of the nature of the audience, for what is part and parcel of ourselves and our own nature cannot be left outside of the comic *kōmos* or made the scapegoat for some other partial truth. To do so is romantic idealism (probably based on the doctrines of Mani),[18] and there we must write tragedy, for in it we kill one of our own, one that it is natural and just for us to love, for it is an intrinsic part of us.

The second distinct *kind* of catharsis, which we should perhaps call the religious comic catharsis, also has two forms. They both are feeling recognitions—perhaps I should say practices of feeling—that there is an ideal realm that checks or overcomes the world of desire even when that realm is fulfilled. That ideal realm bounds the world of desire and does not allow Arden to take itself as utterly absolute, even when everyone in that green world may be satisfied. Only one of its two subtypes can be instantiated in the play, however, for either can only be instantiated on stage by Jaques. He may be understood (and played) as a prototype of Schopenhauerian denial of the world of desire—one who begins in melancholy and ends in resignation of action and desire. A Hindu might call such a Jaques a religious hero, and the play might bring such an audience member to a religious catharsis. Or, more likely for Shakespeare, and as I think Jaques's last speech makes clear, Jaques may be understood and played as someone who comes to recognize desire's goodness in Arden, who blesses the green world, but lets it be. He goes out to the edge of the green world of the heart to look for something that eye has not heard, nor ear seen, nor did it enter the mind of the Bard to represent. That is why he must be got off stage—even Shakespeare's imagination breaks upon the reefs of this shore and cannot enter. At the limit of ordinary human desire and sociality lies something more divine. Aristotle is not uncomfortable with such a view, or with thinking that even what is mindless imitates that divinity insofar as it can. Such a Jaques transfigures the play's beautiful comic resolution into a sublime one, and his recognition may cause its echo,

18. On this parenthetical expression, see Denis de Rougemont's *Love in the Western World.*

and engender its purification, at least in some of the audience. This erotic aim—for an intellectual, or completely spiritual, good—is not only sparked, but proleptically enjoyed by someone contemplating the play. It is interesting to consider that Jaques's expressed motive for not returning to the "real" world—and he is the only one who does so—is that "there is much matter to be heard and learned" in that liminal space where the hermit and the convertites meet (5.2.178–79). His approach to inner transformation seems to be through the mind rather than through the body;[19] through philosophy rather than through mimesis; through thought rather than through passion. But he has been brought to this desire through seeing the actions in the play (and their Hymenal conclusions), though hearing the music of Arden. The music of desire satisfied has satisfied him, cured him of his antisocial humours, and so set him free for a higher eros. That he is one whose further inner transformation will be philosophical is, however, a mimetic inspiration to a certain kind of soul in the audience. Perhaps such an audience member is rare, but I suppose it is possible for him to have been in attendance at a play of Aristophanes—perhaps standing throughout in order to exhibit what is lacking. Such an audience member might be strengthened and similarly purified (perhaps more directly passionally) by listening to late Beethoven or Bach, or Ralph Vaughan Williams, and not be unfamiliar with the thought that a poet who writes excellent tragedy should be able to write fine comedy as well, for what is at stake in both is the natural incompletion of our nature that rouses both fear and desire and finds its truest fulfillment in something more divine that is already active in us (1177b27–33).[20]

2. COMIC CATHARSIS AND CULTURE

So much, then, for the way the kinds of resolution in the play both represent and are imitated in the kinds of catharsis available to the audience. The above section explains how Aristotle's claims that "everybody, when listening to mimeses, is thrown into a corresponding state of feeling" (*Pol.* 1340a13–14) and that all audience members "undergo a catharsis and lighten-

19. I would like to thank Laura Rotunno for this suggestion.

20. We should remember also that, according to Socrates' story (from Diotima), Eros is the child of poverty and wealth, and while he seeks the whole—as Aristophanes said—he seeks the whole of beauty, and in this regard Aristophanes himself does not have a complete view. The Epilogue of this book will return to this problem of Aristophanic art.

ing with pleasure" (1342a14–15) play out in comic drama. It should be clear also how the strength, extent, and direction of that catharsis will depend on the audience member's character—whether we divide such characters into two (the more noble and the meaner, as in *Pol.* 1342a19–21, cf. *Po.* 1448b24–28), or three, according to whether the audience member is excessive, deficient, or at the mean. "It is through vice and virtue that the characters of all men vary" (1448a)—not just characters in plays. Let us now explicate a further point: we can also see that the kinds of catharsis accomplishable *by* the play, and the kinds of resolution reached *in* the play, figure different kinds of culture *outside* the play. The easiest to see is the society of the material fools, symbolized by T and A,[21] for whom everything is merely physiology. Students of physical education come to mind, for whom work is lifting weights, running laps, lines, patterns, plays, and who build a day (and so a life) around such activities, others (philosophy or literature classes) falling in as they may—or not. What kind of thing can be cathartic in such a culture? Things that relax their bodies from the efforts of the day: sex, drugs, rock 'n roll, or lounging at a play. The more such a one dedicates himself to the work, the stronger the catharsis needed to achieve a kind of normal state. Aristotle himself suggests that special competitions and shows must be organized for this kind of person (*Pol.* 1342a20–22). One has to wonder whether or not the comedies of Aristophanes and Shakespeare are the kind of thing he had in mind. Partially, one may hope—though it seems unlikely to be the kind of thing such people would choose on their own. In order to make such art attractive we might have to make it part of a competition in which the whole city participates. It seems more likely that in a culture overweighted with such souls art would be seen as not only not a necessity, but almost an impossibility: *Panem et circenses*, or more modernly translated, sex, drugs, rock 'n roll are more likely candidates for providing the necessary release than Shakespearean comedy, even with a flash of T and A. Soon one will begin to demand New Year's Day games in sunny locales. Sic transit gloria mundi, the body culture, the materialism of atoms and the void. That a whole culture might be this way does not seem impossible, though of course it is, if human beings are more than matter and void.

A second culture is more genuinely social, and may be called moral culture; it exceeds physical culture as the soul, in medieval philosophy, exceeds

21. Lest some ill-humored reader embed me in a context I do not wish to be bedded in, let me say that what I mean by "T and A" is just Touchstone and Audrey.

the body,[22] or as the marriage of true minds surpasses country copulation. This kind of culture may spend its days just as competitively as the first, though the competitions are for things less tangible than physical victory and release, intangibles like love, honor, and perhaps money—which are, after all, bound up with signs. As their competitions and their desires, so must their catharses be, and the catharsis provided by a play may serve to feelingly recall the unity underlying and making possible the single-minded pursuits of the daylight world. For neither love, nor honor, nor even money are possible except that we live among others who recognize and support the reality of such "things," for such are not merely things, but signs, and signs are a social reality. As the competition for such things is largely mimetically induced,[23] one might not unreasonably hope that a mimesis of the excessiveness of the competition and its empowering and empowered desires in a play might also mimetically induce such passions and people to ridicule and reversal (or to emulation and increase if deficient). Such infection and mockery (or arousal) would turn their love and sympathy toward the shared good of their social nature. *The play* is already such an enjoyment: it is the muses' recreation with us. In such a culture, art provides a morally useful and unquestionably legitimate catharsis, a purification with socially important results. As Aristotle would say, such music conduces to moral virtue (*Pol.* 1339a24f). For Aristotle, that catharsis provides the art's political legitimation, though in a day of differing moralists the music's results will be judged differently depending on how the moralist wishes the society to turn: liberals fancy Marx and expect artistic catharses to motivate social revolution (these days watered down to "change"), while conservatives are on the side of Freud, who expects art to work as a substitutive satisfaction for civilization's endemic discontents. But to judge art according to either of these latter standards is to make a baldly political judgment on art, not an artistic or even a moral judgment. It transforms the free and reflective judgment of the beautiful (a judgment based upon the feelings the work arouses, not its structure) into a determination according to a concept of reason, and reason rather parochially understood. As catharsis is not a judgment of theoretical reason, neither is a judgment of excellence in art an affirmation of a public policy or any particular end of practical reason. Rather, art aims at a purifi-

22. See, e.g., Augustine's little treatise, *De quantitate animae*, J. P. Migne, cols. 1035–49.

23. I refer here again to the work of Rene Girard; see, e.g., *Violence and the Sacred* and *Things Hidden from the Foundation of the World*.

cation of feeling and thereby the freedom of reason; we can make judgments about what plays accomplish such purifications, and what plays do not—or worse, accomplish a putrification of them. Such judgments are the business of criticism, which has as its end understanding, not catharsis.

Besides the physical and the moral, there is a third *kind* of culture;[24] let us call it religious, for it posits the world of desire as a completed whole, and *thereby* transcends it. Its vision is of a noncompetitive, infinitely sharable, but intimate and personal good: enlightenment, beatific vision, nirvana, a communion of saints. The version of this culture corresponding to Schopenhauer's resigning catharsis is the unarmed society of Lamaism.[25] The culture corresponding to the more sublime resolution, which does not seek to evaporate the principle of individuation as Schopenhauer does, nor curse the world as mere humorous illusion as a certain way of playing Jaques implies and enacts, is the more traditional religious spirit of the West.[26] For such a person a play itself is the mimesis of just that religious ideal, for without dissolving the principle of individuation, *each* person comes to his or her catharsis *along with* everyone else in the theater. A play is an infinitely sharable, but intimate and personal, good thing.[27] As such, its performance is the beginning through mimesis, and a proleptic passional enjoyment of both vision (*theōria*, the root of theater) and communion. One might well call it a liturgical act, and the culture that enjoys it a liturgical culture.

Even when we are not at a performance but reading a play, the passions

24. If any reader begins to feel like he or she has been climbing up and down a ladder built after a familiar Platonic pattern in these two sections, there is probably something to the thought. For those who are not natural Platonists, there is also Aristotle's remark in the *Ethics* that the three main kinds of life are the life of pleasure; the practical, social life aiming at and practicing moral virtue; and the contemplative life (1095b14–96a5). There is great debate about whether or not he thinks all of these can be joined but it is certain that he thinks there is an order among them. See Chapter 4.1 and 4.2, below.

25. See Georges Bataille, *The Accursed Share*, volume 1, chapter 3.

26. Here we see Nietzsche's cultural debt to Schopenhauer, despite himself, for he evaporates the principle of individuation. In *The Birth of Tragedy*, Nietzsche seems to claim that the principle of individuation is dissolved by tragedy and music: "[T]he transport of the Dionysiac state . . . carries with it a Lethean element in which everything that has been experienced by the individual is drowned" (§7). See also §18 and §21, where he calls the Apollonian charm of art "illusory," "mere appearance" cast upon the darkness, and "the work of Maya."

27. This kind of good so far surpasses the merely physiological or animal good of individual pleasurable satisfaction as to mark an infinite qualitative difference—in other words, that kind of difference to which no amount of merely physiological pleasure can even begin to add up toward. As Kant says, "[H]umanity signifies, on the one hand, the *universal feeling* of sympathy, and, on the other, the faculty of being able to *communicate* universally one's inmost self—properties constituting in conjunction the befitting *social spirit* of mankind, in contradistinction to the narrow life of the lower animals" (*KU* 355).

are moved to and by this universally communicable feeling, and claim (as Kant will say) a universally valid judgment not based on any principle. It is this delight in the mimetic act, not the delight in intellectual recognition of any particular moral principle or insight, nor any particular knowledge about a character's life or a plot's unraveling that allows the claim that art is "a preparation for moral activities of many kinds in life."[28] What is learned from art is not reducible to reference because what is learned is not, in the first place, an "about" or thematic "what." What is learned in the first place is in an important sense not learned but *practiced*; and the part that practices is feeling. Thus understood comedy is far from mere amusement; it is not only a vision or representation but, first of all, a mimesis of ultimate social significance for it is also *the practice* of a shared feeling and *dianoia*, and enjoyment of these communions. It is no wonder that drama was a religious ritual for the Greeks, that species of human being that is a permanent embarrassment to every lower type.

Further, and to the point of our particular culture. It is probably about as accidental as the fact that 3 – 2 = 1 that after the dark political ages of the Pax Romana, and the tiring out of rival football clubs of Vandals, Goths, and Visigoths, that schools and universities were refounded not by states, but by monks and religious communities. The idea of a university is not an idea that a state would have: it does not need them. In particular, it does not need humanities programs. A state, particularly one with a highly mechanized economy, will find it much more useful to keep its citizens under the physiological or directly social understandings of culture and catharsis. Football—I mean physiological catharsis—and fantasy fulfillment are its major tools. Aristotle pointed this out when he said that the bodily pleasures

> are pursued because of their violence by those who cannot enjoy other pleasures, . . . for they have nothing else to enjoy, and, besides, a neutral state is painful to many people because of their nature. . . . Similarly, the youthful, . . . or people of an excitable nature always need relief. (*NE* 1154b3–12)

28. Nussbaum makes this claim in *Poetic Justice* (42), where she is at pains to validate the use of the realistic novel for training in insight and judgment about public life and law. This particular remark, however, defends fairy tales *not* for any insight they engender, but for what they make us *do and feel.* This is the right way to go. Aesthetic enjoyment changes and exercises our affects, it is a practice that exceeds or reverses the practices of ordinary utility and that not only allows the development of certain capacities of thought (what exercise of mind does not?) and affection, but *conjoins pleasure to freedom* and the *pleasure and freedom of one to the pleasure and freedom of all.* It is this kind of emotional practice, not its specific representational content, that makes art morally valuable—or not.

In *Politics* he calls this culture the culture of natural slaves.[29]

But the pursuit of wisdom exceeds both physiology and the pursuit of socially constructed, or socially constructible, desires and virtues, for besides being an activity engaged in for its own sake and without a return to practical or even, necessarily social, use, it is one with which a finite being can never be finished, or even imagine being finished: against physiological desire it is recognized as not having a termination—it is an *energeia* rather than a *kinēsis*.[30] Even if we no longer believe, with Aristotle, that the superlunary world is made of some incorruptible quintessence and so, for us, all theoretical wisdom may have some distant connection to more mundane technical science, and the engineering of earth, water, fire, and air, it is still the case that the pursuit of wisdom is an infinite task, and someone engaged in such a task needs play, for it brings him down to something accomplishable, before he goes back to the task that can never be finished, and into which even his play is taken up. For such a one art is a *necessity*, since only it can grant him the catharsis, the resolution, the feeling of completion and perfection that his infinite spirit—that is, his infinite desires and infinite capacity for knowledge—in its finite weaknesses and limitations, requires. Comic art provides the proleptic accomplishment, the actuality of which could only be seeing God face to face and seeing all things in God. The best comedy is earth's mimesis of heaven's eternal joy.

For a time, persons from all three cultures—physical, moral, religious—can meet at a play like *As You Like It*.[31] It may seem, perhaps, unlikely that we are *meeting* in any other sense than that which any material fool could describe and understand. In a culture less linguistic than imagistic such literalization of "meet" seems even more likely, for it is language that brings us up into the fully human community of thought and feeling—and the mute

29. The slave is distinguished by his (or her) soul, not his (or her) body (*Pol.* 1254b25–37), and the corrupted nature (for whom slavery is both expedient and right) is the one in which "the body appears to rule over the soul" (1254b1). Kant is no doubt referring to the same phenomenon more circumspectly when he says "where the fine arts are not brought into either close or distant connection with moral ideas, which alone bring with them self-sufficing delight [they must] dull the soul, gradually render the object disgusting and make the soul moody and dissatisfied with itself through the consciousness that its disposition is contrary to the purposes of reason" (*KU* 326). Touchstone will find this problem applies to his use of Audrey; indeed, he already intuits the truth of the matter. To live in such a state, or to prefer such recreations, is slavishness.

30. On this distinction, see, e.g., J. L. Ackrill, "Aristotle's Distinction between Energeia and Kinēsis."

31. It is because of this and through this, "fine art . . . has the effect of advancing the culture of the mental powers in the interests of social communication" (*KU* 306).

arts—or those that make themselves so are, in this way, incomplete. Mimesis is that through which we enter into humanity, but it is not our completion. It was once a popular trope to say of certain paintings or pieces of music that they "speak," but the truth is they only wish to. Meeting at a comedy, however, allows us to see and share each other's joy; judgment may grow from this—at least, a desire for judgment may be engendered. In their appreciation of a work of art such as *As You Like It*—in what each enjoys, laughs at, wishes for—an audience necessarily judges itself; in what each member of the audience cheers for he and she show their taste, confess their culture, perhaps even profess their religion. A material fool judges merely the pleasantness of the sensations of the play, and about this there can be no disputing: some prefer Audrey, some prefer sheep. Their pleasures are incommunicable each to each, though the source may be bought, sold, or, in turn, enjoyed by all. Further, like Touchstone, they can't help what they feel, and they think no one else can either—as pigeons bill, marriage is nibbling.

The more noble lovers, and their correlative audience, have an ontological commitment to freedom, understood as freedom from determination by a material humour; that freedom allows them to make commitments to each other that we can expect to last longer than the two-month, or two-hour, cure of a pathological humour. For them, judgments of taste are not merely personal caprice, but are tied to something of greater constancy: they are not merely judgments of physiological taste, but moral commitments freely engaged. The third figure, Jaques, has, under either reading of him, an ontological commitment to freedom understood positively: a transcendental reality is the condition for the happy possibilities of the lovers in the forest of Arden. Of that reality, on the outer and binding edge of our happiness, he would learn more. There his desire seeks its term.

After hearing part of this story about comic catharsis, one of my more Platonic students, Ryan Nelson, suggested that since each person has an element that aims at each type of catharsis, all three kinds of catharsis work on each member of the audience. That idea is more charitable than my own tendency, and, therefore, no doubt, truer. It would be most correct to point out, then, not that Jaques is got off stage for the *kōmos*, but that he is at the very furthest reach of the green world; he shows how far our human celebration extends and his presence exhibits the telos it proposes. He shows that there is something in us that exceeds the social and the political. Art can fail to represent it (Aristophanes seems to miss this), but sometimes even in failing to represent it it can arouse us to love for it (as *what* Jaques seeks is not represented). Further, if art is capable of improving culture, Ryan's idea must be the basis of the how. Someone whose desires run to T and A goes to the play and seeing his Touchstone desire run to its conclusion in Audrey is "feelingly persuaded" that he wants more than that—or something other: something more like Rosalind and Orlando, or Celia and Oliver. His passions have begun their emendation. He has *felt* the ridiculousness of his own physiological reduction, he has laughed at T and A, and that laughter already expresses that he *desires* better. Similarly with Jaques: we may feel something sublime in his abandonment of the green world's goodness. And, if we do, we are already sharing in his passion. Altogether then, like the forest of Arden, the play does not just flatter our desires, but "feelingly persuades" us of what we are (2.1.10), or what we can be and are not yet. What we are is something more than the humourous Touchstone will admit, though his marriage's failure in two month's time will exhibit it—in case the marriage itself hasn't made his pathology plain. Though it may be impolitic (these days) to do so, Aristotle suggests that the culture of such an audience as thinks Touchstone sufficient for comedy is rightly criticized:

> [S]pectators are of two kinds—the one free and educated, and the other a vulgar crowd— . . . [and] their music will correspond to their minds; for as their minds are perverted from their natural state, so there are perverted modes and highly strung and unnaturally colored melodies, etc. (*Pol.* 1342a18–25)

A TV show in which there was nothing but such T and A might be the kind of music such a soul requests, but it is an incomplete and stunted joy for a man (or woman either). But perhaps the more vulgar can also be tempted out of their cave if it is (as Socrates suggested in a famous image) open along its entire width, if, that is, the capacity for virtue is not entirely destroyed in us and the artist is capable of turning our passions—even if slightly—toward the light. The great work of art is such a shadow play in our cave; it mimetically charms us through the fire of our desires rather than merely feeding us as we face a wall away from them (Freud's substitution theory) or dance before the nearer approach of our bright fetish (Marx).

The culture of Touchstone can be reduced to culture embodied in particular unique empirical artefacts, to which the only valid question is "Isn't that interesting?" and the only politically correct answer is "Yes." If you don't say yes, your preference for one artefact rather than another is merely humourous, a different physiological taste. Touchstone makes Audrey; isn't that interesting? Corin makes sheep; isn't that interesting?[32] You now know everything you need to know about multiculturalism except what each culture finds interesting; isn't that interesting? This is culture as a historicist, like Herder, understood it.[33] There are still Herders among us. Isn't that interesting?

The culture of the lovers is one of normative commitments open to moral development. It is a culture that by its very existence asks us "Isn't this good?" And in order to be able to answer that question you have to live in that culture of normative commitments; you have to put *yourself* into such commitments; and the quality of those commitments would be your answer. The play achieves a brief version of this state in the catharsis it produces in the average, or better, audience; but insofar as it is but a two-hour version of moral culture, it is not moral culture, and we must advance from the aesthetic ten-dollar show to the actual life-costing marriage. That is, like the people in Arden, we must now go back to the real world. We have noted earlier in this chapter that the play is not merely a symbol of morality, but also begins the construction of a world closer to the moral heart, for it constructs in the audience that unity of feeling and reason that is the comic catharsis. This is culture as Kant understood it. There are still Kantians among us. Perhaps this book is a Kantian version of play.

Jaques goes to the very edge of culture, and wonders "What is it that allows these cultures to be?" That is, he asks "What are the conditions for the possibility of culture?" And the only proper response is continual wonder. Perhaps this wonder will find its term in reverence.[34] This culture, if there were one, would be the culture of philosophy, if there was any.[35] It is clear that for Aristotle this last culture's highest activity is a religious act, for first philosophy concerns the divine, and philosophy itself is the act of our most

32. Lest some lamb think I am here straying from the folds of Shakespeare's play, recall the interesting discussion between Corin and Touchstone on the cultural differences between the hand-kissing court and the more rural rubbing of sheep (3.2.11–79).

33. On Herder's multiculturalism, see Leventhal, esp. his central brief, "Nine Theses on Johann Gottfried Herder," in *Disciplines of Interpretation*, 230–34; Bluestein, "Herder and Folk Ideology," in *Poplore*, 28–45; or Herder himself, e.g., "On Monuments of the Distant Past."

34. I believe that a similar passional shift (from wonder to reverence) is under the relation and difference between Anselm's *Monologion* and *Proslogion*; see my "The Relation of *Monologion* and *Proslogion*," *Heythrop Journal* 46, no. 2 (2005): 149–66. To think of such prayers as nonmimetic series of truth functional propositions is not to understand them at all.

35. An early version of much that is in these two sections was originally published in *Philosophy and Literature*, 19. I am grateful to the editors for permission to use it here. I am also still grateful to Brenda, Laura, Brett, and Ryan, who worked through many of the matters here with me in a Shakespeare seminar.

divine part. So, in one work of art we ought to find the artifactual, the moral (in a way to be further discussed) and the religious; these are universal aspects of all human art. Though they are universal aspects of art, their forms and moving may and do have particular differences in any case, different cultures may require somewhat different material causes to affect the same finality, and it is certainly true that any so-called work of art—as any artist or audience member—may prove stunted and incapable at one or the other:

I am asham'd: does not the stone rebuke me
For being more stone than it? . . .
There's magic in thy majesty, which has
My evils conjured to remembrance, and
From thy admiring daughter took the spirits,
Standing like stone with thee.

(*Winter's Tale* 5.3.37–42)

3. EMBLEMATIC APPENDIX ON THE CHARACTER OF AUDREY

Modern thinkers tend to find the ancients difficult to treat as serious critics of art because they are thought not to have allowed art to be treated seriously in its own right. That is, they—and Plato is always treated as more criminal than Aristotle in this regard—are considered moralistic: they treat art as subject to morals. They seem not to be able to think of aesthetics as an independent realm, with its own wholly autonomous principles. About such a complaint there are many problems to be raised, not the least of which is to wonder whether some sort of subjection to morals should be considered a problem. And by whom might it be considered so? Particularly in the case of an obviously eudaimonistic thinker like Aristotle, we should turn the question around and wonder what is the problem with the critic—Does he or she think that art neither has nor ought to have any connection to happiness? If art has any power at all in this regard, if it has any connection at all to happiness or misery in human life, then it must be connected to morals. But even for a noneudaimonistic thinker, as Kant is generally considered, we should consider that if, as I have been arguing, art works upon our feelings—about which the law makes no inquiry, requiring, as it does, mere obedience—then art is, in this way, more closely related to morals than the law that is built according to moral principles. Art's concern with justice and equity (among other things) is that we feel appropriately about it; and it enacts its concern by charming forth our feelings; in doing so we practice loving, practice (e.g.) loving justice or equity for its own sake. This the law dare not require even though it is built upon justice as a principle and requires equity in its administration. Art's concern with feeling makes it the subjective counterpart of the law's concern with behavior; and we might say that together the two develop the fully rounded sense of human action. Our opening comparison (Chapter 1.1) between constitutions and poems was neither accidental nor incidental; it is found in Plato's requirement that every law have its prelude (*Laws* 722d–23c), and here it returns again as the aspect of the human moral agent that the law cannot enforce. It seems that Plato's point in *Laws* is that our feelings must be properly organized in order for the laws to even be heard. So then, not only do *nomoi*, whether laws or kitharic melodies, receive preludes, but music (in the broad Greek sense of art of the muses) is the prelude for law (*Laws* 722d–23e). I am not convinced that the process outlined thus far as the work of the work of art, or any of these Platonic, Aristotelian, or Kantian sets of relations just mentioned, reduces art to didacticism, and will show in this section that the reading of *As You Like It* presented here and the Aristotelian understanding of comedy it relies upon do not require a view of art that makes it catechetic or propagandistic in any simple, much less objectionable (—and on what grounds would one make an objection if not moral?), sense. In the next section I will argue in greater length that a view of art that attempts to sever art from morals completely is itself absurd.

As an emblematic appendix of the complex relation between art and morals, we might indicate the difficulty in playing Audrey, who marries Touchstone at the end of the play. (We should note here that every opportunity for a sexual pun in this section should be read as such, starting with the name of the clown, who seems by his very presence to infect the language with second meanings: that indeed is part of the play and part of the human being and problem.) Audrey swears she is honest (3.3.14–33). She is, for Touchstone, the solution to a recently developed humour; that is, he translates her to the vulgar, boorish, and common (5.1; 5.3.51–58)—to be polite. Throughout all their intercourse the naive girl keeps her desire for "honesty" (5.3.3f), and her country virtue. That she is honest and virtuous, though naive next to her more cunning linguistic courtly lover, is probably the truth since Jaques says "*one* of you will prove a shrunk panel and . . . warp" (3.3.76f). Audrey, then, is more σπουδαῖα than Touchstone in the ethical sense, even if she is less so in the social sense. She marries him apparently unaware of his less honest—and ethically more φαῦλος—desiring and nature. It becomes clear in this that the only thing Touchstone can treat as a feeling end in itself is his own feeling end; he is aware, as Kant would put it, of the purposiveness of pleasure. Touchstone is *interested.*[36] It is questionable whether Audrey is treated as anything other than Touchstone's conjunction by anyone in the society with the possible exception of Jaques—who sees what she does not. Touchstone is not the kind of character a good man would imitate (*Rep.* 396d), nor does it seem he is cured in the course of the play. He, his arts, and his success at those arts—fooling and quibbling his way into a naive girl's heart and dress—are not the kind of thing a strongly moralistic critic—say, Augustine—would allow children to see—or have young actors imitate. "Unfortunately," the moralist would say, "he is (as usual) one of the funniest and most memorable characters," and loudly applauded at the end of the play (cf. *Rep.* 397d). Further, he is, unlike the randy clown (Lucio) in *Measure for Measure*, shown as rewarded and happy at the end of the play—as he likes it, which might (according to a certain Socrates) encourage certain audience members to become like him in life.

Why, then, should this be considered a great play, particularly when greatness in art is linked to *ethos*, depending as it does upon catharsis of the feelings of desire and sympathy? To answer this we cannot cut scenes and characters out of their place in the whole as Socrates does for Ion and Glaucon, thereby providing a template for bowdlerizing critics for thousands of years. Catharsis of the emotions depends upon *movements* of the plot, the actions of the characters, and the concomitant passions raised thereby in the audience, and so proper understanding of this work of the work of art must be relational. The right question is not whether Touchstone is a good or bad character who comes to a good or bad end, but what does this conjunction of Audrey's (subjectively recognized) morally honest nature with her (objective and seemingly universal) treatment as the telos of Touchstone's particular pleasure accomplish? And how does this relation affect us in the course of the play?

36. Cf. Kant, "the delight which we connect with the representation of the real existence of an object is called interest" (*KU* 204), and "the judgment on an object by which its agreeableness is affirmed expresses an interest in it [as] is evident from the fact that *through sensation it provokes a desire* for similar objects; consequently the delight presupposes . . . the bearing [the object's] real existence has upon my state. . . . It *gratifies*" (207, italics in Kant).

Audrey's presence in the play is necessary, for without her and Touchstone *As You Like It* would be merely comic melodrama or mystery play, and one constructed along moralizing lines. Perhaps it still is a mystery play, and Audrey makes us consider how love, by covering a multitude of sins, may even convert the sinner himself. But without reaching that far, or guessing at the success of Audrey's marriage beyond the play or the prophecy of Jaques, let us recall that just as the comic drama began by disabling our moral judgment, it here ends with a resolution that achieves almost the status of universal blessing. Despite Jaques's prediction, T and A's wedding party joins the more noble weddings as a part of the moral and comic communion under the exorbitantly superfluous deus ex machina of Hymen. That opening disablement and this concluding absence of moral judgment upon the lower part is a large part of what allows the comedy to exist as art, in a realm "disinterested" and free of constraint by *determinations* of pure practical reason. The play, whatever its effects on our feelings, does not, like a piece of rhetoric, require us to come to judgment about how to act or what sentence to give precisely because it sets itself off as a separate world: a *visible* cosmos, but not one in which we act. Moreover, as we shall see more clearly shortly, the play can accomplish its (multiple) ethical task (catharsis) without catechizing about proper moral judgment; its work is effected through mimesis—as a charm or spell works—more than through representation, which is a sign (and so works through thought about meaning); it works through feeling more than reason; it engages imagination (φαντασία) not choice (προαίρεσις) or decision.

In criticism of a play, however, we attempt to bring into reflective judgment the feelings raised and purified by the play by explicating how the mimesis of action affects the feelings of the morally normal audience member.[37] The play itself moves us through the interplay of light and dark—it is the movement between them—and does not merely present us with well-scoured statues of each sort. The difficulty with criticism is that the critic

37. I have already shown that and how comedy and tragedy work on all three kinds of audience member; what I am now aiming to do is show how what should be a problem for the moralist if the purpose of art were simple didacticism or "animated lecture" (Harbage, 112) is not a problem when we understand that art's aim is to bring us to appropriate feeling. This is the defense Socrates was asking for at the end of *Republic* in order to repatriate Homer and the poets. Socrates had treated art as mere animated lecture; he asks for a defense and Plato hoped that someone saw the error Socrates' attack was based on. Plato has Socrates exhibit the dilemma of such a view of art more briefly and clearly in *Ion*: What *technē* does a poet have that he may teach? If none, then he teaches nothing, or everything badly.

must explain the mimetic representatively—as a sign of . . . ; that is, where the critic aims at clarification of understanding about how the passions are working, the poet aims at catharsis of the passions—that is, at working the passions. The critic is supplementary, not repeating the activity of the poem. The professional hazard of critical readings is that they have the effect of making the poem look as if it works through understanding and is an object for knowledge—an animated lecture, just as a *story* about a passion makes the passion look as if it has a narrative and rational or judgmental structure.[38] The extreme case of thinking this way is to make all music into (unconscious) program music. But if the mimetic is before the rational, as Plato and Aristotle say, then "story" or "program" is a certain kind of Emperor's clothing. A critic makes a poem look like its center is a theme, but its center is its work on the passions through action and character. "*Wrath*, O Muse, sing. . . ."

With that caveat we proceed to the issue. The conflict of feelings an *actress* playing Audrey might have is an emblem of the conflict of feelings the normal *audience* will have in seeing her in the play. The actress must *freely* enter a world in which she will appear as a *mere means*, and the feeling of self-respect that the activity of freedom raises in a human being opposes that feeling—even the plausible pleasure—of being a mere means of pleasure. Just so, Audrey's activity and self-acknowledged honesty, joined to her treatment in the play, raises a similar set of conflicting emotions in the audience; but because she appears in just this way—as the locus of the conflict between respect and pleasure (or between the morally σπουδαῖος and the morally φαῦλος)—the greater community of the play can be both a symbol and mimesis of *a world becoming moral*. The conjunction of Audrey and Touchstone make us *feel* that there is still a desire that needs to be brought around to the side of virtue, a feeling of pleasure that needs to be aligned with the good (namely, Touchstone's); at the same time, their place in the wedding allows us to see and feel a proleptic enjoyment of the unity of desire and imagination, and the pleasures of Touchstone with the loves of the more noble lovers. He has not yet come to this, but Touchstone's place in

38. The first sentence of Martha Nussbaum's first Gifford Lecture (published as *Upheavals of Thought*) is: "The story of an emotion, I shall argue, is the story of judgments about important things." The idea of art as a *mimesis* working on the passions does not mean that the passions themselves have a narrative or judgmental structure, but that stories and drama *take us through* the passions, invoking or provoking them in us. *The story of* an emotion puts it into a judgmental structure that it does not necessarily have in vivo.

the communal joy is already granted, with Audrey, who is holding to her honesty. Their place in the wedding allows us to feel this good as coming to be. In this way, the body and its would-be simple physiological pleasures are taken up into the weddings of the spirit. Thus, "in art man enjoys himself as perfection" (*Beyond Good and Evil,* 519)—even, as here, when we feel the emotive pressure of the "not yet" as a moment within the whole.

Audrey may be explicated then—and I have mentioned this analogy earlier—as a symbol of sensibility, of the imagination; as imagination is, of herself she is a poor virgin, an ill-favored thing, but in play with the moral power (which power is at work in the movement of the play—in which a more moral community is formed), she becomes beautiful, and Audrey's wedding is felt to be a rightful part of the beauty of the comedy.[39] Touchstone does not see this beauty, but he is only seeing Audrey from below (as it were); the audience has a more complete experience. The play is felt to be more beautiful with her in it because it is more human. It is our human task to form such a moral community as she becomes a member of, and imagination and her conjunction—physical desire (the touchstone of which is body pleasure)—are but poor and ill-favored things if they do not come along, *or* if they are ruled out in advance as being of too low a character—one, for example, that is intrinsically tied to a morally intractable body, incapable of refinement and better driven out of the garden or escaped from altogether: the so-called Platonic and certainly Manichaean view. Shakespeare was not such a Manichaean; he could not have been, being Christian; but neither, I think, was Plato.

As an experiment to test this thesis (about Audrey's importance, not Plato's religion), consider the counterpossibility: if the play moved the other way—toward a less moral community, one in which the forest became more vicious than the "normal" world, as it does, for a while, in *Midsummer Night's Dream*—wouldn't Audrey's marriage to Touchstone be felt as suffering, or biting farce?[40] The play would at least become a problem com-

39. Shakespeare seems to be regularly aware of and trying to bring out the relation of morality to imagination; see, e.g., Laura Rotunno and Gene Fendt, "Comic Construction and Comic Purpose: The Unity and Sublimity of *Midsummer Night's Dream.*"

40. The distinction here invoked between the beautiful comic ending of *As You Like It* and the farcical ending of, say, *The Importance of Being Earnest* is still not what Kant would call a determinate judgment of the understanding. It is, rather, a reflective judgment: it is a judgment free from being *directed by* moral reason—because although the play of the moral faculty is involved with imagination in the experience of the play, it is the *feelings* that are aroused that lead to the judgment rather than a set of moral judgments (i.e., judgments of practical reason based on its

edy. Probably it would be worse than that, for in it we would see either an autonomous being (Audrey) become entirely a thing in a world of things (the tool for Touchstone's physiological resolution)—a spaniel (*Midsummer Night's Dream* 2.1.202–10), or a nonautonomous being (farce is never about full-fledged moral beings) somehow *choosing* nonautonomous thinghood—like a girl who wants to marry someone because his name is Earnest. The first of those possibilities (the physiological reduction of the world) Shakespeare plays out in the center of *Midsummer*, in which Hermia is used, battered, and abandoned by the mimetically indistinguishable lovers—all as a result of some misplacing of fluids. And for the Touchstone reductionist, what is love but displacing fluids? One cannot think that a marriage under this physiological dispensation would be a happier ending than abandonment—as Helena's complaints of the love-juice's additional suitors in the *Dream*'s act 3, scene 2 indicate:

> To conjure tears up in a poor maid's eyes
> With your derision! None of a noble sort
> Would so offend a virgin and extort
> A poor soul's patience, all to make you sport.
>
> (157–60)

A *body* would not complain so, nor would a void.

Such togetherness as the juices require and cause would be a malicious mockery of any being higher than a spaniel: Helena rejects it. But in the circumstance that *As You Like It* creates, bringing Audrey's marriage into the noble feast makes palpable—makes us *feel*—the rational ideal of autonomy achieving its end in the world, rather than just *think* or understand the achievement of autonomy's end as disembodied reasons might. In fact, the play makes us *feel* this whether we have the capacity for this kind of philosophical analysis or not; and that is exactly the point. This is the prologue of a ring, a prelude to reason's law: The experience of the beautiful, as in this play, is *a feeling symbol* of reason's moral knowledge. That feeling is one of the requirements of virtue, one that lies beneath the reach of law (*nomos*),

principle) that lead to an aesthetic conclusion. Kant would say that the person who cannot distinguish farce from comedy *by feeling* is morally flawed, for it is an indication of a lack of moral feeling "which we believe ourselves able to impute to everyone and be justified in so doing" (*KU* 266). To attempt to distinguish comedy and farce only on the basis of form, thereby making the judgment a determinate one (theoretically so), suffers from accepting the false premise that art is a purely intellectual exercise. It *is* an intellectual recreation (otherwise it could not be a *technē*), but that is not all it is, or even primarily what it is.

but not a certain melody (*nomos*). The play is cathartic, and a viable work for moral development, not because of any specific *teaching*, but because it arouses a feeling of joy at the imitation of a movement that our moral vocation demands that we make—and make joyfully and continually. A similar feeling lights up the heart in every scene between Levin and Kitty in *Anna Karenina*. To feel pleasure in the good is both the beginning and the end of virtue. To feel pleasure elsewise is another thing entirely. To feel pleasure in the taking up of the less-than-virtuous Touchstone into the celebratory *kōmos* of the more perfect citizens is taking pleasure, mimetically, in our moral vocation. The scene, as well, symbolizes our taking up the physical and our passions (even when less than virtuous) into that vocation.

The difficulty of *playing* Audrey is also emblematic of the difficulty of *arguing* for the freedom of aesthetic judgment (the freedom of judgments of the beautiful), while holding that the final cause of art is catharsis of the passions (or holding that beauty is able to be a symbol of the moral). For just as it is difficult for someone (the actress) who has knowledge of good and evil to play at honest innocence (Audrey) with the bawdy clown—of whose every word the *actress* knows both the *double* and the *entendre*, it is difficult for art to be a symbol of the moral without being moralizing. But because it is difficult to accomplish, it is not thereby made optional or impossible. Dramatic art calls up what Kant would call the moral feeling (respect) along with the other feelings: pity, fear, eros, sympathy. It works upon these feelings not by catechizing, deducing wise principles, or providing pictures at an exhibition of any such deduction, but (though perhaps at times through each of those things) by playing all these feelings against and beside and over one another. Since one of drama's means of mimesis is language, it always calls up our capacity for reason; thereby it is always treading close to practical reasoning and its judgment, though it never calls them forth to act in the world, as rhetoric (and ethics) do. As art knows what morality entails, the actress knows what Touchstone means, but neither understanding what he means nor exhibiting that understanding is her task. So too for art. Art, like the actress, has moral judgments within her, but her task is not improving our casuistry, or our knowledge of principles. A poet is better considered a maker of exercises for the passions than a didact or judge of them. It is a bad coach who gives exercises that make his athletes worse. And it is not a real coach at all who talks about the theory of hurdling rather than getting his charges to hurdle. Art's real business is not theoretical. There are bad coaches and there is bad art; to cut out Audrey and Touchstone (or the nurse in *Romeo and Juliet*, or any number of phrases and scenes from the *Iliad*) would be to make the exercise for the passions worse. A song for a castratus is a different kind of song than one for someone fully human; it requires practices inappropriate for the kind of being most of us are and certainly inappropriate for what we should be. To treat a play as a casuistical presentation of a moral problem is to purposefully shoot cannons at the Parthenon.

When Socrates attempts to turn poetry into philosophy, this running through of the emotions or charming them forth to mimetic action is precisely the activity he *leaves out*.[41] A poem cannot be explicated so.[42] We might consider that Plato wishes us to notice how his Socrates cuts up poems into discrete bits of characterization or action and catechizes with them, but that (if we know them) the poems themselves run feelings into each other and by doing so accomplish quite other things than the Bowdler thinks. No one learned from reading the *Iliad* what Socrates says it teaches; one could only learn those lessons through that poem via a very bad teacher: one who treats art as the childish picture thinking of a more absolute knowing, for example. That picture of art is false. Art accomplishes the shaping of feeling by feeling, as our own Touchstone feelings may be shaped to a better end by desire for the better thing we have seen working together with, and on, that simpler part of us which, like Audrey, hopes to be honest. If you do but seek a hind, there is no need for Rosalind.

Playing Audrey, while difficult, is something any reasonable actress can do—probably without thinking in this much detail about it; those who have the mimetic genius for acting just do it, the complementary genius becomes a philosopher and explains it. Similarly, any reasonable human being can make a judgment of the beautiful without moralizing, while at the same time *feel* the beautiful is symbolic of the moral. It is the feelings that are at stake and brought up in art; art criticism necessarily makes this sound like rational judgment, for in criticism we take what was dramatic and transform

41. E.g., Ion, taking the bait, reads *Iliad* 23:335–340 as accurate and worthwhile advice about chariot driving; he leaves out the nearly murderous result of employing it, from which the Greeks are saved only by the exorbitant generosity of Achilles. Plato is speaking *in this* obvious *absence*, not in the Socratic argument.

42. The extreme position is that a poem cannot be explicated at all. Cf. Cleanth Brooks, "The Heresy of Paraphrase" and "What Does Poetry Communicate?" in *The Well Wrought Urn*. As some other essays in the book indicate, the idea that a poem cannot be explicated at all is a hyperbolic remark, but perhaps it is this mimetic effect that is precisely what is lost in explication.

it into *narrative* or argument—a form that is already more removed from suffering the passions, as Socrates pointed out long ago.[43] I do not mean to imply that passion and reason are entirely disconnected, but feeling and reason are like the concave and the convex surfaces of a lens, as Aristotle says (*NE* 1102a30–34), or, in other (more Kantian) words, the aesthetic judgment of the beautiful is a symbol of moral judgment, not moral judgment itself.

4. THE FREEDOM OF AESTHETIC JUDGMENT, OR "MUCH VIRTUE IN 'IF'"

The emblem explicated above should help to make visible how it is that "taste does not reach out to morality to increase its own security; rather, morality—that is to say the concern for morality which is primary in us all—spreads its wings over the realm of taste in its own behalf," as Paul Guyer puts a point of Kant's.[44] It should be somewhat more clear how the *judgment* of the beautiful can be feeling's "symbolism" for morality, though that judgment is not a deduction from morality. From the side of the *object*, we should see that art is not, nor is it properly called or treated as, proposing an analysis or representation of morality—or any thing else—as some of its critics and defenders alike presume.[45] The feelings art allows us to enjoy are *like* those the moral person enjoys, and art leaves our feelings in a state more adequate to morality, but we have done nothing except go to a play (or to a symphony). At the play or the symphony the interplay of imagination and the intellectual powers is felt to be pleasant, and this pleasant interplay caused by the object is felt to be universally communicable (and pleasantly so). Thus the experience of the beautiful itself arouses feelings *like* those morality engenders (universally communicable, pleasant, having a relation to cognition), but the aesthetic does not require the judgment of practical reason; therefore these feelings can be learned through mimesis before reason becomes an autonomous active power, as we have been arguing is true for Aristotle and Plato.

A mimesis of action and character does not primarily represent the world

43. It will be remembered that Socrates allowed narratives of the bad, but not their mimesis, in *Rep.* 396c–97d.

44. Paul Guyer, *Kant and the Experience of Freedom: Essays on Aesthetics and Morality*, 19.

45. That that presumption is not shared by Plato is our argument in *Platonic Errors*; see esp. the chapter on *Ion*.

we live in in the manner a documentary does, rather more as the triangle on the board represents the triangle we are thinking about—which is "triangle," the universal; nor is a mimesis primarily like the story the rhetorician tells about what happened to the imperial-minded democracy of Athens, presenting through example a general rule for politics, including a political action to be avoided today; but rather the work of art does (primarily and necessarily) work on exactly the real passions. The work of mimetic art makes a visible, hearable, or imaginable world distinct from this one, a heterocosm into which (as through the singing and dancing of a chorus) our passions are called and by which they are turned. It does this by presenting a particular order of events (or tones) and characters (or rhythms) by which passions that are universal or general are called up. For the geometer and rhetorician, this universal or general (presented in their particular drawing or example) is a universal or general rule of theoretical or practical reason, but the work of art, on the other hand, through its particular representations, calls up something different, not a more universal theoretical or practical rule, but a particular passion that is universal to human beings.

Insofar as art arouses the painful and pleasurable passions in its particular ordering, then, it must be connected to morals in some way because, as Aristotle is at pains to show in *NE*'s analysis of virtue, such passions are always excessive, deficient, or at the mean, at the right time and place, or not; suitably directed, or not; and so on. Kant calls such matters pathological, not rational, and he agrees with Aristotle that our passions can be in accord or "cooperate with the rational principle" (*NE* 1144b28–30), though they are not themselves principles (*logoi*). So, from the side of the *subject*, it is clear that the beauty of the play cannot be merely a matter of a certain play of sensation, still less of the play of pure concepts or the (more or less) accurate representation of ideas, but must involve the interaction of sensibility with moral feeling—that feeling that has an intrinsic (or, in Aristotle's terms, natural) connection to reason. While the situation of Audrey and the movement of the play (as the movement of *Acharnians* or *Lysistrata*) arouse certain moral feelings (or the moral feeling as well as many others in Kant's more straitening terminology), our feelings and judgment may still be called "disinterested" because we are not, in suffering those feelings, really bringing that moral community the play builds into the fullness of existence;[46] we are, however, doing so mimetically by our communal enjoyment of the

46. See note 36 for Kant's definition of interest.

shared cosmos, and our shared feeling. We are not making a law for the future action of our polis or our selves, even if our passions are following certain laws or our reason is judging the acts we see in art's world as being in accord with morality or not. We are not *acting* directly in the interest of morality here, nor do the feelings roused move us directly to any action or decision even though the indirect connection to morality is palpable.

Augustine's analysis of what goes on at stage shows, then, is accurate even if we may not agree with his concomitant condemnation of the art. Augustine notes that when we experience pain and suffering in real life we seek to escape it, or when we see it occur to others we are moved to pity and so respond with acts of mercy, but when we experience it on the stage "the auditor is not roused to go to the aid of the others" (*Confessions* 3.2.2): we merely suffer the feelings and return to suffer them again. Neither escape nor acts of mercy ensue, we merely enjoy the sorrow. Agreeing (unbeknownst to himself) with Aristotle, Augustine adds that if we are not made to feel such grief or sorrow, we leave "with disgust and disapproval." That (aesthetic) disgust and disapproval is clearly distinct from the (moral) disgust and disapproval Augustine expresses in the next paragraph (and throughout the book) for his loathsome lusts and sins (among them his love of theater), but it echoes in its key Aristotle's disgust and disapproval of certain forms of tragedy that fail to rouse the emotions properly and carry them through to catharsis but leave us feeling polluted or unmoved. Aristotle's aesthetic disapproval of such plays is distinct from his (moral) disapproval of, say, the tribes who eat their neighbors' children.

This difference in key between moral judgments and aesthetic ones provides a clue to our solution. What keeps aesthetic judgment free from being *subject to* morality (and so becoming what Kant would call a kind of determinative judgment) is, first, that the aesthetic involves feeling, *not only* principles: aesthetic judgment depends on the *felt* relation of reason and feeling, not a logical relation between them, or a logical relation between principles or beliefs: it is not a deduction, as Kant's "deduction" shows.[47] Second, all the judgments we make of the ordering of the theater during the play are what Kant would say are in the "problematic" modality, not the assertoric or apodeictic (cf. A70/B95, A74f/B100f) modalities.[48] Moral judgments, by

47. On the considerable queerness of the third *Critique*'s deduction vis-à-vis the deductions of the principles for practical and theoretical reason, see chapter 1 of *For What May I Hope? Thinking with Kant and Kierkegaard*, 95–111.

48. In contrast, the aesthetic judgment "beautiful," when given of the object (e.g., the whole

contrast, are always the latter. What Kant is after in this tripartite distinction is not a difference in *content* between moral judgments and judgments we may be making while at a play, but a difference in the relation of the mind to the thing. Kant's relation of modality picks out the dynamic relation between the thing and the mind (possibility rather than actuality or necessity), and the heterocosm of art, while it *is* before us, is before us in such a way that it *is not*—it presents a world in which we can do nothing (in contrast to the world in which we actually are thirsty or must help our neighbor escape from the burning theater). A similar stand is implied in Aristotle's choice of the phrasing "mimesis of an action" over, say, "an action." In contrast with art and judgments thereof, Aristotle and Kant agree that real ethical consideration ends in choice, decision, action—the ethical has existential import or "interest" (as the rhetorical does against the poetic in Aristotle's explication) and it speaks apodeicticly about the world (as Kant puts things). Aristotle is on exactly this point of existential import regarding moral matters when he says:

> [T]he result of deliberation is the object of choice. For everyone ceases to inquire how he is to act when he has brought the moving principle back to himself and the ruling part of himself; for this is what he chooses. . . . Choice will be deliberate desire of things in our power. (*NE* 1113a5–12)

Similarly, for Kant, the good will is one that determines itself according to the categorical imperative; it is not a pious desire or sorrowful wish "but the summoning of all the means in our power" (*FMM* 394). As Augustine pointed out, this is not the case in the theater—there we summon no means whatsoever (and that is why he condemns theater). The result of any deliberation we engage in at a play is (merely) a feeling. This feeling is exacerbated or diminished or led to another by the play—no action, no choice; but something is going on, and it can be polluting (as Augustine presumes)—or purifying. Wherever it is not the case in life that we summon all the means in our power, it is a moral flaw; Aristotle calls it softness (*NE* 7.7–8). But the theater is a *visible* cosmos or order, not the cosmos in which we *are* and *act*. In the theater we are passive, we suffer the joy or sorrow, the desiring or the

play) speaks with "the universal voice" (*KU* 216). Though the judgment of the beautiful in fine art is reflective and involves the understanding, it is not determined *by* the understanding; rather, it is "nothing else than the mental state present in the free play of imagination and understanding (so far as these are in mutual accord)" (*KU* 218), which is the source of the judgment "beautiful." It is a certain state of feeling called forth by the work (not necessarily one represented in it) that is at the root of the judgment.

angry passions, but the question of our action is not put. Hence, aesthetic judgments have a different relation to our being than moral judgments, while the moral is yet "spreading its wings" over the former experience and judgment.

When Aristotle begins *Poetics* by talking about mimeses, he carefully distinguishes that way of using language from the kind of speech that makes truth claims or has what we might call existential import—like the writing of Empedocles' poem (1447b18–19), or the speech of a rhetorician. When he says that tragedy aims at a catharsis of the passions, he seconds that motion: it does not aim at *decision* in the world or *truth* about the structure of the universe—or even at presenting the truth about our particular passional habits. Since mimeses do not aim to represent reality, the impossible (what theoretical reason *would* deny the truth of) is a legitimate poetic trope, so is the immoral (what practical reason *would* deny the truth of).[49] We have seen great poetry include the immoral in both tragedy (Ulysses in *Hecuba*) and comedy (Touchstone in *As You Like It*). We see the impossible in (e.g.) Agamemnon's arrival just after the light from burning Troy, and the dung-beetle trip to heaven. The passions pay no mind to these impossibilities, but are charmed into their "as if." The immoral and the impossible are legitimate here only because, and only when, they better serve the cathartic purpose of the art. Notice how I entered the subjunctive (would), when I spoke of mimesis from the point of view of practical and theoretical reason, for aesthetics *is* the subjunctive with regard to them—its virtue is in "if." (Suppose I could fly to heaven on a dung beetle, if I grew one big enough.)

Similarly, when Kant says aesthetic judgments are reflective, he means that we do not arrive at them as we do determinative moral judgments that proceed from moral principles operating upon beliefs about my present situation, but by reflection upon the feeling that the work of art (or, in Kant's

49. Nuttall considers that Aristotle's "believable impossibility" being preferable to an "unbelievable possibility" (1461b11–12) is a cynical comment on "the imperfect apprehension of the audience" (*New Mimesis*, 63). On the contrary, I consider it a revelatory comment on the perfect apprehension of the passions: A private peace in time of war?—Exactly what I want! The descent of Hymen as a god upon four weddings?—Absolutely! Such impossibilities are convincing necessities in art because art appeals to the passions; they answer to passion, not cognition.

Aristotle himself says, "Criticism of both irrationality and depravity is right when they are unnecessary and *no purpose is served* by the irrationality . . . or the wickedness" (*Po.* 1461b18–21). The purpose he speaks of here is purposive for the functionality *of the poem as a poem*: purposeless wickedness of a character *in the poem* might well have a poetic function: Iago comes to mind. (See Auden's fine essay on this character, "The Joker in the Pack.")

usual case, the experience of nature) accomplishes.[50] When he says that the beautiful is the symbol of the moral he does not, then, mean that the beautiful thing symbolically *represents* the moral law or its work upon the world (as a halo represents sanctity); the phrase means that the feeling the beautiful works upon us is in line with the feelings required and raised by morality. This is why he calls the beautiful a hypotyposis rather than a type of the good (*KU* 351–55). Art does not have to represent the complete and unadulterated good in order to do this, as we saw with the case of Audrey and Touchstone. In fact, it doesn't have to *represent* anything at all, which is the case in music generally, and in other arts, like painting and sculpture, with greater or less frequency. One reason Kant chooses most of his examples of beauty from nature is to emphasize this, since nature is *not representing*. It is not purposing anything and yet it still calls up feelings of the beautiful or sublime. The artist, even if not representing, is creating for a purpose (to evoke a certain run of feelings—catharsis), but then it is clear from this point of view that the work of art is not "apart from the representation of an end" (*KU* 236).[51] So we can more accurately say that the play is mimetically symbolic of the moral because the experience of beauty and the judgment that a thing is so depends not on any intellectual or representational relation but on a *felt relation of the thorough harmony* of two powers (feeling and reason) that it raises in us. A play need not be representationally symbolic of the coming to be of the moral community (as *Acharnians* is not), though that kind of *kōmos* is highly successful at arousing and purifying certain erotic and sympathetic feelings. *Everyman* is, after all, at least somewhat cathartic, and *As You Like It* is stupendously so. We would not be likely to accuse many Aristophanic *kōmoi* of directly symbolizing such a community given the scapegoating of (e.g.) Lamachus and Socrates and the more than occasional orgy with flute girls that follows, though the moral power is similarly

50. It is noted by Martha Husain (*Ontology*, 28) that "[b]eauty is not a part of Aristotle's definition of tragedy, and his paradigm of beauty is a living organism rather than a work of art (cf. *De Partibus Animalium* 1.5)." It is interesting that two such distant thinkers as Kant and Aristotle should not want to use the word *beauty* (at least in the first case) in connection with our purposed makings. That parallelism combined with an investigation of wonder as Aristotle discusses it in *Meta.* 1072b and Kant at the end of *KU* is an intrinsically attractive study.

51. It seems from Kant's footnote here that his "purposiveness without a purpose" refers to an objective utility. The work of art does not have this objective utility, rather a purely subjective utility or purposiveness with no connection to real acts (a rhetorician would have an impurely subjective purposiveness, aiming that the subjective change lead to a certain decision in and about objective reality). Kant does say, however, that "judging artistic beauty will have to be considered as a mere consequence of the same principles which ground the judgment of natural beauty" (*KU* 251).

at play in the audience of his plays and the *kōmos* is achieved in a way that allows us to feel it in play.[52]

Having considered the moral import of aesthetic judgment under the figure of Audrey, let us consider further its *freedom* and place this discussion of the "symbol of the moral" in the background. In particular, let us consider, since the ancients are usually considered moralizers about art, whether it is possible for art to be absolutely free of ties to morality as "art for art's sake" defenders might imagine.[53] An aesthetic judgment, if it is not to be a *pure formalism* of the intellectual power (and that it is not so for Aristotle has already been argued), and if it is not to be mere *mystery play for the moral power of reason* (as the Platonic Socrates has been known to argue it should be or is), must have a more complicated structure than either of these two reductionisms are able to admit. The first step in explicating that dialectical structure is to make clear exactly how opposed the elements are. Paul Guyer's summary of Kant's problem of aesthetic judgment is a good starting point. An analysis of an aesthetic judgment reveals it to be made up of two fundamental, and essentially contrasting, claims.

> On the one hand, as *aesthetic*—that is, as essentially connected with feeling or sensibility—a judgment of taste cannot be made on the basis of the subsumption of its object under any determinate concept (or set thereof, for feeling is not conceptual); it must, rather, both be about that aspect of cognition of an object, namely, the pleasure (or in the case of a negative judgment, the displeasure) it produces in an observer, and even be made primarily on the basis of such a feeling. On the other hand, as a *judgment*, an aesthetic judgment claims acceptability not only by the person who asserts it on the basis of her own encounter with its object but by all others who might encounter it (Guyer, 8).

52. The lack of the fullest sort of human community in the Aristophanic *kōmos,* is, I think, Plato's implied criticism of Aristophanes in *Symposium*. This remark will be explicated further in the Epilogue.

53. A more honest defense of "the creed of aestheticism" admits that aestheticism is itself "a moral outlook, one that stresses the values of openness, detachment, hedonism, curiousity, tolerance, the cultivation of the self, and a preservation of a private sphere—in short the values of liberal individualism" (Posner, 2). At this point the argument between us can take place on the correct ground: whether or not that moral system Posner and the aesthete embrace is sound or good. There is a long argument against it being either in MacPherson's *The Theory of Possessive Individualism*. A more mimetic attack is Kierkegaard's *Either/Or*. Aristotle does not name tolerance as a virtue (it is a late invention), argues against hedonism per se, demands cultivation of the self in some directions and for some purposes but not in or for others (see his discussion of musical training in *Politics*), and argues that some people are natural slaves, which implies the lack of a legitimate private sphere in those cases and *for the good of* those people. He also argues that some cultures are destructive of the very possibility of virtue, and as such should not be tolerated. About all of these matters I think Aristotle is true and liberalism false, though an argument about that matter must be a book on ethics or politics (e.g., MacPherson's), not on comedy.

Now if Aristotle considered the catharsis of the passions as the final cause of art, the pleasure of the catharsis of pity and fear being the pleasure appropriate to tragedy particularly (1453a35), and if his judgment about better and worse kinds of plays depends upon that catharsis (as I have argued), then Aristotle is in the same problematic boat as Kant, for his judgment of a play is reflective upon sensibility (its catharsis of the passions) and yet he claims universal validity for his criticism. If he didn't claim such validity, he would not be able to argue that certain connections of events in the plot are better than others based on the way they work on the feelings, as he does. Aristotle does not try to give transcendental deductions of his first principles of either aesthetics or morals, but he does recognize that there is a problem getting agreement about judgments, particularly those involving feeling—which for him includes both moral and aesthetic judgments. To resolve this problem in ethics he defines the mean as being "such as the man of practical wisdom defines it" and this same figure is the source of his claim that certain plots we would find *miaron*, or not arousing philanthropy, or pity, and so on. He is expecting universal agreement among readers within the range of average virtue; when he finds an agreement he thinks is false, he traces its cause to weakness on the part of the audience and pandering on the part of the poet (*Po.* 1453a33–35). We should expect that the barbarians around the Black Sea who invite the neighbor children over for dinner (*NE* 7.5) would not react with any particular disgust to Thyestes' dinner and so would be unlikely to fear the work of the furies upon the house of Atreus. Such extravagances of feeling and behavior as their culture allows are not going to allow the general run of feeling the plays work through in Athens, and we should expect that such people cannot be cured by the arts of the muses, but only by the art of politics that includes force—if they can be cured at all. Not having the right feelings would make such creatures not only incapable of reacting appropriately to art, but also incapable of having an art that is appropriate to humanity except by the supervenient grace of God (in which kind of merciful God Aristotle does not seem to believe). Slaves and barbarians cannot save themselves; one wonders, in fact, if they can even discover they are lost. Such people need masters.

To continue to clarify this subject of aesthetic judgment, let us consider a different kind of "judgment of taste." If we were to discuss the making of a pizza and you wanted anchovies but I didn't, because you like them and I can't stand the way they taste, we would both be making statements about the pleasure or displeasure of the object upon us. These judgments (anchovies are bad/anchovies are good) would not be statements about objects per se so much as statements about the reaction of our respective senses to the salty, oily fish we want or do not want on our pizza, and in this way these statements would not involve our "objective cognition of the object." We would both, of course, have to know what the word *anchovies* refers to; be able to remember, if not their precise taste and texture, at least our reaction to them last time; and in knowing what they are we do have "objective cognition" of them, but to add that they taste vile on pizza is a subjective claim, a claim about how the object affects me, not a claim that grants further knowledge *of the object*—though it does tell you something about me. Objective cognitions are universally communicable and testable, as whether or not a thing is an anchovy. Judgments of taste, in the pizza sense, are not universal in any way: *de gustibus non disputandum*, because the "object" is not a shared object; the object of the judgment is how they affect me.

Feeling and sensibility are, for Kant as for Aristotle, aspects of human existence that line up on the passive rather than the active side of the soul's powers (*dynameis*) and activities (*erga*). To say "anchovies taste vile" or "anchovies taste wonderful" on pizza is to confess a certain kind of sensibility that may be changed by habit (I remember having to learn to like beer) or age (as children frequently grow from bland macaroni and Velveeta to blue corn, goat meat burritos with jalapenos and picante). It is to make a statement about how something in the world affects me, not in the first case to make a statement about something in the world. How it affects me is also a statement about something in the world—namely, me. But where the anchovies are a universally sharable object (even if I would really rather not), the tasting vile or wonderful is not a universally sharable experience (even if I wish it were). If you could experience how they taste to me, you would know how vilely they go down and would cease to disturb me with your requests that we put them on our pizza when we go out. Of course, you know I dislike them, and *that* knowledge is sharable: let the world take note, Gene dislikes anchovies on pizza. But the feeling of pleasure in your case, or of displeasure in mine, is not conceptual or cognitive (and so not, as Kant would say, a judgment), and even when we learn to say what we feel, we do not by that statement share *the feeling*.

An aesthetic judgment is also a judgment about what pleases, but it differs from a statement about anchovies on pizza precisely by asserting that the feeling of pleasure or displeasure has "universal subjective validity," and is not a confession of singular taste, bourgeois or proletarian upbringing, or caused by certain sexual preferences or perversions, be there any. Of course it is possible, and indeed perhaps likely, that when a person is attempting an aesthetic judgment she is expressing a certain political, social, sexual, or racial development or promoting a political, social, sexual, or racial platform. But insofar as a person is doing this, the person is not (Kant would say) making an aesthetic judgment, but a political, social, sexual, or racial confession—or perhaps advertisement. We are left with this dilemma: aesthetic judgment is (really) a judgment determined by a concept (like the structure of an antiphallogocentric politics determining we should revel in Hecuba's murders); or it is (really) a pizza judgment: the *cabritto con jalapeno* is to die for. If art is a different thing from both political, social, sexual, and racial deduction and from confession or advertisement of taste—or as Kant would word this last option, if art is something besides pathological expression of emotion—then there must be such a thing as aesthetic judgment and we need to explicate the conditions for its possibility (as he attempts to do in the third *Critique*). If art is not a different thing than pathological expression, then *all* it is is Herder's artifacts; isn't that interesting? Or else it is more or less adequate conceptualizing; isn't that queer? In short, art is always only the fewmets of political or social or personal physiological construction. Because aesthetic judgment is reflective upon *feeling*, it cannot be reduced to a pure formalism of speculative reason or the picture thinking of practical reason (either of which reductions would make aesthetic judgments determinative through purely logical subsumption under the categories of the operative power). On the other hand, because aesthetic judgment is a *judgment*—engaging all the categories through which we think any object of intuition—and not merely the report of a pathological reaction of sense (as the reaction to anchovies)—we can expect universal agreement of all creatures with such schemata of imagination as we have.

So the argument about art's freedom falls this way: either (1) there is something like what Kant calls "pure aesthetic judgment," or (2) there is not. If there is not such a thing as pure aesthetic judgment, then either (a) art is merely pathological expression and aesthetic judgment pathological confession (as creation and judgment about pizza); or (b) art is a construction of speculative reason and aesthetic judgment is logically determinative by its concepts (a good urinal is one that works, not one that hangs upside down, unconnected to the plumbing, with the label "fountain" beneath it); or (c) art is a construction of practical reason and aesthetic judgment is logically (and directly) determinative by its laws (e.g., Aesop's fable). In cases (a) and (c) it follows that either (i) Socrates' arguments in *Republic* are valid and art is a serious (because infectious) danger to every polity, or (ii) art, while remaining a pathological expression or moral construction, is powerless to infect anyone and so is not a serious venture at all: each to his or her own forever. In the former case, art should be among the first businesses of politics. In the latter case, art may be completely overlooked by a politician, for it is mere entertainment (though of course taking a certain stand on art may make him more electable). That is to say, Plato is wrong about the real power of art as art, but art may have political significance because of popular opinions about it. In case (2b) art's power is similar to that of mathematics (we can practice complex problem solving),[54] although art has the distinct disadvantage of not applying directly to the real world, as mathematics and the sciences directly do. Quaint, but impractical. In all of these circumstances one thing is certain: no one could consider being an artist and spending one's time engaged in art to be a morally worthy use of one's life—not if he was capable of anything *really* useful (*Rep.* 599a,b). Only case (2c) allows such a life to be of any moral significance, and then only when and because the art is constructed as a kind of picture thinking for moral reasoning logically determined by its concepts—exactly the kind of thing Socrates allows in *Republic* for the benefit of the state. No heroes behaving badly, no cursing of the gods (unless followed by lightning strokes), no *Lear*, no *Lysistrata*, no *Iliad.*

Table 3-1 summarizes the argument and provides examples. It should be noted that all of the labels used in the examples refer to both a school of criticism and to a view of art's work. There are some schools of criticism that have produced no art, for example, historicism (new or old), which should be sufficient indication that whatever such critics say about art it has nothing to do with art's function. Historicism merely picks up on art's artifactuality: that its made-ness has a determinate venue; isn't that interesting? Whatever cannot empower an artist certainly cannot be a correct theory about the ground of art's power. In fact, since all of the following examples are actual mistakes about art, a school of criticism without a related type of

54. This seems to be the opinion of Jacques Barzun; see "A Future for the Liberal Arts, If. . . ." Against his view and several others, see my "The Empiricist Looks at a Poem."

art has only an imaginary (in Kant's terms, hypothetical) connection to the work of art. New historicism is an owl of Minerva, a creature of speculative reason, but one curiously incapable of vision or activity during any day: it cannot even be found nesting.

Before continuing with the argument, I have two further thoughts regarding the outline presented here. The argument is noticeably deductive; its first premise (suppressed) is man: the whole four-handed, four-footed, two-headed creature who struck fear into the heart of Zeus (according to Plato's Aristophanes). The whole human being is feeling, reason (both practical and theoretical), and praxis. Most versions of art and criticism presently running around are halvsies, quarters, and unattached fingers looking for the right place to stick themselves. Second, we should notice that the avant garde, which in the last hundred years has run the gamut from expressionism through constructivism and formalism to feminism and Marxism is always a partial and a fragmentary view. That's what it means to be the front of something.

Whether or not one thinks that the Socrates of *Republic* is giving Plato's ideas about art, it is clear that both Plato and Aristotle—along with Kant—consider art to have a real power, and thus the work of the artist to be an important problem. Every artist who thinks an art is worth spending her life on thinks so too, and every critic who is not a dilettante seconds the motion. Let us regard these data as appearances with which we must find some agreement and so rule out the possibility that art is powerless and the problem of aesthetic judgment not a serious one for life. The agreement of these three (the artist, the critic and the great philosophers) on the real power of art effectively eliminates versions 2.a.ii, 2.b.i, and 2.c.ii, reducing the anti-Kantian suggestions to three. Of these, version 2.b.ii replaces aesthetics with expedient construction via technology and experiment: building a better toilet or computer chip. While this doesn't make art powerless or unimportant (unless it means diddling with varieties of Rube Goldberg apparatus), it does make it (and the whole realm of the aesthetic) disappear into technology. That art includes a certain element of technique is given; that a *technē* is sufficient by itself for art is the question; both *Phaedrus* and *Ion* imply the answer is negative. What remains—2.a.i and 2.c.i—while they have their source in different aspects of the human being—feeling (2a) or practical reason (2c)—both make the similar claim that art is (consciously or unconsciously) determined by pathological affect or by political aim, which

Whether or not there is something like "pure aesthetic judgment"?

1. There is (Kant, Aristotle).*
2. There is not.
   a. art is merely pathological (in the generic sense) expression and aesthetic judgment pathological confession (expressionism)
      i. art is infectious (specifically pathological)→Socrates' arguments in *Republic* are valid and art is a serious danger to every polity,

      or

      ii. art is powerless to infect anyone and so is not a serious venture at all (*de gustibus non disputandum*): it is merely expressive, "what I call art" or "I like it."

   OR

   b. art is a construction of speculative reason and aesthetic judgment is logically determinative by its concepts (formalism, constructivism)
      i. art is an esoteric form of mental "exercise" less directly applicable to any activity in the real world than, say, mathematics (formalist)

      or

      ii. "the organizing principle is expedient constructivism, in which technology and experimental thinking take the place of aesthetics" (Varvara Stepanova, constructivist)**

   OR

   c. art is a construction of practical reason and aesthetic judgment is logically (and directly) determinative by its laws (feminism, Marxism, Aesop, others of the *discipline* = *punish* school)
      i. art is infectious (= practically convincing)→Socrates' arguments in *Republic* are valid and art is a serious danger to every polity: we must rewrite the canon to bring about the new world order (feminist, Marxist, Aesopian): that is exactly what Socrates (the secret father of all these others) does.

      or

      ii. art is powerless to infect anyone (= not practically convincing), and so is not a serious venture at all (in morally relativistic times this option is the same as 2.a.ii). The book on this school has not yet been written, but its title is *Whose Feelings? Which Rationality? Who Cares?* It is by rights either a very short book or else an infinitely long one.

---

*I do not mean to say that Aristotle gives a transcendental deduction for his aesthetic judgments, but that he agrees with Kant that judgments of art are not explicated properly by any of the other options, including the social relativist version (c) that might be accepted by a modern virtue ethicist.

**Varvara Stepanova's Essay "On Constructivism" is quoted in *The Great Utopia*, constructed and published by the Guggenheim Museum (1994), 299. The sentence preceding the one quoted runs as follows: "Once purged of aesthetic, philosophical and religious excrescences, art leaves us its material foundation, which henceforth will be organized by intellectual production."

pathology can be explicated in the manner of the schools: Freudian, feminist, Lacanian, Marxist, childhood abuse, and so on. In this case we should perhaps conclude that war is really an aesthetic phenomenon: it is criticism grown thoroughly serious. Art and aesthetic judgment are either this kind of thing or there is pure aesthetic judgment.

Let us hunt one step further down the wrong road. Under condition number 2, how might we *know* what the aesthetic equivalent of "health" is? Or, alternatively, what are the conditions for the possibility of each kind of critique each school (under condition 2) offers, for each has an idea (at least) of sickness? If a deduction for what health or critique is cannot be given, one must suspect that each school is itself merely a self-selecting institution of individuals united in their pathology or their politics: anchovy eaters of the world unite! War against anchovy conditions! This is what we call art! It may be that each pathological view is true for it, but then the only possibilities for art are (a) that it is a temptation, advertisement, and confession of a certain fetishism—economic, political, sexual; or (b) that it is powerless and trivial because each group of pizza eaters is self-selecting and change is merely accident (I am taken by a different sickness). Under either version of this dispensation criticism is not only not a science, it is not possible for it to be in any way scientific; it does not deal with truth, but with one's feeling of pleasure or lack of pleasure in anchovies or certain sexual or political or child abuse positions. Art is merely a sociological effect or event. Consequently, a book of criticism, in this dispensation, is merely a celebration of a particular fetishism (more or less unique), and the only difference between fetishists besides the obscure object of their desire is whether they stroke their respective fetishes with public announcement of their activity—Frank Lentricchia will be doing his thing on Shakespeare's last plays forthcoming from Cambridge—or adamantly deny that they are stroking anything—a kind of critic who, like the old joke about the sadist and the masochist, requires an audience whose fetish is for ostensible but (a priori?) impossible deprivation of all fetishism: "Do that again." "No." "Ohhh . . . Thank you." Unsurprisingly, such criticism, like an esoteric form of spanking, has nothing to say to most people, and to expect to be supported by tax dollars for doing it provides a target no politician can miss. And it would be a serious political error not to shoot.

In short, what Kant once said of metaphysics (and with somewhat less evidence of deep psychosexual disturbance) could then apply to art criticism:

So far are the students of [criticism] from exhibiting any kind of unanimity in their contentions, that [criticism] has rather to be regarded as a battle-ground quite peculiarly suited for those who desire to exercise themselves in mock combats, and in which no participant has ever yet succeeded in gaining even so much as an inch of territory, not at least in such manner as to secure him in its permanent possession. This shows, beyond all questioning, that the procedure of [criticism] has hitherto been a merely random groping, and what is worst of all, a groping among. . . . (Bxv)

We need not finish the details.

My conclusion is against such absurdities as have been played out in the preceding pages and century: aesthetic judgment, while arising from and regarding feeling, is still free from determination either by pathological feeling or theoretical or practical reason. The idea that the purpose of dramatic art is catharsis does not require that the aesthetic be reduced to the ethical, though it notes that the aesthetic cannot exist without the ethical. More comically put: one can make pizza with or without anchovies or anchovy substitutes, but one cannot make sense of aesthetic judgment, nor can one grant it any sort of freedom (for either artist or critic) without something like Kant's view of aesthetic judgment as based on the feeling of the free play of the moral power and sensibility, or Aristotle's idea of catharsis of the passions (which is measured rightly by an experience of the free run of the passions of the virtuous).

There is one further version of aesthetic criticism upon which I must expend some more effort. While Aristotle presumes, and Kant argues, that aesthetic judgment joins two fundamentally distinct powers—feeling or sensibility and reason or judgment—it is possible to consider that art and judgment of art do (or should do) no such thing. Perhaps, that is, art is an act of pure intellection and the idea that it involves feelings is based on the illusion that the feelings themselves are not intellectual judgments. If the feelings are such judgments,[55] then aesthetic judgment does not join two distinct powers of the soul, but it is intellectual or cognitive through and through and so purely formal theoretical procedures of judgment can be developed and such development is precisely the task of the critic.

For example, the arguments of *Republic* 10 hold the position that art is cognitive, though ultimately inaccurate and so untrustworthy. The Platonic Socrates develops a formal procedure for judging the worthwhileness of art that depends in large part on the accuracy of its representation. Those

55. That feelings are judgments is the view taken by Martha Nussbaum in her Gifford lectures, *Upheavals of Thought*.

that picture the gods lying or heroes hiding under the skirts of women are thrown out. The modern postcolonial cognitivist will most probably want to disagree with Socrates about the accuracy and worthwhileness of art's representations and particularly about *which* ones are accurate and which not (Can a lyric that sings the joys of sex with flesh barely twelve years old be accurate or worthwhile? Is it equally accurate and worthwhile if the voice is homosexual or from a more primitive culture? Can a novel that depicts a large number of its economically challenged characters as lazy and talentless be accurate and worthwhile—or is *Hard Times* the truth of the matter?). The point of these insensitive questions is to make it clear that the starting points of Socrates in book 10 and the modern cognitivist are suspiciously equivalent; only what counts as the god one must tell the truth of has changed. We ought to be especially suspicious of this connection because Plato is giving away the fact that such intellectualism is a partial view. Far from summarizing his earlier critique of poetry (as Socrates says), book 10's intellectual critique largely runs on the opposite rail. The earlier critique of mimesis (in books 3 and 4) depended almost entirely on a discussion of the feelings aroused by stories and music in the education of children so that the man

> would blame and hate the ugly in the right way while he's still young, *before he's able to grasp reasonable speech.* And when reasonable speech comes, the man who's reared in this way would take most delight in it, recognizing it on account of its kinship. (*Rep.* 402a)

The literal truth of these stories was not important at all; in fact, Socrates is only concerned with false stories (*Rep.* 377a, 392a–c). Art works on those who don't yet have logos operating. Perhaps both Socrates and Plato want their interlocutors to pick out how mistaken the intellectualist view about art is by virtue of setting it out so baldly and in such distinct contrast to the arguments of the earlier books to which he explicitly (and lyingly) joins them. Between the critique of mimesis in the earlier books (on the basis of the emotions it calls up) and that in the last one (on the basis of its inaccuracy), Plato sets up precisely the dialectical horns Kant and Aristotle are trying to avoid: neither the expression of pathological feeling or ethical propagandizing, nor intellectual formalism or scientific knowledge, but an aesthetic judgment. Thus does all philosophy become a footnote to a dialectic exhibited by Plato and mimetically instantiated in his art.

Plato being as inscrutable as any self-ironizing artist, let us get to the philosophical point: if it were the case that the feelings were nothing but judgments, then art would again be subject to the hegemony of the ideas, and we would be, again, at the same impasse as that which the moral expressionists or varieties of formalist would take us. Each school would promote its favored candidate for God-term among the ideas: phallocentrism/differance, capitalism/socialism, aristocracy/democracy = elitism/equality, and the like—but the choice of any one of them requires either a transcendental deduction of its necessity and primacy, or a demonstration of the impossibility of any such transcendental deduction[56] to both of these positions (either of which requirements may be impossible, though we could not prove so a priori). There is no secure path to science down this cognitivist road either, but an ending of the life of art and culture in the dissipation of a holy war of all against all.

The only possible road to an understanding of art as both of serious importance and universal human (rather than merely pathological) value, as being more than titillation while being other than moral sermon or political screed, is through the Aristotelian-Kantian dialectic that unites judgment and feeling, reason and sensibility as two distinct powers at play in aesthetic judgment. Such judgments must be made by the man of practical wisdom according to Aristotle, because he has the right relation of reason to sensibility; such judgments are free according to Kant because the autonomous reason that makes both speculative and practical laws for itself is at play in art—which is not the case in judgments about pizza (where reason is not involved) or moral action (where reason has apodeictic import and is not playing) or science (where reason gives the rule for how something is to be accomplished).

The idea of a free realm for aesthetics—such as defenders of art for art's sake wish to hold—requires an adequate (i.e., true) idea of freedom; mere arbitrariness of desire doesn't work, but reduces to individual pathology. Similarly, mere random combination of concepts (e.g., aleatory music) is a "freedom" of complete inconsequence. On what other grounds than those we have been exploring as Aristotelian or Kantian could we consider that aesthetic judgment could or should be something that is free from being determined by either pathological feeling or the formal rules of intellection? Between these horns the aesthetician is in the same position a physician would be in who had thirty-seven conflicting ideas of health demanding they be met at once in the same body. This is indeed a sorry situation, and makes

56. Notice how close Derrida comes to this in *Of Grammatology*.

the natural state of criticism the same as Hobbes claimed was the natural state of man.[57] But the classical philosophers do not think Hobbes is correct about the natural state of man, the wholly artificial nature of society, or the way of being of the work of art. Under this (modern) dispensation it is really more honest to confess that art and criticism are dilettantery since they are just politics played out in a realm without any realpolitikal power or consequence. Perhaps art is the activity of the politically disenfranchised, "an expression of revolt? Of plebeian *ressentiment*?" (Nietzsche, *TI* 2.6). Then aesthetic criticism is the ideal newspaper of real slaves.

This road is pointless wherever it is not indecisive. And it is so because the idea of freedom from which it follows is that of arbitrariness of desire or of intellect—the particular desire or fetish of the moment becomes the principle of judgment upon the work of art; and every judgment is interested (and—for a reason known well to the powerless—should be treated as interesting or at least tolerated). If freedom is something other than such arbitrariness, then aesthetic judgment can be so; if there is no freedom other than such arbitrariness, then aesthetic judgment can be nothing else either. But we really ought to pay attention to this fact: only creatures capable of morality make art. What is the condition for the possibility of this fact? As much as truth, art, too, has a debt to freedom.[58]

Kant is well known for having a nonarbitrary view of freedom as reason that gives law to itself, but without tracing out his argument proving the existence of this freedom (from the second *Critique*), we can see that it is *only because there is moral freedom from determination by desire that there can be such a thing as a free aesthetic judgment.* The freedom of art and of judgments of art owes its existence to the fact of moral freedom, but this does not thereby and therefore determine aesthetic judgment according to the content of moral concepts. There are two points to emphasize here. The first is that without moral freedom the idea of a free aesthetic realm or judgment is either delusional or inconsequential; the second is, the fact that aesthetic freedom depends *for its existence* on the existence of moral freedom does not require art to determine itself according to the *content* of ethical dogmatics. The aesthetic realm has a conditional freedom; the artist makes a condition-

57. It is interesting that Judge Posner regards the values of aestheticism to be those of liberalism, the root of which can also be traced to Hobbes; see note 53. See also Chapter 1.1. That both modern politics and modern aesthetics are based on a mistake is a thesis I do not think Aristotle or Plato would have a problem with.

58. Cf. Warner Wick, "Truth's Debt to Freedom."

al cosmos into which charmed circle the passions are called and in which they suffer. The source of the conditional freedom of art is the unconditional freedom of the will. Art's freedom is in "if"; the will's freedom is in the world and actual—it is, as Kant says, a fact—and that freedom is the capacity to act according to a conception of its own that is necessary. A human being is not able to see that actual freedom (in the way we can see an anchovy) because it is what the human being is; the visual field does not include the eye that sees even when we are looking in a mirror. We are able to see something *like* that freedom in drama, where, as Aristotle says, the characters exhibit moral choice (*Po.* 1450a16–19, 1450b7–9).

Aesthetic judgment *cannot* be determined by ethical dogmatics if it is an act that combines feeling and reason (as Kant thinks it does) and is not an act of pure practical reason—which it isn't. Aesthetic and moral judgment agree, but "merely in the rule of [their] procedure, and not in the intuition itself. Hence the agreement is merely in the form of reflection, and not in the content" (*KU* 351). The beautiful is the symbol of the moral not in the sense that the work of art represents what the moral will aims to do in similar specific situations (like a mystery play might), but in the "rule of procedure." The rule is that our feeling and reason play freely and pleasantly together. Our nature being what it is, that under which this occurs is Aristotelian virtue under the condition of no worldly inhibition: it is the joyous activity of the blessed (μακάριος; *NE* 1101a8) given in our recreation with the Muses and Apollo (*Laws* 653d).

An aesthetic judgment is like a moral judgment as a feeling is *like* an intellectual recognition; all four (two judgments, a feeling, and a recognition) can be true. This language is analogical: a true recognition considers the content of the recognition, a true feeling means one properly aimed and tensed though the object may depend upon a dung beetle large enough to fly to Olympus. A true moral judgment considers the content of the judgment, not what is gone through to get there; a true aesthetic judgment may not have the content of a moral judgment, but agrees in the "what is gone through." What is gone through is feeling (*pathē*), and catharsis is feeling's mimesis of getting to true moral judgment. The analogies continue: a disinterested judgment of beauty, that is, a judgment free from answering to pathological desire, is a procedure like moral judgment—which also must be free of being driven by the interests of pathological desire (though aesthetic judgment necessarily also includes such desires); our feeling of enjoyment of this aesthetic capacity of freedom from determination by sense *in the very enjoyment of sense* (at the play or symphony) is a hypotyposis of our moral capacity, for it is a "form of reflection" which, *like* the moral capacity, is not determined to its judgment by interested desire, but unlike the moral capacity is not deducible from reason's principle. If aesthetic judgment were determined by pathological desire (as, say a Freudian substitive satisfaction theory holds), it would not be a *hypotyposis* of moral capacity or even a hypotyposis of a faculty of desire that finds the good to be whatever answers my desire at the moment but merely the *activity* of just such a faculty. I suppose a hedonist or a utilitarian would call that a moral faculty, as would the common run of people who consider pleasure the good.[59]

If beauty is the one spiritual thing we love by instinct, Plato must be meaning not that we have a special sense for it, but that we rise from feeling it even in our childish nature into the more reflective and self-determinative—the more spiritual—activities of full humanity. That is, aesthetic feeling and judgment precede moral feeling and its judgment and development even though moral freedom is the condition for the possibility of aesthetic freedom and judgment. This strange, seemingly self-contradictory, relationship, that a potentiality not yet activated is the condition for the possibility of a certain kind of experience (pleasure in the beautiful), is what makes aesthetic judgment so difficult to reduce to mere feeling or mere reason, as well as making it so tempting to do so. This strange relationship also provides another indication that it is first through mimesis that we learn, not through the acts of reason itself. I suppose one reason music is so important for Plato and Aristotle is because it is a pleasure based (more largely than any other art) on sensation, and that sensation is one whose pleasure has absolutely no relation to appetite; it is thereby a first approximation to the freedom of moral judgment in which we *know* a good that is also free of appetitive determination. Music may be considered one of the finest of the arts because its pleasures can never be of use.

In this final matter of the conditioned (aesthetic enjoyment) preceding in act the condition (moral freedom) for the act we see Kant agreeing with Aristotle's view on the development of virtue. For Aristotle, right upbringing by parents and the laws are necessary if the child is not to be spoiled for

59. I realize I am going beyond Kant's explicit statements here; for a more strict textually based Kantian explication of the way aesthetic judgment is an analogy of moral freedom, see Guyer, esp. chapters 2, 7, and 10.

virtue. That is, the practice of virtuous acts in childhood and youth is required for the development of what is the real condition of virtue: the state of character and characteristic desire and action of the virtuous adult. To have the right start in feeling makes it easier to arrive at true virtue as natural virtue and the spirited character show (*NE* 1107a3–10). The characteristic—virtue—demands choice and Aristotle does not consider that choice is something children exercise, but if they do not get trained in accord with principle, virtuous choice (and so the characteristic) may become impossible for them through bestiality, or good choice may never have the chance to develop or flourish—as happens with barbarians. The largely mimetic training in the conditioned (virtuous acts) precedes in act the condition (fully virtuous choice) at which we hope to arrive and that is naturally possible for our kind of being. Similarly, the feeling of joy in the conditioned freedom (enjoying the beautiful) must precede the acts of unconditioned (moral) freedom. *We start in sensiblity*, and "to beauty alone [of spiritual things] has it been ordained to be most manifest to sense" (*Phaedrus* 250d10). Through it we come to freedom and the good.

Back in the Kantian language, we have seen how aesthetic judgment rises out of feeling without being determined by reason, while yet having a hypotypic (cf. *KU* 352) relation to practical reason and its judgments. On the other hand, insofar as aesthetic judgment requires the combination of feeling *and* reason, moral ideas must necessarily be brought into connection with the sensible intuitions provided by art. Mere theoretical or speculative formal complexity would produce works of art that "only serve for a diversion, of which one continually feels an increasing need in proportion as one has availed oneself of it as a means of dispelling the discontent of one's mind" (*KU* 326). But moral ideas "alone are attended by a self-sufficing delight" (for respect and moral worth are without price, but everything else has a market or affective value). Such rational ideas are concepts to which no intuition *can* be adequate (this is one difference between the ideas of practical reason and the concepts of natural science all of which latter *require* fully adequate intuitions to have any significance), but of which art continually attempts to present mimeses in its concrete and perfecting particulars. All poetry is a raid on the inarticulate; this is not a problem, an indication of inadequacy, or a gnostic credo; it is an indication of the sublimity of our moral vocation and an index of the worth of a man. We could then say that *As You Like It* represents the coming into existence of the community of the good, or is a preamble to the entrance of the communion of saints into paradise, but this would both be saying too much and too little. It would be saying too much because there is—with the exception of Orlando's saving of Oliver from the lion and the snake—little of morally involved choice (and none on the part of the audience) and more than a little that is morally questionable T and A. It is saying too little because the judgment of the beautiful in the work of art is based on *the pleasurable experience of the integration of all our faculties in freedom*, which experience is not an inadequate representation of the preamble to paradise, but a *mimesis of the actual experience* of that communion as it must be—in the flesh, and all of us together.

4

A LOVE SONG FOR THE LIFE OF THE MIND

Arcadia

O you who are within your little bark,
eager to listen, follow then
my ship, crossing the sea—deep, dark,
singing—turn to see your shores again:
. . .
The thirst innate and everlasting
for the godlike realm bears us away
swiftly as the heaven you see is passing.

Paradiso 2.1–21

All men by nature desire to know.

Aristotle (*Meta.* 1.1)

1. OF HAPPINESS, POLITICS, AND ART

Before we know, we desire to know. How can this be? And what a strange desire!—what a strange animal! Before we are happy, and before we know what happiness is, we desire to be happy. But there is a natural pleasure in mimesis, and through mimesis we first learn. One of the first things that happens through mimesis is that we enjoy a pleasure not associated with or caused by the ordinary animal appetites: the pleasure of mimesis. And being naturally mimetic, we enjoy this often. Out of this process the arts first grew, but this natural process is at work in us everywhere, not just in the theater. Repeating and remembering mimeses and their accompanying pleasure is repeating and remembering a "for its own sake" kind of thing. Mimesis is not something we do for the sake of something else. From memory and repetition of these earliest experiences a human being first develops distinctions (cf. *An. Post.* 100a3–6); first develops feelings for certain sorts of activities; and might even develop a preference for a life superior to that of cattle (cf. *NE* 1195b19–22), or not, depending on what he imitates. One might grow up imitating cattle, wolves, barbarians, or slaves, and the pleasure in mimesis will make these acts more and more habitual. Or the opposite; so "we become just by practicing just acts, temperate by temperance, brave by bravery" (*NE* 1103b1–3). To have our feelings turned and tuned in the appropriate way makes all the difference. Mimesis is how we "are ethicked into" (ἐθίζεσθαι; 1103b23–25) them; we aren't syllogized into appropriateness: we don't purposefully practice it at first, though we later can "ethick" ourselves (1119a25–27). A similar story is told in *Laws* where again Plato uses a word (ἀποτυπουμένους: "to stamp" [681b]) that emphasizes the mechanical rather than the cognitive nature of this mimetic process.[1] After this he says that "we have unwittingly, it seems, set foot on the *archē* of legislation" (681c). The first law we follow is that of mimesis of our neighborhood; we follow it not as law, but as nature. Mimesis continues to shape us, however, even after we have our wits about us, and as *technai* the mimetic arts aim at such working on us—aiming at our catharsis. This is Aristotle's teaching about all poetry; that, and how, various catharses are available to variously "ethicked" audience members has been explained. So the real concern of all human culture and all its arts has already been touched upon, but we must now take these matters to their furthest extent. Catharsis is produced through a human *technē* applied to a natural activity. It is then a thing of nature and of art, and so, like constitutions, can be more and less adequate to the nature it affects. In order to judge of more or less adequate poems, we must answer the question, What is that nature and its highest good?

Every art and every inquiry, and similarly every action and every undertaking seems to aim at some good, and if the final good of all our arts and

1. Cf. Fossheim, "Mimesis and Aristotle's Ethics," in *Making Sense of Aristotle: Essays in Poetics.*

undertakings is happiness (*eudaimonia*[2]) as the philosopher has demonstrated, then art, like politics, is not the most final and self-sufficient good. To think that it is so is not only to err about art, but to err about the nature of humanity, and to miss the purpose of life. The purpose of life is happiness, and happiness is not merely pleasant amusement and relaxation, but activity in accordance with virtue—and if there are several with the best and most complete in a complete life. Art is therefore important for life insofar as, and because it contributes instrumentally to or is a constitutive part of, that end: *eudaimonia*, happiness, activity in accordance with virtue. The two questions this section aims to answer are (1) what is *eudaimonia*? and (2) what is the precise relation of art to happiness?

1.1 *Eudaimonia* and Politics: The Errors of Inclusivism

It has become somewhat popular to interpret Aristotle's *Nicomachean Ethics* as a flawed book, significantly diverging in its penultimate chapters with its emphasis on the intellectual life from the detailed and supposedly completely coherent earlier view of happiness as the practice of the moral virtues, or as he calls it, the political life, which discussion takes up most of the book. It would be possible, in an essay with a different aim, to consider at greater length the following three lives as contenders for the best human life: the political life, the intellectual life, and the mixed life of political-moral virtuous activity and intellectual activity. These are the three choices modern critics present as contenders for happiness. To say that the political life is absolutely the best requires one to completely disregard *NE* X.6–7 and the *Eudemian Ethics*. Doing so could hardly be Aristotelian. For the sake of my modern interlocutors, I will therefore consider only the inclusivist (mixed) view and the intellectualist view, despite the fact that Aristotle himself does not consider an inclusivist option in his own argument; rather, he regularly considers the political-moral, the contemplative, and the life of pleasure as the three competitors.

For example, J. L. Ackrill says that Aristotle "seems to give two answers"[3]

2. The opening of this sentence is the incipit of *NE*. On the problems arising from the usual translation of *eudaimonia* as happiness, see Nussbaum (*Fragility*, 6) and Ackrill ("Aristotle on Eudaimonia," 23f). If we keep in mind that what Aristotle has in mind is not merely a feeling, psychological state, or result to be achieved by action but activity itself—doing well, or living well, flourishing—there should be no serious problem.

3. J. L. Ackrill, "Aristotle on Eudaimonia," in *Essays on Aristotle's Ethics*, ed. Rorty, 15. It is invariably the *Nicomachean*, rather than the *Eudemian*, *Ethics* to which this kind of criticism is raised.

to the question about what *eudaimonia* is and concludes that Aristotle's *Nicomachean* account is "broken-backed" (33). He argues that an account of happiness that includes both moral and intellectual virtues seems to be the best one and thinks that these two sets of virtues must be commensurable or comparable in order for such an account to make sense. He does not, however, think that such commensurability is plausible on Aristotle's most complete picture. Nussbaum is, if possible, even less sanguine. She holds that *NE* 10.6–8

> does not fit with its context and . . . is in flat contradiction with several important positions and arguments of the *EN* taken as a whole. (*Fragility*, 375)

She is a trenchant defender of the view that

> intellectual activity is one of many intrinsic goods, . . . that *sophia* is one *part* of *eudaimonia* and also that it is in some way the best part. It is, as it were, the biggest and brightest jewel in a crown full of valuable jewels, in which each jewel has intrinsic value in itself, and the whole composition (made by practical wisdom) also adds to the value of each. (*Fragility*, 374; italics in Nussbaum)

Opposed to this inclusivist explanation of *eudaimonia* is that explication, traditionally labelled "intellectualist," that Thomas Nagel (among others) considers to be Aristotle's. This view of *eudaimonia* agrees with the position Nussbaum sets up as Aristotle's Platonic opposition—"that the best life for a human being is the life of the philosopher, a life devoted to learning and the contemplation of truth" (*Fragility*, 138). Nagel agrees with Nussbaum and Ackrill in holding that "the *Nicomachean Ethics* exhibits indecision between two accounts of *eudaimonia*—a comprehensive and an intellectualist account" (7). He also agrees with them that the latter view is unsatisfactory and would be best challenged by the more inclusivist view, though he (against Nussbaum) thinks that the intellectualist account is, in fact, Aristotle's.

On the contrary, I think that *NE* is a unified text with a single overarching argument concluding in favor of the life of the mind as the best life for a human being. That is, Aristotle considers the best life for human beings to be that which is shared with the gods. But how does a sublunary animal come to share in the life of a Prime Mover who has neither knowledge of nor concern for any changing being? Mimesis is the beginning of Aristotle's answer about this how, but first we must give some argument for our own version of the end. That is, we must give some reasonable explanation both for the historical question of Aristotle's argument about happiness, but also about the philosophical issue: that he is right and that Nagel, Nussbaum, and Ackrill (among others) are wrong about the intellectual life being unsatisfactory. While a complete and detailed defense of this view would require a book of its own,[4] I will more briefly defend the case for this view of *eudaimonia* by emphasizing some elements and implications to which its critics pay too little attention.

It is fairly well agreed upon, Aristotle says, that happiness is the end, "but what constitutes happiness is a matter of dispute; and the popular account of it is not the same as that given by the wise" (1095a21–23). Next to the popular view of happiness as the life of pleasure, he places the political life and the life of contemplation and distinguishes a superficial version of the political life (one that *seeks honor*) from a more adequate one (whose end is the moral virtues: what *is honorable*). These three are the major competitors for the crown throughout the *Nicomachean Ethics*.[5] He rules out of consideration the life of money-making, for money is good only as a means, and happiness—whatever it is—is final and self-sufficient, "or if there are several final ends, the one among them which is most final will be the good which we are seeking" (1097a27–31). The lives Aristotle considers as having a legitimate claim all have this aspect of finality in common, for "honor, pleasure, intelligence and virtue in its various forms we choose indeed for their own sakes (since we should be glad to have each of them though nothing else resulted from it), but we also choose them for the sake of happiness, in the belief that they will be a means of our securing it" (1097b1–5).

The inclusivists are correct to note that this argument holds as well if we understand honor, pleasure, intelligence, and virtue as constitutive parts of happiness rather than as causes of it as his argument seems to consider them in the sentence just quoted. Indeed, it seems that Aristotle *must* understand the practice of the moral and intellectual virtues not as means but as constitutive parts of happiness since no act is fully virtuous unless it is engaged in for its own sake, and Aristotle is most consistent in considering happiness itself is an activity, not a state resultant from activity. Clearly, it is not correct to consider an act fully virtuous even if it is the correct act, if it is done for

4. The best place to begin such an investigation and defense is with Richard Kraut's *Aristotle on the Human Good*. See also Tom Sherman's *The Perfect Happiness of Virtuous Friends*, chapters 1 and 2.

5. These are also the major competitors in the slightly varying account of *Eudemian Ethics*. On the relation of the two books to each other (earlier-later?) and to Aristotle (is he the author or is either book compiled by the person whose name it bears?), there has been division in the scholarship for two millenia. I will follow the current general stream of scholarship in treating the *NE* as primary, but both as Aristotle's.

the sake of avoiding a penalty and winning honor (as in the case of the citizen soldier; 1116a17–29), or for money or some more trifling pleasure (as in the case of the mercenary; 1117b10–19).

But granted all this, and keeping in mind that all of the virtues must be practiced for their own sakes and from a firm and unchangeable character—that is, they all require finality intrinsically—it is surprising that Aristotle (or a modern reader) does not suggest that the life of the artist is a legitimate competitor beside the life of contemplative virtue and the political (or morally virtuous) life.[6] For *technē* too is a virtue, and of the particularly human, rational part of the soul, and one that could bind itself up with the moral virtues. Though it does produce something, it is plausible to think that the acts of *technē*, like those of moral virtue (which may produce victory, etc.) or contemplation, are also enjoyed for their own sake, since, as the others, they are incarnations of human excellence. W. H. Auden makes a good case for their inclusion as a form of the happy life:

> How beautiful it is,
> that eye-on-the-object look.//
> To ignore the appetitive goddesses,
> to desert the formidable shrines//
> of Rhea, Aphrodite, Demeter, Diana,
> to pray instead to St. Phocas,//
> St. Barbara, San Saturnino,
> or whoever one's patron is,//
> that one may be worthy of their mystery,
> what a prodigious step to have taken.//
> There should be monuments, there should be odes
> to the nameless heroes who took it first,//
> to the first flaker of flints
> who forgot his dinner,//
> the first collector of sea-shells
> to remain celibate.//
> Where should we be but for them?
> Feral still, un-housetrained, still//
> wandering through forests without

6. In fact, at *EE* 1215a27–33, Aristotle seems to rule out the life dedicated to *technē* as not able to lay claim to happiness since its business is to pursue what is necessary. In *Meta.* he makes a more fine-grained distinction, saying that, of the inventors of the arts, those who invented the arts directed to recreation "were always naturally regarded as wiser than the inventors of [arts directed to the necessities of life], because their branches of knowledge did not aim at utility" (981b17–26). According to this argument, the life of the person who is a maker of mimeses would seem to approach the requisite finality in a way the maker of couches or shoes would not. For mimesis, being pleasant by nature, partakes of the "for its own sake" sort of activity.

> a consonant to our names,//
> slaves of Dame Kind, lacking
> all notion of a city . . .[7]

We should consider some of the reasons for and implications of this unremarked-upon absence of the life of *technē* from the competitors for the title of *eudaimonia*.

First, let us consider the word. *Technē* might be used in a positive sense as an excellence or in the broader and more neutral sense of an art—a systematic procedure, or rules for such a procedure—for making something, or acting on an object (as a doctor), whether one does that well or badly being a further question.[8] It is most unlikely, however, that a bad or incomplete set of rules or practices for production or action upon an object would be considered a *technē* by Aristotle and the wider, more neutral sense should probably always be treated as focally oriented to the restricted sense. *Technē* "is a rational quality concerned with making that reasons truly. Its opposite, lack of art (*atechnia*) is a rational quality concerned with making that reasons falsely" (1140a21–23). It seems that such a false way of making might, at least occasionally, come to a good result anyway, as, for example, Tynnichus (*Ion* 534d). On the other hand, if it seems more likely that we would say of a doctor that he failed to practice his *technē* perfectly than that we would say his *technē* failed that is because the narrower, more positive sense of *technē* as virtue or excellence centers our thought about what *technē* is in the broader, more neutral sense (cf. *Rep*. 340d–46e, 360e–61d).

A different and somewhat deeper problem with the word is the claim that it is frequently considered that Aristotle's view of *technē* is essentially different from our modern understanding of art.[9] However, if we consider that Aristotle thinks music's three purposes are education, catharsis, and pleasant (including intellectual) recreation, it seems this supposed difference should not be taken for granted: modern artists still attempt to make things that can provide all three. If art has a function (as I have argued throughout), then there are rule-formulable skills one must apply in achieving that function even if the *technē* or skill is not sufficient by itself to make or provide an adequate object;[10] clarifying these rules is the task of *Poetics*. In this

7. W. H. Auden, from "Horae Canonicae," in *Collected Poems*.

8. See Rackham's notes to this effect in his Loeb edition of *NE*, 332, 338.

9. E.g., see R. G. Collingwood, *Principles of Art*, esp. 5–7, 15–35, 47.

10. Aristotle, e.g., says that experience is sometimes more successful than art at *Meta*. 981a12–24.

the later theory of romantic genius (cf. Collingwood's "expression") overemphasizes the obvious: a rule-formulable *technē* is not sufficient.[11] Nonetheless, the good artist does make such things as perform their functions well. When contemporary critics talk about modern art (or romantics talk about theirs) they still consider at least one or the other of Aristotle's three purposes (catharsis, education, recreation) as important elements of their analyses—even if they wish to unburden themselves of one or the other of those purposes or reshape (as Freud) what the significance of catharsis is. At the least we must agree that Aristotle's *modus cognescendi et operandi* in this matter is clearly not illegitimate. His multiple uses of *technē* clearly encompass a wide enough range to include the fine arts as we understand them, and the ancient term *mimesis* encompasses the central meanings of our term *art*.[12] If his idea of *technē* were thoroughly different from our idea of art (as Collingood says), Aristotle would have no application to present art forms, like tragedy or comedy; but he does have such application, so the premise is false. Finally and in any case, we have no other way to deal with Aristotle than by accepting at least a rough and general comparability of the terms "*technē* of mimetic things" and "art" and we should begin to consider that it is a very strange thought to think that Sophocles, Pindar, Aristophanes, and Sappho are doing something thoroughly distinct from Shakespeare, Jonson, Keats, and Kyd, or Stoppard and contemporary artists, and it is equally strange to think that such geniuses could not carry on some discussion of their work with the likes of Aristotle, should they meet with him—or Socrates—on the Islands of the Blest.

I doubt, however, that this richer story about *technē* will convince many Aristotelians to consider its life as a plausible candidate for happiness next to moral virtue and contemplation. Aristotle clearly distinguishes it from *phronēsis*—the other intellectual virtue dealing with changeable things—because making is distinguished from doing (*NE* 1140a1–5, 17), and further by the fact that "making aims at an end distinct from the act of making,

11. Whether or not Aristotle thought skill (*technē*) sufficient for the production of epic, lyric, or dramatic art might be debated by some; clearly he is trying to lay out some general rules in *Poetics*. Just as clearly, he thinks poetry requires a special gift, if not mania (*Po.* 1455a33); the better poets have a kind of genius, the making of fine metaphors being a sign of genius, not science. Similar remarks and implications can be found in Plato (*Phaedrus* 245a and *Ion*). "Romantic genius" might merely be art's way of recovering what was lost to it in the preceding centuries' extreme reduction of the concept of mimesis to mere imitation. See the Propylaia above, and Halliwell's *Aesthetics of Mimesis*. Collingwood's complaint about the ancients, then, is a matter of an overly limiting translation/understanding of mimesis.

12. As shown by Halliwell, *The Aesthetics of Mimesis*.

whereas in doing the end cannot be other than the act itself" (*NE* 1140b3–5). "Where there are ends apart from the actions, the products are better than the activities" (1094a5–7), therefore *technē* is always less final than what it produces and so the life centered on its practice is not a contender for *eudaimonia*, which is both most final and self-sufficient. This argument is why Aristotle never suggests that *technē*, though a virtue, is a contender for happiness. I do not think this argument is sufficient to discount the life of the artist as a genuine competitor for happiness, however. The artist does produce an end apart from his own action (the poem), but that poem's purpose is to invite contemplation and incite a certain kind of passional response and activity in the citizens—so its true end is an activity. In Athens it was an activity in which the entire polis participated, and "to achieve the end for a city is finer and more divine" (*NE* 1094b 10–11). To carry this debate further is not, however, directly *apropos*.

But this argument leads directly back to a problem about the inclusivist idea of happiness, and such an argument against the life of *technē* cannot be made so simply by a pseudo-Aristotelian inclusivist as I have just made it for a strict Aristotelian. For, if the strict Aristotelian argument is accepted, inclusivism cannot be accepted. Consider: insofar as

> the function of man is a certain form of life, namely the activities of soul implying or in accord with a rational principle, and the function of a good man is to perform these activities rightly and well, and since a function is well performed when it is performed in accordance with its own proper excellence, . . . then the human good [happiness], is the active exercise of the soul's faculties in conformity with virtue. (1098a7–17)

The inclusivist takes this to mean that all the virtues—moral as well as intellectual—are essential aspects of the human good because they are the proper excellent activities of the human soul. This implies that *technē*, since it is—like activities of moral and theoretical virtue—an active exercise of the soul's faculty in conformity with a rational principle, must itself be a cause or constituent part of happiness under the inclusivist idea and understanding—no matter that it produces something outside of itself. If one is going to take the inclusivist tack on happiness, *technē* must at least be included along with philia, practices of moral and scientific virtue, and the material wherewithal to practice the moral virtues such as generosity. But Aristotle does not even approach making this suggestion in *NE*. Further, the inclusivist ought to be required to give a reasonable argument why the life of *technē*, like the life of intellectual virtue or the life of political virtue, cannot stand alone. Aristotle does consider that the moral virtues can stand as a separate life and inclusivist arguments take this political option very seriously, *even though this life clearly produces something outside itself*—the well-running of the state and victory being two obvious beneficial results (to say nothing of preparing the way and allowing the time for development of the intellectual virtues, which is where my own and Aristotle's argument is aiming). Aristotle clearly calls the political and the morally virtuous life happy in a secondary way (1178a8–10); that life is not sufficiently final, just as the life of *technē* is not: it produces a good outside itself in redounding to the well-running of the state. The same argument one uses against *technē* standing alone applies to the life of moral virtue. The further good moral virtue aims at and accomplishes must be considered a greater good than the activities themselves, which is perhaps what Aristotle has in mind when he says that "producing the good for a state is nobler and more divine" (1094b11).

There is a second problem we may raise here. The inclusion of *technē* as a constituent part or partial cause of happiness may seem a small addition to the moral virtues, but the wide variety and large number of arts exacerbates a problem with the inclusivist view that Aristotle remarks upon several times. That problem is the problem of competition. For example, in his discussion of pleasure Aristotle notes that each kind of activity has its own pleasure, that these pleasures compete with one another and so

> each person is active about those things and with those faculties that he loves most; the musician exercises his hearing upon musical tunes, the student his intellect upon the problems of philosophy and so on. And the pleasure of these activities perfects the activities and therefore perfects the life. (1175a11–16, cf. 27–29)[13]

Here we come upon another double-edged argument, one of whose edges is popular among contemporary inclusivists. Theoria is hard to "include" among the other virtues, inclusivists like Ackrill say, because in order to do so one has to invent a scale of comparability and compromise between incompatibly different *kinds* of virtue (Ackrill, 30–33). This, they say, makes Aristotle's account broken-backed. But clearly, the problem comparability raises to the inclusivist view Ackrill and others wish to maintain is already present *before* Aristotle defends the contemplative life as the highest human life. At

13. Aristotle would no doubt remember that the competition among the pleasures in one life reaches its zenith in the soul of the democratic man who can only "pretend to be occupied with philosophy" (*Rep.* 561c). Perhaps the (pseudo-Aristotelian) inclusivist view is really merely the modern version of a (Platonic) democrat—the life of pleasure masquerading as something more and presumed to be more defensible than Plato (or Aristotle) allows.

least it is for them. For they must invent a scale of measure and comparability for the moral virtues and *technai*. The inclusivist view does not resolve a problem in Aristotle's account of happiness; it exacerbates it, infinitely. For consider the arts—from pottery to metalworking, from medicine to music, from comedy to tragedy—so many arts, so little time. Now, according to the inclusivist, admitting the worth of both *theōria* and virtuous action along with the claim that the former element is "more divine" leads to the problem "How can there be a coalition between such parties?" (Ackrill, 33). If there can't be, the account is broken-backed since we must have both. Similarly, then, admitting that *phronēsis* and *technē* are excellences of the soul but that those practices that do not admit of ends outside the action (*phronēsis*, ostensibly) are more noble than those that produce an end (*technē*, certainly) leads to the same problem: Is it not ignoble to choose the less noble activities of *technē*? How can there be a coalition with this partner? Yet we must have both. *Technē* is a human and intellectual virtue, one producing necessities. Remembering that the pleasure perfects the life and draws us further into it, how can there be a coalition between such parties? These pleasures compete and differ in kind. Yet the inclusivist *takes it for granted* that all the moral virtues and *technē* have an aspect of finality and are worth practicing and so she must (impossibly) balance incomparables even if (unlike Ackrill) she does not consider intellectual virtue to be the activity of divinity brought into human nature. Aristotle's account must already be broken-backed; book 10 does not introduce a new problem as the inclusivists say.

Or else the inclusivist must admit that there is a legitimate hierarchy of *kinds* of virtue and if *technē* (intellectual virtue aimed at production) is a lower kind than moral virtue (though the life of moral virtue requires *technē*'s practice as supplying means), it is possible that there is also a higher kind of virtue (the purely intellectual) that requires the moral virtues as part of its means. The account of the last chapters of *NE* then hangs together with the rest of the book, as Kraut suggests, under the rubric that every other good is pursued insofar as it promotes the highest activity. This argument has the additional advantage of being in agreement with the *Eudemian Ethics*, which closes thus:

> Whatever mode of choosing and of acquiring things good by nature—whether goods of the body or wealth or friends or the other goods—will best promote the contemplation of God, that is the best mode and that standard is the finest; and any mode of choice and acquisition that either through deficiency or excess hinders us from serv-

ing and contemplating God—that is a bad one. . . . Let this, then, be our statement of what is the standard of nobility. (1249b17–25)

Such a closing, echoing *NE*, would seem to indicate a deeply considered and long-held conviction on Aristotle's part. The main argument for throwing out the intellectualist account (that it breaks the back of an otherwise unified theory) evaporates, and in fact we see more clearly the need for just the wisdom Aristotle describes. For if the highest activity is wisdom, which has as its object what is highest (*NE* 1141a18–22) and most divine (1177a15), then, according to *Metaphysics*, "it is most archetectonic and authoritative and the other sciences, like slave women, may not even contradict her" (996b10–11).[14]

Of course, it is *phronēsis* itself that will tell us that the practice of certain arts is necessary to enable the practice of virtue. *Phronēsis* dictates to *technē* just as political wisdom says which arts are to be practiced in the state and to what extent (*NE* 1994b1). In order to be generous one must have practiced certain productive arts well to produce the wherewithal of generosity.[15] In order to be courageous someone must have practiced arts productive of implements like swords, helmets, and shields, for to enter a battle without such well-made things is foolishness or naked Celtic madness. It would be the case, then, that the activities of the lesser but intrinsically good *technai* "are valuable only insofar as they promote" the higher intrinsically good moral virtues—just what Ackrill suggests (and rejects) as the relation between moral action and wise *theōria* (31). But if such an argument can be used to defend the goose Aristotle never openly discusses—the inclusivist view of happiness—it should certainly be legitimate in defense of the gander he openly prefers—the intellectual life. Aristotle does not openly commit himself to either of these thorough-going reductions of value (*technē* is for moral virtue, moral virtue is for *theōria*) to a relation to a dominant end—if he had there would be nothing to debate. But he does not do so because a means-end reductionism here would miss important points: all the virtues (*technē*, *phronēsis*, *sophia*) are, *first of all*, good for their own sake; they are the excellent activities of human souls only, animals partake in them only by a very weak analogy when they are at the top of their game; all of them except *so-*

14. See also Tom Sherman's account of "good" and "happiness" understood according to *pros hen* homonomy (96–102) and the requirement of the exercise of wisdom (*sophia*) in discerning the end correctly (127–60).

15. Cf. Kraut on the necessity of at least practicing the craft of *oikonomia*, 249–51.

phia are discussed as good for some other purpose as well. My point is that the inclusivist view is not any more able to *get around* the problem of the competition of kinds of virtuous activities and their accompanying pleasures than the intellectualist view is *problematized by* its supposed inattention to metabolic function or political action. If the problem of justifying a "full recipe" for the combination of the virtues (Ackrill, 31) is a problem for the life including *sophia*, it is also a problem for the life including *technē*—and the inclusivist is hoisted with his own petard. The main argument against intellectualism—that it does away with the virtuousness and importance of the moral virtues (the back that would unite the account)—does not hold, or else it holds against inclusivism too. We may conclude with *Metaphysics*, "the science of the end and of the good is of the nature of wisdom, for the other things are for the sake of the end" (996b12–13).

The implications of the conflict of activities and an attempted solution via reference to a more dominant end or focal value raises more involved problems for the inclusivist than for the defender of *sophia* as that to which and for which all others must be related. First of all, as Nussbaum's parenthesis in her crown analogy reveals (cf. 239, above), "the whole composition" of the inclusivist life is made by practical reason. If, as inclusivists wish to claim, the arguments proving the supremacy of theoretical reason are incompatible with the rest of *NE* and must be diluted to bring the intellectual life within the ambit of the more social and political human good, then it seems that practical reason is de facto raised to the position of the highest virtue. Like Charlemagne, it crowns itself. Aristotle, in the middle of *NE*, forthrightly denies that this is the case in 1141a20–1b4, where, among other things he says that "it would be strange to consider politics or practical wisdom the highest kind of knowledge." *Phronēsis* is de facto the most important virtue and highest knowledge in Nussbaum's account because in the inclusivist view no virtue has a position of ultimate supremacy or the quality of being that in reference to which all others are judged, *and phronēsis* is necessary in order to make each possible and to keep them all—competitors as they are—in appropriate relation. Since *phronēsis* does not have a target given to it by nature on this view, it is clear that the target *phronēsis* is aiming at (Nussbaum's crown) is practical wisdom's own creation. On the contrary, the intellectualist holds that *phronēsis* is given a target by nature; for its own nature is not of the best: the divine is higher (*NE* 1141a16–42b2). The target to be aimed at is not adjustable by practical wisdom—which according to Aristotle *never* sets ends, but only finds means (*NE* 1145a5–6). Aristotle clearly allows that *phronēsis* does have responsibility for making the virtues practicable, but just as clearly he sees practical reason as doing all this for the sake of a good far superior to practical concerns: contemplation.[16] If *phronēsis* is not answerable to anything higher and holds the power of legislation as well as the power of execution, it is, in fact, king and unitary executive; there is no court of appeal except itself. *Metaphysics*, we have already seen, disagrees.

Were this a work of literary criticism rather than a work of philosophy, I would point out that Nussbaum's crown analogy itself *announces* the decision her argument defends. For if the three competing lives are differentiated by their ends—pleasure, the noble or fine, and truth—a crown would certainly be the symbol of a noble or fine thing, especially the crown she describes, but it is not necessarily an image of truth. The pleasant, the noble, and the true is more like the way Aristotle differentiates the competing lives and perhaps part of the reason he does not consider the mixed life as a plausible competitor: one cannot serve two masters. This is more clear in the discussion in *EE* 1214a33–b6 where he says that some people think that happiness might come from two of them, others that it consists in one, whence he begins his discussion of finding the target. In that discussion he again separates out the three usual suspects—pleasure, moral virtue, and contemplation (1215b2–5)—according to what they are about. The inclusivist option (i.e., two of the ends combined) simply disappears. If I were I writer of comedies, I would imagine three caskets, and in one of them put the image of the queen; another one has the wedding ring. The way Nussbaum imagines the telos—as a crown—indicates that to which her own soul is drawn: nobility; and her analogy appeals to the same desire in her reader. This desire is not to be condemned, for it is, truly, the desire for something fine, but that is not to say that it is the desire for the finest, or that it rightly clarifies the organization of activity which is, in truth, best for us, given a nature that is capable of participation in the life of the divine. That question, about what is truly finest, is triable only in a higher court than that of practical wisdom. It is a further question whether *we* bring this question into the higher court,

16. Kraut argues that "the best amount of lower goods to have . . . is the amount that most fully contributes to one's ultimate end, [and that this] target . . . helps us determine how much is too much, and how little too little" (12). One might say that his entire book explores the problem of how practical reason could work without an end given by nature, though to make the argument more brief I will quote but part of a sentence: "if someone fails to realize that the philosophical life is best, . . . then he does not have perfect practical reason" (53n).

or whether we must suffer to be tried by it, and our deference to the truth of the matter is a *recognition* of our constitution rather than *our creation* of a crown.

If practical reason has the inclusivist's free reign among all the virtues and is at the service of nothing absolutely superior and end-giving, we must wonder if certain of the ends and activities are being suggested surreptitiously by the ever active knave of hearts (who is incorporated now under the name of Id and given free rein in democratic culture). Further, practical reason's (or Id's?) free rein in combining the elements of life (with no particular end in view) would have the already discussed result of debilitating poetry and the other arts of the muses as well (Chapter 3.3, 3.4). Their purpose would be—whatever we wished it to be at the moment (or perhaps only what Id wished, ourselves all unknowing). We would have to conclude about the making of and attending to drama that it is justifiable only insofar as it, like weapons-making or production of the material wherewithal for generosity, directly provides for the life of moral virtue in the polis. A number of critics apparently think this consequence, which would certainly follow upon practical reason's aim being to invent a balance of all intrinsically valuable activities, is Aristotle's. Amelie Rorty, for example, says, "Aristotle's way of saving the phenomena of tragic drama has a strongly normative turn, beyond that which is implicit in any technical advice. Indeed, his normative agenda may have so focused his analysis of classical drama that he ignored some of its important features."[17] Most inclusivists are more democratic, however, and do not find such a normative view of art companionable, nor do they think it true. Judgment upon the arts, as judgment upon each person's crown, then will be based on. . . . But Aristotle thinks that there is a crown nature means us to have, a crown that is our highest good, at which all our arts and activities aim, and not to achieve it is to fail at human perfection, and not to attempt it is cowardice.

I have already argued that aesthetic judgments have an important freedom from both technical and normative *determination*, while also being naturally and intrinsically connected to *technē* and *ethos*. This freedom, I will shortly argue, connects with Aristotle's view of happiness as the activity of theoretical reason, but first let us give the opposition more rope. Rorty's complaint about the directly dependent relationship of art to politics (and

17. A. O. Rorty, "The Psychology of Aristotelian Tragedy," 3.

ethos) might seem to follow from Aristotle's claim that politics is the master science of the good for man, a science that directs the nature and extent of all the other arts (*NE* 1094a29). In such a case, many literary critics in studying their history have taken a wrong turn. Rather than being an artistic formalist, Aristotle should, under this dispensation, be placed among those more materialist critics who discover in literature only the expression and promotion of the hegemonic values of the society in which it was written. Aristotle, in fact, must be demanding this kind of expression and promotion in the case of what he calls a good society. Now while Aristotle attempts not so relativistic a view as many contemporary critics who hold such views (every society's art is as good as every other society's)—for he seems to think his own is more natural—there would be one underlying agreement between this Aristotle and these relativists about the (incestuous?) mode of relation between politics and art: the virtues of the polis are decisive for the question of the value of art. Aristotle would say that the artist and audience should be joined in their view of what counts as virtue. The underlying relationship between art and politics would then remain the same from the Stagirite through Anatoli Lunacharski, Dollimore and Jameson, and feminist critics, though Aristotle will disagree with the moderns (as they do among themselves) about precisely whose virtues and which politics lead to the best human life. This seems to be the way MacIntyre (mis)understands the issue. But neither the formalist not the cultural materialist is correct, or correct about Aristotle. Aristotle thinks that the particular virtues art should exercise, and what is the basis of the community, can be found by sufficiently discerning the nature of the human psyche and community. He avoids both extremes of formalism and culturally relative materialism because he sees both constitutions and the arts of the muses as natural to our being yet shaped to chosen purposes, and some chosen purposes are naturally superior to others.

The contemporary subjection of art to politics is analogous to, and linked with, a subjection of the individual to the state, which follows necessarily if the intellectual life is not considered the best life for human beings. While the moral virtues are an excellence of the soul (like *technē*) and are yet more final than *technē* because their practice does not aim at a product outside the action, the practice of the moral virtues themselves, including practical wisdom, does *redound to a further good* besides the happiness of the individual whose activity they are, namely, the good functioning of the state.

Far from being a criticism, Aristotle considers this a high good (as he would consider it a good of *technē*). He says that

> even if it be the case that the good is the same for the individual and for the state, nevertheless the good of the state seems greater and more complete both to attain and to preserve. To secure the good for one person alone is something, but to secure the good of a nation or state is nobler (κάλλιον) and more divine (θειότερον). (*NE* 1094b7–11)

We should consider this argument carefully, for while at first reading it seems to valorize the moral or political virtues—and so support the inclusivist view, if it is not a defense of the political life *tout court*—there are several things implied here to which inclusivist interpreters of the *Ethics* ought to pay closer attention. First of all, there is a rather ugly face beneath this mask. If those (moral and political) virtues that also produce something are valued more ("more divine") for what they produce than for their practice (which is also a good thing), it seems that not only is *technē* valued most for its production of things with which the moral virtues may be practiced, but moral virtue must be valued most for its production of a well-functioning state (to which good thing it redounds). If there is nothing higher than political science, then what makes the state run well must be virtue and this virtue is definable by the state in accordance with the light "good running." If practical wisdom fashions the crown of each according to its own light, then political wisdom must do so for the state. If we do not recognize wisdom (*sophia*) as absolutely the highest aim, then there is nothing higher than the state that can allow a corrective to political wisdom's light of efficiency. In such cases political wisdom crowns itself, after making the crown to its own liking: efficiency. Gradgrind becomes prime minister. It is no longer possible to make a distinction between open and closed societies; all societies are closed upon themselves—in one way or another. The Penates are the fasces in small; the fasces are more divine; and there is no higher good to which this organization of goods is naturally ordered.

There are two further problems connected to this (mis)interpretation of Aristotle. The first is that the argument for the primacy of the achievement of the social good over the individual good ("greater and more complete both to attain and to preserve") seems to be predicated on the condition that the good is the same for both society and individual—that we are comparing apples with more apples. More is better. But what if there is a good that is by its very nature more divine, more final and more self-sufficient than the moral virtues which are the good of both the individual and the polis? What if we have to compare apple juice with ambrosia? Further, what if that good is something which may be achieved by an individual only as an, and for that, individual?[18] The practice of the theoretical virtues not only cannot redound to the benefit of society according to Aristotle, they are the most autonomous activities in which human beings participate (*NE* 1177a25–28). Though Aristotle says, in *Politics,* that the polis has an (existential) priority in nature to the household and the individual (1253a19–20, cf. 1337a21–29), it seems the individual has a (moral) priority by virtue of the good of his natural entelechy, for the individual's entelchy, *but not the state's*, shares in the activity that belongs to god.[19] We see here that Aristotle has a more deep and rich individualism than modern philosophy has dreamt of: it is not our own individual invention or the congeries of our individual pathologies, individuality is an achievement (or not) of the individual herself, not given by nature. Like the god, then, "that human being is free who exists for his own sake, and not for the sake of another" (*Meta.* 982b25–26). Individuals are not the foundation of politics, but they are its hoped for result; and a properly organized state will aim to achieve this divine happiness.

Aristotle nowhere considers that the theoretical virtues redound to the good of the community or any other person; in fact it is clear that they cannot since *sophia* contemplates what is unchanging—not the sublunary. "From practical pursuits we look to secure some advantage, greater or smaller, beside the action itself" (*NE* 1177b3–5). Wisdom, on the other hand, contemplates that about which and with which we can do nothing, and, according to *Metaphysics*, among those objects of contemplation is the divine. Man desires to know just in order to know. *Sophia*, as Aristotle understands things, is for her own sweet sake absolutely, and cannot be turned to any earthly purpose. Only because the human being's good goes beyond the good of the society, only because a human being has a happiness which does not redound to the good of the state, or even, necessarily, to any other per-

18. I would not, by this, deny that coinvestigators in wisdom are helpful and pleasant. They, too, have that good (contemplation) as individuals, and do not need us (but, in moral matters, the man who would be just, besides having the virtue, *requires* others on which to practice his virtue).

19. Of course, if Aristotle could imagine a community of saints, as he will through the good offices of Thomas Aquinas a millenium after his death, the individual's entelechy and the human community's entelechy will be found to extend equally far, and then we might be forced to agree that the life of the community is more divine, literally.

son, only because happiness is a higher good than prudence and political science (which rule for its sake), which happiness participates so far as humanly possible in the life of the divine *can* there be an art which is not subject to the demands and direction of a particular politics. Art can have this freedom *insofar as it participates in and shapes our eros to that happiness which is beyond the good and evil of the polis and its virtues.* Thus only can art have freedom; its freedom is, in Kant's terms, conditioned. It comes to be because something else *is* first.

Secondly, the inclusivist should pay attention to the fact that Aristotle throughout 1094b uses the comparative—"nobler and more divine"—to describe a good applying to both individual and society when that good is achieved by the society. When he speaks of contemplation in 10.7 and 10.8 however, his language is full of superlatives. He seeks for the activity which is in accord with the highest (κρατίστην) virtue, the virtue of the best (ἀρίστου) part of us, a part either divine per se (θεῖον . . . αὐτό) or the divinest we have (θειότατον) and so which constitutes final happiness (τελεία εὐδαιμονία; 1177a12–17). For two chapters his argument never slips down to the comparative. If there is a supreme and incomparable good among final human goods, these last chapters are where we will find it. And if there is such a good and such a happiness, only that society which aims to make that happiness possible to the greatest extent (and it does this by requiring practices which build theoretical virtue up) can be called open, virtuous, or magnificent. For politics to aim elsewise is to close upon a lesser good, to close upon itself, and so to fail even at moral virtue. But for a society to truly aim at this . . . —no wonder Socrates wondered how a city could take up philosophy without being destroyed (*Rep.* 497d8). Perhaps, however, it is the divine idea of society, one united in the ecstasy of knowing. If this were possible for human beings, who would aim otherwise?

Against the more popular inclusivist arguments, then, we must affirm the arguments in favor of the intellectual life as the best, as that life in which supreme happiness lies. Aristotle points out that this life has the highest degree of self-sufficiency (αὐτάρκεια; 1177a28). Indeed we should consider that it is the life of contemplation alone which raises the individual and his happiness above the status of "part of" and "partaker in" the good of the state. A close study of our own nature and functions reveals that we have a power that transcends the life of nutrition, *technē,* and even the virtuous ordering of social relations by prudence; it is not unfitting to call that power the capacity to know God. This power is the one which belongs most to the individual per se, not as a member of a society. So when Aristotle arouses us not to

> obey those who enjoin that being human we should think of human things, and being mortal, of mortal things, but rather so far as we can to make ourselves immortal, and strain every nerve to live in accord with what is best in us, for even though it be small in bulk it surpasses all else in power and value (1077b31–1078a1),

we ought not consider that this conclusion contradicts the rest of his *Ethics*, or sits uneasily on its shoulders, but rather that it concludes and perfects it, as the bloom of youth upon the beauteous movement of the dancer, or the long lost head belonging to some archaic torso of Apollo. It may in fact be imprudent to attempt to live in accord with such an ethic, but "it is absurd to think that political science or prudence is the loftiest kind of knowledge, for man is not the highest thing in the universe" (*NE* 1141a21–23). It is, then, not accidental that the first moral virtue Aristotle speaks of is courage (*NE* 1115a6). It is courage which not only risks its life in defense of the good state, but which risks life in the face of the state (perhaps even in the face of the ridicule of its comic poets—those of them who have not yet achieved a complete understanding of the human good), and for a good beyond that state. And such an individual is that, and every state's highest aim. And this is why, as Diotima suggests to Aristophanes (*Sym.* 205e, 212c), becoming whole is not sufficient for the human being, for the whole human being has a telos outside of itself in something more divine.

If the purpose of a state is to make its citizens happy, and contemplation is the highest happiness available to human beings, then it is *necessary* for a state to make possible an end which exceeds it and does not return to it any payment on its capital outlay. The primary virtue of a state, then, is magnificence. Far from being a suitable decision theory for states though not a moral theory for individuals, utilitarian cost-benefit analysis is particularly not suitable for states. It is, rather, a symptom of moral corruption, theoretical ignorance or error, and it is a political error. For Aristotle, the state is at the service of the individual citizen's happiness—which his argument shows may not even be related to his or her desires of the moment, or to the state's better functioning. Aristotle does not share the democrat's inclusivist view of happiness or how we decide about what happiness is, but he does think his arguments will lead most reasonable beings to *know* what happiness is and that this consensus is indicative of a fact about human beings.

> Concerning all these things we must try to seek conviction through argument, using the appearances as our evidences and examples. For the best thing would be if all human beings could come into an evident agreement with what we shall say, but if not, that all shall agree in some way. And this they will do if they are led carefully until they shift their position. For everyone has something of his own to contribute to the truth, and it is from these that we go on to give a sort of demonstration about our own. From what is said truly but not clearly clearness will also be attained if, as we advance, we always move from what is usually said in a jumbled fashion to a more perspicuous view. (*EE* 1216b26–33)

> That is how progress takes place in science too: it is open to anyone to supply what is lacking. (*NE* 1098a25–26)

Since it is not age that makes a child childish, but lack of development of the faculty of reason, Aristotle is unwilling to sacrifice the truth he thinks can be arrived at by the consensus of reason to a compromise patched together from limbs of very different parentage, which child might go under the name of Liberty. In short, he would allow the pursuit of happiness only under the condition that we know what it is, and any other political arrangement than one that aims at happiness—knowing what it is for a human soul (1102a5–17)—is inappropriate for what is best in human nature. It follows that it is also necessary for the most virtuous and happiest of men to be willing to risk their lives in war to defend a state which does allow and make possible the life of contemplation, particularly against a regime which would not allow or encourage it. Such a scholar must, in fact, be considered the most courageous, for he above all others knows what he risks—a life he shares with the god—and what it is worth. But this takes us rather far from the argument about comedy. Perhaps.

1.2. Art and Eudaimonia

We may return now to what was to be our second question (238), one that we have already touched on in passing: the relationship of art to happiness. One of the implications of the inclusivist view seemed to be that art becomes subject to politics as everything in the individual life is subject to practical wisdom. But if contemplation of eternal truth is a more final and complete good than moral action, then it is possible that art—insofar as it prepares the emotions and the mind both to love properly and to participate well in that best of all activities—also transcends that narrowing social and political focus. Music, as Aristotle says, not only provides moral education and catharsis, but intellectual recreation. So, too, the other arts, which can all provide suitable objects for recreative contemplation. If we understand *theōria* as

> an activity that goes on whenever one brings certain truths to mind—it occurs not only when one silently reflects, but also when one lectures or writes about a certain subject, when one reads a book, when one listens to a book being read, or when one hears someone presenting a lecture

—then we should also consider it as an activity that artists and their audiences participate in. Richard Kraut's example, that

> the teacher who is preparing lectures and notes, or who is orally presenting a subject to students and colleagues, is consciously considering truths he has already come to understand, and so he is contemplating (73)

can include the artist insofar as the artist is also consciously considering the truth as he makes his poem.[20]

This adds a level of complexity to the poem's work on the audience. It is not just that in viewing a play we see a character acting morally (or not), certain passions are charmed out of us by mimesis and reaction, and we are inspired (in one way or another) to feel likewise or not. We also see and contemplate a person thinking through—well or not, thoroughly or not—important issues concerning the human good. In Aristophanes' *Clouds* Good and Bad Logic come in person. In Shakespeare's *Henry V* discussion of the king's responsibility the right and wrong are much more darkly and obliquely lit, but in both cases the audience must consider, from their more distant and uninvolved position, the relationship of each argument to the good. If one is not so considering, one does not get the deeper jokes in Aristophanes (the slapstick still works), or feel the deep unease of war in Shakespeare—which feeling is a large part of the purpose of the play. Practice in considering the truth of things in the play and the instigation of laughter at falsity (e.g., laughing at the success of Bad Logic in the crooked world of the comedy) arouses, and is a purifying act of, our love for the truth—a love not merely for the truth in the play, or in some other limited (perhaps politically inscribed) arena.

In Kraut's discussion of Aristotle's claim that we can contemplate our friends' actions better than our own he says,

20. For an argument that the poet could be doing this in Plato's understanding also, see my "Two Views of Imagination."

> too much self-consciousness about the performance of an activity undermines its chances of success. To exercise one's skills in the solution of a practical problem, one must focus on the problem itself, and not reflect on those skills. (143)

This advantage of reflecting on acts other than our own also accrues to art, but in addition, while at the play, we ourselves are not only constantly forced to practice both intellectual judgment and feeling (through reflection on acts other than our own), but we are also *enjoying the practice* of *theōria, and* enjoying it mimetically by taking pleasure in the pleasure of those on stage who may be doing it (as when we take pleasure in Salieri's joy at seeing how Mozart constructs his *Requiem*, though he hates Mozart and is killing him: "Yes! Of course!"). Neither we nor the actor have to understand what Salieri understands in order to *enjoy through mimesis the joy of understanding.* And this is how we always begin, for we learn first by mimesis. One thing we learn here is that there are joys beyond our present ken that are not beyond our entire kenning, and moved by this proleptic, mimetically induced joy some might move actually in the world to achieve it—*but without it no one would.* (Ergo, there must then be a Prime Mover—one who knows . . . whom we imitate first unwittingly, and having found joy in this we are moved to wit the what of it.)

It is true also that if we were not making true judgments and suffering diverse feelings about the worth and working of (e.g.) Wrong Logic, we would neither laugh nor cry at its victory. What happens in the play would merely be a fact. So, we ourselves are, in some aspects of the play, enjoying the intellectual life ourselves. The enjoyment of this practice is one part of our catharsis, for we are practicing and enjoying in the limited cosmos of the play an activity fraught with darkness, difficulty, and concern in the real one. Kraut also says that "when we enjoy seeing our friends use their moral skills, we are seeing something of ourselves, since we have much to do with their accomplishments" (143). This last is not literally true in the case of art, whose characters are not our friends in the sense that we have some part in their accomplishments in the play's world. However, we are seeing *something of ourselves* insofar as we share with the characters the same kinds of desires, pains, pleasures, possible relations to the highest and secondary goods, necessity of choice, and the like; the play puts these things together in a way that draws us out to *feel* them as well as to *contemplate* the interplay of their connections. And so, in this way too, our eros, philia, sympathy are charmed forth to play, to an exercise that can and should shape and strengthen them for those goods our nature aims at: moral feeling and action, the life of contemplation.

It would not be surprising to find that some arts—particularly those concerned with vision (e.g., painting or narrative)—emphasize more the production of objects for intellectual contemplation than they emphasize catharsis or ethical training. For exercise of the passions, as of the body, seems to require movement. Music would be more likely to tend toward the side of ethical education and catharsis, and it seems to most to be more closely tied to the emotions; our bodies respond to music long before our minds begin to figure out what is going on. If music is preeminent among the arts in this particular matter, that would explain why it is Aristotle's example of choice when he talks about catharsis. Drama not only contains the other arts, but seems to hold the middle position with regard to art's possible effects, being as cathartic (musical) as it is intellectually recreative (painterly). Its middle position in this regard, as well as its use of all the means of mimesis that the other arts use alone is why Aristotle chooses it as the center of poetics and brings in other arts insofar as they share elements of drama. Of course all the arts of the muses might well do all three (catharsis, intellectual recreation, moral education)—in one way or another and to one degree or another, partly depending on the art, partly on the artist, and partly on the character of the audience member. I do not doubt, for example, that meditating on one of Rembrandt's late self-portraits, or a sixteenth-century Spanish diptych can be cathartic. I am not sure that I *learn* anything when I return to the museum to look again; I am pretty sure that learning is not the usual impetus for going back to look again. It is practice at *theōria* on an object complete and evocative. Such activity is naturally pleasant, and the made thing arouses the activity, lets it play freely, and so purifies through this recreation.

It may seem that I have here been giving back somewhat to the intellectualist position what I have been at pains to take away in earlier sections. But I have already pointed out how the presence of Touchstone among the noble lovers might lead someone who is excessively drawn by such darker horses to laugh at those desires and increase his desire for the better kind of love. Similarly, the playing of Jaques's conversion in the way I have suggested increases our always inadequate love for the philosophical life.[21] This is

21. When Socrates says that no regime at all of those current is suitable for philosophy (*Rep.* 497b), he implies not only that there are no cities properly arranged for her, but no souls with

so even though we see him solve no problems, nor hear any argument. The purification of desire—art's first and most universal aim—is in no way dismissed as the primary purpose of comedy (or tragedy, or music) by the addition of contemplation and intellectual recreation. Our love for *sophia* must, above all other loves, be purified, for where we live ordinarily

> all is seared with trade; bleared, smeared with toil;
> And wears man's smudge.
>
> (G. M. Hopkins, "God's Grandeur")

In fact, intellectual contemplation is a necessary part of art because, by creating a world in which to practice *theōria* in a freer, simpler, pleasant, and completable way, art *makes us practice* those virtues *and makes pleasant* the practice of that virtue which is most divine. One could hardly purify a passion without engaging it in some way, so only by having elements that exhibit or encourage and reward contemplation (or mock such things as pretend at or abuse it) can comedy lead out our desire for it and give us pleasure in that highest good. By leading us in a mimesis of our real task, art draws forth that activity, and, finding pleasure in it, the desire increases—and so we are returned to our own world, re-created for our own most proper good. Thus does pleasure in the performance of an act perfect the act and thereby perfect the life (*NE* 1174b17–33, 1175a15f), and so our spirit is enlarged and set free from the poverty of utility and the heavy cross of gain. That is a purification devoutly to be wished, frequently to be suffered.

Instead of being locked in an old quarrel, then, we might more accurately see poetry as the handmaid of philosophy. And if, as Socrates wonders in *Republic*, it is a serious question whether or not a state can survive philosophy, it is also an equally serious question whether or not the handmaid (art) can, when true to her heavenly Queen, serve also Caesar. Perhaps only under the condition that Caesar is also the god. I do not think we are there yet. Perhaps Socrates kicked out poetry from Glaucon's republic as a test to see if Glaucon was golden. His inability to defend the handmaid means he is not yet a true subject of the Queen and cannot be expected to defend her adequately either when it is necessary. If, as the previous chapters of this book have argued, the purpose of comedy is to provide a catharsis of desire and sympathy, the greatest comedy should prepare and purify us for our best and

---

the right regime either. The word applies to both parts of the great analogy: the city and the man. That we should find such an expression in the mouth of Plato's Socrates is deeply humiliating.

highest love. Whether or not the artist's story ends with an upward turn of the plot, we know what that desire is which would make us most happy: All men by nature desire to know, therefore paradise must be that *energeic* activity known as contemplation of eternal truth. Dante (in his practice, though not in his criticism)[22] understood perfectly what Aristotle would have said about the function of comedy, its high and most important aim.

2. *ARCADIA*: A LOVE SONG FOR THE LIFE OF THE MIND

In *Arcadia,* Tom Stoppard accomplishes something that does not seem to have even been attempted by Aristophanes, and is only hinted at in Shakespeare (if Jaques is played as the character we have outlined). Nonetheless, it is a latent possibility for comic drama in its nature as the kind of thing that provides a catharsis for the passions that involve pleasure—desire and sympathy standing as metonyms for them all. In this play, besides the usual eros, an eros for the life of the mind is raised and purified in us, an eros for our own highest and most divine life, buried in the life of the more usual and demanding desires that are our quotidian focus. Plato, in *Phaedrus* and *Symposium* most clearly, is his only competitor,[23] so far as I can see. Moreover, in aiming at this catharsis of our highest love—that for the life of the mind—*Arcadia* also provides a catharsis of our other desires and sympathies.

2.1. Plot

Since *Arcadia* is a relatively new and unfamiliar play in comparison with *Iphigenia in Tauris, Acharnians,* or *As You Like It,* it behooves me to spend a bit more time summarizing it.[24] The play is most heuristically set out as a double-plotted one. *Midsummer Night's Dream,* for example, has a courtly plot whose problem is "Will the true lovers be properly sorted and consort-

22. Dante's epistle to Cangrande is disappointingly intellectualist in its understanding of the purpose of art; his art itself is cathartic and seems to recognize this effect (cf. *Inferno* 33:148–50 where, having traveled through hell, his once excessive pity is now properly ordered to justice).

23. A bit of hyperbole. Brecht's *Galileo* has something of this, and the aforementioned *Amadeus*; both predate Stoppard's play. Since then, one might produce *Proof* that this eros still has some box office pull.

24. References to *Arcadia*, by Tom Stoppard (London: Faber& Faber, 1993), will be in the text by the pagination of this edition.

ed?" and a rustic one whose problem is "Will the rude mechanicals be able to pull together a play for the Prince's wedding and be made the preferred entertainment?" These two plots at first just interchange, then overlap, interweave, and come together in the climactic scene. *Arcadia* is similar. In it there is an early-nineteenth-century plot whose central question is "Will the tutor, Septimus, have to duel the would-be poet, Ezra Chater, over the matter of the poet's wife, and, if so, will he survive?" and there is a plot set in the present day whose main question is "Will the contemporary scholars (Bernard and Hannah) discover the truth about the goings-on in the nineteenth-century household?"[25] The first six scenes alternate centuries, allowing characters' lines and stage properties to overlap even as events repeat themselves (with a difference). As Stoppard himself points out, and many critics are fond of emphasizing, the final scene repeats this structure fractally, being composed of six subscenes: "two of only the past, two of only the present, and two where the different periods share the stage."[26] It is a truly beautiful intellectual structure, but there is much more in the comedy than a critic's intellectual recreation, and even someone who does not follow the intricacies of the physics being discussed or note the intricacies of the play's construction can feel it.

We are aware that both Shakespeare's and Stoppard's plays are each a μίμησις φαυλοτέρων early on. In *Midsummer Night's Dream* a father complains to the prince that his only daughter won't marry the man he's chosen and brings her before him to seek the penalty of the law: her death or nunnification. Although the boy is confessed to be fickle while her own chosen lover is not, the Prince threatens the law will be upheld and so the lovers immediately plan an elopement that has no credible threat to its success: the evil threatened is obviously outrageous, the way out simple. Similarly *Arcadia* announces the lightness of its action when it opens in a quiet early nineteenth-century study (a place where we might expect seriousness of plot) with the sudden and outrageous question:

25. More poetically, one might say that the object of the second plot is to discover and restore the "fallen obelisk overgrown with briars" (12) that was raised to Thomasina's discovery in the first plot, except that there never was such an obelisk raised, for the only one who knew of her discovery was her tutor—who was considered mad and became himself her living monument. The obelisk referred to in the play was always fallen, memorializing a nonexistent victory. I shall avoid the temptation to comment on the deeper, resonating significances of such a memorial being found in a garden. The only memorial to Thomasina is in the words of the characters, but that is all right, for Thomasina herself is but a creature of words. So long lives this and this gives life to thee. Though true, this is too poetical a description to be of any help to anyone.

26. See, e.g., Fleming, *Stoppard's Theater*, 195, who quotes Stoppard.

Septimus, what is carnal embrace?

He responds—perhaps without looking up from the poem he is reading—

> Carnal embrace is the practice of throwing one's arms around a side of beef.
> Thomasina: Is that all?
> Septimus: No . . . a shoulder of mutton, a haunch of venison well hugged, an embrace of grouse, . . . caro, carnis; feminine; flesh (1).

The phauloterous roll has begun. As in *Midsummer Night's Dream*, the action of both plots of *Arcadia* invade the same place, first interchanging, then overlapping, then coming together to conclusion. In both plays there are complications leading up to the crux, recognitions with accompanying changes of affection and peripety of plot.

The climactic scene of Stoppard's play takes place on the eve of the nineteenth-century Thomasina's seventeenth birthday and the night of the contemporary Coverly's annual party—which are the same. There the modern professor is caught *in flagrante* with the daughter of the house by her mother (seeking him for similar purposes) and escapes into the night. At the same time Septimus teaches Thomasina to waltz, having given her paper on the (as yet undiscovered) second law of thermodynamics "an Alpha in blind faith" (96). In a scene where multiple times exist impossibly at once we hear how her essay and diagram, discovered by the moderns earlier in the play, outline a thought she supposedly couldn't have thought. As Thomasina *sees* something she couldn't have discovered—"she didn't have the maths, not even remotely, she saw . . . way ahead, like seeing a picture" (93), so the idiot savant (Gus) of the modern house brings the investigating Hannah Thomasina's old drawing (a drawing Hannah could not have known existed and so did not know to search for), which drawing proves that what Hannah *felt* about the garden's significance was literally true: her hermit was real, the change in the emotional tenor of Western culture from Enlightenment order to romantic despair is more than a poem, but was played out in the souls of the living. It is a picture of reality and the reality was pictured (precisely as the change was dawning) by Thomasina. We might say that gardening is a mimesis of the spirit of the age. Hannah's thesis about the changing of that art in the Coverly gardens turns out to have also been instantiated in the life of the most sensitive person who suffered through the change of the garden: Septimus. All the arts of mimesis play themselves out in the bodies and souls of the living, "hardly differing in character" from the realities (*Pol.* 1340a20–25). The play ends in a present we cannot identify where the future(?) (Hannah and Gus) dances—rather awkwardly—with the fluent and long burned-away past(?).

This thumb-nail sketch of the plot (already more poetic than practical . . .), as a similar one for *Midsummer Night's Dream*, makes nothing of the poetry and overlapping imagery of worlds, and tells us little of the passions evoked; nor will the continuing discussion be likely to evoke or catharsize such passions. Representation is not mimesis; therefore every great poem beggars all description. An argument about, or explication of, a poem, like a proof for the existence of God, can at best make you wish to see the thing itself, to experience its work upon your soul, as one might have wished to see Cleopatra in order to fall in love.

2.2. Characters

Eros, as it is popularly understood (feminine, flesh), is obviously directly involved in the first plot of *Arcadia*, and desires for fame, honor, and perhaps even truth are operative as well as the more obvious carnal desires in both the first and the second plot. The characters of *Arcadia* can best be sorted according to their eros, and here, whether he knows it or not, Stoppard has reiterated brilliantly a metaphysics that is both classical and romantic (and the historical source of both): Plato's. The two main objects of desire in the first plot never appear on stage, but only in speech: Mrs. Charity Chater—the poet, Ezra's, erstwhile wife—is spied "in carnal embrace" with Septimus in the gazebo, discovered leaving Lord Byron's bedroom, and is reported to have left the estate with Captain Brice, whom she later marries, on a plant-gathering cruise. "Her chief renown is for a readiness that keeps her in a state of tropical humidity as would grow orchids in her drawers in January" (7). Let us call her the lower Venus. To have her appear in person would be a distraction, for she must be one thing to all men.

The heavenly Aphrodite (who *can* only appear in logos) is the physical (as in the science) and metaphysical truth toward which Thomasina aspires, inspired and aided by her tutor Septimus, whom she loves and surpasses. Thomasina and Septimus share that higher kind of love; they embody love of truth for us, and the love they share is the root of their love for each other. Further, as amazingly as one may share a love of Aristotle across the centuries, their love is shared by the moderns, Valentine and Hannah. Septimus, for his part, shares the lower love with Lord Byron (who doesn't appear on stage), Ezra Chater (the erstwhile poet and husband), Captain Brice (who succeeds, as husband), and his employer, Lady Croom (whose garden is being rearranged, and to whom he confesses that Charity was merely the substitutive satisfaction of his inordinate desire for her ladyship). (P.S. The Lady is pleased, and admits him to her chamber.) All of these latter characters do appear on stage. Of these Ezra Chater seems the most polymorphously erotic and inadequate, by turns concerned (inadequately) with his honor (regarding his wife), his (inadequate) poetry (or his honor as a poet), and his wife (the very figure of insatiability) and, finally, tropical flora. He seems almost completely subject to the lower forms of eros, his inadequacy at the higher form (poetry) spilling over (?) into his inadequacy at all the others, and so he is the butt of this plot. A letter reports he is bitten by a monkey and dies. Not a Bottom *ad litteram*, but 'twill serve.

Between the heavenly and the humid we can place Lady Croom, whose love for her pastorally refined English garden (an object somewhere between the physiological and the realm of pure truth) is being outraged by her husband's employment of Richard Noakes. Noakes is transforming the ordered post-Enlightenment garden into a romantic wilderness in the picturesque style. Her daughter (Thomasina) says she (Lady Croom) has fallen in love with Lord Byron; the mother invites Septimus to tutor her after her bath upon discovering that his noodling of Charity Chater was displaced eros for her; and she later is very friendly with a Polish nobleman and piano tuner (who is heard playing, but not seen). The garden apparently was (according to the twentieth-century scholar, Hannah) very beautiful, unlike Chater's poem, so we must give Lady Croom credit for being somewhat higher on the ladder of eros than her house-guest, Ezra, though she is at least equally poly-. Ezra, Lady Croom, and Septimus share in the common denominator called Charity, but are quite different fractions in the numerator, where only Septimus can really be compared with Thomasina.

Mr. Noakes and Captain Brice have more steady hearts—the one is set on his romantic garden, the other on Mrs. Chater. If purity of heart is to will one thing, these are they who will see God, but the text is not a serious one: Noakes builds a famous garden, Brice takes possession of the Chater. In this each achieves what he most wishes. The remaining characters in the first plot are the butler (who has a function, but no eros)—this, of course, is the definition of butler, the Platonic idea instantiated—and Augustus, the son and lord in waiting, who is interested in finding out about the facts of sexual congress, but exhibits little eros and less interest or wit regarding the heavenly Aphrodite. In this he is the exact opposite of his sister, who is rather disgusted by the facts when she hears them bare (3), though her eros is indubitable.

In keeping with both the rather rundown nature of contemporary houses and culture—at least in Britain, as well as in the second law of thermodynamics—the characters of the present-day plot seem less frequently and less purely moved by the higher eros that moves Thomasina, though we must wonder about the wordless boy genius, Gus. Finding the right thing at the right time, whether in music or symbol, garden or scholarship, seems to be effortless for him: Aristotle would point out that this is a function of his character (*Po.* 1454a33–37). By contrast, the young Lord Augustus of the earlier family lacks breeding, heart, and taste by all available comparison and so contributes mostly to the phauloterous aspects of the plot's action and language. As is the case with the Guses, the remainder of the modern Coverly family is broadly the reverse of its earlier instantiation. The modern daughter, Chloe (the reciprocal of Thomasina), is excited by Professor Nightengale's intellectual excitement, or perhaps just generally excited. She boggles the professor (64), but then the professor (Septimus's reciprocal) is easily boggled. Of him we will have much more to say later. Her brother, Valentine, is doing research on the application of iterated algorithms to populations, specifically of grouse, based on the game books the Coverly men have kept for over a century. He doesn't go hunting; he tries to hunt up its long-dead effects. A foil, like his silent brother, to the stolid vanity of the previous son, Lord Augustus, he (again, like his brother) is attracted by the quiet scholarship of Hannah Jarvis and, largely because of her sympathy for and interest in Thomasina's accidentally rediscovered mathematical project, takes up with his new tool—the computer—the mathematical problems Thomasina could only have spent decades trying to solve on paper (as her abandoned tutor apparently did, going mad in the new romantic garden). Hannah's own first love and research is the history of the famous garden, to which she has been invited by Lady Coverly, whose pride and joy it is. The modern Lady Coverly never appears, though she is apparently rather taken with the university Byron scholar (Nightengale), for she lends him her bicycle: "a form of safe sex, possibly the safest there is" (51), and is looking for him on the night of the party.

So we see each character gravitate to an area of Diotima's ladder—the love of bodies, the love of souls (Plato puts poetry and laws here), the love of ideas—their love is their weight, and they are pulled into or out of the final glorious dance—the dance in which all times meet—by the gravity or sublimity of their loves, or, in Aristotle's terms the ridiculousness or seriousness of their choices. The play, like life, is a test of their reverence, and before the final dance most of the characters are fanned and flown; only the grain remains to flower in the last scene. In sum, we might arrange the objects of eros and the characters in each plot as they appear in Figure 1.

FIGURE 4-1

Arcadia: Characters and Plots

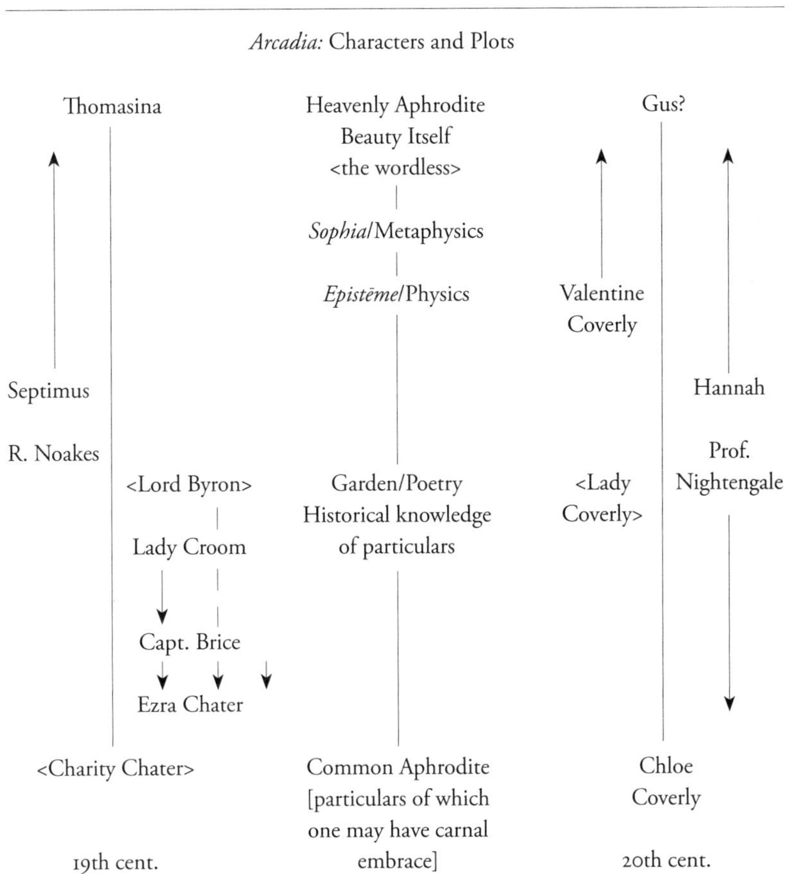

<characters spoken of, but not appearing>
⟶ direction of character's movement/love in the course of the play

2.3. The Comedy as Love Song

All things imitate the Prime Mover so far as they can, and so in *Arcadia* everyone takes part in the intellectual life so far as they are able. It may be that in the case of the wordless Gus the act of contemplation exceeds the adequacy of language. Or it may be that, as in Chloe, the inspirational excitement of the (for her) unreachable intellectual life leads to a more physical consummation (a repetition—after a fashion—of the action Lysias wished to work on Phaedrus). In her case we might see that the mimetic passional effect transfers to the perceiver in accord with the mode of the perceiver: Bernard's intellectual excitement becomes physical excitement in her. But all of the characters in *Arcadia* dance between the Chater—who is what Aristotle would call the purely animal imitation of divinity—and the living flame of Thomasina, or better, the life that Thomasina best embodies and imitates. Her tutor, who dances closest to her, is burned.

Like the intellectual life of which it is a mimesis, *Arcadia* seems timeless; though both life and the play take place in time and take time to take place, this seems accidental. The play itself encompasses all times—at least it lets us feel so—by presenting two random times on a single stage: alternately, interlocking, and finally, simultaneously: How is it that in a play so involved with modern physics something so impossible as simultaneity could be made not just believable, but the structure of the play? What is an impossibility for physics is a recreation for the soul. A world that is impossible calls up all our real passions. The impossibility of simultaneity is believably overcome not because of anything we learn but because it feels like it is.[27] We might, upon reflection, say that time falls out of importance because eros is the principle of movement in the play and under its power characters are as accidents to an Aristotelian substance, or one-time solutions to an iterated algorithm that pulls its answers out of dust, and lets them return to it and reshape the next solution, where eros shapes itself again to beauty. The objects of human eros are eternally the same, only their names are changed. Desire and fear are the two mainsprings of movement of all finite spirits—all crea-

27. This is not the first play that impossibly collapses time. Shakespeare's *Romeo and Juliet* is famous for it; Aeschylus's Agamemnon returns home just barely after the light from burning Troy announces the night of his victory and Clytaemnestra announces her instantaneous knowledge of it (with godlike assurance) to the chorus of disbelieving men. Such instantaneity is the reverse of narrative discursiveness and increases the concentration of the passional movements and so the effectiveness of the play (cf. *Po.* 1462a12–17).

tures with sensation for which pleasure and pain are natural and unavoidable. But this is a comedy, and so, in it, it is desire that is aroused and purified; therefore it is the shaping love not the dissolving strife that is the action of the play. And there is more than this, for the eros that is the highest point of the play seems not to be a movement at all, but the still point's dancing. In the play, Thomasina, by discovering the truth before its time, is made one with that good that Socrates could only imagine as like the sun—that which makes be and makes knowable all that a mind can know. The truth she discovers had always been true, and by reaching it she shares in that good with all others who reach it in all times and places. Further, it is Thomasina (and her notes and drawing) that makes be and be known whatever is true and worthwhile that the later plot discovers. She herself intuits the modern science and seems not so much to move herself by her love of knowledge as to possess it in certainty and merely show it to her teacher in the final paper. She is, in this way, the embodiment on stage of Beauty itself (the Unmoved Mover), to which all the other loves lead and which she comprehends and still exceeds. She is the objective correlative of the end—which is an activity—of the human being; Hopkins saw her before Stoppard named her:

> To what serves mortal beauty . . . ?
> . . . . See: it does this: keeps warm
> Men's wits to the things that are; what good means . . .
>
> (G. M. Hopkins, "To What Serves Mortal Beauty?")

The two sets of characters know of each other only in one direction—that which time allows—though the universality of the power that moves them (and moves us through the play) would have led them to understand the relation of their separated existences. The turtle that remains on the desk across the centuries is the living instantiation of a relation that goes both ways—for souls. As the play goes on we are made to feel not only the inaccuracy and piecemeal nature of the historical knowledge the moderns get of their predecessors, but that even a perfect history or accounting would miss the life and meaning of that past: not "just" its felt significance, but its real significance, which is also felt. History is less than philosophy because all of its experience and knowledge is a lower act: a trivial fond record of singulars about which there can be no science. The poem is more philosophical than history first because its acts are of the nature of universals (the passions, which make all men equal), and second because it draws us to love and practice *sophia* rather than a *technē*, or some lower particular, as Chloe, a body among bodies, does.[28]

That the set is "a schoolroom" opening onto a garden—that primordial and ever-changing place of intersection between nature and the human will—is too rich a symbol to be fully explicated. I can't show you how deep it goes. But we should note that the audience's own seemingly transcendent view of the garden comes only through the comments of various interlocutors, though the garden's changing light falls into the schoolroom constantly through the windows. If the audience is God, we are gods who do not see directly into the garden, but must imagine it according to the reactions of its people and the changing cast of light into our theater. The two people who sit in the study at the opening "are separately occupied" (1) with mathematics (Thomasina) and with poetry (Septimus). In the course of the play we learn that the poetry is bad and the mathematics too simple to resolve the problem Thomasina will soon set for herself. Perhaps the great globe itself is such a schoolroom set in such a garden—or perhaps the garden is just outside the windows of our globe casting its light, as the sun, into it. The work of art is the window through which we see this relation of globe to garden, of will to nature, of love to its variety of possible objects, and the play is that which makes those relations felt, and by so drawing our love through its movements it draws us into a more appropriate garden, purifies and perfects our nature, our will, and our love.

In such a globe as the play lets us, godlike, look into, we might find characters much like those in *Arcadia*, characters who are not only nearer or farther from the best and most complete actualization of the intellectual life—which is humanity's highest happiness—but whose relations to the life of the mind vary in other ways as well. Thomasina, for example, reveals the perfection of her character in the first scene, where her questions move from the meaning of terms—"what is carnal embrace?"—to morals—"is it a sin?" And her desire to know "the true meaning of things" takes her from physics—"when you stir your rice pudding . . . the spoonful of jam spreads itself round making red trails . . . but if you stir backward, the jam will not

28. The status of history is not only debated in the modern academy (social science—and are the social sciences science?—or humanistic study?), but also not a matter about which Aristotle makes a definitive statement. However, since *nous* is the grasping of first principles, and *epistēmē* the ability to put together the steps of a deductive science, history is probably neither for Aristotle, but at best a sort of craft or *technē* (like poetry in that, but unlike poetry in that poetry deals with things that have the nature of universals [*Po.* 1451a39–b12]). It is clear the Prime Mover does not contemplate its dustbin. History is insufficient for Psyche's eros, too.

come together again. . . . Do you think this is odd?"—to theology—"Do you think God is a Newtonian?" and to metaphysics—

> If you could stop every atom in its position and direction, and your mind could comprehend all the actions thus suspended, then if you were really, really good at algebra you could write the formula for all the future; and although nobody can be so clever as to do it, the formula must exist just as if one could. (5)

In her questions she exhibits not only the intensity of her desire to know, but also the rectitude of her mind's flame—for she moves from what we might take as a pun for vulgar curiousity, through morals, to questions about the highest and most important truths. It is impossible for any soul capable of virtue not to love her. Sometimes we are given students like this, and the only proper response is eternal gratitude—immediately and forever.

Her opposite number is the modern professor. Bernard Nightengale, Sussex University, knows the words, but not the way. In his angry argument against Valentine and modern science he says that "if knowledge isn't self-knowledge it isn't doing much," but it is clear that he is not interested in knowledge per se, but as a means to status (61), money (61), fame (31, 56), and greater sexual opportunity (63, 64). When he turns out to be proven wrong about the connections between the curios collected on the table of history, he mourns his tarnished five minutes of fame and continues to hold on to all the errors yet available to him: that he has discovered two essays and four lines of Byron. This may be enough to keep a bit of cachet, but only among scholars and probably not for twenty-year-old girls with the romantic tendencies of large-winged horses. As Hannah says, he is "arrogant, greedy and reckless," not the type for whom knowledge, much less self-knowledge, can be the highest pleasure. The professor has not (as he complains he has) lost the status accorded him in the old world of Aristotle, for unlike Aristotle he does not think knowledge is for its own sake. Rather, the professor has sold his heritage (even as a teacher of literature) for a mess of historical pottage about the acts of the poets (rather than their poems), and the occasional boggling of an undergraduate girl. He is from Sussex, and heading souther.

Bernard (whose name in the classical dispensation was Lysias) is completely perverse in the structure of his desires according to Aristotle. Aristotle says that the intellectual life is something we engage in for its own sake, which results in no further good and so *cannot* be used as a means for anything else. What we want to know the truth for is because it is our nature to desire to know, not because we can do anything with it; and regarding contemplation of Aristotle's principles of physics and the first principles of metaphysics in particular, it is clear that they *can* lead to no new result or better bathroom. Aristotle also thinks that while some people desire fame, they desire it as a sign of their virtue and they seek it in order to promote virtue (*NE* 1095b26–30; cf. Kraut, 234). The professor is opposed on all counts. The purpose of his intellectual life (leaving aside the question of how intellectual a subject we should consider history would be for Aristotle) is to achieve fame, and the purpose of fame is not to prove or be an aid to virtue, but to increase the range of possibilities for sex. For instance, the reason he comes to the Coverly estate in the first place is because he thinks he will find evidence there that will cause other Byron scholars "to get their dicks caught in their zip" (29)—thereby cutting them off from further competition. When his supposed discoveries—among them that Byron killed a poet in a duel over the other man's wife—get him invited to a national morning television show he invites Hannah to come along. For intellectual discussion? To share his fame? To witness it?—"No, no, bugger that. Sex" (63). He thinks that this would free up Hannah's intellect to write the book she is meant to write—a romantic one. His argument to her here is the only place where he even speaks of desire in something like the proper order: "for we have recreation in order to work better" (*NE* 1176b33). Of course his argument is false (empirically, for her book was apparently on the mark without the recreation he suggests would most likely free her up for it) and duplicitous (emotionally, for he is interested in sex for its own sake, not as an aid to intellectual freedom and concentration). His historical arguments about Byron were also false and duplicitous—but maybe he won't get caught (by Hannah or history). She makes him keep his literal (or is it real?) dick in his pants (63), and catches the scholarly one in his zip with the revelation that there was no duel at Sidley Park. Her review of his piece will "be very short, very dry, absolutely gloat-free" (90).

Above Bernard are three other socially recognized scholars—they would be kinds of σπουδαῖος character in a more notable action, but as it is they are something above the level of of the general in *Acharnians*, and nearer the level of Theseus in *Midsummer Night's Dream*. Hannah Jarvis, his contemporary, works, as Bernard does, in what Valentine, agreeing with Aristotle, calls the trivial vein, which is not concerned with *scientific* knowledge: the historical. The free scholar (for Hannah has no tenured position) is more adequate to the life of the mind than the professor however. That she is a free scholar is a sign; she works as an amateur, a lover for the sake of her love, not for money or a full professorship. She is not interested in historical minutiae for their own sake, or for fame, but as important clues to how scientific knowledge and human imagination and passions interact. In this, she is more philosophical then Valentine, who is at first a mere empiricist. For her, the garden is both symbol and history, *res et signum*, of the life of culture and that is why it interests her:

> The history of the garden says it all beautifully. There's an engraving of Sidley Park in 1730 that makes you want to weep. Paradise in the age of reason. By 1760 everything had gone . . . and then Richard Noakes came in to bring God up to date. . . . The decline from thinking to feeling, you see. (27)

Her study of the changing things is still connected to a desire to understand the unchanging, as if, like Valentine, she could find the equation for the acts of spirit and its passions from the record of the garden's changing fate. The equation she seeks in particular is the one that joins the science and garden of the Enlightenment to the passion and garden of romanticism to the science and passion and garden of the present day—from which we are left to determine what will come—with further entropy, or perhaps what we really desire—by nature, forever.

Because she seeks a more important kind of knowledge, one that is connected to self-knowledge and higher truths than history, and because she seeks it for its own sake rather than for the sake of fame or greater sexual opportunity, she is more patient in her research than Bernard, who hears his biological clock ticking. Moral virtue is necessary in order for the intellectual virtues to be able to be practiced, not only because the vices take time and resources away from research, but because—as we see with the professor—his appetites interfere with his vision. Hannah Jarvis's desire for knowledge keeps the would-be hurries and interruptions of the appetites—and their complications (which eventually drive Bernard out the door of the study and away from the garden)—at bay. It is no wonder the dumb genius loves Hannah and presents her with the garden's first fruit (33, 34) and final secret (96). Gus's love is not "a joke," nor is Hannah's classical reserve "only a mannerism, and neurotic" as the contemporary scientist says (75). There is something classical about it—and wise:

> Resplendant and unfading is Wisdom, and she is really perceived by those who love her, and found by those who seek her. . . . For the first step toward discipline is a very

> earnest desire for her; then, care for discipline is love for her; love means the keeping of her laws, to observe her laws is the basis for incorruptibility; and incorruptibility makes one close to God; thus the desire for Wisdom leads up to a kingdom. (Wis 6:17–20)[29]

In the play's conclusion we see that Hannah achieves her desired knowledge of the garden—an ὀπσέως κόσμος—(aided by a gift from Gus) and our sympathy for her who first had sympathy with Thomasina's (historically) impossible desire to understand the mathematics of the real cosmos achieves its satisfaction, and the dance of the wise is enlarged—and by many more than two, for the audience too is drawn into their joy: Wisdom engenders her kingdom, makes it come to be in those who seek her, and engenders desire for her in those who watch the desire and joy of her practices.

By the end of the play Bernard has achieved his desire too, having boggled the daughter. It is (as with Touchstone's wedding) a less permanent or complete satisfaction, and clearly the object is less desired once it is achieved (95). Though he does not realize it, the poverty of his whole order of desires and their satisfaction confesses itself in his desire *not* to take Chloe along with him while bolting out the door. Adam at least was faithful; and Touchstone will take three months. The sexual attractiveness of Chloe and the play's construction of its resolution over and after our dissatisfaction with Bernard's satisfaction, and his driving off by the discovering mother, ridicules and purifies an audience member's darker horse (which Chloe must be full-bodied enough to draw forth). Yes, she has a piece of Beauty, yes she would be a good ride (better than a bicycle), but then one would not get to dance in the same room with Thomasina, who is Beauty entire. So, moral virtues, for the sake of wisdom.

A second scholarly foil to the modern professor is the nineteenth-century tutor. Septimus Hodge, though he causes a disturbance in his own study by the Chater affair, would probably disagree (as would Aristotle) with Hannah's excessively democratic statement that "comparing what we're looking for misses the point," though he and Aristotle would agree with her idea that "it's wanting to know that makes us matter" (75). It is clear that Thomasina loves him and that that love is returned, but their love for each other is born of the more heavenly Venus of their shared search for and contemplation of truth. When he tells Augustus—lately returned from Eton—"I do not rule here, my lord,

29. As far as I know there is no evidence that the writer of Wisdom read the last chapters of Aristotle's *Ethics*, or that Aristotle read Wisdom. Their accidental agreement across culture and history is, then, merely accidental, I am sure.

I inspire by reverence for learning and the exaltation of knowledge whereby man may approach God" (80), he echoes Aristotle (*NE* 10.7) and states what we have already seen and intuited and grown to love in Thomasina and in the relationship between tutor and student: the joy of their communal knowing. This is what philia is for.[30] It sets them in a community apart from the more politic, practical, and carnal unions, the creatures of which understand them not. Unlike knowledge of the Chater (happening off-stage on a regular basis), their knowledge is *infinitely* sharable: "I can't show you how deep it goes." One might wonder if that is not the reason they are so distinct, for to be united in an activity that *cannot come* to a conclusion, cannot achieve a final satisfaction, is perhaps too fearful a thing for most people to enter upon.

> But let us not follow those . . . rather let us, as far as possible, achieve immortality, and do all that we can to live in accord with what is highest in us. (*NE* 1177b34–78a2)[31]

None of the modern scholars seem to be quite able to admit this capacity; the top of the ladder of Eros seems to be missing. In fact, for the moderns, the top seems to have been cut off, making all rungs equal. That would explain Hannah's democratic disclaimer that the matter we direct our minds to doesn't matter. In the argument of this book, then, Hannah, lovely and right as she is, instantiates the democratic inclusivist view of happiness that Nussbaum defends—each makes a crown after her own liking, "comparing what we're looking for misses the point." On the contrary, and in the play, Thomasina is more lovely and more true, and more lovely because more true: there is a crown *in nature*; Thomasina would have it: she is doing metaphysics. Hannah herself *acts* differently than she speaks: she *puts away* her work on the garden in order to work out Thomasina's mathematical question. She is drawn, as if by nature, from the crown she would wish, to a beauty she could not imagine. Thomasina, from a century before, takes her out of herself and the mistaken belief in the equality of all objects of contemplation. In addition, Septimus's claim to Augustus not only describes his position as tutor, but also exhibits how the relation of theoretical reason to practical reason differs from the more practical understanding's view of such matters. The young Augustus, as any emperor or new-crowned lord, understands that practical reason rules for the sake of an end: whatever end he is set in soci-

30. For the scholary argument on this Aristotelian point, see Thomas P. Sherman, S.J., "The Perfect Happiness of Virtuous Friends."

31. Cf., also, the kinds of ecstasy available to human beings, which I have laid out in *Is Hamlet a Religious Drama?*, chapter 3, in the section entitled "Ecstasy?" (92–110).

ety. That is why such sons of such families go to Eton. Augustus does not see that there is another way to rule—he renders everything unto Caesar. Septimus tells him otherwise: theoretical wisdom does not rule in the way that practical or political wisdom does—by ordering—just as the Prime Mover does not will to rule, but is and acts; and each thing seeks to imitate it so far as it can and in the best way that it can. The highest does not rule by ordering, but by being and being imitated; love attaches to it by nature, and all sublunary activities mimic it in the particular sublunary way their own nature allows. Unlike the Chater family and the desires they embody—which demand satisfaction day and night (7), theoretical wisdom and the prime mover draw us by an Eros considerably different, one in whose kingdom the coin of satisfaction is a counterfeit minted by children. Unlike the modern professor, Septimus does not turn the higher power to the service of a lower eros even when Thomasina seems to invite him:

> Th: I will wait for you to come.
> S: I cannot.
> Th: You may.
> S: I may not.
> Th: You must.
> S: I will not.
>
> (96)

He is determined *not* to come to her room, but what can he be determined by? Surely not a heat equation. If the will can only be determined by one thing rather than another because the one is a higher good, then there must be a better knowledge of Thomasina than that provided by carnal embrace, and there must be a determination of choice no heat equation covers or includes. We have already *seen*, by this point in the play, that the community of their minds proves a deeper, more all-embracing, and more perfecting one than any carnal knowledge desired, mentioned, invited, or consummated during the play. Some loves are incomparably better than all others; their dancing is more fluid, more beautiful, and more exacting. Seeing the dance of such perfection makes us want it more: our inadequate eros for it is purified and raised, for this perfection is meant to be our own. Joy is of an entirely different order than satisfaction; we feel that at this play. It is attested to by Septimus's refusal, for such a thing is, for carnal imaginations, a mere blank, a nothing, a thing that eye cannot see nor ear hear.

The remaining researcher in the play is the modern Valentine, who switches projects from the population of grouse to plotting what he calls Thomasina's "Coverly set." The first project would have been a small piece of scientific knowledge—to discover the algorithm that would map the changes in population of grouse from a century ago on a small bit of English park. When Hannah asks him "and then what?," he answers, "I publish" (46). That seems to be the extent of it. On the other hand, mapping out Thomasina's "rabbit" equation is interesting for its own sake, not just because it shows how the universe operates like a heat engine—losing money all the way—and because her work began a hundred years before the mathematics it really needs was invented or the thermodynamic law it illustrates was discovered. Rather, because her patterns make themselves by eating their own progeny—being equations for which the answers of one supply the variables to the next (77)—they provide an endless object for *theōria*. He could have got done with the grouse; he can never be finished with the Coverly set. Thomasina provides an object of contemplation with which he can never be finished; not a bad imitation of the contemplation of God. Not, in the confines of poetry, a bad imitation of God.

The change in Valentine's projects is telling on a number of grounds, for his interest in the second is piqued before the first is given up as lost. Against Bernard, he had argued that scientific progress matters more than personalities (61) or explications of the incidentalia left over in the dustbin of history, but what wakes his second interest is not a new discovery, but rather the idea that what he considers a new opening in science was worked out first, without the proper tools, a century earlier than it supposedly appeared. What wakes his interest is the eternity of truth: its permanent presence everywhere. Having the requisite modern tools, he continues Thomasina's work—as had her tutor, Septimus, by hand, after her death. Thus Thomasina's desire to "draw all the forms of nature through number alone" (43) is shared across several centuries. We dare not think it is only the centuries pictured in the play that are present here, for wisdom draws *all* men to herself. Stoppard presents this everlasting community to us directly in the final scene, where Thomasina, Septimus, Hannah, and Valentine all consider the import of Thomasina's diagram and equations *at once*: one over the shoulders of the other, as has been done for millenia. Their voices mix, they seem, impossibly, to answer each others' questions, sharing in their contemplation outside of the order of time. It is not, as Valentine had said earlier, that *he* is "at the beginning again, knowing almost nothing" (47) and on the road of discovery, but that he *understands* and understands *with* the others how things are. It is hard to imagine a happier community. No, it is impossible.

It is not that personalities matter less either, as Bernard thinks Valentine implies (61). The erotic attraction between Valentine and Hannah *includes* their personalities even as it supercedes them. Nor is the supersession of their personalities brought to its fulfillment through the mere usefulness of the mathematics for understanding the basic physics of the universe. It is not their use that brings Valentine and Hanna to meditate together on "patterns making themselves out of nothing" (76), but their beauty. Their individual wonder ends in a shared reverence. Valentine has exchanged an understanding of the life of science as a *kinēsis* (an activity understood as a project to be completed and aiming at some far-distant result) for an understanding of it as an *energeia*—an activity complete at every moment, like seeing, an activity whose end and worth is wholly in the activity itself.[32]

This later work, too, will be publishable, but that is not its value either. Now Valentine's passions are set properly: publication is for the sake of sharing this thought, the thought is not for the sake of publication. The professor—Bernard—will never get these things ordered correctly, for he values the lesser good excessively. To laugh at him is the proper emotional response, and for that laughter there is much opportunity. Perhaps the humor is even deeper. As Richard Kraut notes,

> Even the choices made by human beings with highly defective conceptions of the ultimate end are, in this way [without realizing it] aiming at contemplation. For example, if they aim at physical pleasure, then they are imitating the way lower animals imitate the unmoved mover. . . . Since there is something divine in all creatures, they all pursue the same pleasure, though the pleasure they are pursuing is not always the one they think it is. (218n)

The humor then is that Bernard, when the natural and the best is easily available to him, seems to look everywhere else to find the good, like a man

32. This distinction is familiar to readers of Aristotle; cf. Peck, Ackrill ("Aristotle's Distinction"), and Polansky, who makes the point that *energeiai* can be affective as well as intellectual.

In *Physics* 5 Aristotle says that the definition of motion (*kinēsis*) as the fulfillment of what exists potentially, insofar as it exists potentially (201a10), implies that "every goal of motion . . . is immovable, as, for instance, knowledge and heat" (224b10–12). In *Metaphysics* (1048b18–34) he distinguishes these actions, which have a limit or end, from those in which the end is present in the action, like thinking and learning. The first he calls *kinēsies*; like housebuilding, they are not completed actions until they reach their term (the house). The second type are *energeia*; such acts are complete at every moment: like vision. Notice that his examples allow that thinking can be understood in both ways. The first is Valentine's early understanding of science, the already finished weight of which crushes Septimus into madness. But this is not the only way to understand *noēsis*.

who is looking for his glasses when they are on his nose and he is already looking through them in order to find them.

Even if the audience does not consciously make the connections I have been making, their emotions *are connected* in this way by the play—the excessive desire for fame and sexual opportunity embodied in the professor is laughed at throughout the play, while Thomasina we grow to love absolutely. This is a good practice for the erotic emotions and cathartic for those of us tempted on the alternative routes of eros, or to deficiency or excess. And for those perfected in virtue, the play allows them to see a perfect student and love their own happiness by seeing it shared in her.

Valentine has found a good that does not lead to any further good. What it leads to is itself: more of the same, an increase in its scope and depth and in his capacity. But this is what only the practice of the best habit can long continue: to grow by what it feeds on. All others sate us, or worse. As we see in Bernard's case, and slightly differently in Septimus's, the attempt to satisfy the appetites of several women (the men's own appetites personified) ends self-destructively. Since this is a comedy, the self-destruction is not a harmful one, but ridiculous: Bernard flurries out (95), Septimus, at his abandonment by Lady Croom for the Polish pianist, sulks (83); both are roundly mocked for it. The good that Valentine finds and enjoys is one Thomasina had never fallen away from. We rejoice in that good when we enjoy Valentine's discovery and happiness. We fall mimetically into joy from the joy we see. That is the direct emotional effect—joy in the vision of unrestrained and unridiculed happiness, which is also our own—unconstrained and celebrated—in the theater; reflecting on the play (as here) gives us the additional pleasure of contemplating the relation of the practice of the intellectual virtues to happiness. In both cases desire is enjoying a proper relation to its highest object: knowledge for its own sake.

We also share Valentine's joy at sharing Thomasina's thought, and sharing its more exactingly drawn out details with Hannah. This is not the pleasure of victory (what Bernard desires vis-à-vis his peers in the Byron Society) but the pleasure of shared contemplation of a truth surpassing the knowers. In this we cannot rejoice too much, and at this exquisite play our natural desire to know finds a mimesis of its completeness which releases us into a festivity Aristophanes seems never to achieve, nor even dream of. The whole of the merely human is insufficient; Eros aims us beyond ourselves to Beauty itself.

Among the things Valentine comes to understand (and we may well come to feel about the play) is that even with a computer he can't show how deep the patterning of nature (or we the play?) goes. This Thomasina already knew, but she wished to follow the dance as fluidly and far as she could. The idea of progress—and its correlative idea of understanding as a *kinēsis*—has no place with Valentine any longer, for there can be no progress to an end if there is no end, no terminus, to what can be known. He must have given up his idea of progress as the aim of every investigation (61) for the more Aristotelian idea that the practices of theoretical virtue are for their own sake. The modern mathematician's confession that he "can't show how deep it goes" (76), is the poetic revelation that understanding is better understood as an *energeia*, not a *kinēsis*, and that it is the *practice* of this *energeia* which is (as he says) "pretty nice" (76), *not the result.* Hannah's response is more adequate: "how beautiful."[33] In the physical world there is universal progress to the final goal—where everything will be at room temperature—but in the life of the mind there is a burning which does not burn down. If what it is that the mind wants to know is infinite, then there is no need to fear that the answers are in the back of the book, for there is no back to the book.

Early on Valentine had voiced an opposite opinion. He clearly thought of science as a kind of motion, like building a house, which is never complete (or finally satisfying) until the house is completely finished, at which point the action, necessarily, stops: the heat death of science. He rejoiced that "everything [we] thought we knew was wrong" (48) because it means the house-building starts over—there is more and bigger stuff to do than merely painting the circumbendibus of the fascia. By contrast, it is not the discovery of the new per se that thrills Thomasina, but coming to know and knowing the true and eternal principles of creation. ("What immortal hand or eye . . .") Thomasina saw the door and walked through it before the house was even thought of, not waiting for Valentine or Einstein to build it (79). The life of the mind is this kind of miracle, and to see this miracle on stage, like seeing a statue come to life, awakens our faith and enkindles our love. The life of the mind cannot be the best, nor can *sophia* be the virtue most to be loved or whose activity is most imitative of the divine if it is one that comes to an end, like building a house. Contemplation is not such an activ-

33. And Kant would agree that "beautiful" is precisely the right word, for the beautiful "must be estimated on the ground of a finality apart from an end" where the good presupposes "the reference of an object to a definite end" (*KU* 226).

ity, but one which is, like vision, complete at every instant. The object of *sophia*'s meditation then cannot be individual truths, historical facts, or finite tasks, but only the kind of thing of which Valentine says "I can't show you how deep it goes" (76). *Et hoc dicimus Deum.*

Perhaps when a poet or a philosopher wishes to provide a representation of an *energeia* he must play it out as a *kinēsis* without end. So an infinite act requires an infinite object, and only such an act with such an object can be our perfect happiness, and this must be our end if we have the power to take part in it. It may be that the world Thomasina's equation describes is not one made for the continuing pleasure of mankind; it may be that it is determined to be unlucky for us, but the fact which so comes to disturb her tutor that he becomes the hermit in the ruined garden seems not to disturb her at all. For the activity of knowing is above lucky pleasures, or unlucky fires and pains. She is as excited about knowing the truth though her equations as she is desirous of the knowledge of waltzing. In both the activity is the end. Her mind, like the well-trained soul in *Phaedrus*, moves fluidly and without constraint through all the lower spheres to the very rim of heaven. Even when just beginning to learn, her body follows easily and fluidly the music she hears, whether from another room and time, or her own, or impossibly, a music outside time itself—the Platonic form of waltz, played by all the superlunary spheres.

If the intellectual life were a kinetic act, then like all other *kinēsies* it would end up at room temperature, and it would not be, in any case, the kind of operation in which we see a very good teacher inspire a much better flame, for that is against the law of increasing entropy. But if the intellectual life is an *energeia*, then we will never know when to expect the spontaneous combustion of flesh into spirit, or the mind's leap to its highest love. It is not sex that is the attraction physics leaves out—that is a heat equation; it is the heavenly Eros which never appears in physics—though the act of understanding physics itself is a piece of her. The eros of the mind for truth is the deepest, strongest, and most stunning of all loves because it is the love of the infinite for its own.

According to Augustine, charity's aim is to call all publicly to her consummation in truth (*Confessions* 12.25.34). Charity Chater understands this in the literal sense, and insofar as it is possible to her, enacts it. But Valentine and Hannah, Thomasina and Septimus understand this in quite the highest sense: the sharing of truth is the communion of souls. And this is required for the happiness of humankind, the former is the lower nature's less perfect and less universal instantiation. The more perfect consummation of charity is also instantiated between the audience and the actors, or among the audience, actors, and Thomas Stoppard, the guiding spirit of this particular sacrament. It is a wedding of minds into which we enter even as we consider here, and perhaps it is a mimetic echo of the wordless Gus, or the silence of Augustine (*Confessions* 1.4.4, 9.10.23–26).

Even though he inspired her to her love for it, her teacher feels the truth as the weight of an absolute answer, not bliss, as a completed fact rather than a dance inviting our continuous participation; but Thomasina participates in a more divine comedy. There is the historical rumour that Thomasina dies that last night in a conflagration in her bedroom, but the investigations of historical materialists never touch the stuff of poetry or the story of her love. Even the most common attendant at the play, however, seeing her dressed in white, bathed and embued in the whirling light, feels not the approach of sorrow, but the birth of joy, as if

> From matter's largest sphere
> we now have reached the heaven of pure light,
> light of the intellect, light filled with love,
> love of true good, love filled with happiness,
> a happiness surpassing every sweetness.
> Here [we] will see both ranks of Paradise
> and see one of them wearing that same aspect
> which [we] will see again at Judgment Day.

As for the fire . . . ,

> The love that calms this heaven always welcomes
> into Itself with such a salutation,
> so to dispose the candle to its flame.
>
> (*Paradiso* 30.38–54)

While the light in which Thomasina participates and which embraces her becomes as oppressive as the repeated answer to a completed equation to Septimus, her love remains untouchable by historical investigation, though it can be, and is, imitated by others who are moved as she is. And she herself is palpable light and lovely to the audience, which is *stuck* neither in history nor physical fact, but placed outside of both by the play and constituted as the community of saints. She charms our eros to dance with hers, and it is we who welcome her through the fire, with our glad hands. The play reconstitutes Thomasina's love and discovery for an audience which (precisely as audience, and exactly as the community of saints) already participates in the truth she wishes to know and know more completely: to know even as we are known. Anytime we attend this play we imitate that community. The theater is the right place for *theōria*—for this seeing and knowing—and in it our highest eros is given its long lost wings. In reconstituting Thomasina's love and knowledge the play reconstitutes the sundry individuals who enter the theater as that community of which Dante speaks. Because it is a mimesis, not an argument or illustration, the poem moves us from (and through) what it says to *the experience* of which it speaks. The mimesis of this life of the mind gives exercise to the wings of our heavenly eros, and such exercise is a required part of the purification of our desire and sympathy. And the good, too, require it, for the world is too much with us.

Even as she turns to flame (which we see almost literally in her final scene's white gown, but have been seeing figuratively throughout the play) Thomasina does not deny the body, but raises desire up through it, as she has from the play's opening and perfectly literal question about 'carnal embrace,' through the irreversible entropy of physics and plot, to the final dance of timeless spirits. By doing so she makes the play enact (not merely represent, not merely picture) the anagogical reading of our state. Under her priesthood the play becomes an outward sign to inward glory, a sacrament in which the whole theater participates. Like baptism or holy orders this sacrament brings about an ontological change. Before she goes to bed Thomasina is already an ecstatic—someone who stands forth from her body—not leaving it, but rising through it. What else could she do but burn? She has been burning from the beginning, irreversibly. And in that burning she is undestroyed, as the play shows, for she takes the whole play up into her dance: "As if, on earth, a living flame stood still" (*Paradiso* 1.141). Her burning is not a sacrifice of the life of the body for the life of the mind, but a sign of the soul's demand that the body be given wholly to that only which is worthy of it: the body is made for the mind, and the mind for infinite knowledge.

> He who does not take wings to reach that realm
> may wait for tidings of it from the mute.
>
> (*Paradiso* 10.74–75)

EPILOGUE

Still Awake and Drinking

Symposium

As soon as a man starts drinking, he finds himself in a merrier, more self-indulgent mood than before, and as he increases the dose, he finds himself entertaining foolish fancies, and begins to think he has powers he does not really possess, and when he is very drunk he thinks he is a philosopher. . . .

Laws 649a–b[1]

Without the ridiculous (γελοίων) it is impossible to learn the serious (σπουδαῖα), or any contrary without its contrary, if one is to be of good judgment (φρόνιμος).

Laws 816d–e

If what I have been arguing for is true about comedy, then it might also have been a thought familiar to that one-time dramatist and lover of Aristophanes, Plato, and so, feeling merry and self-indulgent at the end of this project—it being a season of merriment—and entertaining the fleeting recollection of having been, in a previous life, a flute girl in the house of Agathon, I will make bold in closing to philosophize a little about the famous drinking party. Plato's *Symposium* concludes with the "outrageous paradox"[2] that the same man who can write tragedy can write comedy as well (223d). Unfortunately, the argument has been lost. Unlike Aristotle's second book of *Poetics*, lost due to the accidental slaughters and casual mischances of history, the Socratic argument about comedy and tragedy is lost at its origin.

1. The translation here is that of H. A Mason, from his book *Fine Talk at Agathon's*, 71. It is a little loose, a little freer than usual—in a word, perfect.

2. F. H. Sandbach, *The Comic Theatre of Greece and Rome* (New York: W. W. Norton, 1977), 13.

Aristodemus—the uninvited guest who originally related the speeches and happenings of the *Symposium* to our erstwhile source, Apollodorus—apparently drank too much and fell asleep (like the other revelers) and woke only for the stunning conclusion of the bout between Socrates, Aristophanes, and Agathon (*Sym.* 223c–d). Though little more than a child at the time of the banquet, Apollodorus (who relates the story of the symposium) should himself share some of the blame for the lost argument since he took the trouble to check the story with Socrates much later and had time and opportunity to have him rehearse it—but he didn't, or he did and forgot (173b). And then this is all fiction anyway, so the real nonexistence of the argument is due to the coyness of Plato, author of the comedy we are discussing. Perhaps, on the other hand, the claim was so obviously true that the proof of it is, as they say, trivial, though history is more mendicant than usual in getting the truth to cash out.

Professor Allen, in a footnote to his translation of *Symposium*, says that "the argument must have been that tragedy and comedy are opposites; the same art has knowledge of opposites; therefore, anyone who is by art a tragic poet is a comic poet too."[3] Curiously, he treats the dialogue as ending with the entrance of the revelers in his accompanying commentary (109), thereby skipping both Alcibiades' ecomium and the report of the sleep-soaked argument, and does not discuss the issue of the unity of the arts further. While a critic stuck in the trammels of historicism could only treat Socrates' argument as (given the times and his audience) deliberately provocative and offensive, and Plato's presentation of it as irony (or provocation and offense), in the course of this book it has become clear not only that Professor Allen's suggestion has something to it, but how that something, which he leaves as a bare suggestion, could begin to be fleshed out and dressed.

Let us begin somewhat symbolically: Socrates spends a night drinking in Agathon's house two nights after Agathon's tragedy takes first prize; in the course of the evening's discussion he convinces Agathon and Aristophanes of the "outrageous paradox" and then he leaves early in the morning to spend the day in his usual way (223d). A drinking party in the house of tragedy is apparently an appropriate psychic preparation for, as well as plausible re-creation of, the daylight of philosophy. In the recreation of the philosopher tragedy and comedy discover their deep and original unity, as if they

3. Reginald E. Allen, *The Symposium* (New Haven, Conn.: Yale University Press, 1984), 170n. This agrees with the sort of argument our epigram from *Laws* maintains.

were two halves of one being so long sundered that they cannot believe each is not a complete and independent being. In *Laws* the Athenian Stranger claims that the education (and civic culture) required for a nonlopsided human being must not only train the left hand's shield against improper fear and pity, but also keep the right hand practiced in attacking the excesses of desire by ridicule and pricking up its deficiencies through appropriate pleasure and joy (cf. *Laws* 634a, 635c, 635d). This is so, our slightly less than roman à clef explication runs, because if our passions are not properly ordered and exercised, our thought will not be clear, powerful, or disciplined enough to reach the conclusion we really aim at, our choice will have insufficient erotic power, or incorrect direction, and so we will be defeated in the matter of greatest importance: we will not know what happiness is, or lacking the appropriate love, we will not achieve it insofar as that is possible. For the achievement of happiness is not merely a matter of the intellect and knowing, or of the will and choosing, or of the passions[4] and satisfying, but it is a matter for the whole person and all of these elements must be appropriately synergised.

So then, tragedy and comedy—the left and right hands, respectively—are the arts that make us practice and purify such passions. The catharsis of pity and fear that Aristotle claims is the end of tragedy is matched by a catharsis of desire and sympathy in comedy's working on its audience. Plato also suggests that symposia are appropriate tests and training for eros (*Laws* 634–53). Without such recreations we are likely to be turned by the world into its puppets rather than remain the more subtley tuned divine puppet who follows the golden cord as a lover of wisdom and spirited pursuer of the beautiful. This book's central purpose has been to show that tragedy and comedy—the left and right hands, respectively—are the arts that make us practice and purify such passions.[5]

4. Whether we call the passions fear, pity, desire, and sympathy or libido's cathectic and anticathectic movements, or perhaps—after Kant—*schwärmerei,* is a matter of culturally determined facticity. Though each age's set of terms does confess a connotation about passion's worth and working, there must, in all, be a rightness to their working; there is, in each, an idea of their illness.

5. More formally and metaphysically, the human being is between the most beautiful (κάλλιστος) and the ridiculous (γελοῖος), perhaps

> a divine puppet, put together for their play or for some serious purpose—which we don't know. What we do know is that these passions work in us like tendons or cords, drawing us and pulling against one another in opposite directions toward opposing deeds, struggling in the region where virtue and vice lie separated from one another. (*Laws* 644d, e)

When Alcibiades enters the drinking party he suggests Socrates ought to sit by the ridiculous Aristophanes rather than the good (nominally Agathon), but in his story he is himself revealed to be

If Diotima is right about eros when she includes under its domain not only the desire to make babies in beautiful bodies, but also the desire to procreate with and in beautiful souls—as lawmakers, poets, and teachers do—then the achievement of any one person's desire, or its loss, or its inaccuracy, is a matter of concern—and a proper matter of concern—for each other one. Far from being a principle of individualistic hedonism, Diotima's eros encompasses the desire for justice: to love each as each is worthy of being loved, in accord with what each is due. And in order to do this properly, one must know something about the soul. The movement from one body to bodies ("bringing his passion for the one into due proportion"; 210b) and from there to a soul and to souls is clearly due to recognitions of order ("due succession"; 210e) in the beauties available to men. In her story eros is not *bound by* temperance (though it might look that way to those who are too liberal of their favors, like Phaedrus—who must be convinced there are other horses to ride than his black one). Rather, perfected eros *includes* temperance as an element and brings it along in *her* train, as is perhaps best illustrated by Socrates in the arms of Alcibiades (one who was too liberal with his favors—which is why he cannot understand Socrates).[6] Eros, according to Diotima's theory and Socratic practice, has a built-in reference to the good of others insofar as it aims *to produce* the beautiful with (or bring it forth within) them, *and to keep* it: and the better beauty is psychical, not physical, for it is a nearer approach to the divine source, Beauty itself, even though all beauties participate therein.

The noble pederasts—Phaedrus, Pausanias, Agathon and Eryximachus—suffer from a more self-oriented, and we might say lower, eros. Their eros toils yet under the hybristic tyrant, Satisfaction, whom Eryximachus, like Dr. Freud, thinks he can medicate.[7] They say it is not so, but since they

ridiculous, and he is known in both history and Plato's dialogue as being the one with the most excessive desire. Socrates is, then, in the right metaphysically symbolic place—next to the good (used here only to speak of what is literal—Agathon); he is not moved from it by fear or ridicule. See also Clay, 189f.

6. I agree with Mason that the correct understanding of the episode reported by Alcibides "must somehow get rid of the suggestion of an unworthy sensibility or of a degrading insensibility in Socrates" (84; cf. 83–86). In showing how to do so I will disagree with Martha Nussbaum's *The Fragility of Goodness* (Cambridge, U.K.: Cambridge University Press, 1986), Stanley Rosen's *Plato's Symposium*, 2nd ed. (New Haven, Conn.: Yale University Press, 1987), and C. D. C. Reeve's "Telling the Truth about Love: Plato's *Symposium*," in *Proceedings of the Boston Area Colloquium in Ancient Philosophy*, vol. 8 (Lanham, Md.: University Press of America, 1994), as well as Mary Blundell's following comment, that Socrates is an unerotic monster or inadequate lover of Alcibiades.

7. Eryximachus holds that "we are justified in yielding to the desires of the temperate—and of the intemperate insofar as such compliance will tend to sober them" (187d). Freud advises that

are most eager to share their virtue with the most beautiful boy—rather than with the most adequate soul, one might well raise an eyebrow at their endowing capacity. Further, since their *modus preferendi sexualis* is one that is not naturally productive in the body, and is against the *nomos* of Athens, so counterproductive in ethos as well, one must wonder, after the speech of Socrates-Diotima, whether the "pure lovers of the male" are suffering any eros at all. Perhaps it is merely self-love, as the speeches of the first—Phaedrus—who offers a hymn to the beloved (which he knows himself to be to Eryximachus), and last—Agathon—who presents the most openly narcissistic song of himself, might indicate.[8]

Thus the circle of pederasts closes—on itself, performing a demonstration of the most obvious form of a love that goes nowhere and produces nothing. Aristophanes' story offers them the cure they seek and their cycle of speeches performs: a hermetic welding. If they all were to laugh at his story, we would see a portion of their cure, a catharsis by comic mockery (à la mode overdone fulfillment) of their much-pandered-to eros. But Eryximachus seems to feel Aristophanes' story is magnificent rather than humorous (193e);[9] and the pederasts do not laugh at the aims or results of such eros until the man of utter excess appears in person and tells his story (222c). Apparently, the comic poet had not gone far enough in giving his speech. They *do* laugh at the performance of Alcibiadean eros. To so laugh is to be already in a position of superiority to such eros, though what that position is is a mystery to the pederasts, for each of their eulogies is in part taken up by Alcibiades' explanation of his own love, and so their love is active within that performance. In laughing at the performance of their own kind of eros their feelings have moved toward correction, though their minds are still somewhat retarded. Perhaps they will reflect upon their laughter. Instead, they merely get drunk, unable to control themselves (or survive) in the mimetic contest Alcibiades brings to the circle.

"temptations are merely increased by constant frustration, whereas an occasional satisfaction of them causes them to diminish, at least for the time being"; see Sigmund Freud, *Civilization and Its Discontents*, trans. Thomas Strachey (New York: W. W. Norton, 1962), 87.

8. On these matters see Rosen's analysis of each character's speech and character. E.g., on Phaedrus' selfishness and subordination of political good to individual desire, see 50–55; Eryximachus supports his beloved's desires with his medical *technē*—for a price that it is not necessary to name, though these days it may dare to do so.

9. We should, no doubt, recall that the gods who found Ares and Aphrodite similarly welded by Hephaistos were subject to a fit of uncontrollable laughter. The divine response differs significantly from that of the pederasts.

What the superior position would be, in any case, is also *not* indicated by Aristophanes' story, which was, rather, the perfect satisfaction of their error: a (pseudoepic) narrative mimesis of what they are and seek. Aristophanes' ability to make a story that presents their satisfaction from a view at which even they should laugh exhibits that he is outside the pederastic circle;[10] that they all do laugh at Alcibiades indicates there is something in them that is higher as well, though Aristophanes' audience needs a *performance* of the ridiculous rather than its mere *narration* to begin to be set free in laughter. The polite speech of the symposium is insufficient to begin their cure in laughter; they need a stronger mimesis of the ridiculous. Alcibiades brings their kind of eros itself onto the stage under the laurels of Dionysus, performing—in his drunkenness—just as a character of Aristophanes' would on the Dionysiac stage, and arousing laughter very like that at a comic performance. Still, the pederasts do not grasp the condition for the possibility of their laughter even when they stand in it, laughing. Aristophanes' theatrical *practice*, which also frequently overstepped the bounds of polite speech, is hereby proven worthwhile in Plato's *Symposium* without any argument at all being given in its favor: it shows its worth in Plato's plot.

While I owe much to his analysis of the speeches and erotic character of the other participants, I do not agree with Rosen's view that it is Socrates who is immune to the charm or power of eros (xvii) or disconnected from human things (xviii);[11] he may look that way in comparison to all the speakers preceding him, but it may well be that, as Rosen himself suggests, the pederasty defended[12] by each of the others is a sign of their lack of self-restraint with re-

10. Nussbaum, following Rosen, agrees that Aristophanes is "the only speaker not involved in an erotic relationship with another person present"; see *Fragility*, 467n 27. Both she and Rosen think Socrates is unerotic. Though Aristodemus attaches to him on the way to the party, he leaves Socrates meditating in the neighboring porch: in these pictures neither one seems to be *erastēs* or *erōmenos* of the other. But that Socrates has an eros for something—something perhaps only a Diotima can see—is clear in his long pause a door away from the party.

11. This view is echoed by Nussbaum and Reeve.

12. Aristophanes does not defend pederasty, in fact he seems to be mocking it at 192a,b, in his myth's providing it with a blessed satisfaction—as it does for adultery. In contrast with the first three speakers particularly, the relative silence of Socrates-Diotima about homosexual practices, especially when that is followed by the story of Socrates' "hubristic" refusal of the younger and much-sought-after Alcibiades, speaks volumes about his estimation of that pederastic eros: it is not a practice of Eros. The love of bodies Diotima speaks of aims at fruition: procreation with the beautiful; her love of souls is to bring up into the ethos of the city. The successful pederasts will accomplish neither. It is true that in Aristophanes' story "sexuality replaces logos as the principle of human wisdom" (Rosen, 120), but it is a rather queer sexuality. And it is rather queer of Rosen not to think Aristophanes is aware of this when his happy welded parts are exhibited as being comprised solely

gard to pleasure (as are their hangovers and later collapse or flight under the burden of wine brought in by Alcibiades). If a drinking party is a test to reveal erotic excess and misdirection, as the Athenian Stranger suggests (*Laws* 649a–50b), we might expect that given additional license to speak in praise of eros in a *contest* of speeches each speaker will reveal and praise—to the length and engorgement of his capability—his own particular. That Socrates does not react to eros, the speeches, the wine, or the physical beauty of Agathon or Alcibiades—to say nothing of war and weather—in the way the excessive, misdirected, or soft others do (or would like to) is not necessarily a proof of an unerotic nature. In fact, the claim should be reversed: Socrates is the most and most adequately erotic; the knowledge he claims in this area (and this area only) is virtue.[13] Like the others, but through Diotima, Socrates praises his own eros. However, he starts by mocking himself and then gives the speech through an old woman, a considerably less self-serving, and therefore more truly erotic approach than that of the lovers. It is a narratological arrangement that performs what it argues for: an understanding of eros as a gift rather than as one's own possession. Socrates' practices are not *his own*; indeed, even his understanding comes from elsewhere. It is an eros that, by Socrates' humility in claiming a woman as his teacher, exhibits itself to be aroused and immediately active only under the light of something higher. What *is* true in relation to Rosen's claim is that Socrates' eros is not as easy *to look for* as that of the others because, while it begins with the body (he always seeks out the most beautiful, according to Alcibiades [213c, 216d]—which may of course just be referring to Alcibiades), it does not find its terminal satisfaction there—as Alcibiades himself attests. It *looks* as if it disappears, as if Socrates has been a tease to Alcibiades. The Socratic-Diotimic Eros is difficult for materialists—Eryximachus comes to mind—to follow.

Eros is *rightly* called a philosopher by Diotima (203d7; cf. Rosen, 84), because eros, the philosopher, and Socrates (like all other true lovers) seek a

---

of pederasts, lesbians, and adulterers (191e–92a). Surely it is a joke to consider these to be the whole of humanity. Aristophanes is mocking his fellow symposiasts. He undoubtedly developed the hiccups from trying to control his laughter at their bold self-congratulatory nakedness (cf. Rosen, 120, who thinks he has merely stuffed himself).

13. David Halperin is exactly correct on this matter when he claims that "Plato actually glorifies the transcendental power of eros and praises the madness it brings about: from a traditional Greek perspective Plato appears to want us to be sick [in eros] all the time. For according to Plato eros is the response evoked in us by a higher reality"; see "Plato and the Metaphysics of Desire," in *Proceedings of the Boston Area Colloquium in Ancient Philosophy*, 50. To be sick in this way all the time might be one reason why the city in *Laws* is required to have "no less than 365 festival days" (828b).

good that they do not themselves possess, which they themselves are not. If, in fact, each lover were the good (or each the other's good), then the Aristophanic solution would be true, and the community *a deux* of eros *appropriately* closed in on itself. What is evident from the speeches preceding Socrates', then, is not necessarily what eros is or is not, but how each speaker's evident eros (they should all have comic phalli, appropriately sized and stiffened according to their hubris,[14] and pointing in the direction of their desire) draws his particular speech into . . . contradiction. Aristophanes all but pins such phalli on them with his ironic praise for the kind of man that becomes a politician due to the suppleness of backbone engendered by certain sexual practices in his youth (192a, b). In his comedies he was considerably less circumspect in his locution. Perhaps being in the house of tragedy has been rather purifying and makes him more serious; or perhaps the presence of philosophy civilizes his tongue (unlikely); perhaps, on the other hand, it's his hangover.

Be that as it may, that all the round beings of his happy conclusion are closed in an erotic community utterly incapable of forming any larger community (e.g., a city) is indicated by the kinds of being produced by their splitting: pederasts, lesbians, adulterers, and loose women: no individuals who even form families, much less cities (191e–92a). In fact, all of them are contrary to the civic ethos. Laughter at the exuberance of the round ones and the discovery of their beloved solution is, like laughter at Dicaeopolis' good deal for pussycats, the right feeling being charmed forth: there are better peaces. The gods of Homer, who laugh at a similar scene between Ares and Aphrodite, exhibit the proper passions here. On the contrary, the symposiasts all feel affirmed and even more proud of themselves as parts of "the true male."

As I have already pointed out, Aristophanes' surprisingly light and indirect manner is an important matter. Malcolm Heath points out that comedy's aim as art is distinct from the aims of ordinary discourse in the city:

> [T]herefore, the contents of comedy must deviate from the ethical norms of polite social discourse. . . . [Aristotle] would have disapproved of anyone who spoke in daily life as Aristophanes composed comedies; so, I am sure, would Aristophanes.[15]

Here is (as Heath himself notes) his example of polite Aristophanic discourse; what the pederasts *need*, however, is comedy; *Plato* brings that in

14. Phaedrus's would be very soft, as would his sphincter; Agathon's would reach to his own mouth. See Rosen on the erotic (mis)direction of each character.

15. Malcolm Heath, "Aristotelian Comedy," *Classical Quarterly* 39 (1989): 345.

shortly in the person of Alcibiades. Plato thereby authorizes comic mimesis and is exhibiting its proper function.

Let us consider Diotima's point (that Eros is a philosopher) a little more closely and by way of contrast to the popular reductionism attributable to Freud.[16] According to Freud, the libidinal movement of the psyche aims at physical sexual pleasure; children are a consequence that the reality principle recognizes, but Id would rather not, and libido both can and must be sublimated into other activities in order for society to either begin or long continue.[17] While these activities of sublimated libido—like writing books, or creating works of art—can be very satisfying, the original and continuing repression of the answer direct is a source of permanent discontent, to which state we are bound in and by society.[18] Happiness is therefore impossible, and a certain kind of tragedy (being outside the womb) is our natural state. If man is the eudaimonistic creature Aristotle said, then man is a useless passion according to Freud, for the desire for happiness (= satisfaction of Id's desires) cannot be fulfilled. Just so, selfish and hedonistic, the followers of Phaedrus pipe themselves out of every real city following the sign of the *phallus erectus*.[19] (I have it on the best authority that one need not be gay in following this godlet.)

On the other hand, Diotima says that the desire for sexual pleasure is itself a specification—inchoate and unself-conscious—of the ruling desire

16. The summary that follows is drawn from *Civilization and Its Discontents* and from *The Future of an Illusion*, esp. its first two chapters.

17. Beginning any sublimation is a greater difficulty than Freud (or Thrasymachus, with whose theory of human nature Freud largely agrees) might be willing to acknowledge. How the Id of a powerless (and tasty) infant can call forth Ego from the Id of a more powerful adult—especially one who finds his sexual satisfactions being interfered with—is a question not to be taken lightly. (Rene Girard considers this problem in "The Process of Hominization," chapter 3 of *Things Hidden*.) Given the power of the original father and the interests of his Id, the female's demand "care for me, care for my children" takes on the appearance of a prayer to a god without ears. Like Thrasymachus and Hobbes, Freud's understanding of human nature is made of equal parts hedonism and egoism; the solitary strong like to pretend that this theory is true although it leaves inexplicable how or why the baby Thrasymachus survives infancy or is taught anything. As a moral theory, this is a quick lunch; as science, it is still-born; that it is appealing to certain characters is diagnostic.

18. It is a sign of Plato's genius that the modern discoverer of the *technē* for easing the pleasure principle should be a physician. Eryximachus, a physician, is Freud's John the Baptist; cf. notes 7 and 8 above. It is as if Plato could discover the truth before its time, or walk into a modern garden before the plans for it are even drawn.

19. Again, Rosen is excellent at pointing out the (particularly sexual and political) contradictions of the earlier speakers. Aristophanes story of the split men, who would find their perfect happiness in being knit together with their other half, is as much a mockery of their erotic self-deception as it is an expression of it. They seem already to be hopping about on only one leg.

of the soul to make the beautiful its own forever (204d–205b). Though trial and error does have its pleasures, before jumping on the first thing that moves us, we should seek some enlightenment on the active element in our ecstatic emotion. Since mortal being cannot attain to immortality but only its semblance, the procreative activity is loved and pursued for the pleasure of attaining this token of immortality: the child. According to Diotima, Freud (as Aristophanes' split human) does not recognize what he and we are truly seeking, but mistakes what we really seek for its mere concomitant: the physical pleasure of release and fulfillment. It is certainly not obvious to Dick that what he really wants of Jane is the token of immortality she will present him with a few months down the road. Freud denies that it is so, and his reading of eros is much more naively literalist in this regard. But where the great difficulty in Freud is to explain how sublimation begins, Diotima teaches that, far from being *sublimations* of original libidinal forces, art, law making, and science are *more adequate specifications* of our original psychic desire both because they are longer lasting and because they work within a more adequate object: the soul itself, the kind of thing that can not only possess beauty, but the only kind of thing that can *recognize* it, attain to it at least through thought of eternal things, and which, according to some, might be itself *immortal*.[20] A body can at best possess beauty for a time, but never recognize it, or possess it forever. The creative demiurge, itself an image of psyche, can both recognize beauty and possess it forever. But that is to speak of higher things.

Let us speak only of those lower things about which we might be expected to have some expertise. But that is the question, isn't it: What end does human expertise, human knowledge, intend? A happiness that might best be imagined as the ever increasing pleasure of a womblike Orgasmatron?[21] Or,

20. Like Eryximachan physicalism, Freud's reductive hedonism is a *program* masquerading as a metaphysical truth. One cannot expect the doctor to point this out, for to do so undermines his glory and his usefulness (and then he will obtain fewer satisfactions from his younger beloved—Phaedrus). Perhaps, in fact, he doesn't know; his *logoi* of love are an expression of ignorance and he impregnates those who accept his virtue with wind—at least we might suspect that Phaedrus has been so impregnated by his blow-hard lover.

21. This was a joke in a well-known early comedy of Woody Allen's; ought we have taken it seriously? If I am right to take it as a joke, what we are laughing *at* when Woody gets pulled away from reentering the machine is our own desire to be simply and quickly and constantly physically satisfied; but if such satisfaction is *the real secret of life*, we should be full of pity and fear for him when he is pulled away. If we saw the best of all possible goods being lost, could we laugh so heartily? Eryximachus, the doctor of *Symposium*, is well noted as the "spokesman for 'technicism'" (Rosen, 91; the whole chapter should be read), and no doubt would consider Woody's machine the perfect cure for everything (though, again, it would put him out of work). He does not

well, something higher. The question between Freud and Diotima is a religious one, it is a question of whether or not there are higher things. If the answer is yes, then that collection of practical sciences, that—if we were Utilitarians—we might call by the name of Orgasmatronics, is itself a red herring, and the sciences themselves have, *first of all*, another aim: they are disciplines aimed at allowing and perfecting the activity of souls, and perfecting is not sublimating, but leading out of the natural slavery to pleasure and into joy in the Beauty of which the body is one part. This perfecting activity—for the practices of science do make the soul more capable of vision—might have the concomitant advantage of producing pleasure and even more regular means of physical satisfaction, but we should not—like some split human being hopping around on one leg—consider the pleasure concomitant to two-leggedness (= regular satisfaction) the true end. It is the perfect activity of the soul in communing with Beauty that should itself be called happiness; and this happiness is not impossible. All the arts of the muses lead us to love it, and the disciplines of philosophy and science are the practices that make it up, or lead us to the point where the god may make something of us after all: "then, if ever, it might be given" (*Sym.* 212a). The tragic sense of life would be a comic mistake were it not about so serious a matter.

The difference between the ancients and the moderns here could not be more remarkable. We might say that the Freudian theory of libidinal sublimation is the tragedy of the body, Diotima's erotic ladder of specifications the comedy of the soul. Only one of them can be true. This is more than merely a difference in direction. R. E. Allen describes a further implication of the Socratic-Diotimic critique of the libidinal theory:

> If Eros is the wish for happiness and implies desire for generation according to body or soul, much sexual desire is not Eros. Specifically, Alcibiades' desire for sexual intercourse with Socrates was not Eros, because it was sterile. (108)

In fact *none* of the earlier speakers (excepting Aristophanes)—pederasts all—are erotic in just so far as they are pederasts. Aristophanes' story exhibits the

---

seem to know—as Plato does—that he cures Aristophanes' hiccups in order for a greater good than bodily pleasure or health to be allowed. His cure allows Aristophanes to speak his wonderful poem; the doctor can make no such beauty (though he can, given enough time, cure the hiccups). If comedy were a medical treatment, Eryximachus's treatments could replace it, and the work of the Hephaestean surgeon Aristophanes suggests would be the final telos of life. But comedy works on the soul, or rather the whole person. Medicine is no substitute, nor will surgery suffice for what our poverty-mothered soul requires.

sterility of their desires and portrays all nonpederastic desire as lower versions of the same thing, for the pederasts were part of the real man, while lesbians were merely the original woman and adulterers were the even more questionable hermaphrodite. He probably developed the hiccups from trying so hard not to laugh at the seriousness with which his fellow partiers gave their speeches. Perhaps one or another of the younger beloveds hangs with his lover for an increase in virtue, but one wonders in what this virtue consists (besides Aristophanes' suggestion about preparing one for the required positions of politics).

Professor Allen seems to speak Socrates' own opinion as well, if, as he says, he agrees with Diotima about the signal importance and source of the mortal's desire for generation, and this might also well be the grounds for Socrates' refusal of Alcibiades' advances and his seeming agreement with the laws of Athens that such fulfillments are not a practice of virtue. No doubt he hopes Alcibiades might learn from this refusal that there is not just a better way, but a different one: the way of eros and the way of pleasure are distinguishable—though not, very often, to one who is the slave of pleasure. One cure for an inordinate desire is mockery, such as that to which a comic poet might raise a politician with visions of empire, or a matched set of pederasts by welding them together more tightly than Ares and Aphrodite.

It may be that Alcibiades could only begin to feel that eros and pleasure are different *in the absence* of what he desired and fully expected—knowing nothing more, incapable of imagining other. Absence, rejection, and ridicule then conjure the only shape he is capable of praising: Socrates' (214d). As the disembodied souls of Purgatory knew there was more to Dante than to themselves because the light *did not go through* to the wall behind him, so Alcibiades sees there is more to Socrates (and so to love) than he finds in himself or his desire because of what does *not* happen. To be sure, he does not see it clearly; he is perhaps too much drawn to fire to see its light, but he knows it's there. It hurts his eyes, casts down his proud head. Alcibiades, in a mixture of tragic and serious legal language, accuses Socrates of making him learn by suffering (222a, b)[22]—the suffering is that Socrates wouldn't take him from behind. It is in keeping with the comedy that the terrible

22. On the tragic phrasing of this section, see Nussbaum (*Fragility*, 185); on its legal ramifications see Mason, 76–78. We should also remember that in turning the cave dweller around to face and walk through the fire of desire the philosopher faces similar accusations. On the other hand, Socrates *requests* such suffering from Thrasymachus, if it is necessary (*Rep.* 337d).

and unjust suffering Alcibiades complains of should be *a nonevent.*[23] Both the accusation and the tragedy are heartily laughed at by the audience. But how on earth can they do this? If they were fully convinced of their speeches oughtn't they join in support of Alcibiades' charges against Socrates?[24] Their laughter indicates that their feelings are not quite as perfectly twisted as their speeches—or their backbones. Having been set up more properly by the speeches of Aristophanes and Socrates, their passions react rightly to the comic excess Plato brings in as the next scene. Since that night even Alcibiades seems to have developed some feeling for the eros Socrates has for him—an erotic feeling that does not demand feeling up—and is not satisfied by it. Though he is not yet able to practice or explain it, his image of the Silenus opening to figures of the gods mimetically expresses the erotic reverence his own (very small, very weak) white-winged horse has been brought to. That image also figures a main point of the Socratic-Diotimic understanding of eros: that lovers do not know what they desire, what they seek, because they do not know God: Eros is not a god; all of the previous speakers mistook him for one.

We can agree, then, that Alcibiades "sums up in his own person the human condition insofar as it is not liberated by understanding of the aims and purposes of human life" (Allen, 103), but he is also worse off than that, for he also lacks the catharses that liberate *to* understanding. He has suffered insufficiently under the ministrations of the muses, including Socratic refusals. This is marked by the fact that he enters *after* the speeches. Among other things, he has not heard the comic reduction of his hopes in the speech of Aristophanes. He is still a slave to his (lowest) fears and desires; he has been drinking all night already—and apparently in an unmeasured and unmusical manner. But Alcibiades seems at least to feel his enslavement somewhat, for he is ashamed at no longer following Socrates like a slave (216b; cf. 219e). We can even agree with Nussbaum that there is a "sudden light" (198) illuminating the dialogue at the breaking in of Alcibiades, but it is due to the flint of passionate ignorance being struck by the steel of psychic beauty; the flint of Alcibiades' nature is not a light on his own account (contra Nuss-

23. Recalling that, according to Aristotle, comedy is a mimesis of a fault that is not productive of pain or harm (*Po.* 1449a31–36).

24. Though the audience in *Symposium* laughs rather than seconds him, Alcibiades' charges *are* seconded in their way by numerous modern critics: Rosen, Nussbaum, Reeve, Blundell, and, perhaps their common source, Vlastos; see his "The Individual as Object of Love in Plato's Dialogues," *Platonic Studies*, 2nd ed., 1–34. Plato clearly disagrees.

baum). A presentation of the ridiculous or deformed can only be cathartic when rubbed against those already wise or straight enough to feel the foolishness (though that feeling may not yet have become knowledge of its cause or source). The comedy must be more, and more obviously outrageous for those who are less straight.

On the other hand, if all libido is originally undifferentiated sexual desire, then there is nothing that can be ruled out as failing to answer it—in some form; judgment about what answers libido best is left up to a reality principle the principle of which is "most continuous and consistent satisfaction with least possible repression." Eryximachan technicism answers this call; Freud, too, was a physician of this school. This principle Aristophanes would recognize as the principle of the loose sphincter (*Clouds* 1079–1105, p. 131). It is possible to think that all of civilized life—lawyers, lawmakers, and tragic poets alike—springs from thence, but to think so has been a joke of Bad Logic's for over two millennia. The modern mistake about desire's nature now requires us to take this joke seriously, and disallows that there can be anything like Socrates' "principled disdain" (Allen, 108) for *any* desire. The modern says Alcibiades *should* be ashamed of nothing, should be pitied for having been refused. Plato thought otherwise, and, curiously, *all the pederasts laugh at Alcibiades*, rather than seconding his suit of tort against Socrates. To call Socrates unerotic on this ground is to confess membership in the church of a different and lower god—and let us add that it is common. No wonder comedy (and most other drama) has been reduced from religious festival to mere entertainment, and *de gustibus non disputandum* is the rule for art. Religion will follow suit, if it has not lead the way.

In fact, if Diotima is correct about the productive aim of eros, then at least two-thirds of what Aristophanes describes as the function of eros is not really eros, but a humourous form of busyness that doesn't produce so much as a wind-egg[25]—like Diogenes pushing his barrel through the streets at top

25. The informal mathematical estimate given here is based on Diotima's definition of love as procreative and Aristophanes' story of three kinds of original roundmen (those from the original man, the original woman, and the original—but now disappeared—androgyne) who are attempting to find their other halves. The first two will absolutely fail at procreation. The last group (when split) produces adulterers and loose women; any children, it seems, would be abandoned. Some chicks might hatch, but they would have to peck for themselves. So, Aristophanes is not making a merely homophobic pronouncement: that human erotic intercourse is such an unproductive, misfunctioning desire is applicable to heterosexuals as well as homosexuality in toto; all three kinds of people are excessively eager to jump on their kind—and do so until finding each their "original" other half. All three, then, need comedy to help cure them of their inappropriate desires. Mocking

speed. If we judge by Diotima's principle, only the adulterous former androgynes have eros, since only they procreate; those split from the whole male and the whole female hug each other for naught. The stuff of comedy is just this kind of crooked, misfiring, excessive or deficient desire; sex is just one of the places where it hangs out most obviously, and both physical and intellectual humor play with it because it is there. To think that sexual libido (not identical with eros) is the driving force of human desire is to worship the fallacy *de hoc ergo propter hoc*. This, in fact, is both the implicit and explicit criticism Diotima's speech makes of Aristophanes' wonderfully comic story about a thoroughly sexualized eros: some things that look like eros are not the real or final aim of eros, some wholes are not sufficiently satisfying for the whole person. But the comic poet is not himself that kind of foolish halvsie (in fact, he is the only speaker at the table without a lover or beloved), and Aristophanes' story itself recognized the fact Diotima points out: that the whole is not sufficient object for human eros (205e).[26] According to his own story, the reason we are divided in the first place is because *when we were whole we were still not satisfied*, but sought the place of the gods.[27] Perhaps Aristophanes' point is that pederasts, lesbians, and adulterers lack proper awe—that is how they got produced in any case; the eros of the round ones was already way too big for their being. But to take the story more generally, it is one kind of foolishness to think that we are whole and com-

---

perversity is a social function we cannot do without, for without it perversity takes itself seriously—and in fact (perhaps) is all that is left: the original androgyne is entirely disappeared and remembered only as a mythic name (189e). If we read literally, we would conclude that Aristophanes is even less sanguine about the possibility of "healthy" sexuality than Diotima (who is not at all disbelieving). For in fact, *Aristophanes mentions no such case*. From the androgyne come adulterers and loose women, from the female come lesbians, and from the male come the glorious pederasts; those are the existential options—but of course Aristophanes is making a joke, not a philosophical point . . . right?

26. In fact, Aristophanes is perhaps about to point out that his story implicitly understands this point of Diotima's, but the festive brawler enters (212c).

27. Because Eros has not yet been mentioned by Aristophanes, Rosen thinks that this attack upon the gods "takes place despite the absence of Eros" (140). Drew Hyland similarly considers the round ones were not erotic (115, 116), and so eros is a source of consolation, but not nobility (121). But it is one thing not to speak of something and another for it to be absent, as Rosen recognizes in another context: "Although the *Symposium* does not actually mention the Ideas, it leads us upward to the boundary of their domain. . . . This upward Eros is associated regularly with hybris, and so with injustice" (155). That is inexact: it is an overweening Eros to *be* God rather than just to *know and worship* him that must be constrained. In the story Aristophanes tells, Zeus does constrain that overweening eros; and the moral effect of the story is to get us to constrain it ourselves, so perhaps for this higher reason the overweening desire that led to our splitting is not mentioned as being active in the newly reunited and blissful round ones. As we might at comedy, they have learned by having their sides split. Their hybris has been broken; their eros is whole.

plete beings by ourselves (as the gods are), Aristophanes' story began; it is the foolishness of a creature that thinks it can be god. But it is another (and new) kind of foolishess to think that the human being can be satisfied by the welding together of his and/or her body to the appropriate source of satisfaction. The humor and sublimity of Aristophanes' story is that it makes us *feel* these contradictions: our desire for wholeness—which isn't enough. How can it be that being whole is (and was) insufficient? What kind of whole is that? A whole with a God-sized hole? (Do not let Aristophanes hear that.)

That Aristophanes shares with Socrates the distinction of having no lover speaking at the dinner (at least until Alcibiades shows up and tries to put Socrates with Aristophanes) might repeat—as a film negative—what the moral of Aristophanes' own story seems to show, namely, that the criticism Plato is making of the Aristophanic *kōmos* and liturgical action is precisely the limitation of its emphasis to the political and interpersonal: the Aristophanic *As You Like It* has no Jaques. He does not create an action with a Thomasina. Aristophanes is right to point out that Diotima's story refers to his, but it refers to his in order to go beyond it and to show him the direction his art must take; for the loves he seeks to purify have their source deeper than he has yet drawn. The eros of the pederasts cannot reach a city; the eros of Aristophanes can, but it *does not reach beyond it*, which is necessary for it to be just to the human being, who, according to Plato and Aristotle, has an end beyond the political. *Plato's comedy* points out, as well as makes us feel, the lack in the catharses of Aristophanes. The boundary of human eros is not only not drawn by the interpersonal, it is not drawn by the human world, or found within it, for its aim is essentially higher. Comedy is rooted in what, in Kant's terms, is called the sublime, and it is because this is so that from within its own terms the story of the city looks like "the most beautiful, best . . . and truest tragedy": one which "can only be completed by true law" (*Laws* 816b, c), the true writer of which "exists at present nowhere at all, except in small degree" (875d). The human city, *limited to its own terms* is a tragedy; it must be completed, as the individual soul whose journey Diotima traced, by something being given, and it can only be given by god.[28]

Most scholars do not consider the question of an implicit Platonic criticism of Aristophanic comedy here, and they misconceive the problem of the round man's original eros. For example, Stanley Rosen thinks that Diotima's speech is an "account of the cessation of Eros" (2), and that

28. And with this ending word I mean to touch also the first word of Plato's *Laws*.

> it is clear from the details of Aristophanes' speech that if this longing [for our original nature] were to be altogether satisfied . . . , man would no longer be erotic. . . . To the extent that we grasp the eternal, we must cease to be erotic. A fulfillment of Eros would lead, according to both Aristophanes and Diotima, to the disappearance or overcoming of human nature. (3)

But what kind of being would it be that could fully "grasp the eternal" and so cease to be erotic? The details of Aristophanes' speech seem to make it clear that it is impossible even to imagine the whole human being without imagining it as erotic—for something other or more than wholeness; and Diotima's story does not indicate that our erotic nature, in moving up the ladder, becomes less erotic, but rather *better* at erotic functioning. The idea that we "grasp" the eternal is also rather more active than Diotima's language of touching, being struck, and being given, (211b,c, d), and fails to note that our *coitus* with the Beautiful itself seems always to be *interruptus*—unless the god himself should bring us up into his own uninterrupted life. "And then if ever it is given to a man to become immortal." (*Sym.* 212a)

The myth in *Phaedrus* similarly gives the impression that a taste of this divine life *increases* our Eros for it even as it momentarily satisfies; it increases eros so much that it drives dark and unrestrained horses into frenzies. We should note that Aristophanes' moral for our present split state—that we worship the gods and not act contrary to such piety (193b, d)—would have saved our original parents from being halved, but they desired to *be* gods rather than to *know* them. They desired to be the creators of virtue and Beauty—giving it to their lover or beloved—rather than—more humbly—to reproduce themselves eternally with and in it. The moral and religious practices incumbent upon our eros in our present split nature will serve us well should the god ever deign to make us whole. Perhaps the comedy that cures our hubris through ridicule in our fractured state is internalized as irony by the more complete and pious creature. If laughing at excesses, deficiencies, and mistook purposes in comedy purifies our own desires, perhaps purity of heart is a self-irony born of singleness of vision for what transcends us.

Martha Nussbaum misses the point with less nuance than Rosen[29] in her essay on *Symposium* in *The Fragility of Goodness*. She says that for Aristo-

29. Where Rosen allows that the satisfaction of Aristophanic eros would replace mankind with a race of hybristic monsters, Nussbaum says this monster is Socrates. But the fact that our original round nature is not "something simply good or praiseworthy" (Rosen, 3) means that it too must have had both a part of the good—at least the resourceful (Poros)—as well as that Penia, that neediness, attributable to things erotic.

phanes' lovers to be welded together by Hephaestus as they desire is the expression of "a second order desire that all desires be cancelled," which they would be were the divided lovers answered by the god (176). She further thinks that Socrates, following Diotima's teaching, is "an example of a man in the process of making himself self-sufficient" (184), a man for whom Eros is no longer a living daemon, but a dead godlet. The stories told by each speaker, however, mark both complaints as false. Aristophanes' own story noted that the original round beings entertained more than mortal thoughts (190b) and had an eros—before they were halved—that was at least as outrageous as that which Alcibiades accuses Socrates of having (217e, 219c). Socrates' repetition of Diotima's story in no way suggests that the person who is educated in the things of love and who beholds things rightly and in due order will become self-sufficient. In fact, what such a one is likely to realize more and more clearly is his absolute neediness of the Beautiful, and his utter incapacity to attain or hold it on his own, no matter how ascetic or disciplined his practices: "it is there, *if anywhere*, that human life is to be lived" (211d). As Diotima herself concludes, "for then if ever *it will be given* to him to become immortal" (212a). One might say that the practices of rightly loving the beautiful in the world turn the person to know ever more perfectly, and feel ever more completely, his absolute need for God.

Comedy and tragedy, then, which enact the relationships of philia and eros of human beings within the city, can only fully purify our pity and fear, our desire and sympathy when the eros that they free to its natural motion is one that exceeds the personal and political that their *mythoi* enact and represent. Just so, according to *Laws*, the laws also are to create a space for a constant festival with the gods. Diotima's philosophical eros does not start from or finish at the point of human, or even civic, self-sufficiency or adequacy, so all three arts (comedy, tragedy, philosophy) must agree in their view that we human beings are insufficient to ourselves; and philosophy makes clear that this insufficiency is neither a matter of chance or fate, nor merely a concomitant of posture, or deficiencies and excesses of character, but rather a matter of being. As such, philosophy recognizes our need and insufficiency as neither comic nor tragic, but as the source of both arts, and perhaps as our highest perfection.[30] For what is wonder but the recognition of incapacity before a beauty that neither judges nor condemns? (Recall that it is

30. Or, echoing Plato rather than Kierkegaard, "what is human has been devised as a kind of plaything of god, and this is really the best thing about it" (*Laws*, 803c).

not Socrates who judges Alcibiades, but Alcibiades who judges himself when faced by the beauty of Socrates—as if we were ourselves compelled even to the very teeth and forehead of our faults to give in evidence.)[31] What other kind of creature could wonder except one that can recognize beauty and desire it to be his own forever? What higher perfection could a mortal have than the need of God? One might begin to consider that wonder does have an opposite passion; that passion is hubris. The round ones suffered from it and were split; Socrates suffers wonder (e.g., in the porch before the symposium) and is whole. Socrates and Alcibiades are the head and the tail of the coin—*anthrōpos.*

Though I think she is wrong about Plato's, Socrates', and Diotima's points in this dialogue, I think that Nussbaum is correct about how the dialogue works[32] and (inadvertently) explains why this dialogue is an imbedded narrative rather than a straight discussion like *Meno*, *Euthyphro*, or the less clearly imbedded *Republic*. I think Plato, Socrates, and Diotima would agree with Nussbaum that

> there are some truths about love that can be learned only through the experience of a particular passion of one's own. If one is asked to teach those truths, one's only recourse is to *recreate that experience* for the hearer: to tell a story, to appeal to his or her imagination and feelings by the use of vivid narrative. Images are valuable in this attempt to make the audience share the experience, *to feel, from the inside*, what it is *like* to be that. (*Fragility*, 185; last italic original, others mine)

This means that if *Symposium* is successful as a work of art, it brings us closer in feeling to the feeling of *Plato's* own eros, an eros that is announced (literally) by "honor to the God"—Diotima. It does this partly through the comic mockery of those erotic pretenders whose satisfaction we—more or less frequently—accept as our real erotic be-all and end-all. To laugh at such satisfactions is already to be on the other side of them, to be drawn past them. Even when such mockery is indecent (αἰσχρός) or abusive (ψόγος), as in Aristophanic comedy it frequently is, that we are laughing on the side of the mocker of a certain satisfaction indicates that our own love has its weight elsewhere. The other part of *Symposium*'s catharsis is achieved

31. Recall also Rilke, "For beauty is nothing / but the beginning of terror we can just barely endure / and we are driven to wonder at it so [*wir bewundern es so*] / because it calmly disdains to destroy us" ("Die Erste Elegie," *Duino Elegies*).

32. Rosen's introductory methodological essay on reading Plato, in his commentary on *Symposium*, is perhaps one of her inspirations and is well worth rereading.

through its presentation of Diotima's depiction of the way to that which is most worthy of all eros: Beauty Itself.[33]

Not only does Alcibiades re-create the experience of his eros in telling his story about Socrates, but Diotima re-creates hers in the young Socrates by telling about the ladder, and Socrates wins over his fellow symposiasts by telling the story of his own foolishness about love before Diotima (which story frames her story while overturning Agathon's and all the pederasts). Plato himself raises our love of the beautiful whole by having the story of the symposium narrated by a rather offputting chap who, despite his lapses and those of his source (the Silenic outside of the dialogue), gives us a narrative complete, humorous, beautiful to contemplate, and wonder-waking to suffer through (the Socratic inside): and so a catharsis of desire and sympathy is accomplished. The narrative puts everything off at the distance of a burnished and long-burned-away youth, so that even though all the characters are historical personages (and still alive at the dramatic start of the dialogue), they are characters more than they are themselves; partial and doubly inflected: a story of Aristodemus as told by Apollodorus. If one were, on the other hand, to say straight out what one thinks about love, and to prove it by book and footnote, it would read, and perhaps be experienced, as an exercise of hubris more likely to arouse the hubris of the reader into competition (by the usual mimetic mechanism) than to create a stage for the free exercise of her own eros. Philosophical writing and the agon of dialectics is dangerous to the soul; we are tempted to fall into its patterns of feeling and behavior. If this dialogue were a portrait of Socrates we would identify it as late Rembrandt.

As a mimesis, comic poetry attempts to re-create *the experience*; as an art that aims at catharsis, it must make us feel or experience certain passions we imitatively run through; and as comic, its particular emotional target is our desire and sympathy. *Symposium* re-creates the whole range of desire—from the drunken and sensual to the philosophic, poetic, and religious; it makes us feel the ridiculous or the sublime aspects of such eros, and by doing so it exercises our love and sympathy appropriately[34] and they become thereby

33. This combination of mockery and beauty, of castigation and representation of a more perfect sociality, or eros, or philia is visible in all great comedy, from Aristophanes through Shakespeare to Stoppard (to say nothing of the *Divine Comedy*, or for that matter Augustine's *Confessions*).

34. For instance, it does not let us love sexual conjunction as the meaning of life, for while Aristophanes suggests this, the suggestion is couched in ridiculous terms and we must laugh at it even while envisioning its happiest, welded satisfaction bowling through the world.

more perfectly oriented and adequately roused or damped. Alcibiades does tell the truth about Socrates, as well as show the truth about Alcibiades' own particular version of love, but *in laughing* at his story—as he does in telling it—both his and our feelings *confess* another, superior love, a love more like Socrates', a love more finely aware and richly responsible than the most sensitive tissues of the young Alcibiades' body. Socrates explained the condition for the possibility of this laughter in the speech Alcibiades missed; Alcibiades clearly does not yet understand it.

> Alcibiades does *want to claim* that through a lover's intimacy he can produce accounts (stories) that are more deeply and precisely true . . . than any account that could be produced by a form-lover who denied him the cognitive resources of the senses and emotions (*Fragility*, 191, my emphases),

but the story of the symposium itself makes clear that he doesn't and can't produce them. The eros he was suffering does not prove itself in accounts, but in pleasures. The truth or accuracy of the story he does produce is precisely because of nonintimacy, or, better, an intimacy he does not yet know how to recognize. The speech of Diotima lets us see the cause of Alcibiades' failure; it is as clear as the distinction between pleasure and joy.

Let us stipulate that Nussbaum is correct that a

> lover can be said to understand the beloved when, and only when, he knows how to treat him or her: how to speak, look, and move at various times and in various circumstances; how to give pleasure and how to receive it; how to deal with the loved one's complex network of intellectual, emotional and bodily needs (191),

but then is anything clearer in the whole course of the dialogue than that it is Socrates who truly loves Alcibiades and not Alcibiades who loves him?—Unless she meant merely give pleasure, presuming all pleasures are proper and all desires fine. But barring that clearly inadequate notion, can anything be more certain than that among all the true things Alcibiades says, this one truth—Socrates' love for him—is revealed, and hangs like an echo in the affirmative silence of Socrates?[35] Is anything more certain than that Alcibiades does not know himself what he sought, for he knows not himself, nor love, nor what it is to love himself—even though of all the Athenians of his age he was most full of himself and most desired?

Through Alcibiades' speech Plato takes us into that kind of love that

35. Alcibiades invites Socrates to interrupt the story if at any time he says anything false at 214e; Socrates is silent throughout.

cannot begin to give an account of itself, it lets us experience it from the inside and feel its confusion and unintelligible frustration; but the dialogue lets us do that without becoming unintelligible to ourselves—we become *like* it, we undergo a mimesis of such a love and lover, and our own laughter wakes us from becoming so in being and in truth. Joy is more possible for us than for Alcibiades; in fact, perhaps we have already begun to suffer it in our laughter at Alcibiades. To become such a person as he in real life would be tragic; but the mimesis of such a person in the comedy of *Symposium* allows those passions in us that are like him to come out and play, and in our laughter at what happens to him we are freed from being the blind feeling-following slave of that part of (that eros in) ourselves—for we have followed that feeling into laughter, and the wag and wander of that passion hereafter will be recognized as leading to such a conclusion. That is the comic catharsis; it is a service to the individual, the city, and the god. Unless we do not take laughter seriously. At least the image of all the others around the table laughing at Alcibiades' story should free us from taking his passion at the inestimable face value it gives itself. To *feel* this truth (about Alcibiades and his passion) is to be well on the way to being able to speak it, but most importantly, eros is already, thereby, better aimed; it has been trued by the comedy. For it is only by the presence of an already better aimed eros (even if unrecognized or unnamed) that we are able to laugh at this one before us: our laughter is this better eros enjoying its free play. We can laugh at a great pleasure rebuffed only via participation in a community that is already in a joy that is higher. Thus laughter is a sign of superiority, but the laughter's source is not necessarily pride or self-sufficiency, for the superiority is not founded in our person; rather the joy in which *we have been granted participation* is a naturally superior state; from it, the demanding partiality of our other erotic satisfactions is experienced as a ridiculous hubris. The golden cord of the divine puppet moves freely again, unconstrained by the cords of iron and bronze. To feel shame or to laugh are already emotional recognitions of the truth, and the beginning of freedom from a passion we have served perhaps too often and too well.

The purpose of comic art is to bring us to that state of desire and feeling in which we not only *wish* to speak the truth (like Alcibiades—this is the best thing in him), but also are free enough from the crimped or overpowerful lines of the less adequate desires and stronger fears to be *able* to do so. And Diotima, the prophetess, reveals something of what that truth may be which we will come to see. What could be more erotic, or more purifying of our eros, than to see the Beautiful itself playing in the body, soul, words, or face of the person next to us? Alcibiades is afraid of this hideous strength, and runs out into the night to deface the herms of the god, but even a headless torso can be a reminder, and Socrates dead is more distressing than his presence (216c), for what we are lacking is now visible everywhere, precisely by its absence.

SELECTED BIBLIOGRAPHY

Ackrill, J. L. "Aristotle on Eudaimonia." In *Essays on Aristotle's "Ethics,"* edited by A. O. Rorty, 15–33. Berkeley and Los Angeles: University of California Press, 1980.

———. "Aristotle's Distinction between Energeia and Kinesis." In *New Essays on Plato and Aristotle,* edited by Renford Bambrough, 121–42. New York: Humanities Press, 1965.

Adkins, A. W. H. "Aristotle and the Best Kind of Tragedy." *Classical Quarterly* 16 (1966): 78–102.

———. *Merit and Responsibility.* Oxford, U.K.: Oxford University Press, 1960.

Adrados, Francisco. *Festival, Comedy and Tragedy: The Greek Origins of Theatre.* Translated by Christopher Holme. Leiden: Brill, 1975.

Allen, Reginald E. *The Symposium.* New Haven, Conn.: Yale University Press, 1984.

Alighieri, Dante. *The Divine Comedy.* Translated by Allen Mandelbaum. Camp Hill, Pa.: Quality Paperback Book Club, 1982.

Andersen, Øivind, and Jon Haarberg, eds. *Making Sense of Aristotle: Essays in Poetics.* London: Duckworth, 2001.

Aristophanes. [*Plays*]. 3 vols. Translated by Benjamin Bickley Rogers. Cambridge, Mass.: Harvard University Press (Loeb Classical Editions), 1937.

———. *The Complete Plays.* Edited and translated by Moses Hadas. New York: Bantam Books, 1962.

———. *"Acharnians," "Lysistrata," "Clouds."* Translated with an introduction and notes by Jeffrey Henderson. Newburyport, Mass.: Focus Classical Library, 1997.

———. *Acharnians.* With translation by Jeffrey Henderson. Cambridge, Mass.: Harvard University Press (Loeb Classical Editions), 1998.

Aquinas, St. Thomas. *Commentary on Aristotle's "De Anima."* Translated by Kenelm Foster, O.P., and Silvester Humphries, O.P. Notre Dame, Ind.: Dumb Ox Books, 1994.

———. *Commentary on Aristotle's "Nicomachean Ethics."* Translated by C. I. Litzinger, O. P. Notre Dame: Dumb Ox Books, 1993.

Auden, W. H. *Collected Poems.* Edited by Edward Mendelson. New York: Random House, 1976.

———. "The Joker in the Pack." In *The Dyer's Hand,* 256–72. New York: Random House, 1962.

Augustine, St. *City of God.* Translated by Marcus Dods. New York: Modern Library, 1950.

———. *Confessions.* Translated by John K. Ryan. Garden City, N.J.: Doubleday Image, 1960.

Barber, C. L. *Shakespeare's Festive Comedy.* Princeton, N.J.: Princeton University Press, 1972.

Barzun, Jacques. "A Future for the Liberal Arts, If . . ." *Academic Questions* (Fall 1994): 74–76.

Bataille, Georges. *The Accursed Share.* Vol. 1. Translated by Robert Hurley. New York: Zone Books, 1988.

Belfiore, Elizabeth S. *Tragic Pleasures: Aristotle on Plot and Emotion (Pleasures).* Princeton, N.J.: Princeton University Press, 1992.

———. "Aristotle and Iphigenia." In *Essays on Aristotle's "Poetics,"* edited by A. O. Rorty, 359–78. Princeton, N.J.: Princeton University Press, 1992.

Bennett, Robert B. "Reform of a Malcontent: Jaques and the Meaning of *As You Like It.*" *Shakespeare Studies* 9 (1976): 183–204.

Bernays, Jacob. *Zwei abhandlungen über die aristotelische Theorie des Drama.* Berlin, 1880; repr. Darmstadt: Wissenschaftliche Buchgesellschaft, 1968.

Berry, Edward. *Shakespeare's Comic Rites.* Cambridge, U.K.: Cambridge University Press, 1984.

Berry, Wendell. *Sex, Economy, Freedom and Community.* New York: Pantheon Books, 1992.

Bluestein, Gene. *Poplore.* Amherst: University of Massachusetts Press, 1994.

Blundell, Mary Whitlock. "Comment on C. D. C. Reeve." *Proceedings of the Boston Area Colloquium in Ancient Philosophy* 8: 115–33. Lanham, Md.: University Press of America, 1992.

Bremer, John. *Plato's "Ion": Philosophy as Performance.* Richland Hills, Texas: BIBAL Press, 2005.

Brooks, Cleanth. *The Well Wrought Urn: Studies in the Structure of Poetry.* New York: Harcourt, Brace Co., 1947.

Burnett, Anne Pippin. *Catastrophe Survived: Euripides' Plays of Mixed Reversal.* Oxford, U.K.: Clarendon Press, 1971.

Butcher, S. H. *Aristotle's Theory of Poetry and Fine Art.* 4th ed. London: Macmillan, 1932.

Butterworth, Charles E. *Averroes' Middle Commentary on Aristotle's "Poetics."* Princeton, N.J.: Princeton University Press, 1986.

Clay, Diskin. "The Tragic and Comic Poet of the Symposium." In *Essays in Ancient Greek Philosophy,* edited by John P. Anton and Anthony Preus, 2:186–202. Albany: SUNY Press, 1983.

Coghill, Nevill. "The Basis of Shakespearian Comedy." In *Essays and Studies of the English Association,* n.s., 3:1–28. London: John Murray, 1950.

Collingwood, R. G. *The Principles of Art.* Oxford, U.K.: Clarendon Press, 1938.

Cooper, Lane. *An Aristotelian Theory of Comedy.* New York: Harcourt, Brace, 1922.

———. *Aristotle On the Art of Poetry.* An amplified version with supplementary illustrations. Ithaca, N.Y.: Cornell University Press, 1947.

Cornford, Francis M. *The Origin of Attic Comedy.* 2nd ed. Cambridge, U.K.: Cambridge University Press, 1934.

Crane, R. S. *The Languages of Criticism and the Structure of Poetry.* Toronto: Toronto University Press, 1953.

Davis, Michael. *Aristotle's "Poetics": The Poetry of Philosophy.* Lanham, Md.: Rowman & Littlefield, 1992.

de Duve, Theirry. *Kant after Duchamp.* Cambridge, Mass.: MIT Press (October Books), 1999.

Demastes, William. "Re-inspecting the Crack in the Chimney: Chaos Theory from Ibsen to Stoppard." *New Theatre Quarterly* 10 (August 1994): 242–54.

Derrida, Jacques. 1984. *Dissemination.* Translated by Barbara Johnson. Chicago: University of Chicago Press, 1984.

Dillon, Matthew. "Tragic Laughter." *The Classical World* 84, no. 5 (1991): 345–55.

Dodds, E. R. *The Greeks and the Irrational.* Berkeley and Los Angeles: University of California Press, 1964.

Dollimore, Jonathan. *Radical Tragedy: Religion, Ideology and Power in the Drama of Shakespeare and His Contemporaries.* Chicago: University of Chicago Press, 1984.

Donaldson, John William. *The Theatre of the Greeks: A Treatise on the History and Exhibition of the Greek Drama.* 7th ed. New York: Haskell House, 1973 (reprint).

Dover, K. J. *Aristophanic Comedy.* Berkeley and Los Angeles: University of California Press, 1972.

Dufrenne, Mikel. *The Phenomenology of Aesthetic Experience.* Translated by Edward S. Casey, Albert Anderson, Willis Domingo, and Leon Jacobson. Evanston, Ill.: Northwestern University Press, 1973.

Dunn, Allen. "Tragedy and the Ethical Sublime in *The Fragility of Goodness.*" *Soundings* 72, no. 4: 657–74.

Eliot, T. S. *The Use of Poetry and the Use of Criticism.* London: Faber & Faber, 1933.

Else, Gerald F. *Aristotle's "Poetics": The Argument.* Cambridge, Mass.: Harvard University Press, 1957.

———. *Plato and Aristotle on Poetry*. Chapel Hill: University of North Carolina Press, 1986.

Euripides. *Bacchae*. Translated by Daniel Mark Epstein in *Euripides, I*. Edited by David R. Slavitt and Palmer Bovie. Philadelphia: University of Pennsylvania Press, 1998.

———. *Hecuba*. Edited and translated by David Kovacs. Cambridge, Mass.: Harvard University Press (Loeb Classical Editions), 1995.

———. *Hecuba*. Translated by William Arrowsmith in *The Complete Greek Tragedies: Euripides 3*. Edited by David Grene and Richmond Lattimore. Chicago: University of Chicago Press, 1958.

———. *Hecuba*. Translated by Janet Lembke and Kenneth J. Reckford. Oxford, U.K.: Oxford University Press, 1991.

———. *Iphigenia in Tauris*. Translated by Witter Bynner in *Euripides II*. Edited by David Grene and Richmond Lattimore. Chicago: University of Chicago Press, 1956.

Evans, James E. *Comedy: An Annotated Bibliography of Theory and Criticism*. Metuchen, N.J.: Scarecrow Press, 1987.

Feibleman, James. *In Praise of Comedy: A Study in Its Theory and Practice*. New York: Russell & Russell, 1962.

Fendt, Gene. "The Empiricist Looks at a Poem." *Philosophy and Literature* 21 (October 1997): 306–18.

———. *For What May I Hope?: Thinking with Kant and Kierkegaard*. New York: Peter Lang, 1990.

———. "*Ion*: Plato's Defense of Poetry." *International Studies in Philosophy* 29, no. 4 (1997): 23–50.

———. "Intentionality and Mimesis: Canonic Variations on an Ancient Grudge, Scored for New Mutinies." *Sub/Stance* 75 (1994): 46–74.

———. *Is Hamlet a Christian Tragedy?: An Essay on a Question in Kierkegaard*. Milwaukee, Ill.: Marquette University Press, 1999.

———. "The Others in/of Aristotle's *Poetics*" ("Others"). *Journal of Philosophical Research* 22 (1997): 245–60.

———. *Platonic Errors: Plato, A Kind of Poet*. Westport, Conn.: Greenwood Press, 1998.

———. "The Relation of *Monologion* and *Proslogion*." *Heythrop Journal* 46, no. 2 (April 2005): 149–66.

———. "Resolution, Catharsis, Culture: *As You Like It*." *Philosophy and Literature* 19 (1995): 248–60.

———. "Sublimity and Human Works: Kant on Tragedy and War." *Proceedings of the Eighth International Kant Congress*, 2.2.509–17. Milwaukee, Wisc.: Marquette University Press.

———. "Two Views of the Imagination and Their Consequences for the Arts." *Soundings* 88, nos. 1–2 (Spring–Summer 2005): 179–97.

Fleming, John. *Stoppard's Theatre: Finding Order Amid Chaos*. Austin: University of Texas Press, 2001.

Fossheim, Hallvard. "Mimesis in Aristotle's *Ethics*." In *Making Sense of Aristotle: Essays in Poetics*, edited by Andersen and Haarberg, 73–86. London: Duckworth, 2001.

Frede, Dorothea. "The Cognitive Role of *Phantasia* in Aristotle." In *Essays on Aristotle's "De Anima,"* edited by Nussbaum and Rorty, 279–96. Oxford, U.K.: Clarendon Press, 1992.

Freud, Sigmund. *The Future of an Illusion*. Translated by W. D. Robson-Scott. Garden City, N.Y.: Doubleday, 1964.

———. *Civilization and Its Discontents*. Edited and translated by James Strachey. New York: W. W. Norton, 1961.

Frye, Northrop. *The Anatomy of Criticism* (*Anatomy*). Princeton, N.J.: Princeton University Press, 1957.

———. "The Argument of Comedy." In *English Institute Essays, 1948*, edited by D. A. Robertson Jr., 58–73. New York: Columbia University Press, 1949.

Gassner, John. "Catharsis and the Modern Theater." In *Aristotle's "Poetics" and English Literature,* edited by Elder Olson, 108–13. Chicago: University of Chicago Press, 1965.

Genette, Gerard. *The Architext: An Introduction.* Translated by Jane E. Lewin. Berkeley and Los Angeles: University of California Press, 1992.

Girard, Rene. *Violence and the Sacred.* Translated by Patrick Gregory. Baltimore: Johns Hopkins University Press, 1977.

———. *"To Double Business Bound": Essays on Literature, Mimesis, and Anthropology.* Baltimore: Johns Hopkins University Press, 1978.

———. *Things Hidden from the Foundation of the World.* Translated by Stephan Bann and Michael Metteer. Stanford, Calif.: Stanford University Press, 1987.

———. *Oedipus Unbound.* Stanford, Calif.: Stanford University Press, 2004.

———. "The Anthropology of the Cross: A Conversation with Rene Girard." In *The Girard Reader,* edited by James G. Williams, 262–88. New York: Crossroads, 1996.

Glanville, I. M. "Tragic Error." *Classical Quarterly* 43 (1949): 47–57.

Golden, Leon. "Aristotle on Comedy" ("On Comedy"). *Journal of Aesthetics and Art Criticism* 42 (1984): 283–90.

———. "Aristotle on the Pleasure of Comedy." In *Essays on Aristotle's "Poetics,"* edited by A. O. Rorty, 379–86. Princeton, N.J.: Princeton University Press, 1992.

———. *Aristotle on Tragic and Comic Mimesis* (*Tragic and Comic*). Atlanta, Ga.: Scholars Press, 1992.

———. "Epic, Tragedy, and Catharsis." *Classical Philology* 71 (1976): 77–85.

———. "Mimesis and Katharsis." *Classical Philology* 64 (1969): 145–53.

Gould, Thomas. *The Ancient Quarrel between Poetry and Philosophy.* Princeton, N.J.: Princeton University Press, 1990.

Gregory, Justina. *Euripides and the Instruction of the Athenians.* Ann Arbor: University of Michigan Press, 1991.

Gum, Coburn. *The Aristophanic Comedies of Ben Jonson.* The Hague: Mouton, 1969.

Gurewitch, Morton. *The Irrational Vision.* Ithaca, N.Y.: Cornell University Press, 1975.

Guyer, Paul. *Kant and the Experience of Freedom: Essays on Aesthetics and Morality.* Cambridge, U.K.: Cambridge University Press, 1993.

Halliwell, Stephen. *The Aesthetics of Mimesis: Ancient Texts and Modern Problems.* Princeton, N.J.: Princeton University Press, 2002.

———. "Aristotelian Mimesis and Human Understanding." In *Making Sense of Aristotle,* edited by Andersen and Haarberg, 87–108. London: Duckworth, 2001.

———. *Aristotle's "Poetics."* London: Duckworth, 1986.

———. "Epilogue: *The Poetics* and Its Interpreters." In *Essays on Aristotle's "Poetics,"* edited by A. O. Rorty, 409–24. Princeton, N.J.: University Press, 1992.

———. "Pleasure, Understanding and Emotion in Aristotle's *Poetics.*" In *Essays on Aristotle's "Poetics,"* edited by A. O. Rorty, 241–60. Princeton, N.J.: Princeton University Press, 1992.

———. *"The Poetics" of Aristotle,* a translation and commentary. Chapel Hill: University of North Carolina Press, 1987.

———. "The Uses of Laughter in Greek Culture." *Classical Quarterly,* n.s., 41, no. 2 (1991): 279–96.

Halperin, David. "Plato and the Metaphysics of Desire." In *Proceedings of the Boston Area Colloquium in Ancient Philosophy,* 7:27–51. Lanham, Md.: University Press of America, 1991.

Harbage, A. E. *As They Liked It: A Study of Shakespeare's Moral Artistry.* Philadelphia: University of Pennsylvania Press, 1972.

Hardison, O. B., with Leon Golden. *Aristotle's "Poetics": A Translation and Commentary for Students of Literature.* Englewoood Cliffs, N.J.: Prentice-Hall, 1968.

Harmon, Gilbert, and Judith Jarvis Thompson. *Moral Relativism and Moral Objectivity.* Oxford, U.K.: Blackwell, 1996.

Hassell, R. Chris Jr. *Faith and Folly in Shakespeare's Romantic Comedies.* Athens: University of Georgia Press, 1980.

Heath, Malcolm. "Aristotelian Comedy." *Classical Quarterly* 39 (1989): 344–54.

———. "Aristotle and the Pleasures of Tragedy." In *Making Sense of Aristotle*, edited by Andersen and Haarberg, 7–24. London: Duckworth, 2001.

———. *The Poetics of Greek Tragedy.* Stanford, Calif.: Stanford University Press, 1987.

Henderson, Jeffrey. *The Maculate Muse: Obscene Language in Attic Comedy.* New Haven, Conn.: Yale University Press, 1975.

Herder, Johann Gottfried. "On Monuments of the Distant Past." In *On World History*, edited by Hans Adler and Ernest A. Menze, 63–80. Translated by Ernest Menze and Michael Palma. Armonk, N.Y.: M. E. Sharpe, 1997.

Herodotus. *The Histories.* Translated by Aubrey de Selincourt. Revised by A. R. Burn. London: Penguin Books, 1954.

Hobbes, Thomas. *Leviathan.* Edited by Richard Tuck. Cambridge, U.K.: Cambridge University Press, 1991.

House, Humphry. *Aristotle's "Poetics."* Westport, Conn.: Greenwood Press, 1978.

Husain, Martha. *Ontology and the Art of Tragedy: An Approach to Aristotle's "Poetics."* Albany: SUNY Press, 2002.

Janko, Richard. "Aristotle on Comedy, Aristophanes, and Some New Evidence from Herculanaeum." In *Making Sense of Aristotle*, edited by Andersen and Haarberg, 51–72. London: Duckworth, 2001.

———. *Aristotle on Comedy: Towards a Reconstruction of Poetics II* (*On Comedy*). Berkeley and Los Angeles: University of California Press, 1984.

———. "From Catharsis to the Aristotelian Mean." In *Essays on Aristotle's "Poetics,"* edited by A. O. Rorty, 341–58. Princeton, N.J.: Princeton University Press, 1992.

Jones, John. *On Aristotle and Greek Tragedy.* Stanford, Calif.: Stanford University Press, 1962.

Kant, Immanuel. *The Critique of Judgement* (*KU*). Translated by James Creed Meredith. Oxford, U.K.: Clarendon Press, 1952.

———. *Critique of Pure Reason* (A . . ./B . . .). Translated by Norman Kemp Smith. New York: St. Martin's Press, 1929.

———. *Foundations of the Metaphysics of Morals* (*FMM*). Translated by Lewis White Beck. Indianapolis, Ind.: Bobbs-Merrill, 1959.

Kerenyi, Karoly. *Dionysus.* Translated by Ralph Manheim. Princeton, N.J.: Princeton University Press, 1976.

Kierkegaard, Søren. *Either/Or.* Translated by Howard Hong and Edna Hong. Princeton, N.J.: Princeton University Press, 1987.

———. *The Concept of Irony, with Constant Reference to Socrates.* Translated by Lee M. Capel. New York: Harper & Row, 1965.

———. "Man's Need of God Constitutes His Highest Perfection." Translated by David F. Swenson and Lillian Marvin Swenson. New York: Harper-Torchbooks, 1958.

Kitto, H. D. F. *Greek Tragedy.* London: Methuen, 1984.

Kraut, Richard. *Aristotle on the Human Good.* Princeton, N.J.: Princeton University Press, 1989.

Lauter, Paul. *Theories of Comedy.* Garden City, N.Y.: Anchor Books, 1964.

Lear, Jonathan. "Katharsis." In *Essays on Aristotle's "Poetics,"* edited by A. O. Rorty, 315–40. Princeton, N.J.: Princeton University Press, 1992.

Leventhal, Robert S. *The Disciplines of Interpretation: Lessing, Herder, Schlegel and Hermeneutics in Germany 1850–1800.* Berlin: Walter de Gruyter, 1994.

Livingston, Paisley. *Models of Desire: Rene Girard and the Psychology of Mimesis.* Baltimore: Johns Hopkins University Press, 1992.

Lucas, D. W. *Aristotle's "Poetics," with an Introduction, Commentary and Appendixes.* Oxford, U.K.: Clarendon Press, 1968.

Lucas, F. L. *Tragedy*. London: Hogarth Press, 1927.

MacCary, W. Thomas. *Friends and Lovers: The Phenomenology of Desire in Shakespearean Comedy*. New York: Columbia University Press, 1985.

MacCormack, Sabine. *The Shadows of Poetry: Vergil in the Mind of Augustine*. Berkeley and Los Angeles: University of California Press, 1998.

MacIntyre, Alisdair. *After Virtue*. South Bend, Ind.: University of Notre Dame Press, 1981.

MacPherson, C. B. *The Political Theory of Possessive Individualism: Hobbes to Locke*. London: Oxford University Press, 1964.

Marcel, Gabriel. "On the Ontological Mystery." In *The Philosophy of Existentialism*, translated by Manya Harari, 9–46. Secaucus, N.J.: Citadel Press, 1956.

Mason, H. A. *Fine Talk at Agathon's: A Version of Plato's "Symposium."* Cambridge, U.K.: Cambridge Quarterly Publications, 1992.

Matthaei, Louise E. *Studies in Greek Tragedy*. Cambridge, U.K.: Cambridge University Press, 1918.

McKim, Richard. "Shame and Truth in Plato's *Gorgias*." In *Platonic Readings/Platonic Writings*, edited by Charles L. Griswold Jr., 34–48. New York: Routledge, 1988.

McLeish, Kenneth. *The Theatre of Aristophanes*. London: Thames & Hudson, 1980.

Migne, J. P. *Patrologia Latina*. Vol. 32. Paris: 1845.

Miola, Robert S. *Shakespeare and Classical Comedy*. Oxford, U.K.: Clarendon Press, 1994.

Moles, John. "Notes on Aristotle, *Poetics* 13 and 14." *Classical Quarterly* 29 (1979): 77–94.

———. "Philanthropia in the *Poetics*." *Phoenix* 38 (1984): 325–35.

Montrose, Louis A. "The Place of a Brother in *As You Like It*: Social Process and Comic Form." *Shakespeare Quarterly* 32 (1981): 40–54.

Mossman, Judith. *Wild Justice: A Study of Euripides' "Hecuba."* Oxford, U.K.: Clarendon Press, 1995.

Murray, Gilbert, trans. *Iphigenia in Tauris*. Oxford, U.K.: Oxford University Press, 1915.

———. *Euripides and His Age*. Oxford, U.K.: Oxford University Press, 1946.

Nagel, Thomas. "Aristotle on Eudaimonia." In *Essays on Aristotle's "Ethics,"* edited by A. O. Rorty, pp. 7–14. Berkeley and Los Angeles: University of California Press, 1980.

Nehamas, Alexander. "Pity and Fear in the *Rhetoric* and *Poetics*." In *Essays on Aristotle's "Poetics,"* edited by A. O. Rorty, 291–314. Princeton, N.J.: Princeton University Press, 1992.

Nevo, Ruth. *Comic Transformations in Shakespeare*. London: Methuen, 1980.

Nietzsche, Friedrich. *Beyond Good and Evil* (*BGE*). Translated by Walter Kaufmann. New York: Vintage Books, 1966.

———. *The Birth of Tragedy*. Translated by Francis Golffing. New York: Doubleday, 1956.

———. *Twilight of the Idols* (*TI*). Translated by Walter Kaufmann. In *The Portable Nietzsche*, 463–563. New York: Penguin Books, 1959.

Nussbaum, Martha C. *The Fragility of Goodness* (*FG*). Cambridge, U.K.: Cambridge University Press, 1986.

———. *Love's Knowledge*. Oxford, U.K.: Oxford University Press, 1990.

———. *Poetic Justice: The Literary Imagination and Public Life*. Boston: Beacon Press, 1995.

———. *The Therapy of Desire: Theory and Practice in Hellenistic Ethics* (*TD*). Princeton, N.J.: Princeton University Press, 1994.

———. "Tragedy and Self-sufficiency: Plato and Aristotle on Fear and Pity." In *Essays on Aristotle's "Poetics,"* edited by A. O. Rorty, 261–90. Princeton, N.J.: Princeton University Press, 1992.

———. *Upheavals of Thought: The Intelligence of Emotions* (*UT*). Cambridge, U.K.: Cambridge University Press, 2001.

Nussbaum, Martha C., and A. O. Rorty, eds. *Essays on Aristotle's "De Anima."* Oxford, U.K.: Clarendon Press, 1992.

Nuttall, A. D. *A New Mimesis: Shakespeare and the Representation of Reality.* London: Methuen, 1983.

———. "Two Unassimilable Men." In *Shakespearian Comedy,* Stratford-Upon-Avon Studies 14, edited by David Palmer and Malcolm Bradbury, 210–40. London: Edward Arnold, 1972.

Olson, Elder. "The Poetic Method of Aristotle: Its Powers and Limitations. " In *Aristotle's "Poetics" and English Literature,* edited by Elder Olson, 175–91. Chicago: University of Chicago Press, 1965.

———. *Tragedy and the Theory of Drama.* Detroit, Mich.: Wayne State University Press, 1966.

———. *The Theory of Comedy* (*Theory*). Bloomington: Indiana University Press, 1968.

———, ed. *Aristotle's "Poetics" and English Literature.* Chicago: University of Chicago Press, 1965.

Otto, Walter, F. *Dionysus: Myth and Cult.* Translated by R. B. Palmer. Bloomington: Indiana University Press, 1965.

Pangle, Thomas L. *"The Laws" of Plato: Translation, with Notes and Interpretive Essay.* New York: Basic Books, 1980.

Peck, Arthur L. "Aristotle on Κίνησις." In *Essays in Ancient Greek Philosophy,* edited by John P. Anton and G. L. Kustas, 478–90. Albany: SUNY Press, 1971.

Pickard-Cambridge, Arthur. *The Dramatic Festivals of Athens.* 2nd ed. Edited by John Gould and D. M. Lewis. Oxford, U.K.: Oxford University Press, 1968.

Pickstock, Catherine. *After Writing: On the Liturgical Consummation of Philosophy.* Oxford, U.K.: Blackwell, 1998.

Plato. *The Collected Dialogues of Plato.* Edited by Edith Hamilton and Huntington Cairns. Princeton, N.J.: Princeton University Press, 1973.

———. *"The Laws" of Plato.* Translated with an interpretive essay by Thomas L. Pangle. New York: Basic Books, 1980.

———. *Laws.* Translated by R. G. Bury. Cambridge, Mass.: Harvard University Press (Loeb Classical Library), 1926.

———. *Phaedrus.* Translated by Walter Hamilton. London: Penguin Books, 1973.

———. *"The Republic" of Plato.* Translated with an interpretive essay by Allan Bloom. New York: Basic Books, 1968.

———. *Republic.* Translated by Paul Shorey. Cambridge, Mass.: Harvard University Press (Loeb Classical Library), 1935.

———. *The Symposium.* Translated with commentary by Reginald Allen. New Haven, Conn.: Yale University Press, 1984.

———. *Two Comic Dialogues: "Ion" and "Hippias Major."* Translated by Paul Woodruff. Indianapolis, Ind.: Hackett, 1983.

Polansky, Ronald. "*Energeia* in Aristotle's *Metaphysics* IX." In *Essays in Ancient Greek Philosophy V: Aristotle's Ontology,* edited by Anthony Preus and John P. Anton, 211–25. Albany: SUNY Press, 1992.

Posner, Richard A. "Against Ethical Criticism." *Philosophy and Literature* 21: 11–27.

Preminger, Alex, O. B. Hardison Jr., and Kevin Kerrane, eds. *Classical and Medieval Literary Criticism: Translations and Interpretations.* New York: Frederick Ungar, 1974.

Rabinowitz, Nancy Sorkin. *Anxiety Veiled: Euripides and the Traffic in Women.* Ithaca, N.Y.: Cornell University Press, 1993.

Radcliff-Umstead, Douglas. *The Birth of Modern Comedy in Renaissance Italy.* Chicago: University of Chicago Press, 1969.

Raphael, D. D. *The Paradox of Tragedy.* Freeport, N.Y.: Books for Libraries Press, 1971.

Reckford, Kenneth J. *Aristophanes' Old-and-New Comedy.* Chapel Hill: University of North Carolina Press, 1987.

———. "Concepts of Demoralization in the *Hecuba* ("Concepts")." In *Directions in Euripidean Criticism,* edited by Peter Burian, 112–28. Durham, N.C.: Duke University Press, 1985.

———. "Introduction" in *Hecuba*. Translated by Janet Lembke and Kenneth J. Reckford. Oxford, U.K.: Oxford University Press, 1991.

Reeve, C. D. C. "Telling the Truth about Love: Plato's *Symposium*." *Proceedings of the Boston Area Colloquium in Ancient Philosophy* 8 (1992): 89–114. Lanham, Md.: University Press of America.

Ricoeur, Paul. *Interpretation Theory: Discourse and the Surplus of Meaning*. Fort Worth, Texas: TCU Press, 1976.

Ridley, Aaron. *Music, Value and the Passions*. Ithaca, N.Y.: Cornell University Press, 1995.

Rilke, Rainer Maria. *Duino Elegies*. With a translation by C. F. MacIntyre. Berkeley and Los Angeles: University of California Press, 1961.

Rotunno, Laura, and Gene Fendt. "Comic Construction and Comic Purpose: The Unity and Sublimity of *Midsummer Night's Dream*." Unpublished manuscript.

Rorty, Amelie Oksenberg. "The Psychology of Aristotelian Tragedy." In *Essays on Aristotle's "Poetics,"* edited by A. O. Rorty, 1–22. Princeton, N.J.: Princeton University Press, 1992.

———, ed. *Essays on Aristotle's "Ethics"*. Berkeley and Los Angeles: University of California Press, 1980.

———, ed. *Essays on Aristotle's "Poetics."* Princeton, N.J.: Princeton University Press, 1992.

Rosen, Stanley. *Plato's "Symposium."* 2nd ed. New Haven, Conn.: Yale University Press, 1987.

Salingar, Leo. *Shakespeare and the Traditions of Comedy*. Cambridge, U.K.: Cambridge University Press, 1974.

Sandbach, F. H. *The Comic Theatre of Greece and Rome*. New York: W. W. Norton, 1977.

Schofield, Malcolm. "Aristotle on the Imagination." In *Essay's on Aristotle's "De Anima,"* edited by Martha C. Nussbaum and A. O. Rorty, 249–77. Oxford, U.K.: Clarendon Press, 1992.

Schollmeier, Paul. "Ancient Tragedy and Other Selves." *Revue de Metaphysique et de Morale* 103, no. 2 (1998): 175–88.

———. "The Purgation of Pitiableness and Fearfulness." *Hermes* 122 (1994): 289–99.

Segal, Charles. "Aristophanes' Cloud-Chorus." *Arethusa* 2 (1969): 143–61.

———. *Dionysiac Poetics and Euripides' "Bacchae."* Princeton, N.J.: Princeton University Press, 1997.

Shakespeare, William. *The Complete Pelican Shakespeare*. Edited by Alfred Harbage. New York: Viking Press, 1969.

———. *A Midsummer Night's Dream*. Edited by Madeleine Doran. New York: Viking Press, 1969.

———. *As You Like It*. Edited by Ralph M. Sargent. New York: Viking Press, 1969.

———. *Julius Caesar*. Edited by John E. Hankins. New York: Viking Press, 1969.

———. *Love's Labor's Lost*. Edited by Alfred Harbage. New York: Viking Press, 1969.

———. *Romeo and Juliet*. Edited by John E. Hankins. New York: Viking Press, 1969.

———. *Sonnets*. Edited by Douglas Bush. New York: Viking Press, 1969.

———. *The Winter's Tale*. Edited by Baldwin Maxwell. New York: Viking Press, 1969.

Sherman, Thomas P., S.J. "The Perfect Happiness of Virtuous Friends: The Nature and Place of Perfect Friendship in the Happy Life of the Virtuous in Aristotle's Practical Philosophy." Ph.D. dissertation, University of Toronto, 1999.

Silk, M. S. *Aristophanes and the Definition of Comedy*. Oxford, U.K.: Oxford University Press, 2000.

Smith, Barbara Herrnstein. *Contingencies of Value: Alternative Perspectives for Critical Theory*. Cambridge, Mass.: Harvard University Press, 1988.

Smith, Kendall K. "Aristotle's 'Lost Chapter on Comedy.'" *Classical Weekly* 21, no 19: 145–48; 21, no. 20: 153–56.

Snyder, Susan. *The Comic Matrix of Shakepeare's Tragedies*. Princeton, N.J.: Princeton University Press, 1979.

The Solomon R. Guggenheim Foundation. *The Great Utopia: The Russian and Soviet Avant-Garde, 1915–1932*. New York: Guggenheim Museum Publications, 1992.

Sorabji, Richard. *Man and Beast*. Ithaca, N.Y.: Cornell University Press, 1991.

———. "Intentionality and Physiological Processes: Aristotle's Theory of Sense Perception." In *Essays on Aristotle's "De Anima,"* edited by Martha C. Nussbaum and A. O. Rorty, 195–225. Oxford, U.K.: Clarendon Press, 1992.

Spariosu, Mihai I. *God of Many Names: Play, Poetry and Power in Hellenic Thought from Homer to Aristotle*. Durham, N.C.: Duke University Press, 1991.

Stanford, W. B. *Greek Tragedy and the Emotions: An Introductory Study*. London: Routledge & Kegan Paul, 1983.

———. *Enemies of Poetry*. London: Routledge & Kegan Paul, 1980.

Stinton, T. C. W. "Hamartia in Aristotle and Greek Tragedy." *Classical Quarterly* 25 (1975): 221–54.

Stoppard, Tom. *Arcadia*. London: Faber & Faber, 1993.

Strauss, Leo. *Socrates and Aristophanes*. Chicago: University of Chicago Press, 1980.

Sutton, Dana F. *The Carthsis of Comedy*. Lanham, Md.: Rowman & Littlefield, 1994.

Tuozzo, Thomas M. "Aristotelian Deliberation Is Not of Ends." In *Essays in Ancient Greek Philosophy IV: Aristotle's "Ethics,"* edited by John Anton and Anthony Preus, 193–212. Albany: SUNY Press, 1991.

Vanden Heuvel, Michael. "The Politics of Paradigm: A Case Study in Chaos Theory." *New Theatre Quarterly* 9, no. 35 (1993): 255–66.

Vellacott, Philip. *The Logic of Tragedy: Morals and Integrity in Aeschylus' "Oresteia."* Durham, N.C.: Duke University Press, 1984.

Vernant, Jean-Pierre, and Pierre Vidal-Naquet. *Myth and Tragedy in Ancient Greece*. Translated by Janet Lloyd. New York: Zone Press, 1988.

Vlastos, Gregory. "The Individual as Object of Love in Plato's Dialogues." In *Platonic Studies*, 2nd ed., 1–34. Princeton, N.J.: University Press, 1973.

White, Stephen A. "Aristotle's Favorite Tragedies." In *Essays on Aristotle's "Poetics,"* edited by A. O. Rorty, 221–40. Princeton, N.J.: Princeton University Press, 1992.

Whitman, Cedric H. *The Heroic Paradox: Essays on Homer*. Ithaca, N.Y.: Cornell University Press, 1982.

Welton, William. "Divine Inspiration and the Origins of the Laws in Plato's *Laws*." *Polis* 14, nos. 1–2 (1995): 53–83.

Wick, Warner. "Truth's Debt to Freedom." *Mind* 73 (1964): 527–37.

Williams, James G., ed. *The Girard Reader*. New York: Crossroads, 1996.

Woodruff, Paul. *Plato: "Hippias Major."* Translated, with commentary, and essay. Indianapolis, Ind.: Hackett, 1982.

INDEX

Love Song for the Life of the Mind: An Essay on the Purpose of Comedy was designed and typeset in Garamond by Kachergis Book Design of Pittsboro, North Carolina. It was printed on 60-pound House Natural Smooth and bound by Sheridan Press of Ann Arbor, Michigan.